GROWING OLD
IN AMERICA

ISSN 1538-6686

GROWING OLD IN AMERICA

Elizabeth Vierck

INFORMATION PLUS® REFERENCE SERIES
Formerly published by Information Plus, Wylie, Texas

GALE GROUP
—✦—
™
THOMSON LEARNING

Detroit • New York • San Diego • San Francisco
Boston • New Haven, Conn. • Waterville, Maine
London • Munich

GROWING OLD IN AMERICA

Elizabeth Vierck, *Author*

The Gale Group Staff:
Coordinating Editors: Ellice Engdahl, *Series Editor*; Charles B. Montney, *Series Graphics Editor*
Managing Editor: Debra M. Kirby
Contributing Editors: Elizabeth Manar, Kathleen Meek
Contributing Associate Editors: Paula Cutcher-Jackson, Prindle LaBarge, Heather Price, Michael T. Reade
Imaging and Multimedia Content: Barbara J. Yarrow, *Manager, Imaging and Multimedia Content*; Dean Dauphinais, *Imaging and Multimedia Content Editor*; Kelly A. Quin, *Imaging and Multimedia Content Editor*; Robyn Young, *Imaging and Multimedia Content Editor*; Leitha Etheridge-Sims, *Image Cataloger*; Mary K. Grimes, *Image Cataloger*; David G. Oblender, *Image Cataloger*; Lezlie Light, *Imaging Coordinator*; Randy Bassett, *Imaging Supervisor*; Robert Duncan, *Imaging Specialist*; Dan Newell, *Imaging Specialist*; Luke Rademacher, *Imaging Specialist*; Christine O'Bryan, *Graphic Specialist*
Indexing: John Magee, *Senior Indexing Specialist*
Permissions: Shalice Shah-Caldwell, *Permissions Associate*; Maria Franklin, *Permissions Manager*
Product Design: Michelle DiMercurio, *Senior Art Director and Product Design Manager*; Michael Logusz, *Graphic Artist*
Production: Evi Seoud, *Assistant Manager, Composition Purchasing and Electronic Prepress*; Keith Helmling, *Buyer*; Dorothy Maki, *Manufacturing Manager*

Cover photo © PhotoDisc.

ISBN 0-7876-5103-6 (set)
ISBN 0-7876-6058-2 (this volume)
ISSN 1538-6686 (this volume)
Printed in the United States of America
10 9 8 7 6 5 4 3 2 1

TABLE OF CONTENTS

CHAPTER 1

This chapter introduces the reader to today's older Americans. It defines terms used when discussing the elderly, and explains why America is rapidly growing older. In addition, a demographic portrait is painted of older America, the increasingly positive attitudes of the elderly are documented, and their power as a consumer market is described. Aging trends worldwide are also discussed.

CHAPTER 2

Chapter 2 begins with a discussion of some measures used to determine economic security, such as net worth and median income. Both ends of the spectrum, poverty and wealth, are covered. A lengthy section details income sources for the elderly, and looks closely at pension funds. Consumer spending trends among older Americans are documented, and in-depth coverage of the Social Security program rounds out the chapter.

CHAPTER 3

This chapter details the many housing arrangements elderly people have, including living with family members (some caring for grandchildren), living alone, or being homeless. Alternatives to living at home, such as nursing homes, assisted living, shared housing, or retirement communities, are also covered. A section on homeownership analyzes characteristics of housing and neighborhoods, as well as hazards older Americans may face in houses. Public housing is also touched upon.

CHAPTER 4

Older Americans often make great contributions to society in both paid and unpaid roles. Discussed in this chapter are changes in lifestyles (from linear to cyclic life paths) and the economy (from agricultural to industrial to service-oriented) that make these contributions possible. Labor participation is covered, including common stereotypes about older workers, as well as age discrimination. Also described are the increasing options the elderly have in retirement, among them work, leisure, and volunteering.

CHAPTER 5

Greater numbers of older Americans are choosing to fill their time with educational and political pursuits. This chapter outlines the educational levels of today's older citizens and discusses trends toward lifetime learning and growing computer knowledge. Also explored is the political power of the elderly: their voting conduct and party affiliation; their force as a political bloc; and their participation in grass-roots politics, such as Silver-Haired Legislatures and town councils.

CHAPTER 6

About one in seven American drivers is age 65 or older. Chapter 6 discusses this phenomenon, examining safety issues (including vision impairment and driving habits), suggested strategies to make driving easier for the elderly, and alternatives for older Americans who cannot, or choose not to, drive themselves.

CHAPTER 7

Documented here are the ways the body's functioning changes with age. Leading causes of death among the elderly are cataloged, as are the numerous chronic ailments that can beset older people. Additional sections deal with disability, dementia (including Alzheimer's disease), prescription drug use, preventive health measures, sexuality, and geriatric medicine.

CHAPTER 8

This chapter examines the state of mental health among today's elderly, shedding light on such topics as state of mind (including life satisfaction and the "survivor" syndrome), depression, and suicide. The last segment of the chapter discusses alcohol abuse among the elderly, including its characteristics, physical consequences, and the difficult nature of diagnosis and treatment.

CHAPTER 9

Older Americans may not always be able to care fully for themselves. This chapter documents differing dependency levels as perceived by the elderly and their caretakers, and provides a composite of the "average" American caretaker, including demographic characteristics, the types of care provided, and the physical, psychological, and financial burdens of caretaking. Also included are alternatives to home caretaking, and an examination of the consequences caretaking has for the corporate world.

PREFACE

Growing Old in America is one of the latest volumes in the Information Plus Reference Series. Previously published by the Information Plus company of Wylie, Texas, the Information Plus Reference Series (and its companion set, the Information Plus Compact Series) became a Gale Group product when Gale and Information Plus merged in early 2000. Those of you familiar with the series as published by Information Plus will notice a few changes from the 2000 edition. Gale has adopted a new layout and style that we hope you will find easy to use. Other improvements include greatly expanded indexes in each book, and more descriptive tables of contents.

While some changes have been made to the design, the purpose of the Information Plus Reference Series remains the same. Each volume of the series presents the latest facts on a topic of pressing concern in modern American life. These topics include today's most controversial and most studied social issues: abortion, capital punishment, care for the elderly, crime, health care, the environment, immigration, minorities, social welfare, women, youth, and many more. Although written especially for the high school and undergraduate student, this series is an excellent resource for anyone in need of factual information on current affairs.

By presenting the facts, it is Gale's intention to provide its readers with everything they need to reach an informed opinion on current issues. To that end, there is a particular emphasis in this series on the presentation of scientific studies, surveys, and statistics. These data are generally presented in the form of tables, charts, and other graphics placed within the text of each book. Every graphic is directly referred to and carefully explained in the text. The source of each graphic is presented within the graphic itself. The data used in these graphics is drawn from the most reputable and reliable sources, in particular the various branches of the U.S. government and major independent polling organizations. Every effort has been made to secure the most recent information available. The reader should bear in mind that many major studies take years to conduct, and that additional years often pass before the data from these studies are made available to the public. Therefore, in many cases the most recent information available in 2002 dated from 1999 or 2000. Older statistics are sometimes presented as well, if they are of particular interest and no more recent information exists.

Although statistics are a major focus of the Information Plus Reference Series, they are by no means its only content. Each book also presents the widely held positions and important ideas that shape how the book's subject is discussed in the United States. These positions are explained in detail and, where possible, in the words of their proponents. Some of the other material to be found in these books includes: historical background; descriptions of major events related to the subject; relevant laws and court cases; and examples of how these issues play out in American life. Some books also feature primary documents, or have pro and con debate sections giving the words and opinions of prominent Americans on both sides of a controversial topic. All material is presented in an even-handed and unbiased manner; the reader will never be encouraged to accept one view of an issue over another.

HOW TO USE THIS BOOK

American society is aging at an increasing rate. In the last 100 years the percentage of Americans over the age of 65 has more than tripled. This book explores the current condition of growing old in the United States. Included is a general overview on growing old in America; the economic status of older people; the Social Security program; the living arrangements of the elderly; working and retirement; and the education levels, voting trends, and political behavior of the elderly. General health and health problems, including physical and mental health; drug and alcohol abuse; caring for the elderly; crime; and death, dying, funerals, and burials are also covered.

Growing Old in America consists of twelve chapters and three appendices. Each of the chapters is devoted to a particular aspect of growing old. For a summary of the information covered in each chapter, please see the synopses provided in the Table of Contents at the front of the book. Chapters generally begin with an overview of the basic facts and background information on the chapter's topic, then proceed to examine sub-topics of particular interest. For example, Chapter Seven: General Health and Health Problems begins with a discussion of life expectancy, the three leading causes of death, and the general health of older Americans. It then goes on to detail the chronic physical problems of the elderly including arthritis, diabetes, malnutrition, hearing and vision loss, dementia, and Alzheimer's disease. Drug use among the elderly, getting and staying healthy, and sexuality in aging are also included. Readers can find their way through a chapter by looking for the section and sub-section headings, which are clearly set off from the text. Or, they can refer to the book's extensive index if they already know what they are looking for.

Statistical Information

The tables and figures featured throughout *Growing Old in America* will be of particular use to the reader in learning about this issue. These tables and figures represent an extensive collection of the most recent and important statistics on growing old, as well as related issues—for example, graphics in the book cover median income, number of persons over age 65, major reasons for working after retiring, homeownership rates by age of householder, labor force participation, senior volunteer activity, reported voting and registration, leading causes of death, instrumental activities of daily living performed by caregivers, suicide rates, number of Medicare beneficiaries, and violent crime rate. Gale believes that making this information available to the reader is the most important way in which we fulfill the goal of this book: to help readers understand the issues and controversies surrounding growing old in the United States and reach their own conclusions.

Each table or figure has a unique identifier appearing above it, for ease of identification and reference. Titles for the tables and figures explain their purpose. At the end of each table or figure, the original source of the data is provided.

In order to help readers understand these often complicated statistics, all tables and figures are explained in the text. References in the text direct the reader to the relevant statistics. Furthermore, the contents of all tables and figures are fully indexed. Please see the opening section of the index at the back of this volume for a description of how to find tables and figures within it.

In addition to the main body text and images, *Growing Old in America* has three appendices. The first is the Important Names and Addresses directory. Here the reader will find contact information for a number of government and private organizations that can provide information on growing old. The second appendix is the Resources section, which can also assist the reader in conducting his or her own research. In this section, the author and editors of *Growing Old in America* describe some of the sources that were most useful during the compilation of this book. The final appendix is the index. It has been greatly expanded from previous editions, and should make it even easier to find specific topics in this book.

COMMENTS AND SUGGESTIONS

The editors of the Information Plus Reference Series welcome your feedback on *Growing Old in America*. Please direct all correspondence to:

Editors
Information Plus Reference Series
27500 Drake Rd.
Farmington Hills, MI 48331-3535

ACKNOWLEDGEMENTS

The editors wish to thank the copyright holders of material included in this volume and the permissions managers of many book and magazine publishing companies for assisting us in securing reproduction rights. We are also grateful to the staffs of the Detroit Public Library, the Library of Congress, the University of Detroit Mercy Library, Wayne State University Purdy/Kresge Library Complex, and the University of Michigan Libraries for making their resources available to us.

Following is a list of the copyright holders who have granted us permission to reproduce material in Information Plus: Growing Old in America. *Every effort has been made to trace copyright, but if omissions have been made, please let us know.*

Acknowledgements are listed in the order the tables and figures appear in the text of Growing Old in America. *For more detailed citations, please see the sources listed under each table and figure.*

Figure 1.1. From "Figure 1: Number of Persons 65+, 1900-2030," in *A Profile of Older Americans: 2000.* U.S. Department of Health and Human Services, Administration on Aging, Washington, DC. 2000.

Table 1.1. Hetzel, Lisa and Annetta Smith. From "Table 1. Population 65 Years and Over by Age: 1990 and 2000," in *The 65 Years and Over Population: 2000.* U.S. Census Bureau, Washington, DC. October 2001.

Table 1.2. Krach, Constance A. and Victoria A. Velkoff. From *Centenarians in the United States.* U.S. Census Bureau, Washington, DC. 1999.

Figure 1.2. From "Projected Resident Population of the United States as of July 1, 2000, Middle Series," "Projected Resident Population of the United States as of July 1, 2025, Middle Series," "Projected Resident Population of the United States as of July 1, 2050, Middle Series," and "Projected Resident

Population of the United States as of July 1, 2100, Middle Series," in *Population Projections* [Online]. http://www.census.gov/ population/www/projections/natchart.html [accessed September 26, 2001]. U.S. Census Bureau, Population Division, National Projections Program, Washington, DC.

Table 1.3. Hetzel, Lisa and Annetta Smith. From "Table 2. Number of Men per 100 Women by Age, for the 65 Years and Over Population: 1990 and 2000," in *The 65 Years and Over Population: 2000.* U.S. Census Bureau, Washington, DC. October 2001.

Table 1.4. Fields, Jason and Lynne M. Casper. From "Table 5. Marital Status of People 15 Years and Over: March 1970 and March 2000," in *America's Families and Living Arrangements: March 2000.* U.S. Census Bureau, Washington, DC. 2001.

Table 1.5. From "Table 8. Foreign-Born Population Age 55 Years and Over by Sex, Citizenship Status, Year of Entry, and Age: March 2000," in *The Older Population in the United States: March 2000: Detailed Tables (PPL-147)* [Online]. http://www.census.gov/ population/socdemo/age/ppl-147/tab08.txt [accessed September 26, 2001]. U.S. Census Bureau, Washington, DC. June 1, 2001.

Table 1.6. Hetzel, Lisa and Annetta Smith. From "Table 3. Population 65 Years and Over for the United States, Regions, and States, and for Puerto Rico: 1990 and 2000," in *The 65 Years and Over Population: 2000.* U.S. Census Bureau, Washington, DC. October 2001.

Table 1.7. From "Projections of the Population, By Age and Sex, of States: 1995 to 2025," in *State Population Projections* [Online]. http://www.census.gov/population/ projections/state/stpjage.txt [accessed September 26, 2001]. U.S. Census Bureau, Washington, DC.

Table 1.8. *Innovations: The Journal of the National Council on the Aging,* no. 1, 2001, for "NCOA Survey Heralds New Age of Old Age" by Michael Reinemer. National Council on the Aging.

Table 1.9. From "Table 7. Median Age by Major Area, 1950, 2000 and 2050 (medium variant)," in *World Population Prospects: The 2000 Revision—Highlights.* United Nations, Department of Economic and Social Affairs, Population Division, New York, NY. February 28, 2001.

Table 1.10. From "Table 3. Expectation of Life at Birth for the World, Major Development Groups and Major Areas, 1995-2000 and 2045-2050," in *World Population Prospects: The 2000 Revision—Highlights.* United Nations, Department of Economic and Social Affairs, Population Division, New York, NY. February 28, 2001.

Table 2.1. Davern, Michael E. and Patricia J. Fisher. From "Table F. Percent Distribution of Net Worth of Households, by Age of Householder and Asset Type: 1993 and 1995," in *Household Net Worth and Asset Ownership: 1995.* U.S. Census Bureau, Washington, DC. February 2001.

Table 2.2. Davern, Michael E. and Patricia J. Fisher. From "Table 1. Median Net Worth and Median Net Worth Excluding Home Equity of Households, by Type of Household and Age of Householder: 1993 and 1995," in *Household Net Worth and Asset Ownership: 1995.* U.S. Census Bureau, Washington, DC. February 2001.

Table 2.3. From "Table 7. Median Income of People by Selected Characteristics: 2000, 1999, 1998," in *Income 2000* [Online]. http://www.census.gov/hhes/income/income00/ inctab7.html [accessed October 2001]. U.S. Census Bureau, Washington, DC.

Table 2.4. From "Table 4. Median Income of Households by Selected Characteristics,

Race, and Hispanic Origin of Householder: 2000, 1999, and 1998," in *Income 2000* [Online]. http://www.census.gov/hhes/income/income00/inctab1.html [accessed October 2001]. U.S. Census Bureau, Washington, DC.

Figure 2.1. Dalaker, Joseph. From "Figure 2. Poverty Rates by Age: 1959 to 2000," in *Poverty in the United States: 2000*. U.S. Census Bureau, Washington, DC. September 2001.

Table 2.5. From Dalaker, Joseph "Table A. People and Families in Poverty by Selected Characteristics: 1999 and 2000," in *Poverty in the United States: 2000*. U.S. Census Bureau, Washington, DC. September 2001.

Figure 2.2. From "Poverty Status, 1999," in *Fast Facts & Figures About Social Security*. Social Security Administration, Washington, DC. June 2001.

Figure 2.3. From "Aggregate Income by Source, 1999," in *Fast Facts & Figures About Social Security*. Social Security Administration, Washington, DC. June 2001.

Figure 2.4. From "Ratio of Social Security to total income," in *Fast Facts & Figures About Social Security*. Social Security Administration, Washington, DC. June 2001.

Table 2.6. From "Expected and Actual Retirement Age: 2001," in *The 2001 Retirement Confidence Survey Summary of Findings*. Employee Benefit Research Institute, American Savings Education Council, and Mathew Greenwald & Associates, Inc. May 10, 2001.

Table 2.7. From *Retirement in America* [Online]. http://www.ebri.org/rcs/2001/01rcsf1.pdf [accessed October 17, 2001]. Employee Benefit Research Institute.

Table 2.8. From "Percentage Having Saved for Retirement," in *The 2001 Retirement Confidence Survey Summary of Findings*. Employee Benefit Research Institute, American Savings Education Council, and Mathew Greenwald & Associates, Inc. May 10, 2001.

Table 2.9. From "Table 3. Age of Reference Person: Average Annual Expenditures and Characteristics, Consumer Expenditure Survey, 1999" [Online]. http://www.bls.gov/cex/1999/Standard/age.pdf [accessed October 22, 2001]. Bureau of Labor Statistics, Washington, DC.

Table 2.10. From *Fast Facts & Figures About Social Security*. Social Security Administration, Washington, DC. June 2001.

Figure 2.5. "Hypothetical Benefit Amounts," in *Fast Facts & Figures About Social Security*. Social Security Administration, Washington, DC. June 2001.

Figure 2.6. "Adult Beneficiaries by Sex," in *Fast Facts & Figures About Social Security*. Social Security Administration, Washington, DC. June 2001.

Figure 2.7. From "Average monthly payment," in *Fast Facts & Figures About Social Security*. Social Security Administration, Washington, DC. June 2001.

Figure 2.8. From *Social Security: Individual Accounts as an Element of Long-Term Financing Reform*. U.S. General Accounting Office, Washington, DC. 1999.

Table 2.11. From "Confidence in Social Security and Medicare," in *The 2001 Retirement Confidence Survey Summary of Findings*. Employee Benefit Research Institute, American Savings Education Council, and Mathew Greenwald & Associates, Inc. May 10, 2001.

Table 3.1. Fields, Jason and Lynne M. Casper. From "Table 1. Households by Type and Selected Characteristics: March 2000," in *America's Families and Living Arrangements: March 2000*. U.S. Census Bureau, Washington, DC. 2001.

Table 3.2. From "Table 15. Home Ownership Rates for the United States by Age of Householder and by Family Status: 1982 to 1999," in *Housing Vacancies and Homeownership Annual Statistics: 1999* [Online]. http://www.census.gov/hhes/www/housing/hvs/annual99/ann99ind.html U.S. Census Bureau, Washington, DC. February 2001.

Table 3.3. From "Least Affordable States," in *Out of Reach, September 2001* [Online]. http://www.nlihc.org/oor2001/table1.htm [accessed October 24, 2001]. National Low Income Housing Coalition (NLIHC), Washington, DC.

Table 3.4. From "Least Affordable Metropolitan Statistical Areas (MSAs)" in *Out of Reach, September 2001* [Online]. http://www.nlihc.org/oor2001/table2.htm [accessed October 24, 2001]. National Low Income Housing Coalition (NLIHC), Washington, DC.

Table 4.1. *Monthly Labor Review Online*, v. 123, n. 10, October 2000, for "Table 2. Labor Force Participation Rates by Age and Sex, 1950-2008," in "Older Workers: Employment and Retirement Trends" by Patrick J. Purcell.

Table 4.2. From "American Seniors, 1998," in *The New Nonprofit Almanac in Brief*. Independent Sector, Washington, DC. 2001. Reproduced by permission.

Figure 4.1. From "Where Seniors Volunteer, 1998," in *The New Nonprofit Almanac in Brief*. Independent Sector, Washington DC. 2001. Reproduced by permission.

Table 5.1. From "Table 1. Educational Attainment of the Population 15 Years and Over, by Age, Sex, Race, and Hispanic Origin: March, 2000," in *Educational Attainment in the United States: March 2000*. U.S. Census Bureau, Washington, DC. December 2000.

Table 5.2. Wirt, John, et al. From "Table 7-1. Percentage of adults age 18 and above who participated in learning activities in the past 12 months, by educational attainment and age: 1991, 1995, 1999," in *The Condition of Education: 2001*. U.S. Department of Education, National Center for Education Statistics, Washington, DC. 2001.

Table 5.3. Newburger, Eric C. From "Table A. Households With Computers and Internet Access by Selected Characteristics: August 2000," in *Home Computers and Internet Use in the United States: August 2000*. U.S. Census Bureau, Washington, DC. September 2001.

Table 5.4. From "Table 1. Reported Voting and Registration, by Sex and Single Years of Age: November 1998," in *Voting and Registration in the Election of November 1998, Detailed Tables for Current Population Report, P20-523* [Online]. http://www.census.gov/population/socdemo/voting/cps1998/tab01.txt [accessed October 2001]. U.S. Census Bureau, Washington, DC. November 2000.

Table 5.5. From "Table 12. Reasons for Not Voting, by Sex, Age, Race, and Hispanic Origin, and Educational Attainment: November 1998," in *Voting and Registration in the Election of November 1998, Detailed Tables for Current Population Report, P20-523* [Online]. http://www.census.gov/population/socdemo/voting/cps1998/tab01.txt [accessed October 2001]. U.S. Census Bureau, Washington, DC. November 2000.

Table 7.1. From "Table 33. Leading causes of death and numbers of deaths, according to age: United States, 1980 and 1999," in *Health, United States, 2001*. Centers for Disease Control and Prevention, National Center for Health Statistics, Hyattsville, MD. 2001.

Table 7.2. *National Vital Statistics Reports*, v. 49, n. 8, September 21, 2001, for "Table 8. Death Rates by age and age-adjusted death rates for the 15 leading causes of death in 1999: United States, 1998, modified 1998, and 1999," in "Deaths: Final Data for 1999" by D.L. Hoyert, et al.

Table 7.3. From "Table 37. Death rates for diseases of the heart, according to sex, race, Hispanic origin, and age: United States, selected years 1950-99," in *Health, United States, 2001*. Centers for Disease Control and Prevention, National Center for Health Statistics, Hyattsville, MD. 2001.

Table 7.4. From "Table 38. Death rates for cerebrovascular diseases, according to sex, race, Hispanic origin, and age: United States, selected years, 1950-99" in *Health, United States, 2001*. Centers for Disease Control and Prevention, National Center for Health Statistics, Hyattsville, MD. 2001.

Table 7.5. From "Table 58. Respondent-assessed health status according to selected characteristics: United States, selected years 1991-99," in *Health, United States, 2001*. Centers for Disease Control and Prevention, National Center for Health Statistics, Hyattsville, MD. 2001.

Table 7.6. *Morbidity and Mortality Weekly Report*, v. 50, n. 7, February 23, 2001, for "Table 1. Number and prevalence rates of civilian noninstitutionalized persons aged 18 years and older with disability, by age group—Survey of Income Program and Participation, United States, 1999," in "Prevalence of Disabilities and Associated Health Conditions Among Adults—United States, 1999."

Table 7.7. From "Table 72. Health care visits to doctor's offices, emergency departments, and home visits within the past 12 months, according to selected characteristics: United States: 1997-99," in *Health United States: 2001: Updated Tables* [Online]. http://www.cdc.gov/nchs/products/pubs/pubd/hus/tables/2001/01hus072.pdf [accessed October 2001]. Centers for Disease Control and Prevention, National Center for Health Statistics, Hyattsville, MD. September 2001.

Table 7.8. Adams, P.F., et al. From "Table 57. Number of selected reported chronic conditions per 1,000 persons, by age: United States, 1996," in *Current Estimates from the National Health Interview Survey, 1996*. Centers for Disease Control and Prevention, National Center for Health Statistics, Hyattsville, MD. 1999.

Figure 7.1. From "Figure 14. Prevalence of reduced hip bone density among persons 65 years of age and over by age, sex, and severity: United States, 1988-94," in *Health, United States, 1999*. Centers for Disease Control and Prevention, National Center for Health Statistics, Hyattsville, MD. 1999.

Table 7.9. *Family Economics and Nutrition Review*, v. 8, n. 4, 1995, for "How Does Living Alone Affect Dietary Quality?"

Table 7.10. *Family Economics and Nutrition Review*, v. 8, n. 4, 1995, for "How Does Living Alone Affect Dietary Quality?"

Figure 7.2. *Aging Trends*, n. 2, March 2001, for "Percent of elderly who reported currently having hearing impairments by age, sex, and race, 1995," in "Trends in Vision and Hearing Among Older Americans" by Mayur Desai, et al.

Figure 7.3. *Aging Trends*, n. 2, March 2001, for "Percent of elderly who reported being visually impaired by age, sex, and race, 1995," in "Trends in Vision and Hearing Among Older Americans" by Mayur Desai, et al.

Figure 7.4. From "Figure 6.2. Self-reported prevalence of obesity among adults aged 20 years and older, by age group and sex: United States, 2000," in *Early Release of Selected Estimates from the National Health Interview Survey: Data from Year 2000 and Early 2001* [Online]. http://www.cdc.gov/nchs/data/nhis/measure06.pdf [accessed October 2001]. Centers for Disease Control and Prevention, National Center for Health Statistics, Hyattsville, MD. October 2001.

Table 7.11. From "Table 68. Serum cholesterol levels among persons 20 years of age and over, according to sex, age, race, and Hispanic origin: United States, 1960-62, 1971-74, 1976-80, and 1988-94," in *Health, United States, 2001*. Centers for Disease Control and Prevention, National Center for Health Statistics, Hyattsville, MD. 2001.

Figure 8.1. From "U.S. suicide rates by age, gender, and racial group," in *In Harm's Way: Suicide in America* [Online]. http://www.nimh.nih.gov/publicat/harmaway.cfm [accessed October 2001]. National Institute of Mental Health, Bethesda, MD. January 1, 2001.

Table 8.1. From "Table 47. Death Rates for Suicide, According to Sex, Race, Hispanic Origin, and Age: United States, Selected Years, 1950-1999," in *Health, United States, 2001*. Centers for Disease Control and Prevention, National Center for Health Statistics, Hyattsville, MD. 2001.

Figure 8.2. From "Figure 9.2. Percentage of adults aged 18 years and older with excessive alcohol consumption, by age group and sex: United States, 2000," in *National Health Interview Survey: Data from Year 2000 and Early 2001* [Online]. http://www.cdc.gov/nchs/data/nhis/measure09.pdf [accessed October 2001]. Centers for Disease Control and Prevention, National Center for Health Statistics, Hyattsville, MD. September 20, 2001.

Table 9.1. Pandya, Sheel M. and Barbara Coleman. From "Figure 1. Caregiver characteristics, 1997," in *Caregiving and Long-Term Care*. AARP, Washington, DC. December 2000.

Figure 9.1. From "Figure 7. Activities of daily living performed," in *Who Cares? Families Caring for Persons with Alzheimer's Disease*, Alzheimer's Association and National Alliance for Caregiving, Washington, DC, and Bethesda, MD. 1999.

Figure 9.2. From "Figure 8. Instrumental activities of daily living performed," in *Who Cares? Families Caring for Persons with Alzheimer's Disease*, Alzheimer's Association and National Alliance for Caregiving, Washington, DC, and Bethesda, MD. 1999.

Figure 9.3. From "Figure 9. Level of care index," in *Who Cares? Families Caring for Persons with Alzheimer's Disease*, Alzheimer's Association and National Alliance for Caregiving, Washington, DC, and Bethesda, MD. 1999.

Figure 9.4. From "Figure 10. Medication management," in *Who Cares? Families Caring for Persons with Alzheimer's Disease*, Alzheimer's Association and National Alliance for Caregiving, Washington, DC, and Bethesda, MD. 1999.

Figure 9.5. From "Figure 2. Relationship between caregiver and care recipient," in *Who Cares? Families Caring for Persons with Alzheimer's Disease*, Alzheimer's Association and National Alliance for Caregiving, Washington, DC, and Bethesda, MD. 1999.

Figure 9.6. From "Figure 21. Impact of caregiving on work," in *Who Cares? Families Caring for Persons with Alzheimer's Disease*, Alzheimer's Association and National Alliance for Caregiving, Washington, DC, and Bethesda, MD. 1999.

Figure 9.7. From "Figure 17. Coping behavior," in *Who Cares? Families Caring for Persons with Alzheimer's Disease*, Alzheimer's Association and National Alliance for Caregiving, Washington, DC, and Bethesda, MD. 1999.

Figure 9.8. From "Figure E. Helpfulness of information," in *The Caregiving Boom: Baby Boomer Women Giving Care*. National Alliance for Caregiving, Bethesda, MD. 1998. Reproduced by permission.

Table 9.2. From "Table 3. Influence of caregiving on thinking about future," in *The Caregiving Boom: Baby Boomer Women Giving Care*. National Alliance for Caregiving, Bethesda, MD. 1998. Reproduced by permission.

Figure 9.9. From "Figure J. Actions taken to plan for own long term care needs," in *The Caregiving Boom: Baby Boomer Women Giving Care*. National Alliance for Caregiving, Bethesda, MD. 1998. Reproduced by permission.

Figure 9.10. *Health Affairs*, v. 18, n. 2, March/April 1999, for "Economic value of informal caregiving, 1997," in "The Economic Value of Informal Caregiving" by Peter S. Arno, Carol Levine, and Margaret M. Memmott. Reproduced by permission.

Figure 9.11. *Health Affairs*, v. 18, n. 2, March/April 1999, for "Home care, nursing home care, informal caregiving, and total national health care spending, 1997," in

"The Economic Value of Informal Caregiving" by Peter S. Arno, Carol Levine, and Margaret M. Memmott. Reproduced by permission.

Table 9.3. From "Replacement costs for employees who quit," in *The MetLife Study of Employer Costs for Working Caregivers*. Metropolitan Life Insurance Company, Westport, CT. 1997. Reproduced by permission.

Table 9.4. From "Costs due to absenteeism," in *The MetLife Study of Employer Costs for Working Caregivers*. Metropolitan Life Insurance Company, Westport, CT. 1997. Reproduced by permission.

Table 9.5. From "Costs Due to partial absenteeism," in *The MetLife Study of Employer Costs for Working Caregivers*. Metropolitan Life Insurance Company, Westport, CT. 1997. Reproduced by permission.

Table 9.6. From "Costs due to workday interruptions," in *The MetLife Study of Employer Costs for Working Caregivers*. Metropolitan Life Insurance Company, Westport, CT. 1997. Reproduced by permission.

Table 9.7. From "Costs Due to Eldercare Crises," in *The MetLife Study of Employer Costs for Working Caregivers*. Metropolitan Life Insurance Company, Westport, CT. 1997. Reproduced by permission.

Table 9.8. From "Costs Associated with Supervising Caregivers," in *The MetLife Study of Employer Costs for Working Caregivers*. Metropolitan Life Insurance Company, Westport, CT. 1997. Reproduced by permission.

Table 9.9. From "All Costs to Employers," in *The MetLife Study of Employer Costs for Working Caregivers*. Metropolitan Life Insurance Company, Westport, CT. 1997. Reproduced by permission.

Table 10.1. From "Table 90. Discharges, Days of Care, and Average Length of Stay in Short-Stay Hospitals, According to Selected Characteristics: United States: 1997-1999," in *Health, United States, 2001: Updated Tables* [Online]. http://www.cdc.gov/nchs/products/pubs/pubd/hus/tables/2001/01hus090.pdf [accessed October 2001]. Centers for Disease Control and Prevention, National Center for Health Statistics, Hyattsville, MD. September 2001.

Table 10.2. From "Table 124. Nursing Home Average Monthly Charges Per Resident and Percent of Residents, According to Primary Source of Payments and Selected Facility Payments: United States, 1985, 1995, 1997 and 1999," in *Health, United States, 2001: Updated Tables* [Online]. http://www.cdc.gov/nchs/products/pubs/pubd/hus/tables/2001/01hus124.pdf [accessed October 2001]. Centers for Disease Control and Prevention,

National Center for Health Statistics, Hyattsville, MD. September 2001.

Table 10.3. From "Table 2. National Health Expenditure Amounts, and Average Annual Percent Change by Type of Expenditure: Selected Calendar Years 1980-2010," in *National Health Care Expenditure Projections: 2000-2010* [Online]. http://www.hcfa.gov/stats/nhe-proj/proj2000/tables/t2.htm [accessed October 2001]. Centers for Medicare and Medicaid Services, Baltimore, MD.

Table 10.4. From "Table 131. Health Care Coverage for Persons 65 Years of Age and Over, According to Type of Coverage and Selected Characteristics: United States: Selected Years 1989-1999," in *Health, United States, 2001: Updated Tables* [Online]. http://www.cdc.gov/nchs/products/pubs/pubd/hus/tables/2001/01hus131.pdf [accessed October 2001]. Centers for Disease Control and Prevention, National Center for Health Statistics, Hyattsville, MD. September 2001.

Figure 10.1. From "Figure 1. Number of Medicare Beneficiaries, CY 1970-2030," in *Medicare: A Profile* [Online]. http://www.hcfa.gov/stats/35chartbk.pdf [accessed October 2001]. Health Care Financing Administration. July 2000.

Figure 10.2. From "Figure 5. Medicare Spending for Fee-For-Service Beneficiaries by Income, 1997," in *Medicare: A Profile* [Online]. http://www.hcfa.gov/stats/35chartbk.pdf [accessed October 2001]. Health Care Financing Administration. July 2000.

Figure 10.3. From "Figure 20. National Personal Health Expenditures by Type of Service and Percent Medicare Paid, 1998," in *Medicare: A Profile* [Online]. http://www.hcfa.gov/stats/35chartbk.pdf [accessed October 2001]. Health Care Financing Administration. July 2000.

Figure 10.4. From "Figure 3. Average Prescriptions Filled by Medicare Beneficiaries, with and without Drug Coverage, by Selected Characteristics, 1998," in *Medicare and Prescription Drugs* [Online]. http://www.kff.org/content/2001/1583-03/1583_03rx.pdf [accessed October 2001]. The Henry J. Kaiser Family Foundation, Washington, DC. May 2001.

Figure 10.5. From "Figure 10. Sources of Payment for Medicare Beneficiaries' Use of Medical Services, 1997," in *Medicare: A Profile* [Online]. http://www.hcfa.gov/stats/35chartbk.pdf [accessed October 2001]. Health Care Financing Administration. July 2000.

Figure 10.6. From "Figure 9. Where the Medicare Dollar Went, 1980 and 1998," in *Medicare: A Profile* [Online]. http://www.hcfa.gov/stats/35chartbk.pdf [accessed Octo-

ber 2001]. Health Care Financing Administration. July 2000.

Figure 10.7. From "Figure 1.9. Distribution of Persons Served Through Medicaid, by Basis of Eligibility, Fiscal Years 1973 and 1998," in *A Profile of Medicaid* [Online]. http://www.hcfa.gov/stats/2Tchartbk.pdf [accessed October 2001]. Health Care Financing Administration. September 2000.

Figure 10.8. From "Figure 4.4. Medicaid Nursing Home Expenditures as a Percent of Total U.S. Nursing Home Care Expenditures, Calendar Years 1968 and 1998," in *A Profile of Medicaid* [Online]. http://www.hcfa.gov/stats/2Tchartbk.pdf [accessed October 2001]. Health Care Financing Administration. September 2000.

Table 10.5. From "Supplemental Table 3. National Veteran Population by Age (1990-2020)," in *Veteran Data and Information* [Online]. http://www.va.gov/vetdata/Demographics/Vpwelcome.htm [accessed October 2001]. Department of Veterans Affairs, Washington, DC. July 31, 2001.

Figure 10.9. From "Long-term care population, 1996," in *Covering Health Issues: Campaign 2000 and Beyond*. Alliance for Health Reform, Washington, DC. 2000.

Figure 10.10. From "Projection of national long-term care expenditures for the elderly, 2000-2040," in *Covering Health Issues: Campaign 2000 and Beyond*. Alliance for Health Reform, Washington, DC. 2000.

Figure 10.11. From "Long-term care financing 1997," in *Covering Health Issues: Campaign 2000 and Beyond*. Alliance for Health Reform, Washington, DC. 2000.

Figure 10.12. From "Figure 5. Medicaid spending for long-term care, 1990 and 1997," in *Defining Common Ground: Long Term Care Financing Reform in 2001* [Online]. http://www.citizensforltc.org/whitepapers.html [accessed October 2001]. Citizens for Long Term Care, Washington, DC. February 2001.

Table 10.6. From "Long-term care insurance average annual premium," in *Covering Health Issues: Campaign 2000 and Beyond*. Alliance for Health Reform, Washington, DC. 2000.

Table 11.1. Klaus, Patsy. From "Victimizations of persons age 65 or older or of households with a head of household age 65 or older," in *Crimes Against Persons Age 65 or Older, 1992-97*. U.S. Department of Justice, Bureau of Justice Statistics, Washington, DC. 2000.

Figure 11.1. Klaus, Patsy. From "Violent crimes per 1,000 persons age 65 or older," in *Crimes Against Persons Age 65 or Older,*

1992-97. U.S. Department of Justice, Bureau of Justice Statistics, Washington, DC. 2000.

Figure 11.2. Klaus, Patsy. From "Property crimes per 1,000 households with a household head age 65 or older," in *Crimes Against Persons Age 65 or Older, 1992-97*. U.S. Department of Justice, Bureau of Justice Statistics, Washington, DC. 2000.

Figure 11.3. Klaus, Patsy. From "Rates of murder against persons age 65 or older declined after 1976 while those against persons ages 12-24 fluctuated," in *Crimes Against Persons Age 65 or Older, 1992-97*. U.S. Department of Justice, Bureau of Justice Statistics, Washington, DC. 2000.

Figure 11.4. Klaus, Patsy. From "Rates of nonfatal violence against persons age 65 or older declined, 1973-97," in *Crimes Against Persons Age 65 or Older, 1992-97*. U.S. Department of Justice, Bureau of Justice Statistics, Washington, DC. 2000.

Figure 11.5. Klaus, Patsy. From "For a household with a person age 65 or older as head, property crimes in 1997 occurred at half the 1973 rate," in *Crimes Against Persons Age 65 or Older, 1992-97*. U.S. Department of Justice, Bureau of Justice Statistics, Washington, DC. 2000.

Table 11.2. Klaus, Patsy. From "Relatives of intimates committed more than 1 in 4 of the murders and 1 in 10 of the incidents of nonlethal violence against persons age 65 or older," in *Crimes Against Persons Age 65 or Older, 1992-97*. U.S. Department of Justice, Bureau of Justice Statistics, Washington, DC. 2000.

Figure 11.6. Klaus, Patsy. From "43% of nonlethal violence against persons over age 64 occurred in or near the victim's home," in *Crimes Against Persons Age 65 or Older, 1992-97*. U.S. Department of Justice, Bureau of Justice Statistics, Washington, DC. 2000.

Figure 11.7. Klaus, Patsy. From "70% of nonlethal violence against persons over age 64 occurred during the day," in *Crimes Against Persons Age 65 or Older, 1992-97*. U.S. Department of Justice, Bureau of Justice Statistics, Washington, DC. 2000.

Figure 11.8. Klaus, Patsy. From "Among households with an elderly head of household, property crime rates were higher in those having annual incomes over $50,000," in *Crimes Against Persons Age 65 or Older, 1992-97*. U.S. Department of Justice, Bureau of Justice Statistics, Washington, DC. 2000.

Figure 11.9. Klaus, Patsy. From "White women age 65 or older had the lowest rate of nonlethal violent victimization, 1992-1997," in *Crimes Against Persons Age 65 or Older, 1992-97*. U.S. Department of Justice, Bureau of Justice Statistics, Washington, DC. 2000.

Figure 11.10. Klaus, Patsy. From "Households with a white female head of household age 65 or older had the lowest property crime rates, 1992-97," in *Crimes Against Persons Age 65 or Older, 1992-97*. U.S. Department of Justice, Bureau of Justice Statistics, Washington, DC. 2000.

Figure 11.11. Klaus, Patsy. From "On average each year 1992-97, of persons age 65 or older who reported being a victim of violence, 22% were injured and 1% were hospitalized overnight," in *Crimes Against Persons Age 65 or Older, 1992-97*. U.S. Department of Justice, Bureau of Justice Statistics, Washington, DC. 2000.

Figure 11.12. Klaus, Patsy. From "Victims age 65 or older were more likely than younger victims to report nonlethal violence and personal theft to the police," in *Crimes Against Persons Age 65 or Older, 1992-97*. U.S. Department of Justice, Bureau of Justice Statistics, Washington, DC. 2000.

Figure 11.13. From "Breakdown of Confirmed Perpetrators," in *Elder Abuse Awareness Kit: A Resource Kit for Protecting Older People and People with Disabilities* [Online]. http://www.elderabusecenter.org/basic/speakers.pdf [accessed October 2001]. National Association of Adult Protective Service Administrators/National Center on Elder Abuse, Washington, DC. April 2001.

CHAPTER 1
OLDER AMERICANS—A DIVERSE AND GROWING POPULATION

AMERICA GROWS OLDER

Old age is the most unexpected of all the things that happen to a man.

— Leon Trotsky (1879–1940)

America is growing older. Since 1900 the percentage of Americans aged 65 years and older has more than tripled and the number has increased by a factor of 11. In 2000, of an estimated U.S. population of 281.4 million people, 35 million (12 percent) were over the age of 65. (Unless otherwise noted, the statistics in this chapter are from the U.S. Census Bureau.)

Fewer children per family and longer life spans have transformed the elderly's share in the population. By 2030

there will be about 70 million older persons, more than twice the number in 2000. (See Figure 1.1.) At that time one in five Americans will be elderly. The growth in the number of older residents is expected to be among the most important developments in the United States in the twenty-first century.

Historic Slow Rate of Growth in the 1990s

While the burgeoning of the elderly population over the twentieth century was historic and equally significant growth is predicted for the future, in the 1990s the increase in the older population was the lowest recorded in any decade. The slower growth reflected the relatively low

FIGURE 1.1

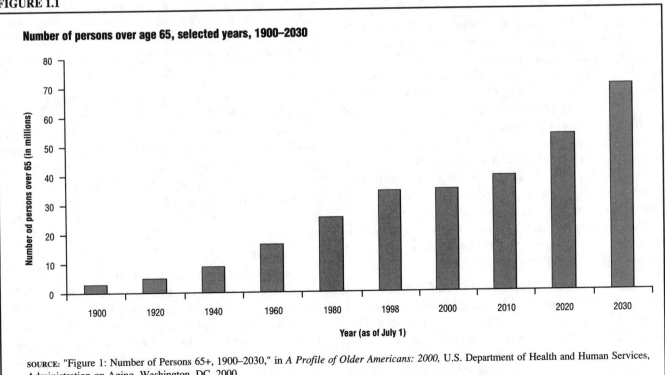

Number of persons over age 65, selected years, 1900–2030

SOURCE: "Figure 1: Number of Persons 65+, 1900–2030," in *A Profile of Older Americans: 2000*, U.S. Department of Health and Human Services, Administration on Aging, Washington, DC, 2000

TABLE 1.1

Population 65 years and over by age, 1990 and 2000

Age	1990		2000		Percent of U.S. total		Percent change, 1990 to 2000
	Number	Percent	Number	Percent	1990	2000	
65 years and over	**31,241,831**	**100.0**	**34,991,753**	**100.0**	**12.6**	**12.4**	**12.0**
65 to 74 years	18,106,558	58.0	18,390,986	52.6	7.3	6.5	1.6
65 to 69 years	10,111,735	32.4	9,533,545	27.2	4.1	3.4	-5.7
70 to 74 years	7,994,823	25.6	8,857,441	25.3	3.2	3.1	10.8
75 to 84 years	10,055,108	32.2	12,361,180	35.3	4.0	4.4	22.9
75 to 79 years	6,121,369	19.6	7,415,813	21.2	2.5	2.6	21.1
80 to 84 years	3,933,739	12.6	4,945,367	14.1	1.6	1.8	25.7
85 to 94 years	2,829,728	9.1	3,902,349	11.2	1.1	1.4	37.9
85 to 89 years	2,060,247	6.6	2,789,818	8.0	0.8	1.0	35.4
90 to 94 years	769,481	2.5	1,112,531	3.2	0.3	0.4	44.6
95 years and over	250,437	0.8	337,238	1.0	0.1	0.1	34.7

SOURCE: Lisa Hetzel and Annetta Smith, "Table 1. Population 65 Years and Over by Age: 1990 and 2000," in *The 65 Years and Over Population: 2000*, U.S. Census Bureau, Washington, DC, October 2001

number of births in the late 1920s and early 1930s. Between 1990 and 2000 the total population increased 13.2 percent, while the aged 65-plus population increased only 12 percent. (See Table 1.1.) The 2000 U.S. Census counted almost 35 million people aged 65 years and over. This number represented a decrease from 12.6 percent (in 1990) to 12.4 percent (in 2000) of the total U.S. population.

DEFINING OLDER AGE

When do the elderly years begin? The problem of defining old age is reflected in the terminology used to describe those who are no longer "young" adults: for example, middle-aged, elder, elderly, older, aged, mature, or senior.

When Social Security was created in 1935, the government assigned a person's 65th birthday as the age when he or she would become eligible for benefits. The age of 65 was not selected by a scientific process. It followed a precedent set by Chancellor Otto von Bismarck (1815–1898) of Germany in 1889. In that year, Germany became the first Western government to assume financial support of its older citizens by passing the Old Age and Survivors Pension Act. Although he was an active and vigorous 74 years old at the time, Chancellor von Bismarck arbitrarily decided that eligibility for benefits would begin at age 65. The United Nations (UN) Population Division has adjusted its definition of "elderly" to mean those 85 and older, rather than 65 and up, which is most commonly used in the United States to define the elderly population.

Many researchers distinguish between various stages of the later years: young-old (ages 65 to 74), middle-old (ages 75 to 84), and oldest-old (ages 85 and over). This book uses this terminology. In addition, the terms "older," "65-plus," and "elderly" are used interchangeably to describe people aged 65 years and older, although in a few specific cases, ages 55 and older may be used.

AGE GROUPS WITHIN THE OLDER POPULATION

In 2000 over half of the elderly population were in the young-old bracket (ages 65 to 74). There were 18.4 million people in this age group, equaling 53 percent of the 65-plus population. Thirty-five percent of the 65-plus population was in the middle-old bracket (ages 75 to 84). This group numbered 12.4 million. Twelve percent were the oldest-old, aged 85 and over. In 2000 there were 4.2 million people in this age group. (See Table 1.1.)

The Oldest-Old

During the 1990s the oldest age group within the elderly population grew more rapidly than did the aged 65 to 74 population. The 85-plus population increased nearly 38 percent between 1990 and 2000. In contrast, the middle-old increased nearly 23 percent and the young-old increased less than 2 percent.

By 2050 the 85-plus age group will make up 5 percent of the total U.S. population and 22 percent of the 65-plus age group. Among the oldest-old, women outnumber men by a ratio of five to two. Because women will continue to live longer into the middle of the twenty-first century, they will make up an even larger proportion of the older population and thereby a larger percentage of the total population in the future.

Centenarians

During the first half of the twenty-first century, America will experience a "centenarian boom." The chances of living to age 100 have increased by 40 percent since 1900. The centenarian population more than doubled during the 1980s and reached 69,000 on November 1, 2000. According to the U.S. Census Bureau's middle series projections, America will have 131,000 centenarians by 2010 and 834,000 by 2050 (see Table 1.2), a phenomenal growth

TABLE 1.2

Projected number of centenarians, 2000–50[1]

Year	Total (lowest series)[2]	Total (middle series)	Total (highest series)[3]	Percent male[4]	Percent female	Percent Hispanic[5]	Percent Non-Hispanic			
							White	Black	American Indian, Eskimo, and Aleut	Asian and Pacific Islander
2000	69,000	72,000	81,000	16.7	83.3	5.6	77.8	12.5	1.4	2.8
2010	106,000	131,000	214,000	15.3	84.7	7.6	72.5	14.5	2.3	2.3
2020	135,000	214,000	515,000	15.4	84.6	9.8	69.2	13.1	2.8	4.7
2030	159,000	324,000	1,074,00	16.4	83.6	14.5	62.3	12.7	2.8	8.0
2040	174,000	447,000	1,902,000	17.4	82.8	17.7	56.2	13.2	2.7	10.5
2050	265,000	834,000	4,218,000	18.0	82.0	19.2	55.4	12.7	2.2	10.6

[1] Projections are based on a July 1, 1994 estimate of the resident population, which is based on the enumerated 1990 census population modified by age and race. As a result of these modifications, the April 1, 1990 population of centenarians is assumed to be 36,000.
[2] Assumes low fertility, low life expectancy, and low net migration in comparison to the middle series values.
[3] Assumes high fertility, high life expectancy, and high net migration in comparison to the middle series values.
[4] Percentage values are based on middle series projections.
[5] Persons of Hispanic origin may be of any race.

SOURCE: Constance A. Krach and Victoria A. Velkoff, *Centenarians in the United States*, U.S. Census Bureau, Washington, DC, 1999

when compared to the 4,000 centenarians living in the United States in 1960. Not surprisingly, most centenarians do not live long after age 100. Ninety percent do not reach 105 years of age.

LIFE EXPECTANCY

Life expectancy (the anticipated average length of life) has changed throughout history. The average life expectancy of an ancient Greek was 18 years. Native Americans in the pre-Columbian Southwest could expect to live 33 years, with the low life expectancy caused by a high infant mortality rate. According to the National Center for Health Statistics, the life expectancy of a baby born in the United States in 1900 was 47.3 years. For a baby born in 2000 life expectancy reached a record high of 76.9 years.

THE "AGE WAVE"

Why is America getting older? One of the main reasons is that in the 20 years (1945–65) after World War II, as soldiers returned home eager to start families, as the world political climate stabilized, and as the U.S. economy prospered, there was an explosion of births. Children born during these years make up what is called the baby boom generation. The baby boomers, who were heading into their forties and fifties at the start of the twenty-first century, will begin to turn 65 around 2010. The aged 65-plus population will increase dramatically between 2010 and 2030 as the baby boomers complete their transition from "middle-aged" to "older."

In addition to the large number of births after World War II, there are a number of other reasons for aging of the American population. Foremost are medical advances that have greatly reduced infant mortality and death from childhood diseases. (An extremely high infant and child mortality rate and deaths due to childbirth were the main reasons that average life expectancy was so low in early civilizations.) At the other end of life, medical advances, life-sustaining technologies, and a greater awareness of and desire for a healthy lifestyle have helped lengthen the lives of Americans.

The Median Age of the Population

Figure 1.2 shows the projected change in the age structure of the American population for the twenty-first century. When those born during the post–World War II baby boom begin to turn age 65-plus in 2011, the result will be a growth in the older population. The number of people aged 65 years and over is projected to swell from 39.7 million in 2010 to 53.7 million in 2020 and 81.9 million in 2050. About 1 in 6 Americans will be elderly in 2020, compared with 1 in 8 in 2000. This ratio will reach 1 in 5 in 2030, where it will remain through 2050. Incredibly, in 2100 it is projected that there will be 131.2 million 65-plus persons. This is equivalent to the total U.S. population in 1940.

The Future Growth of the Older Population

Initially, the birth of the baby boomers reduced the median age of the population. (The median age means that half the population is older and half is younger.) In 1970 the median age was 28. It increased by nearly two and a half years between 1990 and 2000. At the start of the twentieth century it was 35.3. As they grow older, the baby boomers are moving the median age upward in what is being termed an "age wave." According to middle series projections by the Census Bureau, the median age will be 38.9 in 2030.

FIGURE 1.2

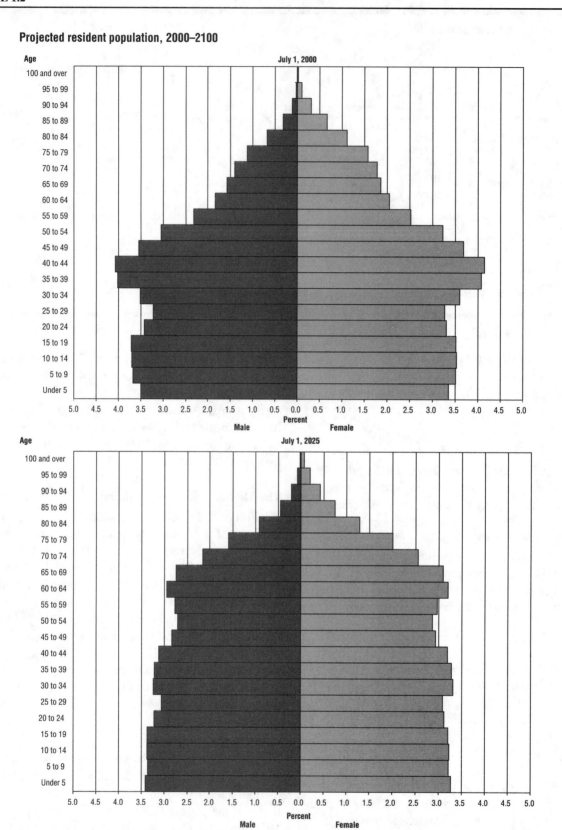

Projected resident population, 2000–2100

SOURCE: "Projected Resident Population of the United States as of July 1, 2000, Middle Series," "Projected Resident Population of the United States as of July 1, 2025, Middle Series," "Projected Resident Population of the United States as of July 1, 2050, Middle Series," and "Projected Resident Population of the United States as of July 1, 2100, Middle Series," in *Population Projections*, U.S. Census Bureau, Population Division, National Projections Program, Washington, DC [Online] http://www.census.gov/population/www/projections/natchart.html [accessed September 26, 2001]

FIGURE 1.2

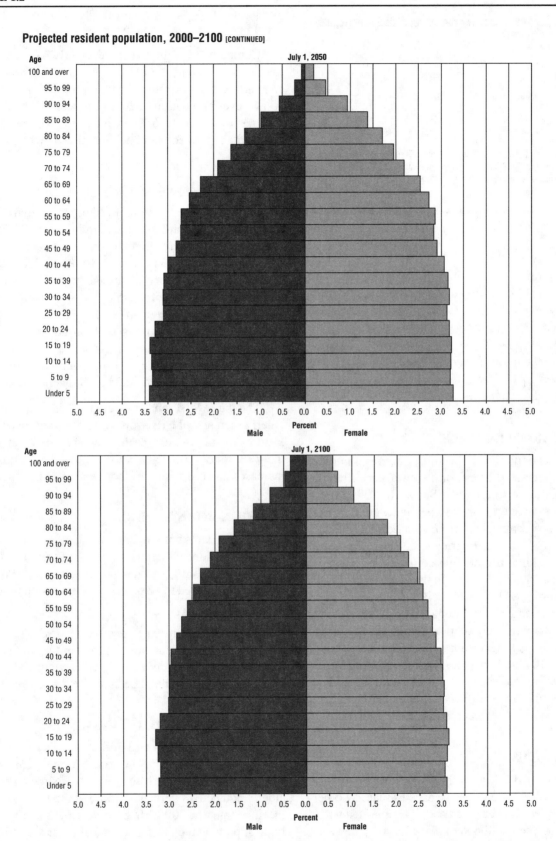

Projected resident population, 2000–2100 [CONTINUED]

July 1, 2050

July 1, 2100

SOURCE: "Projected Resident Population of the United States as of July 1, 2000, Middle Series," "Projected Resident Population of the United States as of July 1, 2025, Middle Series," "Projected Resident Population of the United States as of July 1, 2050, Middle Series," and "Projected Resident Population of the United States as of July 1, 2100, Middle Series," in *Population Projections,* U.S. Census Bureau, Population Division, National Projections Program, Washington, DC [Online] http://www.census.gov/population/www/projections/natchart.html [accessed September 26, 2001]

TABLE 1.3

Number of men per 100 women for the 65 years and over population, by age, 1990 and 2000

Age	1990	2000
65 years and over	**67**	**70**
65 to 74 years	78	82
75 to 84 years	60	65
85 years and over	39	41

SOURCE: Lisa Hetzel and Annetta Smith, "Table 2. Number of Men per 100 Women by Age, for the 65 Years and Over Population: 1990 and 2000," in *The 65 Years and Over Population: 2000,* U.S. Census Bureau, Washington, DC, October 2001

MALE-FEMALE RATIO

Women outnumber men in all older age groups. In 2000 there were 14.4 million elderly men and 20.6 million elderly women—7 men for every 10 women. (See Table 1.3.) In the 85-plus age group, there were 2 men for every 5 women. Higher female life expectancy, combined with the fact that men are generally older than their wives are, contributes to a higher proportion of women living alone—widowed or unmarried.

RACIAL CHARACTERISTICS

The older population is becoming more ethnically and racially diverse, although at a slower pace than the overall population of the United States. In 1999, of the total population over 65, about 84 percent were non-Hispanic white; 8 percent were African American; less than 1 percent were Native American; 2 percent were Asian/Pacific Islanders; and 5 percent were of Hispanic origin (who may be of any race). In the twenty-first century, the minority elderly, especially Hispanics and Asian/Pacific Islanders, are predicted to increase more rapidly than the white population. The Census Bureau reported that although races other than white now constitute about 1 in 10 elderly persons, by 2050 that proportion is expected to increase to 2 in 10. The elderly African American population will likely increase to 10 percent, and elderly Hispanics to 15 percent.

MARITAL STATUS

According to the March 2000 Current Population Survey (CPS) conducted by the Census Bureau, 54.6 percent of people aged 65 years and over were married with a spouse present. The likelihood of being married, however, decreases for older age groups. And, as would be expected, the likelihood of being a widow or widower increases.

About two-thirds, or 66.3 percent, of the young-old were married and living with their spouses. For the 70 to 74 age group, 60.7 percent were married and living with a spouse and 25.6 were widowed. And for the 75-plus age group, 43.8 percent were married and living with a spouse and 45.6 percent were widowed.

Compared to younger people, elderly Americans have low rates of marriage with the spouse absent, divorce, or separation, and low rates of never marrying. For the aged 65 and over population in 2000, 1.5 percent were married with a spouse absent, 6.7 percent were divorced, 1.1 percent were separated, and 3.9 percent were never married. (See Table 1.4.)

Men, Women, and Marital Status

Older men are much more likely to be married than older women. According to the March 2000 CPS, 72.6 percent of 65-plus men were married with a spouse present, compared to only 41.3 percent of women in this age group. And 14.4 percent of men in this age group were widowers, while 45.3 percent of 65-plus women were widows. Women in the oldest age groups have the highest rates of widowhood. Two-thirds of aged 75-plus men were married with a spouse present and 22.7 percent were widowers, while only 28.8 percent of 75-plus women were married with a spouse present and 60.5 percent were widowed.

The large discrepancy between the percentage of elderly men and elderly women who are widowed results from women living longer than men and the tendency for men to marry younger women. As life expectancy increases, the proportion of those widowed may decline.

FOREIGN-BORN ELDERLY

U.S. residents born in foreign countries are slightly less likely to be elderly than native residents are. In 2000, 11 percent of the foreign-born population were aged 65 years and over, compared to 12 percent of the native population.

Among the foreign-born elderly in 2000, more than half entered the United States before 1970. (See Table 1.5.) About 14 percent came to the United States during the 1990–2000 decade. Among elderly naturalized citizens, two-thirds entered the United States before 1970.

WHERE OLDER AMERICANS LIVE

About half (52 percent) of the nation's elderly live in nine states—California, New York, Florida, Pennsylvania, Texas, Illinois, Ohio, Michigan, and New Jersey. The elderly equaled 14 percent or more of the total population in nine states in 2000. (See Table 1.6.) Florida has the highest percentage (17.6 percent) of elderly compared to its total population, while California has the largest number of elderly. Alaska has the fewest elderly residents both in number and in percentage (5.7 percent) of population.

The regional pattern of growth in the elderly reflects that of the entire population. In the 1990s the West had the

TABLE 1.4

Marital status of people 15 years and over, 1970 and 2000

(In thousands)

Characteristic	Total	March 2000 Number Married spouse present	Married spouse absent	Sepa-rated	Divorced	Widowed	Never married	Percent never married	March 1970 percent never married[1]
Both sexes									
Total 15 years old and over	213,773	113,002	2,730	4,479	19,881	13,665	60,016	28.1	24.9
15 to 19 years old	20,102	345	36	103	64	13	19,541	97.2	93.9
20 to 24 years old	18,440	3,362	134	234	269	11	14,430	78.3	44.5
25 to 29 years old	18,269	8,334	280	459	917	27	8,252	45.2	14.7
30 to 34 years old	19,519	11,930	278	546	1,616	78	5,071	26.0	7.8
35 to 44 years old	44,804	29,353	717	1,436	5,967	399	6,932	15.5	5.9
45 to 54 years old	36,633	25,460	492	899	5,597	882	3,303	9.0	6.1
55 to 64 years old	23,388	16,393	308	441	3,258	1,770	1,218	5.2	7.2
65 years old and over	32,620	17,827	485	361	2,193	10,484	1,270	3.9	7.6
Males									
Total 15 years old and over	103,113	56,501	1,365	1,818	8,572	2,604	32,253	31.3	28.1
15 to 19 years old	10,295	69	3	51	29	3	10,140	98.5	97.4
20 to 24 years old	9,208	1,252	75	70	101	-	7,710	83.7	54.7
25 to 29 years old	8,943	3,658	139	170	342	9	4,625	51.7	19.1
30 to 34 years old	9,622	5,640	151	205	712	15	2,899	30.1	9.4
35 to 44 years old	22,134	14,310	387	585	2,775	96	3,981	18.0	6.7
45 to 54 years old	17,891	13,027	255	378	2,377	157	1,697	9.5	7.5
55 to 64 years old	11,137	8,463	158	188	1,387	329	612	5.5	7.8
65 years old and over	13,885	10,084	197	171	849	1,994	590	4.2	7.5
Females									
Total 15 years old and over	110,660	56,501	1,365	2,661	11,309	11,061	27,763	25.1	22.1
15 to 19 years old	9,807	276	33	52	35	10	9,401	95.9	90.3
20 to 24 years old	9,232	2,110	59	164	168	11	6,720	72.8	35.8
25 to 29 years old	9,326	4,676	141	289	575	18	3,627	38.9	10.5
30 to 34 years old	9,897	6,290	127	341	904	63	2,172	21.9	6.2
35 to 44 years old	22,670	15,043	330	851	3,192	303	2,951	13.0	5.2
45 to 54 years old	18,742	12,433	237	521	3,220	725	1,606	8.6	4.9
55 to 64 years old	12,251	7,930	150	253	1,871	1,441	606	4.9	6.8
65 years old and over	18,735	7,743	288	190	1,344	8,490	680	3.6	7.7

- Represents zero or rounds to zero.

[1] The 1970 percentages include 14-year-olds, and thus are for 14+ and 14-19.

SOURCE: Jason Fields and Lynne M. Casper, "Table 5. Marital Status of People 15 years and Over: March 1970 and March 2000," in *America's Families and Living Arrangements: March 2000,* U.S. Census Bureau, Washington, DC, 2001

---

highest percentage increase in the older population, almost 20 percent. The South's older population grew by 16 percent. In contrast, the older population grew by only about 7 percent in the Midwest and about 5 percent in the Northeast. (See Table 1.6.)

The number of aged 65-plus residents will increase in all regions of the United States in the twenty-first century, with the South gaining the greatest number and the Midwest the fewest. According to projections by the Census Bureau, by July 1, 2025, California is expected to be home to over 6 million elderly. (See Table 1.7.) Over 5 million elderly will live in Florida. Twenty-four states are expected to have over 1 million elderly residents. Alaska and the District of Columbia will be tied for the smallest number of elderly, with only 92,000 elderly residents each.

Most older Americans still live in, or have returned to, their native states. Older Americans are less likely than the average American to move across state lines. They tend to remain where they spent their adult lives. In 1997, according to *Americans 55 and Older: A Changing Market* (Sharon Yntema, ed., 2nd ed., New Strategist Publications, Ithaca, NY, 1999), 16 percent of all Americans moved, which was three times the proportion of those aged 55 years and older who moved. Only 7 percent of people aged 60 to 64 moved in that year, and 5 percent of those aged 65 to 69. Mobility was least common among those aged 70 to 74 (3.8 percent), but then rose to more than 6 percent at 85 years and older.

According to the Census Bureau's 2000 CPS, half of the nation's elderly lived in the suburbs. Twenty-seven percent lived inside metropolitan areas and 23 percent lived in rural areas.

Boomer Movers: From Metropolis to Rural America

Many researchers suggest that baby boomers are making retirement plans that include settling down in

TABLE 1.5

Foreign-born population, age 55 years and over, by sex, citizenship status, year of entry, and age, March 2000

(Numbers in thousands)

Citizenship, year of entry, and sex	Total		55 to 59 years		60 to 64 years		65 to 74 years		75 to 84 years		85 years and over	
	Number	Percent	Number	Percent	Number	Percent	Number	Percent	Number	Percent	Number	Percent
Total												
Total	5,736	100.0	1,420	100.0	1,201	100.0	1,778	100.0	965	100.0	373	100.0
1990 – 2000	789	13.8	242	17.0	185	15.4	244	13.7	94	9.7	25	6.7
1980 – 1989	892	15.6	244	17.2	203	16.9	282	15.9	129	13.4	35	9.4
1970 – 1979	1,035	18.0	414	29.2	240	20.0	239	13.4	109	11.3	32	8.7
Before 1970	3,019	52.6	521	36.7	573	47.7	1,013	57.0	632	65.6	280	75.3
Naturalized Citizen												
Total	3,737	100.0	786	100.0	764	100.0	1,195	100.0	695	100.0	297	100.0
1990 – 2000	142	3.8	31	4.0	38	5.0	52	4.4	19	2.7	2	0.8
1980 – 1989	417	11.2	96	12.2	101	13.2	124	10.4	76	10.9	20	6.7
1970 – 1979	695	18.6	263	33.5	174	22.8	155	13.0	79	11.4	22	7.6
Before 1970	2,483	66.4	395	50.3	450	59.0	864	72.3	521	75.0	252	84.9
Not a citizen												
Total	1,999	100.0	634	100.0	437	100.0	582	100.0	269	100.0	75	100.0
1990 – 2000	647	32.4	211	33.2	147	33.7	192	32.9	75	27.9	22	29.9
1980 – 1989	475	23.8	148	23.3	102	23.3	158	27.1	53	19.7	15	20.0
1970 – 1979	340	17.0	151	23.8	66	15.0	84	14.4	30	11.1	10	13.0
Before 1970	536	26.8	125	19.8	123	28.0	149	25.6	111	41.3	28	37.1
Male												
Total	2,539	100.0	656	100.0	537	100.0	799	100.0	406	100.0	142	100.0
1990 – 2000	353	13.9	116	17.7	75	13.9	102	12.8	54	13.3	5	3.9
1980 – 1989	407	16.0	111	16.9	102	19.0	117	14.7	61	15.0	17	11.6
1970 – 1979	452	17.8	175	26.7	109	20.3	115	14.5	42	10.3	11	7.7
Before 1970	1,327	52.3	254	38.7	251	46.8	464	58.1	249	61.4	109	76.9
Naturalized Citizen												
Total	1,659	100.0	364	100.0	332	100.0	543	100.0	299	100.0	121	100.0
1990 – 2000	70	4.2	18	4.9	11	3.2	29	5.4	10	3.5	1	1.1
1980 – 1989	203	12.2	42	11.5	58	17.5	52	9.5	39	12.9	13	10.4
1970 – 1979	290	17.5	109	29.9	73	22.0	71	13.1	31	10.3	6	4.7
Before 1970	1,097	66.1	195	53.6	190	57.3	391	72.0	219	73.4	101	83.8
Not a citizen												
Total	880	100.0	291	100.0	205	100.0	256	100.0	107	100.0	21	100.0
1990 – 2000	283	32.2	98	33.7	64	31.3	73	28.5	43	40.7	4	19.9
1980 – 1989	205	23.3	69	23.7	44	21.5	65	25.6	22	20.8	4	18.7
1970 – 1979	162	18.4	66	22.5	36	17.5	44	17.3	11	10.6	5	24.7
Before 1970	230	26.1	58	20.0	61	29.7	73	28.6	30	28.0	8	36.7
Female												
Total	3,197	100.0	764	100.0	664	100.0	979	100.0	559	100.0	231	100.0
1990 – 2000	437	13.7	126	16.4	110	16.6	141	14.4	40	7.1	19	8.4
1980 – 1989	485	15.2	133	17.4	101	15.2	165	16.8	68	12.2	18	8.0
1970 – 1979	583	18.2	239	31.3	131	19.8	124	12.6	67	12.0	21	9.3
Before 1970	1,692	52.9	267	34.9	322	48.4	549	56.1	383	68.6	171	74.3
Naturalized Citizen												
Total	2,078	100.0	421	100.0	432	100.0	652	100.0	396	100.0	176	100.0
1990 – 2000	73	3.5	13	3.2	27	6.3	23	3.5	8	2.1	1	0.6
1980 – 1989	214	10.3	54	12.8	43	10.0	72	11.1	37	9.5	7	4.2
1970 – 1979	405	19.5	154	36.6	101	23.5	84	12.9	49	12.3	17	9.5
Before 1970	1,386	66.7	200	47.4	260	60.2	473	72.5	302	76.2	151	85.7
Not a citizen												
Total	1,119	100.0	343	100.0	233	100.0	327	100.0	163	100.0	54	100.0
1990 – 2000	364	32.5	112	32.7	83	35.7	119	36.3	32	19.5	18	33.8
1980 – 1989	271	24.2	79	22.9	58	24.8	92	28.3	31	19.0	11	20.5
1970 – 1979	178	15.9	85	24.8	30	12.9	40	12.1	19	11.5	5	8.5
Before 1970	306	27.4	67	19.5	62	26.5	76	23.3	81	50.0	20	37.3

SOURCE: "Table 8. Foreign-Born Population Age 55 Years and Over by Sex, Citizenship Status, Year of Entry, and Age: March 2000," in *The Older Population in the United States: March 2000: Detailed Tables (PPL-147),* U.S. Census Bureau, Washington, DC, June 1, 2001 [Online] http://www.census.gov/population/socdemo/age/ppl-147/tab08.txt [accessed September 26, 2001]

rural areas. Upcoming retirees have more income, independence, and motivation for migrating than in the past. As a group, they are wealthier, better educated, and younger. They have benefited from the real estate boom of the 1970s and 1980s and the healthy 1990s economy.

Many are dual-career couples. They generally participate in physical activities longer and may have identified with rural areas since their "hippie" days. In addition, this generation has traveled more for work and education in their lifetimes than have previous genera-

TABLE 1.6

Population 65 years and over, by region, state, and Puerto Rico, 1990 and 2000

Area	1990 Total population	Population 65 years and over Number	Population 65 years and over Percent	2000 Total population	Population 65 years and over Number	Population 65 years and over Percent	Change, 1990 to 2000 Number	Change, 1990 to 2000 Percent
United States	248,709,873	31,241,831	12.6	281,421,906	34,991,753	12.4	3,749,922	12.0
Region								
Northeast	50,809,229	6,995,156	13.8	53,594,378	7,372,282	13.8	377,126	5.4
Midwest	59,668,632	7,749,130	13.0	64,392,776	8,259,075	12.8	509,945	6.6
South	85,445,930	10,724,182	12.6	100,236,820	12,438,267	12.4	1,714,085	16.0
West	52,786,082	5,773,363	10.9	63,197,932	6,922,129	11.0	1,148,766	19.9
State								
Alabama	4,040,587	522,989	12.9	4,447,100	579,798	13.0	56,809	10.9
Alaska	550,043	22,369	4.1	626,932	35,699	5.7	13,330	59.6
Arizona	3,665,228	478,774	13.1	5,130,632	667,839	13.0	189,065	39.5
Arkansas	2,350,725	350,058	14.9	2,673,400	374,019	14.0	23,961	6.8
California	29,760,021	3,135,552	10.5	33,871,648	3,595,658	10.6	460,106	14.7
Colorado	3,294,394	329,443	10.0	4,301,261	416,073	9.7	86,630	26.3
Connecticut	3,287,116	445,907	13.6	3,405,565	470,183	13.8	24,276	5.4
Delaware	666,168	80,735	12.1	783,600	101,726	13.0	20,991	26.0
District of Columbia	606,900	77,847	12.8	572,059	69,898	12.2	-7,949	-10.2
Florida	12,937,926	2,369,431	18.3	15,982,378	2,807,597	17.6	438,166	18.5
Georgia	6,478,216	654,270	10.1	8,186,453	785,275	9.6	131,005	20.0
Hawaii	1,108,229	125,005	11.3	1,211,537	160,601	13.3	35,596	28.5
Idaho	1,006,749	121,265	12.0	1,293,953	145,916	11.3	24,651	20.3
Illinois	11,430,602	1,436,545	12.6	12,419,293	1,500,025	12.1	63,480	4.4
Indiana	5,544,159	696,196	12.6	6,080,485	752,831	12.4	56,635	8.1
Iowa	2,776,755	426,106	15.3	2,926,324	436,213	14.9	10,107	2.4
Kansas	2,477,574	342,571	13.8	2,688,418	356,229	13.3	13,658	4.0
Kentucky	3,685,296	466,845	12.7	4,041,769	504,793	12.5	37,948	8.1
Louisiana	4,219,973	468,991	11.1	4,468,976	516,929	11.6	47,938	10.2
Maine	1,227,928	163,373	13.3	1,274,923	183,402	14.4	20,029	12.3
Maryland	4,781,468	517,482	10.8	5,296,486	599,307	11.3	81,825	15.8
Massachusetts	6,016,425	819,284	13.6	6,349,097	860,162	13.5	40,878	5.0
Michigan	9,295,297	1,108,461	11.9	9,938,444	1,219,018	12.3	110,557	10.0
Minnesota	4,375,099	546,934	12.5	4,919,479	594,266	12.1	47,332	8.7
Mississippi	2,573,216	321,284	12.5	2,844,658	343,523	12.1	22,239	6.9
Missouri	5,117,073	717,681	14.0	5,595,211	755,379	13.5	37,698	5.3
Montana	799,065	106,497	13.3	902,195	120,949	13.4	14,452	13.6
Nebraska	1,578,385	223,068	14.1	1,711,263	232,195	13.6	9,127	4.1
Nevada	1,201,833	127,631	10.6	1,998,257	218,929	11.0	91,298	71.5
New Hampshire	1,109,252	125,029	11.3	1,235,786	147,970	12.0	22,941	18.3
New Jersey	7,730,188	1,032,025	13.4	8,414,350	1,113,136	13.2	81,111	7.9
New Mexico	1,515,069	163,062	10.8	1,819,046	212,225	11.7	49,163	30.1
New York	17,990,455	2,363,722	13.1	18,976,457	2,448,352	12.9	84,630	3.6
North Carolina	6,628,637	804,341	12.1	8,049,313	969,048	12.0	164,707	20.5
North Dakota	638,800	91,055	14.3	642,200	94,478	14.7	3,423	3.8
Ohio	10,847,115	1,406,961	13.0	11,353,140	1,507,757	13.3	100,796	7.2
Oklahoma	3,145,585	424,213	13.5	3,450,654	455,950	13.2	31,737	7.5
Oregon	2,842,321	391,324	13.8	3,421,399	438,177	12.8	46,853	12.0
Pennsylvania	11,881,643	1,829,106	15.4	12,281,054	1,919,165	15.6	90,059	4.9
Rhode Island	1,003,464	150,547	15.0	1,048,319	152,402	14.5	1,855	1.2
South Carolina	3,486,703	396,935	11.4	4,012,012	485,333	12.1	88,398	22.3
South Dakota	696,004	102,331	14.7	754,844	108,131	14.3	5,800	5.7
Tennessee	4,877,185	618,818	12.7	5,689,283	703,311	12.4	84,493	13.7
Texas	16,986,510	1,716,576	10.1	20,851,820	2,072,532	9.9	355,956	20.7
Utah	1,722,850	149,958	8.7	2,233,169	190,222	8.5	40,264	26.9
Vermont	562,758	66,163	11.8	608,827	77,510	12.7	11,347	17.2
Virginia	6,187,358	664,470	10.7	7,078,515	792,333	11.2	127,863	19.2
Washington	4,866,692	575,288	11.8	5,894,121	662,148	11.2	86,860	15.1
West Virginia	1,793,477	268,897	15.0	1,808,344	276,895	15.3	7,998	3.0
Wisconsin	4,891,769	651,221	13.3	5,363,675	702,553	13.1	51,332	7.9
Wyoming	453,588	47,195	10.4	493,782	57,693	11.7	10,498	22.2
Puerto Rico	3,522,037	340,884	9.7	3,808,610	425,137	11.2	84,253	24.7

SOURCE: Lisa Hetzel and Annetta Smith, "Table 3. Population 65 Years and Over for the United States, Regions, and States, and for Puerto Rico: 1990 and 2000," in *The 65 Years and Over Population: 2000,* U.S. Census Bureau, Washington, DC, October 2001

tions, and as a result, have been exposed to more places. Rarely do people move to a place previously unknown to them.

Where will baby boomers go to retire? The Milken Institute in Santa Monica, California, predicted that the states in the West would lead the nation in elderly

TABLE 1.7

Projections of the population aged 65 and up by state, 1995–2025

(Numbers in thousands - Resident population.)

	July 1, 1995	July 1, 2000	July 1, 2005	July 1, 2015	July 1, 2025
Alabama	552	582	613	785	1,069
Alaska	30	38	46	67	92
Arizona	560	635	707	967	1,368
Arkansas	360	377	402	533	731
California	3,463	3,387	3,454	4,465	6,424
Colorado	375	452	523	745	1,044
Connecticut	467	461	456	526	671
Delaware	91	97	101	124	165
District of Columbia	77	69	65	71	92
Florida	2,631	2,755	2,911	3,825	5,453
Georgia	718	779	852	1,175	1,668
Hawaii	150	157	164	211	289
Idaho	132	157	182	261	374
Illinois	1,484	1,484	1,494	1,735	2,234
Indiana	734	763	794	963	1,260
Iowa	432	442	452	533	686
Kansas	350	359	366	447	605
Kentucky	487	509	538	686	917
Louisiana	494	523	555	705	945
Maine	173	172	173	219	304
Maryland	572	589	611	763	1,029
Massachusetts	861	843	827	965	1,252
Michigan	1,182	1,197	1,211	1,421	1,821
Minnesota	573	596	627	794	1,099
Mississippi	331	344	363	456	615
Missouri	740	755	774	942	1,258
Montana	114	128	143	198	274
Nebraska	228	239	248	303	405
Nevada	176	219	257	350	486
New Hampshire	136	142	148	194	273
New Jersey	1,091	1,090	1,093	1,279	1,654
New Mexico	183	206	228	310	441
New York	2,424	2,358	2,321	2,627	3,263
North Carolina	899	991	1,081	1,445	2,004
North Dakota	93	99	103	126	166
Ohio	1,491	1,525	1,554	1,807	2,305
Oklahoma	443	472	504	654	888
Oregon	426	471	522	741	1,054
Pennsylvania	1,916	1,899	1,867	2,092	2,659
Rhode Island	156	148	143	162	214
South Carolina	440	478	517	696	963
South Dakota	105	110	114	137	188
Tennessee	658	707	760	994	1,355
Texas	1,915	2,101	2,297	3,089	4,364
Utah	172	202	234	338	495
Vermont	71	73	77	101	138
Virginia	737	788	845	1,109	1,515
Washington	628	685	757	1,081	1,580
West Virginia	279	287	296	360	460
Wisconsin	683	705	730	893	1,200
Wyoming	54	62	71	101	145

SOURCE: Adapted from "Projections of the Population, By Age and Sex, of States: 1995 to 2025," in *State Population Projections,* U.S. Census Bureau, Washington, DC, [Online] http://www.census.gov/population/projections/state/stpjage.txt [accessed September 26, 2001]

migrants beginning around 2010. The states with the greatest projected growth of people aged 65 years and older from 2000 to 2025 are Utah, Alaska, Idaho, Wyoming, Colorado, and Washington—states with relatively small populations, lots of rural space, and natural beauty. Southern states will likely grow as well (notably Georgia, Texas, and the Carolinas), but more slowly than the West.

ENJOYMENT OF OLDER AGE

People now see themselves as 10 to 15, maybe 20 years, younger than their real age.... A person turning 50 may still have half of his or her adult life ahead. There may be as many years of life after 50 as there were between 18 and 50.

— Charles Allen, *Modern Maturity,* 1999

The Best Years of Their Lives: The NCOA Study

According to a study by the National Council on the Aging (NCOA) titled *Myths and Realities of Aging 2000,* almost half (44 percent) of people aged 65 years and over said that their current years were the best years of their lives—a 32 percent increase over 1974 results. (See Table 1.8.) In the same survey of more than 3,000 adults, the vast majority of Americans of all ages (84 percent) said they would be happy to live to age 90.

The number of aged 65-plus Americans who agreed with the statement "these are the best years of my life" rose dramatically since NCOA's first survey in 1974, when only 32 percent of older Americans held this belief. NCOA's survey results in 2001 showed that, compared to older whites, much larger proportions of older African Americans and Hispanics agreed with that statement. (See Table 1.8.) The NCOA suggested that this may be because some ethnic groups are more likely than whites to have strong family and religious ties that provide a sense of connection and purpose, which are especially important in older years.

Other important findings from the NCOA survey include:

- Most Americans favored spending more—not less— on older people.

- Older people were less worried about their health, their finances, and the threat of crime than they were 25 years ago.

- For many respondents, "old age" begins with a decline in physical or mental ability, rather than with the arrival of a specific birthday.

- Younger people tended to overstate the financial and social isolation problems of older people.

- Sixty percent of respondents took responsibility for key financial decisions.

- Forty-four percent of married respondents had never discussed with their spouse when they would retire; 40 percent had never discussed where they would live; and 45 percent had never talked about how much money they would need.

Happiness in the Face of Trauma

According to the book *Americans 55 and Older*, older Americans are the happiest of any age group. In fact, the percentage of people who said they were "very happy" peaked in the 65–74 age group. Older Americans are also the ones who are most happily married. Seventy-two percent of couples aged 65 to 74 said their marriage was "very happy," compared to 61 percent of all couples.

In contrast to the good news about marriages later in life, those aged 65 to 74 had a high rate of traumatic events, which include death, divorce, unemployment, hospitalization, and disability. Of people aged 65 to 74, 52 percent had experienced at least one such traumatic event in the past five years, compared to 35 percent for all adults. Another 27 percent of those aged 65 to 74 had experienced two or more such events, and 52 percent had experienced the death of one or more relatives in the past five years.

ATTITUDES ABOUT AGING

In nonindustrialized countries, older people are often held in great respect and esteem. Not only have they weathered years of what may have been harsh living conditions, but they have also accumulated wisdom and knowledge that younger generations need to survive and carry on the traditions of their cultures. In many industrialized societies, such as the United States, a person's worth may sometimes be measured by the type of work he or she does and the amount of wealth accumulated. When people retire from full-time employment, they may lose status because they are no longer working, earning money, or "contributing" to society. People's identity is often bound to their former jobs, and without them, they may feel worthless. Their lifetime of experience may not seem relevant in an ever-changing world where even computers become outdated every year.

Challenging the Myth

As more people have been joining the ranks of older Americans, a revolution has been taking place. People aged 65 years and over are no longer content to be regarded as "old." They want to be recognized as individuals rather than stereotypes. Many are healthier and better educated, and many are wealthier, than at any time in history. They ask for the respect and recognition they have earned. Older activists are involved in causes ranging from job retraining to long-term care to saving historical buildings, and changing the public's perception of old age.

CHANGING THE MARKETPLACE

Because spending power has traditionally been in the hands of young adults and their children, manufacturers and retailers targeted these age groups almost exclusively. Now a whole new market has surfaced. Today's older

TABLE 1.8

Survey responses about enjoyment of old age

Statement: These are the best years of my life. (Base: Age 65 and older)

Agree	44%
African Americans	60%
Hispanic	57%
White	42%

Question: If you knew you would live to be 90, would that make you very happy, somewhat happy, or not very happy at all? (Base: 18-85 years old)

Very + somewhat happy	84%
Not at all happy	13%
Don't know	2%

SOURCE: Michael Reinemer, "NCOA Survey Heralds New Age of Old Age," from *Innovations: The Journal of the National Council on the Aging*, issue 1, 2001

adults worked in the prosperous post–World War II years, generally earned good wages, and were often conscientious about saving. Having completed child-rearing responsibilities, many now have considerable discretionary money.

Ken Dychtwald, in *Age Power: How the 21st Century Will Be Ruled by the New Old* (Putnam, New York, 1999), enumerated the economic power of Americans aged 50 and older. Today's mature consumers:

• Control in excess of $7 trillion in wealth—70 percent of all wealth

• Own 77 percent of all financial assets

• Comprise 66 percent of all stockholders, own 40 percent of all mutual funds and 60 percent of all annuities, and represent 50 percent of individual retirement account holders

• Own their own homes (79 percent), own 46 percent of home equity loans, and transact more than 5 million car loans per year

• Represent almost half of all credit-card use, making up 40 million card owners

• Buy 41 percent of new cars sold and 48 percent of all luxury cars, totaling more than $60 billion

• Account for 51 percent of all over-the-counter drug sales and consume 74 percent of all prescription drugs

A Three-Segment Mature Market

Research by one marketing research firm, Media Matrix (New York City), reported that the mature market constitutes not one but three markets—ages 55 to 64, ages 65 to 79, and ages 80-plus.

Those aged 55 to 64 constitute the "working mature" market. They are the youngest and most active of the so-called mature market. They are approaching retirement and are at the peak of their earning and spending potential. They are generally anticipating retirement with enthusiasm, but greet age with defiance.

Those aged 65 to 79 are the "young retirees." They have the highest discretionary income of any age group. Their homes are often paid for, and their children are grown. Although health is beginning to become a concern, they have made their peace with the aging process. They are as active and involved in leisure, volunteer, family, and second careers as their health and finances allow.

America's oldest elderly population consists of those 80 and older. They generally view themselves as 10 to 15 years younger than they actually are and view 50 year olds as nearly as young and naïve as 20-somethings may appear to 50 year olds.

As a whole, the 21 percent of the population aged 55 and older control about 75 percent of the nation's financial assets. Approximately 80 percent of mature Americans own their own homes and are gradually liquidating and spending their assets. They give more than any other age group to charity, educational organizations, and family members. They spend more on travel, financial services, and health care. They are responsible for 71 percent of all prescription drug purchases. They spend more hours watching television and listening to radio than do younger audiences, and they read more newspapers and magazines. Media Matrix found that retirees spent far more time with their computers than did members of any other age group. Those aged 55 to 64 spent more annually on computers and related equipment than did householders overall.

New Marketing Approaches

Television commercials may look very different in the years ahead. The emphasis on youthfulness may find less acceptance in a generally aging community. Modeling and advertising agencies increasingly demand the over-50 model. Magazines aimed at the mature audience, such as *Modern Maturity,* published by the AARP (formerly the American Association of Retired Persons), almost exclusively use advertisements with older models. The increasing number of elderly, the hours they spend watching television and otherwise attuned to the media, and the considerable discretionary income available to many of them are making the elderly a prime target for consumer marketing.

To appeal to this group, publications targeting those over 50, such as *Modern Maturity,* and *New Choices,* have redesigned their magazines to make them cleaner, brighter, and more youthful. *Modern Maturity* announced a new design featuring two editions of its magazine—one for readers who work and one for those who are retired. In January 2001 AARP started a new magazine called *My Generation* to appeal to younger readers.

Growth in retirement-related industries is expected to continue to increase as businesses seek to fill the needs of the older population. Health and fitness concerns will demand additional geriatricians (physicians specializing in the treatment of elderly persons), physical therapists, cataract and hearing specialists, and nutritionists. A market has emerged for pagers, remote controls, and monitoring devices for those living alone.

Most recreation centers and community programs have expanded their post-55 services. The hotel and travel industries now offer discounts and accommodations tailored to the needs of the increasingly mobile mature market and its discretionary income. Some restaurants offer smaller food portions and lower prices on senior citizen menus. Many rural towns, and indeed states, have found it profitable to attract retirees, with their pensions, savings, and fewer demands on expensive local public services, such as schools.

GLOBAL AGING

Population aging is not confined to the United States. The size of the world's older population has been growing for centuries. What is new is the accelerated pace of aging. Over the first half of the twenty-first century, countries in the developed world will experience unprecedented growth in the number of their elderly and an equally unparalleled decline in the number of their youth.

According to the UN's world population estimates, in 2000 there were 606 million people aged 60 years or older in the world. That figure was expected to triple to nearly 2 billion in 2050.

As fertility levels decline and life expectancy increases, the world will age faster in the next 50 years than it did during the past 50 years. Demographers use median age as an indicator of the youthfulness or aging of a population. From 1950 to 2000 the median age for the world increased by three years, from 23.6 to 26.5. (See Table 1.9.) Over the first half of the twenty-first century, this measure was expected to rise to 36.2.

The UN predicted that there would be a large difference between the median age of the world's developed countries and that of countries that were less developed. The median age of the developed world was expected to reach 46.4 years in 2050, compared to 35 for less developed countries, and 26.5 for the least developed countries.

Proportion of Elderly in the World Population

According to the UN's estimates, between 1950 and 2000 the proportion of people aged 60 and over in the world population rose from 8 to 10 percent. In 2050, 21 percent of the people in the world will be age 60 or older.

Japan is currently the "oldest" country, with a median age of 41 years in 2000. Yemen is the "youngest," with a median age of 15.

TABLE 1.9

Median age by major world area, 1950, 2000, and 2050

	Median age (years)		
	1950	**2000**	**2050**
World total	23.6	26.5	36.2
Less developed regions	21.4	24.3	35.0
More developed regions	28.6	37.4	46.4
Least developed countries	19.5	18.2	26.5
Africa	19.0	18.4	27.4
Asia	22.0	26.2	38.3
Europe	29.2	37.7	49.5
Northern America	29.8	35.6	41.0
Latin America and Caribbean	20.1	24.4	37.8
Oceania	27.9	30.9	38.1

SOURCE: "Table 7. Median Age by Major Area, 1950, 2000 and 2050 (medium variant)," in *World Population Prospects: The 2000 Revision—Highlights,* United Nations, Department of Economic and Social Affairs, Population Division, New York, NY, February 28, 2001. The United Nations is the author of the original material.

TABLE 1.10

Expectation of life at birth for the world, major development groups, and major areas, 1995–2000 and 2045–2050

Major area	1995-2000	2045-2050
World	65.0	76.0
More developed regions	74.9	82.1
Less developed regions	62.9	75.0
Least developed countries	50.3	69.7
Other less developed countries	65.5	76.6
Africa	51.4	69.5
Asia	65.8	77.1
Latin America and Caribbean	69.3	77.8
Europe	73.2	80.8
Northern America	76.7	82.7
Oceania	73.5	80.6

SOURCE: "Table 3. Expectation of Life at Birth for the World, Major Development Groups and Major Areas, 1995–2000 and 2045–2050," in *World Population Prospects: The 2000 Revision—Highlights,* United Nations, Department of Economic and Social Affairs, Population Division, New York, NY, February 28, 2001. The United Nations is the author of the original material.

The growth of aging populations around the world reflects major social and economic achievements: declines in infant mortality, declines in fertility, decreases in infectious diseases, and improvements in nutrition and education. The unprecedented growth challenges social planners, since the oldest-old use disproportionate amounts of health and long-term care services.

The UN, noting the sobering projections, named 1999 the International Year of Older Persons and launched a campaign to raise awareness of the needs of the elderly. Their growing needs—and the smaller base of younger people to support and provide for those needs—highlight the increasing vulnerability of these older societies.

The World's 80-Plus Population

People aged 80 and over make up the fastest-growing population segment in the world. In 2000 there were 69 million people in this age group in the world. By 2050 the 60-plus population is expected to increase 5.5 times to 379 million. Although this age group now represents a very small portion of the world population (1 percent), it is expected to rise to 4 percent in 2050.

In 2000 there were an estimated 180,000 centenarians in the world, but by 2050 there are expected to be 3.2 million.

Global Life Expectancy

The more developed regions of the world have lower death rates than the less developed regions, and, therefore, have higher life expectancies. In the period 1995–2000 life expectancy in the developed part of the world reached 74.9 years. (See Table 1.10.) In less developed regions, it was 62.9 and in the least developed it was 50.3. Although the gap is expected to narrow during the first half of the twenty-first century, the developed world will still be far ahead in life expectancy. In 2045–50 the more developed regions will have a life expectancy of 82.1 years, compared to 75 for less developed regions, and 69.7 for the least developed.

CHAPTER 2

THE ECONOMIC STATUS OF OLDER AMERICANS

As a group, the elderly have a lower economic status than other adults do. When they retire, older Americans lose income from earnings. Most rely on Social Security supplemented by pensions and assets. Some must depend on Supplemental Security Income, a benefit for low-income people provided by federal and state governments.

With limited potential to improve their income through work, older persons become vulnerable to circumstances that are not under their control, such as the loss of a spouse, a prolonged illness, legislative changes in Social Security and Medicare (the federal health insurance program), inflation, and the status of the economy.

The economic status of older Americans is more varied than that of any other age group. While many have limited resources, others are well-off. An all-too-common scenario is that of the couple that does well financially during the early years of retirement, but then runs through all of their assets to pay for a long-term illness for one of them. That partner then dies and leaves his or her spouse impoverished. As an adage goes, the elderly are only one illness away from poverty. Comparisons of average statistics often conceal such facts.

NET WORTH

There are two important measures of how individuals are doing financially. One is income: the flow of money from a job, transfer program, interest on investments, and other sources. The other is asset accumulation or wealth: the economic resources that an individual or household possesses at any given time.

The following excerpt from the U.S. Census Bureau publication *Household Net Worth and Asset Ownership: 1995* (Michael E. Davern and Patricia J. Fisher, February 2001) explains the importance of looking at net worth as well as income measures:

> Because the economic well-being of households depends upon both income and wealth, income by itself is an imperfect measure. A household, for example, may be in the top 10 percent of the income distribution, but may be burdened with a large amount of debt. Consequently, examining the components of wealth, such as equity in a home, savings accounts, certificates of deposit, and mutual funds, provides a better understanding of the economic health of households than considering income data alone.

Below are data from an analysis published by the Census Bureau in 2001. The analysis presents data on the wealth and asset holdings of U.S. households in 1995. A comprehensive portrait of net worth, the data are from the Survey of Income and Program Participation (SIPP).

- In 1995 the median household net worth increased with the age of the householder, rising from $7,428 for householders under the age of 35 to $92,399 for householders aged 65 years of age and older.

- The increasingly positive association between age and net worth occurred up to age 70.

- Median net worth excluding home equity is another important measure of net worth. In 1995, this measure increased until age 70 and then fell.

- For all age groups, home equity was the most important source of net worth, equaling 44.4 percent for people aged 65 years and over. (See Table 2.1.)

- People in the older age ranges were less likely than those who were younger to have equity in motor vehicles, businesses, and individual retirement accounts (IRAs).

- Married-couple households had the largest median net worth in all age categories. (See Table 2.2.) Male householders and female householders trailed far behind.

MEDIAN INCOME

Unlike median household net worth, the elderly have the lowest median income of all age groups. (See Table

TABLE 2.1

Percent distribution of net worth of households, by age of householder and asset type, 1993 and 1995

[Excludes group quarters]

Asset type	1995						1993					
	Total	Less than 35 years	35 to 44 years	45 to 54 years	55 to 64 years	65 years and over	Total	Less than 35 years	35 to 44 years	45 to 54 years	55 to 64 years	65 years and over
Total net worth	**100.0**	**100.0**	**100.0**	**100.0**	**100.0**	**100.0**	**100.0**	**100.0**	**100.0**	**100.0**	**100.0**	**100.0**
Interest-earning assets at financial institutions	9.6	8.2	6.6	7.2	6.7	14.6	11.4	10.9	7.9	7.7	9.6	16.7
Other interest-earning assets	4.5	4.0	1.6	3.0	4.6	6.9	4.0	2.1	2.5	2.6	4.1	6.1
Checking accounts	0.6	1.4	0.7	0.6	0.3	0.4	0.5	1.2	0.7	0.5	0.4	0.4
Stocks and mutual fund shares	8.4	6.3	7.9	7.8	9.4	8.6	8.3	8.9	6.4	8.1	8.8	9.1
Own home	44.4	42.0	48.3	43.6	42.8	44.4	44.4	43.8	47.7	45.3	42.4	43.6
Rental property	6.2	3.2	4.3	6.9	9.6	5.3	6.7	5.3	6.4	7.2	9.1	5.2
Other real estate	4.3	6.4	4.1	5.8	5.0	2.6	4.6	5.1	5.0	5.5	4.9	3.6
Vehicles	8.3	25.3	11.9	8.3	6.4	4.4	6.4	18.2	8.8	6.5	4.9	3.7
Business or profession	5.6	11.9	10.9	7.9	3.5	1.4	6.4	10.6	9.5	9.0	6.1	2.4
U.S. savings bonds	0.8	0.7	0.9	0.6	0.7	0.8	0.8	1.0	1.2	0.7	0.7	0.8
IRA or Keogh accounts	8.3	5.2	7.1	10.1	10.2	7.3	6.7	3.9	6.3	7.4	8.8	5.7
Other financial investments[1]	2.8	1.9	2.0	2.3	2.7	3.8	3.0	3.6	2.9	2.6	3.0	3.2
Unsecured liabilities[2]	−3.6	−16.0	−6.5	−4.1	−1.9	−0.6	−3.4	−14.5	−5.3	−3.3	−2.8	−0.6

[1]Includes mortgages held for sale of real estate, amount due from sale of business or property, and other financial assets.
[2]Because net worth is assets less liabilities, unsecured liabilities are subtracted from the distribution of net worth and are shown as negative.

SOURCE: Michael E. Davern and Patricia J. Fisher, "Table F. Percent Distribution of Net Worth of Households, by Age of Householder and Asset Type: 1993 and 1995," in *Household Net Worth and Asset Ownership: 1995*, U.S. Census Bureau, Washington, DC, February 2001

TABLE 2.2

Median net worth of households, including and excluding home equity, by type of household and age of householder, 1993 and 1995

[Excludes group quarters]

Type of household by age of householder	1995			1993		
	Number of households (thousands)	Median net worth (dollars)		Number of households (thousands)	Median net worth (in 1995 dollars)	
		Total	Excluding equity in own home		Total	Excluding equity in own home
Married-couple households	54,685	64,694	19,010	52,891	65,204	17,960
Less than 35 years	11,753	14,299	7,700	12,141	13,631	5,980
35 to 54 years	25,949	63,107	18,973	23,983	65,171	18,365
55 to 64 years	7,495	126,725	41,248	7,568	134,560	45,863
65 years and over	9,487	138,249	47,741	9,199	136,706	46,776
Male householders	16,044	16,346	7,375	15,397	14,219	5,432
Less than 35 years	5,402	5,425	4,311	5,285	4,529	3,044
35 to 54 years	6,336	22,150	7,899	6,157	19,408	6,484
55 to 64 years	1,539	39,045	9,849	1,437	47,050	11,486
65 years and over	2,767	67,697	15,374	2,518	63,978	13,616
Female householders	28,359	14,949	4,400	28,180	14,002	3,542
Less than 35 years	6,937	2,580	1,850	6,935	1,414	832
35 to 54 years	8,869	11,233	3,948	8,908	8,853	2,793
55 to 64 years	3,305	44,400	6,849	3,286	47,147	6,820
65 years and over	9,248	61,549	11,100	9,050	60,753	10,069

SOURCE: Michael E. Davern and Patricia J. Fisher, "Table 1. Median Net Worth and Median Net Worth Excluding Home Equity of Households, by Type of Household and Age of Householder: 1993 and 1995," in *Household Net Worth and Asset Ownership: 1995*, U.S. Census Bureau, Washington, DC, February 2001

2.3.) For example, in 2000 the median income of men aged 65 and over was half that of men aged 45 to 54, or $19,168 compared to $41,072. (Median income is the level at which half the population has less than that amount and the other half has more.)

There is a large disparity between the incomes of older men and women. In 2000 the median income for women aged 65 years and over was about half that for men in the same age group—$10,899 compared to $19,168. Full-time female workers aged 65 and over also

TABLE 2.3

Median income, by age, 2000, 1999, 1998

[People 15 years old and over as of March of the following year. An asterisk (*) preceding percent change indicates statistically significant change at the 90-percent confidence level.]

	2000 Median income			1999 Median income			1998 Median income			Percent change in real median income (1999-2000)
	Number with income (1,000)	Value (dollars)	Standard error (dollars)	Number with income (1,000)	Value (dollars)	Standard error (dollars)	Number with income (1,000)	Value (dollars)	Standard error (dollars)	
TOTAL Male										
Age										
Under 65 years	83,038	30,675	122	82,336	29,776	229	81,447	28,355	226	-0.3
15 to 24 years	14,476	9,557	221	14,428	8,302	212	14,079	8,190	222	*11.4
25 to 34 years	17,822	30,634	195	17,974	29,864	310	18,330	28,117	379	-0.8
35 to 44 years	21,684	37,087	247	21,654	36,217	258	21,539	35,177	287	-0.9
45 to 54 years	18,156	41,072	271	17,477	40,939	299	16,821	38,922	587	*-2.9
55 to 64 years	10,900	34,412	702	10,804	33,648	721	10,678	32,776	627	-1.1
65 years and over	13,938	19,168	233	13,686	19,079	239	13,501	18,166	224	*-2.8
65 to 74 years	8,060	21,361	396	7,931	21,305	342	7,902	19,734	329	-3.0
75 years and over	5,879	17,023	296	5,755	16,779	257	5,599	16,479	289	-1.8
TOTAL Female										
Age										
Under 65 years	81,647	18,332	158	81,322	16,943	110	80,501	16,096	119	*4.7
15 to 24 years	14,018	7,746	197	13,957	6,689	129	13,875	6,534	120	*12.0
25 to 34 years	17,140	20,937	213	17,411	19,396	279	17,773	18,257	281	*4.4
35 to 44 years	20,971	21,861	213	21,098	20,683	229	20,970	20,285	224	*2.3
45 to 54 years	18,117	24,196	373	17,579	22,588	323	16,915	21,588	244	*3.6
55 to 64 years	11,400	16,465	317	11,277	15,917	319	10,968	14,675	309	0.1
65 years and over	18,319	10,899	115	18,291	10,943	110	18,193	10,504	114	*-3.6
65 to 74 years	9,378	10,793	190	9,476	10,964	190	9,545	10,453	185	*-4.8
75 years and over	8,941	10,982	143	8,815	10,928	130	8,648	10,545	141	*-2.8
FULL-TIME, YEAR-ROUND WORKERS Male										
Age										
Under 65 years	57,391	38,793	298	56,234	37,430	193	55,912	36,170	144	0.3
15 to 24 years	4,676	20,825	226	4,457	19,515	336	4,571	19,510	334	*3.2
25 to 34 years	14,095	34,218	558	14,136	32,599	368	14,353	31,600	190	1.6
35 to 44 years	17,896	41,560	258	17,603	40,916	242	17,510	39,226	509	*-1.7
45 to 54 years	14,360	46,674	410	13,813	46,228	436	13,286	43,482	612	*-2.3
55 to 64 years	6,365	46,752	610	6,224	44,264	967	6,192	44,095	1,025	2.2
65 years and over	1,347	47,985	1,651	1,285	45,781	1,789	1,039	43,157	1,915	1.4
65 to 74 years	1,097	48,185	1,582	1,063	46,933	2,235	877	43,060	1,997	-0.7
75 years and over	249	45,578	6,308	222	40,622	3,155	162	43,750	7,911	8.6
FULL-TIME, YEAR-ROUND WORKERS Female										
Age										
Under 65 years	40,927	28,739	205	39,734	27,337	122	38,230	26,838	123	*1.7
15 to 24 years	3,822	18,960	346	3,330	17,851	340	3,182	17,348	257	2.8
25 to 34 years	9,775	27,953	353	9,791	26,670	228	9,663	26,301	215	1.4
35 to 44 years	12,053	30,471	262	11,875	29,155	418	11,587	28,585	370	1.1
45 to 54 years	10,790	31,981	283	10,380	30,848	244	9,684	30,027	334	0.3
55 to 64 years	4,487	30,282	423	4,358	28,764	716	4,113	27,783	612	1.9
65 years and over	656	34,159	1,485	687	30,013	1,294	580	28,326	1,444	*10.1
65 to 74 years	548	33,276	1,906	554	30,297	1,452	486	27,438	1,493	6.3
75 years and over	109	36,846	3,020	134	28,191	3,880	94	33,716	3,792	26.5

SOURCE: Adapted from "Table 7. Median Income of People by Selected Characteristics: 2000, 1999, 1998," in *Income 2000*, U.S. Census Bureau, Washington, DC [Online] http://www.census.gov/hhes/income/income00/inctab7.html [accessed October, 2001]

earned less than full-time male workers in the same age group—$34,159 versus $47,985.

The trend in household income parallels that for individuals. In 2000 the median income for a household headed by an individual aged 65 years and older was $32,854, less than half the income of those 45 to 54 years of age, $68,084. (See Table 2.4.)

THE ELDERLY POOR

Poverty standards are based on the "Economy Food Plan," developed by the U.S. Department of Agriculture (USDA) in the 1960s. The plan calculates the cost of a minimally adequate household food budget for different types of households by age of householder. Since USDA surveys showed that the average family spends one-third of its income on food, it was decided that a household with an income three times the amount needed for food was living fairly comfortably. The poverty level, then, is calculated by multiplying the cost of a minimally adequate food budget by three.

The overall economic position of those aged 65 years and over has improved significantly since the 1970s. (See Figure 2.1.) In 1959 more than one in every three elderly

TABLE 2.4

Median income of households, by age, 2000, 1999, and 1998

[Families as of March of the following year. An asterisk (*) preceding percent change indicates statistically significant change at the 90-percent confidence level.]

	2000 Median income			1999 Median income			1998 Median income			Percent change in real median income (1999-2000)
	Number (1,000)	Value (dollars)	Standard error (dollars)	Number (1,000)	Value (dollars)	Standard error (dollars)	Number (1,000)	Value (dollars)	Standard error (dollars)	
ALL RACES										
All families	72,383	50,891	239	72,031	48,950	300	71,551	46,737	241	0.6
Age of Householder										
Under 65 years	60,777	55,194	312	60,443	52,564	305	60,053	50,259	239	*1.6
15 to 24 years	3,488	26,508	603	3,353	24,031	841	3,242	21,918	576	*6.7
25 to 34 years	12,823	45,890	523	13,009	43,309	637	13,226	41,074	466	2.5
35 to 44 years	18,580	58,086	615	18,708	54,933	514	18,823	51,883	463	*2.3
45 to 54 years	16,224	68,084	609	15,804	65,303	629	15,127	61,833	586	0.9
55 to 64 years	9,661	55,717	940	9,569	54,249	681	9,635	52,577	665	-0.6
65 years and over	11,607	32,854	446	11,588	33,148	413	11,498	31,568	394	*-4.1
65 to 74 years	7,038	36,319	603	7,025	36,300	528	7,051	34,719	594	*-3.2
75 years and over	4,569	28,664	452	4,562	28,638	479	4,447	27,717	454	*-3.2
WHITE										
All families	60,218	53,256	349	60,256	51,224	258	60,077	49,023	283	0.6
Age of Householder										
Under 65 years	49,919	58,471	395	49,957	55,686	322	49,846	52,550	297	*1.6
15 to 24 years	2,559	29,293	969	2,470	26,426	530	2,504	24,283	637	*7.2
25 to 34 years	10,110	49,054	686	10,378	46,558	570	10,522	43,970	674	1.9
35 to 44 years	15,233	61,099	437	15,571	57,117	519	15,619	54,682	584	*3.5
45 to 54 years	13,692	70,706	603	13,302	68,280	867	12,845	64,119	634	0.2
55 to 64 years	8,326	57,978	907	8,238	55,804	962	8,356	54,476	771	0.5
65 years and over	10,299	33,467	471	10,299	33,795	433	10,231	32,398	429	*-4.2
65 to 74 years	6,219	37,016	619	6,171	37,033	556	6,249	35,784	622	*-3.3
75 years and over	4,080	29,092	476	4,128	29,031	492	3,982	28,205	474	*-3.0
BLACK										
All families	8,812	34,204	788	8,664	31,778	603	8,452	29,404	713	4.1
Age of Householder										
Under 65 years	7,821	35,275	705	7,692	33,027	985	7,489	30,946	598	3.3
15 to 24 years	734	18,484	1,181	709	12,590	1,257	587	11,212	847	*42.0
25 to 34 years	1,999	28,849	857	1,960	26,091	831	2,040	25,165	1,258	*7.0
35 to 44 years	2,399	39,661	1,060	2,326	37,309	1,284	2,323	32,839	1,609	2.8
45 to 54 years	1,758	47,112	1,771	1,759	44,433	1,495	1,642	45,785	2,139	2.6
55 to 64 years	931	37,747	1,782	938	39,435	1,763	898	34,749	1,792	-7.4
65 years and over	991	27,952	1,196	972	25,992	1,205	962	22,102	1,081	4.0
65 to 74 years	628	30,324	1,836	623	27,938	1,958	605	22,419	1,539	5.0
75 years and over	364	23,650	1,366	349	23,823	1,348	357	21,589	1,607	-4.0
HISPANIC ORIGIN[1]										
All families	7,728	35,050	600	7,561	31,663	490	7,273	29,608	568	*7.1
Age of Householder										
Under 65 years	7,081	35,935	546	6,938	32,355	605	6,683	30,363	542	*7.5
15 to 24 years	718	27,725	1,896	671	22,525	1,507	659	19,738	1,106	*19.1
25 to 34 years	2,069	31,987	950	2,068	29,296	1,278	2,008	27,587	831	5.6
35 to 44 years	2,167	37,372	1,115	2,187	34,420	1,100	2,128	32,299	1,050	5.0
45 to 54 years	1,366	42,912	1,631	1,288	42,593	1,899	1,194	39,277	1,876	-2.5
55 to 64 years	762	38,451	2,417	724	35,342	2,755	693	33,872	1,732	5.3
65 years and over	647	24,330	1,362	623	23,634	1,164	591	21,935	1,353	-0.4
65 to 74 years	428	25,849	1,619	421	25,119	1,683	409	24,115	2,264	-0.4
75 years and over	218	21,510	2,235	202	21,385	1,089	181	20,420	1,888	-2.7
NON-HISPANIC WHITE										
All families	52,879	56,442	326	53,071	54,121	355	53,107	51,607	260	0.9
Age of Householder										
Under 65 years	43,202	62,003	287	43,372	59,483	385	43,449	56,064	304	0.8
15 to 24 years	1,882	30,101	1,136	1,844	27,208	690	1,884	26,078	719	*7.0
25 to 34 years	8,162	52,314	612	8,425	50,966	489	8,615	48,133	653	-0.7
35 to 44 years	13,187	64,520	646	13,480	60,916	512	13,578	57,942	554	*2.5
45 to 54 years	12,379	73,410	962	12,078	71,138	670	11,695	66,388	683	-0.2
55 to 64 years	7,591	60,147	832	7,545	57,879	951	7,677	56,272	835	0.5
65 years and over	9,678	34,037	493	9,700	34,417	441	9,658	33,095	471	*-4.3
65 to 74 years	5,814	37,751	630	5,769	37,859	678	5,850	36,592	630	*-3.5
75 years and over	3,864	29,424	485	3,930	29,417	498	3,808	28,612	475	*-3.2

[1]People of Hispanic origin may be of any race.

SOURCE: Adapted from "Table 4. Median Income of Households by Selected Characteristics, Race, and Hispanic Origin of Householder: 2000, 1999, and 1998," in *Income 2000*, U.S. Census Bureau, Washington, DC [Online] http://www.census.gov/hhes/income/income00/inctab1.html [accessed October, 2001]

FIGURE 2.1

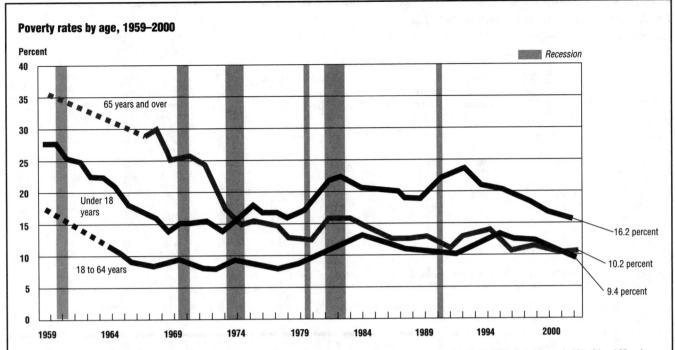

Poverty rates by age, 1959–2000

Percent

Recession

40

35 ····· 65 years and over

30

25

20 Under 18 years

15

10 18 to 64 years

5

0

1959   1964   1969   1974   1979   1984   1989   1994   2000

16.2 percent

10.2 percent

9.4 percent

Note: The data points represent the midpoints of the respective years. The latest recession began in July 1990 and ended in March 1991. Data for people 18 to 64 and 65 and older are not available from 1960 to 1965.

SOURCE: Joseph Dalaker, "Figure 2. Poverty Rates by Age: 1959 to 2000," in *Poverty in the United States: 2000,* U.S. Census Bureau, Washington, DC, September 2001

Americans lived in poverty. During the 1960s and early 1970s, the average income of the elderly increased. This was largely due to increases in Social Security and pension benefits. As a result, by 1989 the poverty rate of those aged 65 years and older had dropped to 11.4 percent. In 2000 the poverty rate for this group was 10.2 percent, up from 9.7 percent in 1999. (See Table 2.5.) In comparison, the poverty rate of the nation's population in 2000 as a whole was 11.3 percent. The elderly, however, were more likely than the nonelderly to have incomes just above the poverty level, in other words, to be "near poor." According to statistics for 2000 from the Census Bureau, 16.9 percent of the elderly had incomes below 125 percent of the poverty level, compared to 9 percent of those aged 45 to 54.

Social Security has played a significant role in reducing poverty among the aged. In 1999, 8 percent of the aged receiving Social Security were poor; without Social Security, the overall poverty rate would have been 48 percent. (See Figure 2.2.)

The Debate—Old-Poor Versus Young-Poor

In 2000 the poverty rate among the elderly (10.2 percent) was below that of the general population (11.3 percent) and well below that of those younger than age 18 (16.2 percent). (See Table 2.5.) Many people use these statistics to support the argument that the elderly do not need as much support, especially from the government, as

they currently receive. Some people assert that the elderly get benefits at the expense of the young. Other sources vigorously challenge this claim, noting that many elderly people have incomes that barely cover their needs (if they cover them at all) and that the oldest-old are among the poorest poor. In addition, many elderly are near poor.

A Different Standard for the Elderly

The Economy Food Plan used in determining poverty levels assumes that a healthy elderly person has lower nutritional requirements than a younger person does and, therefore, an elderly person needs less money for food. This assumption has resulted in different poverty standards for the old and for the young. For example, in 2000, the Census Bureau's statistical poverty level for a single adult under 65 years of age was $8,959; for a single adult aged 65 years or older, it was $8,259. A 64-year-old woman, then, with a yearly income of $8,300 is poor, but on her sixty-fifth birthday, she becomes "not poor."

This method of defining poverty does not recognize the specialized problems of the elderly. For example, no household costs other than food are counted, even though the elderly spend a much greater percentage of their income on health care than younger people do. In addition, the Economy Food Plan considers only the nutritional needs of a healthy person; many of the elderly are in poor health and may need special diets or nutritional supplements.

TABLE 2.5

People and families in poverty by age, 1999 and 2000

(Numbers in thousands.)

Characteristic	2000 below poverty				1999 below poverty				Change[1] 1999 to 2000			
	Number	90-pct. C.I. (±)	Percent	90-pct. C.I. (±)	Number	90-pct. C.I. (±)	Percent	90-pct. C.I. (±)	Number	90-pct. C.I. (±)	Percent	90-pct. C.I. (±)
PEOPLE												
Total	31,139	880	11.3	0.3	32,258	893	11.8	0.3	*−1,119	931	*−0.5	0.3
Age												
Under 18 years	11,633	461	16.2	0.6	12,109	467	16.9	0.7	−476	487	*−0.7	0.7
18 to 64 years	16,146	648	9.4	0.4	16,982	663	10.0	0.4	*−836	688	*−0.6	0.4
18 to 24 years	3,893	192	14.4	0.7	4,603	207	17.3	0.8	*−710	211	*−2.9	0.8
25 to 34 years	3,892	199	10.4	0.5	3,968	201	10.5	0.5	−75	209	−0.1	0.6
35 to 44 years	3,678	192	8.2	0.4	3,733	194	8.3	0.4	−55	204	−0.1	0.5
45 to 54 years	2,441	158	6.4	0.4	2,466	158	6.7	0.4	−25	166	−0.3	0.4
55 to 59 years	1,175	110	8.8	0.8	1,179	110	9.2	0.9	−4	117	−0.4	0.9
60 to 64 years	1,066	105	10.2	1.0	1,033	104	9.8	1.0	33	110	0.4	1.0
65 years and over	3,360	179	10.2	0.5	3,167	174	9.7	0.5	*192	186	0.5	0.6

− Represents zero. * Statistically significant at the 90-percent confidence level. C.I. = Confidence interval.
[1]As a result of rounding, some differences may appear to be slightly higher or lower than the differences of the reported rates.

SOURCE: Adapted from Joseph Dalaker, "Table A. People and Families in Poverty by Selected Characteristics: 1999 and 2000," in *Poverty in the United States: 2000*, U.S. Census Bureau, Washington, DC, September 2001

When comparing the percentage of old and very young people who live in poverty, it is important to note that the same poverty standard is not applied to both groups. If it were, the percentage of elderly poor would increase relative to the younger poor. In addition, most young people are poor for a limited period of time; as they become old enough to enter the workforce, they often have the opportunity to increase their income. Poor older people, on the other hand, have almost no option but to remain poor, and may be poor for the rest of their lives.

Differences in Poverty among Subgroups

According to the Census Bureau, there are significant differences in poverty levels among elderly subgroups. In 2000 women aged 65 years and over were more likely than men aged 65 and over to live below the poverty level—12.2 percent of older women lived in poverty, compared to 7.5 percent of older men. Elderly people who did not live with relatives had a poverty level of 20.8 percent, compared to 4.4 percent for married couple families.

Poverty rates are higher among elderly minority groups. In 2000 the poverty rate for African American women aged 65 and older was 25.8 percent, compared to 19.6 percent for Hispanic women and 10.8 percent for white women. The poverty rate for African American men aged 65 years and older was 22.3 percent, compared to 17.6 percent for Hispanic men and 8.9 percent for white men.

The states with the highest poverty among the elderly in 2000 were Alabama (17.9 percent), Louisiana (16.4 percent), Arkansas and Mississippi (both with 15.3 percent), and Kentucky (15 percent). The states with the lowest poverty among this age group in 2000 were Delaware (4.4 percent), New Hampshire (4.7 percent), Connecticut (5.3 percent), and Hawaii and Montana (both with 6.3 percent).

Elderly people of advanced age are more likely to be poor than the young-old. In 2000, 8.9 percent of the young-old were poor, compared to 11.7 percent of those 75 years and over, and 13.7 of those 85 years and over.

THE WELL-OFF ELDERLY

More older Americans live comfortably today than at any other time in history. People now in their seventies and eighties were children of the Great Depression, which began in 1929 and lasted through the 1930s. Many of them learned to economize and save. In their twenties and thirties, the members of the military returned from World War II (1939–45) to inexpensive housing and G.I. bills that provided a free or inexpensive college education. During their forties and fifties, their peak earning years, they participated in an unprecedented economic expansion. Today, many of them have raised their children, paid off their mortgages, invested wisely, and are in relatively good health. In addition, Social Security payments are larger than ever.

While these factors have contributed to a better economic status for the elderly than they would have otherwise enjoyed, most are not wealthy. According to the Current Population Survey (CPS), conducted by the Census Bureau, in 2000, 5.3 percent of elderly households had total money incomes of $100,000 or more compared to 15.4 percent of people under 65 years of age. The number of elderly households in the $100,000-and-higher income bracket, however, is not trivial. In 2000 there were 1,157,000 elderly households with total money incomes

FIGURE 2.2

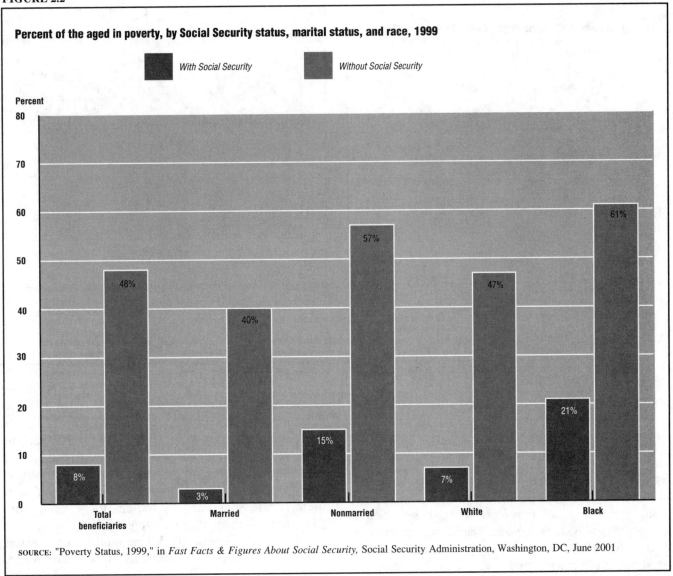

Percent of the aged in poverty, by Social Security status, marital status, and race, 1999

■ With Social Security   ■ Without Social Security

SOURCE: "Poverty Status, 1999," in *Fast Facts & Figures About Social Security*, Social Security Administration, Washington, DC, June 2001

over $100,000. (Money income includes money before taxes and does not include the value of noncash benefits such as food stamps and subsidized housing.)

SOURCES OF INCOME

Unlike younger people, who get most of their income from regular paychecks, the elderly rely on a variety of sources to meet the expenses of daily living. As a group, in 1999 the elderly derived 38 percent of their income from Social Security benefits, 21 percent from earnings, 19 percent from assets (returns on stock investments, interest from savings accounts, etc.), 10 percent from private pensions, 8 percent from government pensions, and 4 percent from other sources. (See Figure 2.3.) Very few elderly people receive income from all these sources at any one time.

Social Security

The elderly depend on Social Security for their incomes more than on any other source. In 1999 the

Social Security program paid benefits to 90 percent of those over age 65. For 64 percent of the elderly, Social Security provided more than 50 percent of their income, and for 18 percent of the elderly, it was the only source of income. (See Figure 2.4.) As the number of elderly increases in the upcoming decades, the number of Social Security participants will rise.

Earnings

The trend toward earlier retirement has led to a decline in the role of earnings in supporting the aged. According to a report titled *Older Workers: Employment and Retirement Trends,* by Patrick J. Purcell (*Monthly Labor Review,* October 2000), the percentage of employed men aged 65 years and older declined in the second part of the last century and then stabilized in the mid-1980s. Between 1950 and 1985 the labor force participation rate for men aged 65 years and older fell from 46 percent to about 16 percent. Since the mid-1980s

FIGURE 2.3

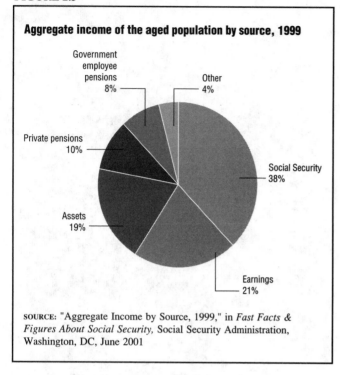

Aggregate income of the aged population by source, 1999

Government employee pensions 8%

Other 4%

Private pensions 10%

Social Security 38%

Assets 19%

Earnings 21%

SOURCE: "Aggregate Income by Source, 1999," in *Fast Facts & Figures About Social Security,* Social Security Administration, Washington, DC, June 2001

FIGURE 2.4

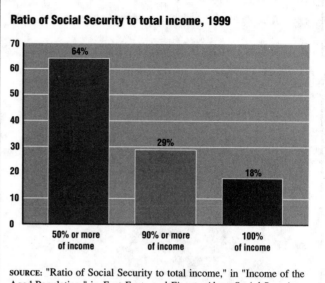

Ratio of Social Security to total income, 1999

	50% or more of income	90% or more of income	100% of income
	64%	29%	18%

SOURCE: "Ratio of Social Security to total income," in "Income of the Aged Population," in *Fast Facts and Figures About Social Security, 2000,* Social Security Administration, Washington, DC, June 2001 [Online] http://www.ssa.gov/statistics/fast_facts/2001/ff2001.pdf [accessed October 24, 2001]

about 15 to 16 percent of elderly men have been employed at any one time. For elderly women, labor force participation has ranged from 8 to 11 percent since the 1950s.

Earnings are much more common among the young-old than the oldest-old. According to the Social Security Administration (SSA), 41 percent of "aged units" headed by people aged 65 to 69 have earnings compared to 3 percent of those headed by people aged 85 and over. (An aged unit is either a married couple living together, with husband or wife aged 65 years or older, or a person that age who does not live with a spouse.)

Work Expectations after Age 65

According to the 2001 *Retirement Confidence Survey* conducted by the Employee Benefit Research Institute (EBRI; a nonprofit public policy research organization), the American Savings Education Council, and Matthew Greenwald and Associates, over half (53 percent) of today's workers expect to retire at age 65 or later, or to never retire. In contrast to these expectations, however, most retirees (65 percent) report actual retirement ages younger than age 65. (See Table 2.6.)

In the summary of findings from the survey, the authors of the report asserted that this early retirement is not by design: "Four in 10 of today's retirees say they retired earlier than planned (39 percent). This is frequently due to negative reasons beyond their control, such as health problems (51 percent), changes at their company (25 percent), or other work-related reasons (25 percent)."

While many current workers retire early, in 2001, 26 percent of retirees reported that they had worked since they retired (2 percent worked full time, 18 percent part time, 2 percent both full and part time, and 3 percent worked seasonally or sporadically). Most retired workers enjoy working and want to stay involved. Table 2.7 lists the major reasons cited by retirees for working after retirement. They include enjoying work and wanting to stay involved (53 percent), having money to buy extras (30 percent), and keeping health insurance and other benefits (24 percent).

Assets

As earnings have accounted for a smaller proportion of income among the elderly, assets and pensions have become more important. As mentioned above, assets represent about one-fifth of the income of the elderly. It must be emphasized that this is an average figure; while some elderly have large assets, one-third of the elderly have no income from assets. Assets include interest-earning accounts, checking accounts, stocks and bonds, and related financial instruments.

Not surprisingly, the elderly with income from assets are better off financially than those who do not have assets. According to the Social Security Administration's *Income of the Aged Chartbook* (June 2000), in 1998 the median income of those with asset income was more than twice as large as that of those with no asset income ($24,423 compared to $10,041). Among those with asset income in 1998, 40 percent had annual incomes of $30,000 or more, while 10 percent had a total income less

TABLE 2.6

Expected and actual retirement age, 2001

Retirement age	Expected (percentage of workers)	Actual (percentage of retirees)
Ages 54 or younger	5%	15%
Ages 55–59	12	16
Age 60	10	5
Ages 61–64	13	29
Age 65	30	14
Ages 66 or older	16	12
Never retire	7	NA

Note: 2001 data are based on a survey conducted in January and February of 2001 through 20-minute random digit dialing telephone interviews with 1,000 individuals (762 workers and 238 retirees) age 25 and older in the United States. In theory, each sample of 1,000 yields a statistical precision of plus or minus 3 percentage points (with 95 percent certainty) of what the results would be if all Americans age 25 and older were surveyed with complete accuracy. There are other possible sources of error in all surveys, however, that may be more serious than theoretical calculations of sampling error. These include refusals to be interviewed and other forms of nonresponse, the effects of question wording and question order, and screening. While attempts are made to minimize these factors, it is difficult or impossible to quantify the errors that may result from them.

SOURCE: "Expected and Actual Retirement Age: 2001," in *The 2001 Retirement Confidence Survey Summary of Findings,* Employee Benefit Research Institute, American Savings Education Council, and Matthew Greenwald & Associates, Washington, DC, May 10, 2001

TABLE 2.7

Major reasons for working after retiring cited by retirees

Reason	Percent of retirees
Enjoy work and want to stay involved	53
To have money to buy extras	30
To keep health insurance or other benefits	24
To have money to make ends meet	22
To try a different career	15
To help support children or other household members	5

SOURCE: *Retirement in America,* Employee Benefit Research Institute, Washington, DC [Online] http://www.ebri.org/rcs/2001/01rcsf1.pdf [accessed October 17, 2001]

than $10,000. For those with no asset income, only 8 percent received annual incomes of $30,000 or more, and 49 percent had annual incomes of less than $10,000.

In all age groups, including the elderly, home equity accounts for most of the household's net worth. In 1995 home ownership represented 44.4 percent of net worth of households headed by an elderly householder, up slightly from 43.6 percent in 1993. (See Table 2.1.) Other key assets include interest-earning accounts at financial institutions, which equaled 14.6 percent of net worth in 1995; stocks and mutual funds (8.6 percent); IRAs (7.3 percent); other interest-earning assets (6.9 percent); and rental property (5.3 percent).

Estimates such as net worth do not always accurately describe the financial condition of elderly people. Some older people in the United States are, indeed, very rich. When their wealth is averaged into income and asset statistics, it masks the fact that a large number of old people live near or below the poverty level.

Pension (Retirement) Funds

Many large companies, along with most local and state governments and the federal government, offer pension plans, or retirement plans. The first employer-provided retirement plan in the United States was started in 1875.

Employers are not required to provide pensions. In addition, pension plans do not have to include all workers; they may exclude certain jobs and/or individuals. Before 1976 pension plans could require an employee to work a

lifetime for one company before being eligible for pension benefits. As required by the Employee Retirement Income Security Act of 1974 (ERISA; PL 93-406), starting in 1976 an employee became eligible after 10 years of service. Most current plans require five years of work before an employee becomes vested (eligible for benefits).

For those companies that have pension plans, employees are eligible for benefits when they retire or leave a company if they have worked for the company for a designated number of years and/or have reached a specified age. According to 1995 data (Michael E. Davern and Patricia J. Fisher, *Household Net Worth and Asset Ownership 1995,* U.S. Census Bureau, February 2001), pensions are much more common among the young-old than the oldest-old: 46 percent of "aged units" headed by people aged 65 to 69 have pensions, compared to 34 percent of those headed by people aged 85 and over.

DEFINED BENEFIT PLANS AND DEFINED CONTRIBUTION PLANS. There are two major types of pension plans: defined benefit plans and defined contribution plans. A defined benefit plan promises the employee a specified monthly benefit at retirement. Until recent years, these pension plans were the traditional plan offered by most employers. A defined benefit plan may state the promised benefit as an exact dollar amount, such as $100 per month at retirement. Or, more commonly, it may calculate a benefit through a plan formula that considers such factors as salary and service—for example, 1 percent of an average salary for the last five years of employment for every year of service with the employer.

A defined contribution plan does not promise the employee a specific amount of benefits at retirement. In these plans, the employee and/or employer contribute to an individual account under the plan, sometimes at a set rate, such as 5 percent of earnings annually. These contributions generally are invested on the employee's behalf. An example of a defined contribution plan is the 401(k).

During the last half of the twentieth century, the prevalence of defined benefit plans decreased and defined contribution plans began flourishing. According to the EBRI, total retirement plan assets in the United States were estimated at about $9.5 trillion in 1998, of which the largest portion (23 percent) was in defined contribution plans. IRAs equaled 21.4 percent of the $9.5 trillion and defined benefit plans accounted for 21.2 percent.

PRIVATE PENSIONS AND FEDERAL PENSIONS. The SSA reported that in 1962 private pensions accounted for 3 percent of income for the elderly. By 1999 private pensions supplied 31 percent of the income of aged units. (The spouse of a person who participated in a pension plan is also considered a recipient.) Government employee pensions also provided 13 percent of the total income of the aged.

The number of private and federal pension plans has risen. In 1975 private industry offered 311,094 retirement plans. According to the Pension and Welfare Benefits Administration, there were 720,000 private pension plans in 1997. The number of active participants in pension plans in 1997 was 70.7 million.

Employees in larger firms are more likely to be covered than those in smaller firms. Highly paid workers and workers in industries covered by union contracts are most likely to have coverage. White-collar workers were somewhat more likely to receive pensions than blue-collar workers. Pension coverage is greater among whites than African Americans or Hispanics and is strongly related to a worker's wage level. Also, employer pensions are more prevalent in goods-producing industries than in service industries. There are fewer government pension plans than private plans, but the average benefits of the former are substantially larger than those of the latter.

Women do not fare as well as men in the pension system. In 1999, according to the EBRI, 45.7 percent of men over age 65 received an annuity and/or pension income, compared to only 28.2 percent of women in that age group. And males receive, on average, a higher benefit payment. In 1999 males aged 65 years and older received on average $14,046 in benefits, compared with females' average amount of $8,224.

Unlike Social Security, most pension plans do not provide automatic cost-of-living adjustments, which can gradually erode retirees' incomes. Persons receiving pensions from the military, the government, or Railroad Retirement were more likely to receive increases than were those receiving pensions from the private sector.

FEDERAL PENSION LAWS. A company that has a pension plan will often invest its funds in vehicles such as stocks and bonds, much as a bank does with its depositors' money. If the investment choice is a good one, the company makes a profit on the money in the fund; a bad investment results in a loss. During the early 1970s, several major plans collapsed, leaving retirees without benefits even though they had contributed to a plan for many years.

These collapses led to the passage in 1974 of ERISA. ERISA established participation and vesting guidelines and standards to ensure that funds are managed in the best interest of plan participants. It also created the Pension Benefit Guaranty Corporation, a federal agency, to take over benefit payments when underfunded plans are terminated.

Before 1983 some plans paid lower monthly benefits to women because statistically women lived longer than men and, on average, collected pension benefits for a longer time. In 1983 the U.S. Supreme Court, in *Arizona Governing Committee for Tax Deferred Annuity and Deferred Compensation Plan v. Natalie Norris* (463 U.S. 1073), ruled that pension plans must make payments based on gender-neutral actuarial tables (statistical calculations for insurance purposes).

The Retirement Equity Act of 1984 (PL 98-397) requires pension plans to pay a survivor's benefit to the spouse of a deceased vested plan participant. Prior to 1984 some spouses received no benefits unless the employee was near retirement age at the time of death. Under the 1984 law, pension vesting begins at age 21 or after five years on the job, and employees who have a break in employment for reasons such as maternity leave will not lose any time already accumulated.

PROBLEMS WITH PENSION MANAGEMENT. A variety of flaws bedevil the American pension system, some of which may deprive retired workers of part, or all, of their pensions. A 1995 audit by the federal Pension Benefit Guaranty Corporation, found an 8 percent error rate in the administration of pension payments, and some sources believed it was higher.

A major trouble spot arises from corporate mergers and downsizings. Employees may lose out when dissimilar pension plans are consolidated. Problems also arise when widowed and divorced spouses fail to get a rightful share of their spouses' pensions. Spouses are often entitled to pension benefits, but terms must be included in divorce decrees or filed with a plan administrator. Divorce lawyers or judges may fail to include pensions when dividing assets, or spouses may unknowingly sign away their rights. Pension calculations are often very complicated, and errors are easily made in calculating amounts due.

401(K)S. The most common type of defined contribution plan is the 401(k). In a 401(k), employers establish a plan that is a cash or deferred arrangement. Employees can elect to defer receiving a portion of their salaries, which is instead contributed on their behalf, before taxes, to the 401(k) plan. Sometimes the employer may match the contributions. There are special rules governing the operation of a 401(k) plan. The plans take their name from Section 401(k) of the Internal Revenue Code.

The Investment Company Institute (ICI), a national association of investment industry groups, reported in 1999 that in companies offering 401(k) plans, approximately 77 percent of employees were enrolled. Eighty-nine percent of companies offering 401(k) plans match employees' contributions, most commonly at the rate of $0.50 per dollar.

The EBRI conducted a study with the ICI (*The EBRI-ICI 401(k) Plan Participant-Directed Retirement Plan Data Collection Project*) on worker pension investments. The EBRI reported in 1999 that 401(k) plans provided substantial retirement income for workers with long participation in the plans. For example, workers in their sixties with 30 years tenure had an average account balance in excess of $156,000. Those in their fifties had balances in excess of $117,000.

IRAs

IRAs are tax-deferred plans that individuals contribute to independently of an employer. An estimated 30 million households—30 percent—had IRAs in 1998. IRAs can provide tax-deferred retirement savings for self-employed workers or those not in the labor force. IRAs have become very popular. According to the EBRI, assets in IRAs totaled $2.47 trillion in 1999, up 21.9 percent from a year earlier. Often IRAs are way stations to store retirement money that has accumulated somewhere else, such as through a rollover (the transfer of funds from one savings program to another) from a pension plan.

Family Support

While the contribution of the family to an elderly parent or relative, both in financial support and the value of the care and time they give, is difficult to statistically determine, numerous studies suggest that it is substantial. According to these studies, income from Social Security plays a minor role compared to the amount of support contributed by family members. When elderly persons outlive their family members, they are often faced with serious problems of financial security and personal care.

Although nobody knows the exact extent of financial support given to aging parents by their children, most sources believe that 10 to 12 percent of the workforce are caring for older parents in some capacity. Andrew Scharlach, a professor in the School of Social Welfare at the University of California at Berkeley, predicted that by 2020 one in three people would have to provide care for an elderly parent, with much of that care in the form of financial assistance.

Personal Savings

The more personal savings workers can put aside for retirement, the higher their retirement income. According to a 2001 study conducted by the EBRI, the American

TABLE 2.8

Percentage of survey respondents having saved for retirement, 1994–2001

1994	61%
1995	58
1996	60
1997	66
1998	59
1999	68
2000	75
2001	71
2001 (revised)	65

Note: 2001 data are based on a survey conducted in January and February of 2001 through 20-minute random digit dialing telephone interviews with 1,000 individuals (762 workers and 238 retirees) age 25 and older in the United States. In theory, each sample of 1,000 yields a statistical precision of plus or minus 3 percentage points (with 95 percent certainty) of what the results would be if all Americans age 25 and older were surveyed with complete accuracy. There are other possible sources of error in all surveys, however, that may be more serious than theoretical calculations of sampling error. These include refusals to be interviewed and other forms of non-response, the effects of question wording and question order, and screening. While attempts are made to minimize these factors, it is difficult or impossible to quantify the errors that may result from them.

SOURCE: "Percentage Having Saved for Retirement," in *The 2001 Retirement Confidence Survey Summary of Findings*, Employee Benefit Research Institute, American Savings Education Council, and Matthew Greenwald & Associates, Washington, DC, May 10, 2001

Savings Education Council (ASEC), and Matthew Greenwald and Associates, the percentage of people who said they had personally saved for retirement decreased from 75 percent in 2000 to 65 percent in 2001. (See Table 2.8.) (The 2001 figure is based on a revised number.)

INCOME INEQUALITY BETWEEN THE SEXES

Women of all ages lag behind men in wages and income. According to the Older Women's League, women spend an average of 11.5 years out of the workforce before they retire, providing care for children or elderly parents. As a result, most women work in lifetime low-wage jobs that give them the flexibility to move in and out of the workforce. Three out of five working women today have sales, clerical, or retail jobs. Service, part-time, and contingent jobs are low-waged and rarely provide the benefits, such as pensions, that women require to ensure a secure retirement.

According to the CPS, conducted by the Census Bureau and U.S. Department of Labor, in 2000 women's wages were about 76 percent those of men. The median weekly earnings in 2000 of male full-time wage and salary workers were $646, compared to $491 for women. This wage gap increases with age.

CONSUMER EXPENSES

The elderly tend to spend their money differently from younger people. On average, older households spend less than younger households because they generally have less money to spend, fewer dependents to support, and different needs and values. In 1999 the annual per capita

TABLE 2.9

Average annual expenditures and characteristics, by age, 1999

Item	All consumer units	Under 25	25-34	35-44	45-54	55-64	65 and over	65-74	75 and over
Number of consumer units (in thousands)	108,465	8,164	19,332	24,405	20,903	13,647	22,015	11,578	10,437
Consumer unit characteristics:									
Income before taxes [1]	$43,951	$18,276	$42,470	$53,579	$59,822	$49,436	$26,581	$28,928	$23,937
Income after taxes [1]	40,652	17,431	39,405	49,616	54,459	45,193	25,325	27,567	22,800
Age of reference person	47.9	21.4	29.7	39.5	49.2	59.1	74.8	69.3	80.8
Average number in consumer unit:									
Persons	2.5	1.8	2.9	3.2	2.7	2.2	1.7	1.9	1.5
Children under 18	.7	.4	1.1	1.3	.6	.2	.1	.1	(2)
Persons 65 and over	.3	(2)	(2)	(2)	(2)	.1	1.4	1.4	1.3
Earners	1.3	1.3	1.5	1.7	1.8	1.3	.4	.6	.2
Vehicles	1.9	1.1	1.7	2.1	2.5	2.2	1.5	1.8	1.2
Percent distribution:									
Sex of reference person:									
Male	55	46	56	58	59	58	49	54	43
Female	45	54	44	42	41	42	51	46	57
Housing tenure:									
Homeowner	65	13	45	67	77	80	80	82	77
With mortgage	38	7	37	54	54	40	16	22	9
Without mortgage	27	6	8	13	22	40	64	60	68
Renter	35	87	55	33	23	20	20	18	23
Race of reference person:									
Black	12	13	15	13	12	11	9	10	7
White and other	88	87	85	87	88	89	91	90	93
Education of reference person:									
Elementary (1-8)	6	2	3	3	4	8	15	12	19
High school (9-12)	39	35	37	38	33	43	46	47	46
College	55	64	60	59	62	50	38	42	34
Never attended and other	(3)	(3)	(3)	(3)	(3)	(3)	(3)	(3)	(3)
At least one vehicle owned or leased	87	70	87	91	92	90	82	87	76
Average annual expenditures	$36,995	$21,704	$36,158	$42,792	$46,511	$39,394	$26,521	$29,864	$22,884
Food	5,031	3,354	5,140	6,109	5,945	5,056	3,511	4,146	2,841
Food at home	2,915	1,828	2,890	3,537	3,340	2,920	2,266	2,575	1,943
Cereals and bakery products	448	271	432	561	509	433	357	399	314
Cereals and cereal products	160	102	170	211	175	140	116	130	101
Bakery products	288	169	262	350	335	294	242	269	213
Meats, poultry, fish, and eggs	749	469	751	897	878	761	563	664	457
Beef	220	155	221	266	257	230	154	187	119
Pork	157	93	154	185	185	165	121	146	95
Other meats	97	61	95	119	111	94	77	94	60
Poultry	136	82	148	162	160	136	96	109	82
Fish and seafood	106	59	103	125	130	102	87	98	77
Eggs	32	19	31	40	34	35	27	30	24
Dairy products	322	195	322	410	354	305	255	289	220
Fresh milk and cream	122	78	124	158	130	107	99	108	89
Other dairy products	200	117	198	252	224	198	156	181	131
Fruits and vegetables	500	283	475	572	563	525	450	497	401
Fresh fruits	152	77	136	173	173	161	149	165	131
Fresh vegetables	149	79	146	161	168	171	131	148	114
Processed fruits	113	77	105	133	129	108	100	106	93
Processed vegetables	86	49	87	104	93	86	71	78	63
Other food at home	$896	$610	$910	$1,097	$1,037	$895	$641	$726	$551
Sugar and other sweets	112	71	99	134	128	118	93	106	80
Fats and oils	84	54	80	96	96	86	70	81	59
Miscellaneous foods	420	300	463	517	464	401	290	322	258
Nonalcoholic beverages	242	167	236	301	301	241	158	176	139
Food prepared by consumer unit on out-of-town trips	39	19	32	49	47	50	29	42	15
Food away from home	2,116	1,526	2,250	2,572	2,605	2,136	1,245	1,571	898
Alcoholic beverages	318	369	365	384	320	330	172	219	122
Housing	12,057	6,585	12,519	14,215	14,513	12,093	8,944	9,607	8,223
Shelter	7,016	4,140	7,612	8,606	8,534	6,660	4,576	4,931	4,181
Owned dwellings	4,525	596	3,935	6,110	6,203	4,812	2,971	3,426	2,466
Mortgage interest and charges	2,547	311	2,694	3,990	3,641	2,328	745	1,038	420
Property taxes	1,123	168	751	1,297	1,444	1,380	1,149	1,222	1,069
Maintenance, repairs, insurance, other expenses	854	117	489	823	1,118	1,104	1,076	1,166	977
Rented dwellings	2,027	3,296	3,447	2,121	1,532	1,206	1,182	968	1,420
Other lodging	465	248	230	375	799	642	423	538	295

TABLE 2.9
Average annual expenditures and characteristics, by age, 1999 [CONTINUED]

Item	All consumer units	Under 25	25-34	35-44	45-54	55-64	65 and over	65-74	75 and over
Utilities, fuels, and public services	2,377	1,166	2,249	2,586	2,819	2,608	2,145	2,369	1,897
Natural gas	270	92	238	283	304	326	284	290	277
Electricity	899	426	811	969	1,074	997	848	933	753
Fuel oil and other fuels	74	14	47	72	94	80	102	117	86
Telephone services	849	562	924	950	1,008	869	614	711	506
Water and other public services	285	72	229	313	339	335	298	318	275
Household operations	666	181	772	830	606	476	746	458	1,065
Personal services	323	121	573	500	148	60	311	87	559
Other household expenses	343	60	199	330	459	416	435	371	505
Housekeeping supplies	498	221	441	604	574	570	423	493	349
Laundry and cleaning supplies	121	64	117	149	135	124	102	118	85
Other household products	250	86	211	315	298	296	199	231	166
Postage and stationery	127	71	113	139	141	149	122	144	98
Household furnishings and equipment	1,499	877	1,445	1,590	1,980	1,779	1,054	1,356	730
Household textiles	114	41	101	114	169	111	106	143	67
Furniture	365	283	435	403	446	382	205	265	138
Floor coverings	44	11	37	37	52	94	31	32	30
Major appliances	183	91	176	192	215	196	175	190	158
Small appliances, miscellaneous housewares	102	47	82	90	131	144	99	147	49
Miscellaneous household equipment	692	405	615	754	968	853	438	578	288
Apparel and services	1,743	1,192	2,047	2,053	2,048	1,722	1,070	1,235	901
Men and boys	421	238	519	517	517	406	219	300	134
Men, 16 and over	328	209	387	331	438	364	195	266	120
Boys, 2 to 15	93	29	133	186	79	41	24	34	13
Women and girls	655	422	709	764	817	671	416	525	301
Women, 16 and over	548	377	579	561	687	625	394	491	292
Girls, 2 to 15	107	45	130	203	130	46	22	34	9
Children under 2	67	99	139	80	40	41	17	22	⁴11
Footwear	303	234	374	373	327	308	165	219	108
Other apparel products and services	297	199	306	319	347	296	253	169	347
Transportation	7,011	5,037	7,150	8,041	9,010	7,330	4,385	5,457	3,196
Vehicle purchases (net outlay)	3,305	2,859	3,500	3,807	4,117	3,406	1,911	2,422	1,344
Cars and trucks, new	1,628	857	1,377	1,722	2,079	2,109	1,304	1,661	907
Cars and trucks, used	1,641	1,974	2,034	2,058	1,988	1,283	606	758	437
Other vehicles	36	⁴28	89	27	51	⁴14	⁴2	⁴3	(5)
Gasoline and motor oil	1,055	708	1,066	1,259	1,349	1,093	644	807	463
Other vehicle expenses	$2,254	$1,253	$2,249	$2,565	$3,085	$2,339	$1,443	$1,724	$1,131
Vehicle finance charges	320	209	402	394	431	320	104	146	57
Maintenance and repairs	664	402	554	743	890	724	519	596	434
Vehicle insurance	756	408	705	806	1,052	803	566	638	485
Vehicle rental, leases, licenses, other charges	513	234	588	620	712	493	255	344	155
Public transportation	397	217	335	411	459	492	387	504	258
Health care	1,959	551	1,170	1,631	2,183	2,450	3,019	2,991	3,052
Health insurance	923	233	597	746	942	1,063	1,554	1,572	1,534
Medical services	558	184	351	531	754	751	601	574	632
Drugs	370	97	162	254	368	497	706	696	719
Medical supplies	109	36	60	101	118	139	158	149	168
Entertainment	1,891	1,149	1,776	2,254	2,367	2,175	1,238	1,567	874
Fees and admissions	459	262	395	528	578	559	336	438	222
Television, radios, sound equipment	608	485	636	707	741	578	412	477	340
Pets, toys, and playground equipment	346	185	375	454	418	354	186	250	117
Other entertainment supplies, equipment, and services	478	217	369	565	631	684	305	403	194
Personal care products and services	408	254	381	471	475	449	333	370	295
Reading	159	70	116	157	210	195	163	184	141
Education	635	1,277	453	637	1,125	552	139	165	111
Tobacco products and smoking supplies	300	220	295	370	395	329	148	204	86
Miscellaneous	867	353	727	946	1,089	1,021	790	775	807
Cash contributions	1,181	182	585	1,067	1,415	1,750	1,627	1,663	1,588
Personal insurance and pensions	3,436	1,110	3,433	4,455	5,415	3,941	980	1,280	647
Life and other personal insurance	394	61	238	418	616	533	333	429	226
Pensions and Social Security	3,042	1,049	3,195	4,037	4,799	3,408	647	851	421
Sources of income and personal taxes: [1]									
Money income before taxes	43,951	18,276	42,470	53,579	59,822	49,430	26,581	28,928	23,937
Wages and salaries	34,456	16,210	39,372	48,616	52,224	34,521	5,406	8,169	2,295
Self-employment income	2,603	304	1,448	2,835	3,957	5,463	1,304	1,809	735

Item	All consumer units	Under 25	25-34	35-44	45-54	55-64	65 and over	65-74	75 and over
Social Security, private and government retirement	4,798	129	354	649	1,870	6,922	16,217	16,498	15,901
Interest, dividends, rental income, other property income	1,104	97	300	388	681	1,495	3,092	1,713	4,645
Unemployment and workers' compensation, veterans' benefits	177	88	182	210	290	169	70	86	51
Public assistance, supplemental security income, food stamps	320	271	365	300	321	480	228	301	146
Regular contributions for support	262	636	255	380	222	153	105	92	120
Other income	230	542	195	202	256	226	158	259	43
Personal taxes	3,299	845	3,065	3,963	5,363	4,243	1,256	1,361	1,137
Federal income taxes	2,513	630	2,316	3,037	4,178	3,312	827	905	739
State and local income taxes	616	208	671	797	955	691	169	178	159
Other taxes	170	7	78	128	230	241	260	278	240
Income after taxes	40,652	17,431	39,405	49,616	54,459	45,193	25,325	27,567	22,800
Addenda:									
Net change in total assets and liabilities	$142	- $617	$123	- $920	$5	$1,402	$966	$44	$1,989
Net change in total assets	6,478	2,715	10,479	9,070	6,770	5,146	2,035	1,220	2,939
Net change in total liabilities	6,336	3,332	10,357	9,990	6,765	3,745	1,069	1,176	950
Other financial information:									
Other money receipts	651	327	1,021	301	721	1,402	305	396	204
Mortgage principal paid on owned property	-1,366	-95	-897	-1,584	-2,009	-2,828	-494	-745	-215
Estimated market value of owned home	87,582	11,079	52,188	94,517	108,963	124,609	96,093	101,196	90,433
Estimated monthly rental value of owned home	592	93	393	646	735	772	645	686	598
Gifts of goods and services	1,083	515	739	956	1,690	1,537	884	948	814
Food	83	19	40	48	194	138	43	63	22
Housing	292	139	238	275	425	375	238	278	196
Housekeeping supplies	41	14	39	52	44	48	32	37	27
Household textiles	17	[4]3	11	11	27	21	22	33	11
Appliances and miscellaneous housewares	32	5	19	23	46	58	36	38	33
Major appliances	9	[4]2	4	6	13	14	10	4	17
Small appliances and miscellaneous housewares	24	2	15	17	34	44	25	34	16
Miscellaneous household equipment	66	42	48	61	83	102	58	79	37
Other housing	136	75	120	128	225	146	90	92	89
Apparel and services	210	118	206	190	269	298	160	176	143
Males, 2 and over	54	24	49	39	70	88	51	65	36
Females, 2 and over	71	35	46	58	110	99	67	55	79
Children under 2	33	23	43	45	30	38	14	17	11
Other apparel products and services	52	36	67	47	59	74	29	40	18
Jewelry and watches	27	22	53	25	23	26	11	18	3
All other apparel products and services	25	[4]14	14	22	36	48	18	22	[4]14
Transportation	63	65	30	56	90	93	57	64	49
Health care	40	[5]5	9	24	46	43	90	57	128
Entertainment	98	63	74	89	106	142	107	99	115
Toys, games, hobbies, and tricycles	32	10	23	28	41	52	30	42	16
Other entertainment	66	53	51	61	65	90	77	57	99
Education	166	42	31	126	422	254	78	78	63
All other gifts	131	65	111	148	138	193	110	120	99

[1] Components of income and taxes are derived from "complete income reporters" only; see glossary.
[2] Value less than 0.05.
[3] Value less than 0.5.
[4] Data are likely to have large sampling errors.
[5] No data reported.

SOURCE: "Table 3. Age of Reference Person: Average Annual Expenditures and Characteristics, Consumer Expenditure Survey, 1999," Bureau of Labor Statistics, Washington, DC [Online] http://www.bls.gov/cex/1999/Standard/age.pdf [accessed October 22, 2001]

expenditure for those older than age 65 was $26,521, lower than all other age groups except those under the age of 25. (See Table 2.9.) Those over 75 spent only $22,884. The greatest amounts were spent on housing (including utilities), food, transportation, and health care. Not surprisingly, the elderly spent more of their money on health care than any other age group, both in actual dollars and in percentage of expenditures. They spent less on entertainment, tobacco and smoking products, alcoholic bever-

ages, apparel, food eaten away from home, and vehicle-related items than other groups.

One measure of the economic differences among the elderly is shown in those who have discretionary income—that is, money left over after the person has paid everything needed to maintain his or her standard of living. Many sources believe that those over the age of 65 have a smaller percentage of discretionary income than all groups except persons under 24, although most experts estimate that at least one-quarter of the elderly have some discretionary income. In 1999 the Conference Board, a marketing research firm, estimated that those aged 45 to 54 accounted for 19 percent of all households and 20 percent of all discretionary income. Those aged 55 to 64 made up 13 percent of households and held 13 percent of discretionary income. Americans aged 65 to 74 were 11 percent of households and had 10 percent of the discretionary income. Those aged 75 and over, who were 10 percent of households, held 8.5 percent of all discretionary income.

Spending by Older Householders Grows

Some sources believe that householders aged 65 years and older are spending more. *Americans 55 and Older: A Changing Market* (Sharon Yntema, ed., 2nd ed., New Strategist Publications, Ithaca, NY, 1999), a study designed to promote marketing among older Americans, reported that while average annual spending per household actually fell .1 percent from 1990 to 1997 and spending by householders aged 55 to 64 grew by just 1 percent, spending by those aged 65 to 74 grew 8.3 percent, and that of those aged 75 and older grew 6.9 percent. Older householders spent more than ever before in a number of categories for which the average householder's spending dropped. For example, while the average household spent 14 percent less on alcoholic beverages in 1997 than in 1990, those headed by people aged 65 to 74 and 75-plus spent 32 percent and 27 percent more, respectively. Entertainment expenses among people aged 75 and above increased 66 percent, while for the population as a whole, they rose just 4 percent.

Smaller Households Are More Expensive to Run

Almost all elderly households are made up of fewer persons than younger households are. While larger households, in general, cost more to operate, they are less expensive on a per capita basis. For example, the Census Bureau reported that the basic cost of living for two people was less than twice as much as the cost for one person living alone; the living cost of four people was significantly less than four times that of someone living alone.

Larger, younger households often have multiple incomes. Repairing a leaky roof or buying a new refrigerator costs the same for any household, but the larger the household, the less cost there is per person. Buying small quantities of food for one or two persons may be almost as expensive as buying in bulk for three or four. Because the elderly often have limited mobility, they may be forced to buy food and other necessities at small neighborhood stores that generally charge more than supermarkets.

THE SOCIAL SECURITY PROGRAM—AMERICA'S MOST POPULAR GOVERNMENT PROGRAM

On January 31, 1940, Vermont resident Ida May Fuller became the first person to receive an old-age monthly benefit check—$22.54—from Social Security. She would collect a total of $22,889 in Social Security benefits—on her payroll contribution of $24.75—by the time she died in 1975 at age 100.

Congress passed the Social Security Act in 1935 to provide economic assistance to retirees, the blind, and mothers and their dependent children. It has since been amended many times and is currently composed of numerous sections, including Medicare and Supplemental Security Income. The section authorizing the Old Age, Survivors, and Disability Insurance (OASDI) program finances Social Security, which provides monthly benefits to retired and disabled workers and their dependents, and to survivors of insured workers. Today about 150 million workers are protected by Social Security.

According to the SSA, in 1999 more than 9 in 10 persons aged 65 or over received OASDI. Benefits are funded through a mandatory tax (the Federal Insurance Contributions Act, or FICA) that is withheld from workers' earnings and is matched by the employer. (Self-employed people also pay a FICA tax.) When covered workers retire (or are disabled), they draw benefits based on the amount they have contributed to the fund. The longer the time of employment and the higher the earnings, the larger the benefit. Today, worker and employer each contribute 7.65 percent of the worker's salary up to $76,200 to the fund. Self-employed workers pay 15.3 percent of wages up to $76,200. In 2000 the trust fund took in $568 billion and paid out $415 billion for old-age and disability insurance combined.

Although Social Security was not initially presented as a full pension, many elderly people depend almost solely on it. The SSA reported that the program enables 38 million Americans to live above the poverty level and that it is the country's most effective antipoverty program.

Workers can retire as early as age 62 and get reduced Social Security benefits. Or they can wait until full retirement age and receive full benefits. The full retirement age has been 65, but starting in 2003, it will increase gradually until it reaches age 67 for people born in 1960 or later. In addition, a special credit is given to people who delay retirement beyond their full retirement age. This credit, which is a percentage added to the Social Security benefit, varies depending on the retired person's date of birth. For people reaching full retirement age in 2001, the rate is 6 percent per year. That rate gradually increases in future years, until it reaches 8 percent per year for people reaching full retirement age in 2008 or later. Beneficiaries do not earn the delayed retirement credit after age 70.

Average Benefits

In 2000 the average monthly Social Security check for retired male workers was $951 per month. The average benefit for spouses of retired male workers was $243 per month. (See Table 2.10.) This together equals approximately $14,328 per year for the couple. Retired male workers received the highest amount on average, and spouses of disabled male workers the least. (Four hypo-

thetical examples of benefits received by retired workers are shown in Figure 2.5.)

Ever since 1940, when Americans first received Social Security checks, monthly retirement benefits have steadily increased, but in the early 1970s they soared. In 1972 the average benefit was indexed to keep up with inflation as reflected by the Consumer Price Index. This meant that recipients received periodic "raises" or cost of living adjustments that were based upon the economic situation at that particular time. The 1970s were characterized by growing inflation, and within a few years, the whole system was facing serious long-range financial troubles, which many observers linked to the 1972 amendments.

Some legislators felt that indexing vastly overcompensated for inflation, causing relative benefit levels to rise higher than at any previous time in the history of the program. In many cases, if the formula had remained in effect, benefit levels for some future retirees would be higher than their earnings before retirement. In an attempt to prevent future Social Security benefits from rising to

TABLE 2.10

Average monthly Old-Age, Survivors, and Disability Insurance (OASDI) benefit by sex and type of beneficiary, December 2000

	Men	Women
All beneficiaries	$928	$696
Retired workers	951	730
Spouses	243	431
Disabled workers	883	661
Spouses	156	199
Survivors		
Nondisabled widows and widowers	607	812
Disabled widows and widowers	362	524
Mothers and fathers	503	600

SOURCE: *Fast Facts & Figures About Social Security,* Social Security Administration, Washington, DC, June 2001

FIGURE 2.5

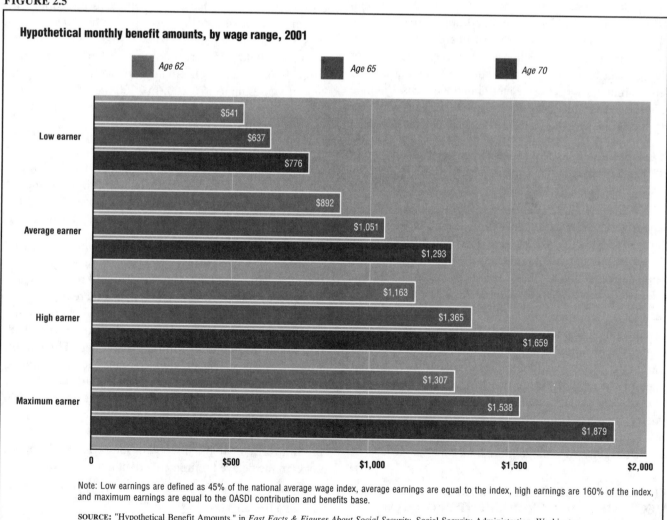

Hypothetical monthly benefit amounts, by wage range, 2001

Note: Low earnings are defined as 45% of the national average wage index, average earnings are equal to the index, high earnings are 160% of the index, and maximum earnings are equal to the OASDI contribution and benefits base.

SOURCE: "Hypothetical Benefit Amounts," in *Fast Facts & Figures About Social Security,* Social Security Administration, Washington, DC, June 2001

FIGURE 2.6

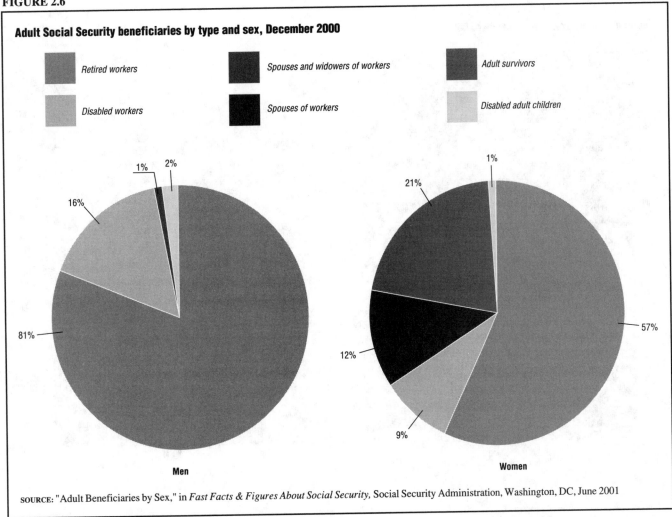

Adult Social Security beneficiaries by type and sex, December 2000

Retired workers
Disabled workers
Spouses and widowers of workers
Spouses of workers
Adult survivors
Disabled adult children

Men

1%
2%
16%
81%

Women

1%
21%
12%
9%
57%

SOURCE: "Adult Beneficiaries by Sex," in *Fast Facts & Figures About Social Security,* Social Security Administration, Washington, DC, June 2001

what many considered excessive levels, Congress passed the Social Security Amendments of 1977 (PL 95-216) to restructure the benefit plan and design more realistic formulas for benefits. Among other things, the 1977 amendments raised the payroll tax slightly, increased the wage base, and reduced benefits slightly.

Benefits and Beneficiaries

According to the SSA, more than 4.3 million persons signed onto Social Security in 2000. In that year, the SSA made payments to more than 45 million persons. Retired workers made up 46 percent of all beneficiaries, and 14 percent were disabled workers. The remaining 40 percent were survivors and/or dependents of workers.

Of all adults receiving monthly Social Security benefits in 2000, 43 percent were men and 57 percent were women. About one-fifth of the women received survivor benefits. (See Figure 2.6.)

Dual Entitlement of Spouses

The proportion of women among retired worker beneficiaries has quadrupled since 1940, while the number of

women who are receiving benefits as dependents (based on their husband's earnings) has been declining. At the same time, the number of women with dual entitlement (based on both their own earnings and their husbands') has risen from 5 percent in 1960 to 28 percent in 2000. This does not mean they get two Social Security payments, but that they are eligible for either and normally get the larger of the two possibilities.

The Earnings Test

A new law, effective January 1, 2000, changed the way Social Security determined how benefits affect how much beneficiaries can work while receiving retirement or survivors benefits. Benefit amounts are now reduced only until beneficiaries reach their full retirement age (currently age 65), not up to age 70 as the previous law required.

SUPPLEMENTAL SECURITY INCOME

Supplemental Security Income (SSI) is a joint federal-state welfare program designed to supply monthly cash payments to low-income aged, blind, or disabled Americans. Instituted in 1974, it replaced many local public

FIGURE 2.7

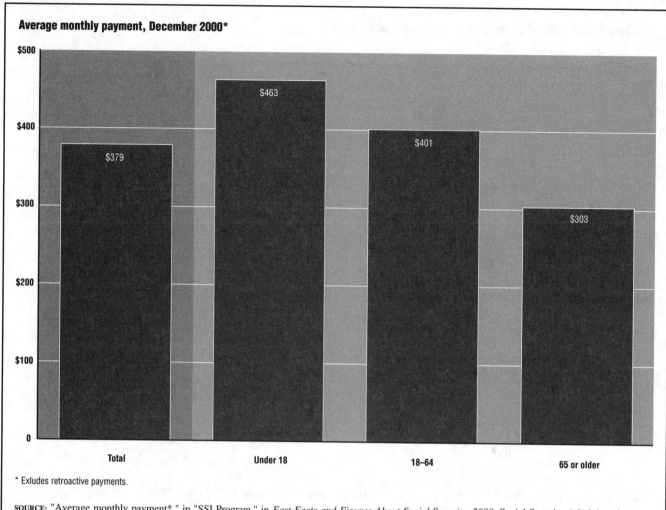

Average monthly payment, December 2000*

* Exludes retroactive payments.

SOURCE: "Average monthly payment*," in "SSI Program," in *Fast Facts and Figures About Social Security, 2000,* Social Security Administration, Washington, DC, June 2001 [Online] http://www.ssa.gov/statistics/fast_facts/2001/ff2001.pdf [accessed October 24, 2001]

assistance programs. SSI benefits are financed from general revenues, not from the Social Security trust fund. Individual payments vary from state to state, depending on whether the federal or state government administers the program.

According to the SSA, about 6.6 million persons, over 2 million of whom were aged 65 or older, received SSI payments in December 2000. SSI payments vary by age group. The average payment to an aged individual was $303 in December 2000. (See Figure 2.7.)

One-fifth (20 percent) of SSI beneficiaries have been awarded compensation based on age. Nevertheless, about one-third (30 percent) of all beneficiaries are aged 65 and older. The difference is accounted for by the fact that persons awarded benefits based on disability convert to Old Age Assistance when they reach age 65, but are still classified as disabled.

The percentage of SSI recipients under 65 years of age increased between 1974 and 2000, while the percent-

age of recipients over age 65 decreased. Critics of the program believe that the SSI program could do more to help the elderly. For one thing, it provides enough income only to bring an individual to 70 percent (and a couple to 90 percent) of the poverty level. Its strict assets test excludes many elderly people from receiving benefits, and many low-income people are unaware of the program.

THE FUTURE OF THE SOCIAL SECURITY PROGRAM

Most experts believe that the Social Security program faces a shaky future and that its solvency is threatened in the next decades. In 1982 the OASDI trust fund almost went bankrupt. Then-President Ronald Reagan and Congress instituted higher Social Security taxes, along with increased contributions and a one-time delay in the cost-of-living adjustment.

Social Security is a "pay-as-you-go" program, with the contributions of present workers paying the retirement benefits of those currently retired. The program is solvent at this time, the result of a larger number of employees contributing funds to the system and fewer retirees than expected. The earliest wave of baby boomers, those individuals born between 1946 and 1964, is still in the workforce and reaching their peak earning years.

At the same time, people who are now retiring were born during the low birthrate cycle of the Great Depression of the 1930s, so there are now fewer retirees depleting funds than there are workers contributing to it. The federal government has been using some of the current surplus in the Social Security fund to make the federal deficit appear smaller. By using this money to pay current non-Social Security expenses, there will be less money for Americans when they retire.

At the present time, a retiree who has paid approximately $25,000 into the system will have that amount returned in about three years. That will not be the case, however, for retired workers in the future. They will have paid considerably more money into the system and get back much less. Furthermore, since there will be a much higher percentage of retirees as the baby boomers reach age 65, starting in 2011, the younger generation of workers will face greater financial responsibility for the support and care of an increasing population of older Americans.

At the same time that the elderly population is growing, life expectancy is increasing, resulting in even more elderly who will become eligible for Social Security. Additionally, the falling birthrate means there will be fewer workers contributing to Social Security for each aged, disabled, dependent, or surviving beneficiary. (Figure 2.8 shows the declining ratio of workers to beneficiaries.)

Currently, because there are more contributing to the system and fewer elderly to use the funds, contributions to the system exceed expenses paid out to the aging by roughly $30 billion each year. That excess goes into a trust fund, which helps reduce the federal budget deficit. According to the SSA, benefit payments will begin to exceed Social Security taxes paid in 2015, and the trust fund will be exhausted in 2037. At that time, Social Security will be able to pay only about 72 percent of benefits owed if no changes are made.

Restoring Social Security's long-term financial balance will require a combination of increased revenues and reduced expenditures. Some ways to reduce expenditures include:

- Reducing initial benefits to retirees
- Raising the retirement age (currently scheduled to rise from 65 to 67 by 2027)
- Lowering cost-of-living adjustments
- Limiting benefits based on the beneficiaries' other income and assets

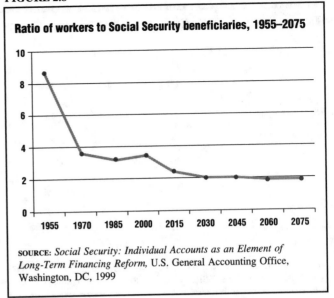

FIGURE 2.8

Ratio of workers to Social Security beneficiaries, 1955–2075

SOURCE: *Social Security: Individual Accounts as an Element of Long-Term Financing Reform,* U.S. General Accounting Office, Washington, DC, 1999

Ways to increase revenues include:

- Increasing Social Security payroll taxes
- Investing trust funds in securities with potentially higher yields than the government bonds in which they are currently invested
- Increasing income taxes on Social Security benefits

In addition to those measures, or a combination of them, some sources suggest it may be possible to return funds to workers in the form of tax rebates, which they could then invest in stock and bond markets through individual accounts, with the proceeds going to finance their retirement benefits, a concept called privatization.

Linking Social Security in some way to the performance of the stock market is one of the key issues in the current debate about rescuing Social Security. In general, such plans would give beneficiaries some degree of responsibility for their retirement investments. Critics of such plans point out that many groups, particularly low-income workers and women, would avoid the risks and invest in lower-yielding investments, reducing their earnings. Other sources believe such systems would expose less educated or inexperienced investors to the dangers of investment scams.

The existing "pay-as-you-go" pension system means that current workers finance the retirement of the elderly. Some sources have predicted that with fewer workers to pay for more retirees, national pension systems in the United States and Europe are headed for trouble. Prior to the September 11, 2001, attacks by terrorists on the World Trade Center and the Pentagon, these issues were being hotly debated in Congress. Most discussions of these issues went on hold as the United States, and indeed the world, focused on the war in Afghanistan.

TABLE 2.11

Worker confidence in Medicare and Social Security, 1993–2001

	Medicare								
	1993	**1994**	**1995**	**1996**	**1997**	**1998**	**1999**	**2000**	**2001**
Very confident	3%	3%	2%	3%	3%	4%	7%	6%	7%
Somewhat confident	21	24	19	20	21	24	24	29	32
Not too confident	43	32	38	38	37	34	38	38	31
Not at all confident	30	37	38	37	34	36	30	27	26

	Social Security								
	1993	**1994**	**1995**	**1996**	**1997**	**1998**	**1999**	**2000**	**2001**
Very confident	4%	4%	3%	3%	5%	6%	7%	7%	8%
Somewhat confident	19	18	16	17	17	16	21	21	26
Not too confident	41	38	42	40	36	31	38	39	33
Not at all confident	33	39	38	38	39	44	33	33	32

SOURCE: "Confidence in Social Security and Medicare," in *2001 Retirement Confidence Survey Summary of Findings,* Retirement Confidence Survey, Employee Benefit Research Institute (EBRI) Online, Washington, DC [Online] http://www.ebri.org/rcs/2001/01rcses.pdf [accessed October 24, 2001]

Confidence in the Future

The EBRI reported in its 2001 *Retirement Confidence Survey* that worker confidence in Social Security and Medicare has continued to rise steadily after lows measured in 1995. In 2001 one-third of workers reported that they were confident the Social Security program would continue to provide benefits of at least equal value to the benefits received by retirees that year. In addition, 39 percent were very or somewhat confident that Medicare would continue to provide benefits of at least equal value to those received in 2001. (See Table 2.11.)

THE AGING CONSUMER—A GROWING MARKET

Today's elderly (and their caregivers) have proven to be a lucrative market for many products. In addition to the products traditionally offered to the aging, such as health and life insurance and burial plots, marketers have discovered the elderly are interested in a new range of products and services. Today's healthier, more affluent aging population desires products that make dressing and other routine tasks simpler, and products that promote health, travel, and recreation. Direct marketers find that elderly consumers readily shop mail-order catalogs. Many older shoppers expect more attractive and comfortable clothing and footwear.

Mature consumers respond to marketing that reflects autonomy and self-sufficiency, social and spiritual connections, altruism (unselfishness), personal growth, and revitalization. Older customers are often suspicious of claims about a product's attributes and are less influenced by peers and less materialistic.

The Emerging "Silver" Market

The aging of the baby boomers is expected to change the consumer marketplace. Boomers are more interested in health and in postponing aging than any generation before. They will search for medical, technological, hormonal, and genetic answers to cure ailments and promote vitality and longevity. They invest in foods, medications, and products that promote energy, relaxation, and sexuality.

Boomers have also embraced technological advances and financial innovation. They will seek innovation in home design and operations. They are accepting of lifestyle changes. All these suggest that they will be voracious consumers when they reach retirement age.

CHAPTER 3
LIVING ARRANGEMENTS OF THE ELDERLY

ELDERLY HOUSEHOLDS

The U.S. Bureau of the Census reported one household in five was headed by a person aged 65 years or older in March 2000 (21.7 million households out of 104.7 million households). (See Table 3.1.) These figures, based on the Census Bureau's Current Population Survey (CPS), include both family and nonfamily households (where the members are unrelated to the head of the household). Most elderly Americans are adequately housed, but housing situations range from the affluent young-old homeowner to the very poor oldest-old nursing home resident.

LIVING WITH A SPOUSE OR OTHER RELATIVES

According to the CPS, the number of elderly people living with a spouse varies greatly between men and women. In 2000, 72.6 percent of all men aged 65 years or over who were not living in institutions lived with their spouse, compared to only 41.3 percent of women. The difference is also dramatic in the 75 to 84 age group: 76.7 percent of men lived with a spouse, compared to 52.9 percent of women. By the age of 85, 67.1 percent of men lived with a spouse, while only 28.8 percent of women did. This disparity occurs because women tend to live longer than men, are generally younger than the men they marry, and are far less likely to remarry after the death of a spouse. With increasing age, both men and women have a greater chance of living alone.

In 2000 about 18 percent of people over age 65 lived with a relative other than a spouse. Again, the difference between men and women was significant: 15 percent of women lived with a relative other than a spouse, but only 4 percent of men did.

MULTIGENERATIONAL HOUSEHOLDS

Multigenerational households, such as grandparents living with children and grandchildren, raised a great deal of interest in the 1990s. Many of these households include older relatives such as grandparents, great-grandparents, and uncles and aunts. The Census Bureau pointed out that many multigenerational households are located in areas where new immigrants live with relatives, where housing shortages or high costs force families to double up their living arrangements, or in areas that have high rates of out-of-wedlock children, where unwed mothers live with their parents and their children.

The 2000 U.S. Census found 3.9 million multigenerational family households, making up 3.7 percent of all households. Hawaii had the highest percentage, with 8.2 percent of all households in the state being multigenerational. Other states exceeding 5 percent in 2000 were California (5.6 percent) and Mississippi (5.2 percent). Puerto Rico also had a high percentage, with 7.4 percent. North Dakota had the smallest percentage, with 1.1 percent.

Almost two-thirds (65 percent, or 2.6 million households) of multigenerational households include the head of the household, a child or children, and a grandchild or grandchildren. The remaining third of multigenerational households (1.3 million households) consist primarily of a householder, the householder's parents or parents-in-law, and the householder's children. Four-generation households are rare, making up only 2 percent of multigenerational households (or 78,000 households).

GRANDPARENTS TAKING CARE OF GRANDCHILDREN

The 2000 census found 5.6 million grandparents living with grandchildren under 18 years of age. Forty-one percent of them (2.3 million) had responsibility for their grandchildren, which means that they had the primary parenting role. This figure includes 1.5 million grandmothers and over 889,000 grandfathers.

TABLE 3.1

Households by type and selected characteristics, March 2000

(In thousands, except average size)

Characteristic	All house-holds	Family households				Nonfamily households		
					Other families			
		Total	Married couple	Male house-holder	Female house-holder	Total	Male house-holder	Female house-holder
All households	104,705	72,025	55,311	4,028	12,687	32,680	14,641	18,039
Age of householder								
15 to 24 years old	5,860	3,353	1,450	560	1,342	2,507	1,286	1,221
25 to 34 years old	18,627	13,007	9,390	886	2,732	5,620	3,448	2,172
35 to 44 years old	23,955	18,706	14,104	1,102	3,499	5,250	3,261	1,989
45 to 54 years old	20,927	15,803	12,792	713	2,299	5,123	2,583	2,541
55 to 64 years old	13,592	9,569	8,138	351	1,080	4,023	1,533	2,490
65 years old and over	21,744	11,587	9,437	416	1,735	10,157	2,530	7,626
Race and ethnicity of householder								
White	87,671	60,251	48,790	3,081	8,380	27,420	12,204	15,215
Non-Hispanic	78,819	53,066	43,865	2,468	6,732	25,753	11,278	14,475
Black	12,849	8,664	4,144	706	3,814	4,185	1,876	2,309
Asian and Pacific Islander	3,337	2,506	1,996	179	331	831	432	399
Hispanic (of any race)	9,319	7,561	5,133	658	1,769	1,758	974	783
Presence of related children under 18								
No related children	67,350	34,670	28,919	1,826	3,924	32,680	14,641	18,039
With related children	37,355	37,355	26,392	2,202	8,762	(X)	(X)	(X)
One related child under 18	15,493	15,493	9,897	1,321	4,275	(X)	(X)	(X)
Two related children under 18	14,020	14,020	10,567	644	2,809	(X)	(X)	(X)
Three related children under 18	5,510	5,510	4,238	185	1,087	(X)	(X)	(X)
Four or more related children under 18	2,332	2,332	1,690	52	591	(X)	(X)	(X)
Presence of own children under 18								
No own children	70,100	37,420	30,062	2,242	5,116	32,680	14,641	18,039
With own children	34,605	34,605	25,248	1,786	7,571	(X)	(X)	(X)
With own children under 1	2,939	2,939	2,264	174	501	(X)	(X)	(X)
With own children under 3	8,786	8,786	6,784	441	1,561	(X)	(X)	(X)
With own children under 6	14,986	14,986	11,393	706	2,887	(X)	(X)	(X)
With own children under 12	25,885	25,885	19,082	1,235	5,568	(X)	(X)	(X)
Size of households								
1 person	26,724	(X)	(X)	(X)	(X)	26,724	11,181	15,543
2 people	34,666	29,834	22,899	1,730	5,206	4,832	2,607	2,225
3 people	17,152	16,405	11,213	1,106	4,086	746	570	177
4 people	15,309	15,064	12,455	682	1,927	245	179	66
5 people	6,981	6,894	5,723	307	864	87	70	17
6 people	2,445	2,413	1,916	130	366	32	26	6
7 or more	1,428	1,415	1,105	73	237	13	8	5
Average size	2.62	3.24	3.26	3.16	3.17	1.25	1.34	1.17

X Not applicable.

SOURCE: Jason Fields and Lynne M. Casper, "Table 1. Households by Type and Selected Characteristics: March 2000," in *America's Families and Living Arrangements: March 2000,* U.S. Census Bureau, Washington, DC, 2001

A Strong Bond

The state of American grandparenting is strong.

— Gretchen Shaw, AARP Research Group, 2000

Many grandparents "stay in touch" with their grandchildren, spend time with them, and give gifts to them. Despite the belief that generational family relationships have suffered in recent decades, the AARP's (formerly the American Association of Retired Persons) *Grandparenting Survey* (January 2000), conducted by ICR Research Group (Media, PA), found that most interact with grandchildren and view their relationships as "very positive." Eighty-two percent said they had seen their grandchild in the previous month, and 85 percent said they had talked to that child on the phone in that period. In the past month, 72 percent had

shared a meal and an equal number reported they had bought a gift for their grandchild within that month.

The activities most often shared with a grandchild were eating together, watching a television comedy, staying overnight, shopping for clothes, and engaging in a sport or exercise. When asked about the roles they played when interacting with their grandchildren, 49 percent said they served as companion/friend, and 35 percent reported they gave advice. Approximately one-third of respondents talked about family history, told what their parents did as a child, served as a confidant, or "talked about the old days." Grandparents spent a median of $489 a year on clothes, books, toys, and other items for their grandchildren. The survey found that a typical grandparent had five grandchildren/great-grandchildren (one-fourth of grandparents had great-grandchildren).

Grandparents' Rights

The high rate of divorce in the United States has caused many grandparents to become separated from their grandchildren. As a result, some grandparents are seeking visitation rights to grandchildren. Since the 1980s more and more cases have made their way into courtrooms, leading most states to develop laws to decide how and when grandparents can see their grandchildren. At issue is whether fit parents can be forced to allow grandparents to visit grandchildren. In most states, grandparents must show that it is in the best interest of the child. In one state, Georgia, they must show that the child would suffer harm if they were denied visits.

In 2000 the U.S. Supreme Court, in *Troxel v. Granville,* heard arguments to decide whether grandparents have a legal right to visit grandchildren over the objections of the child's parents. On June 5 of that year the Court issued a narrow decision in the case that surprised many because it did not affect most state visitation laws. The plurality of the Court, in an opinion written by Justice Sandra Day O'Connor, struck down a state of Washington visitation statute as too broad. The Court limited its ruling to this specific statute, which allowed "any interested person," not just grandparents or other relatives, to petition the courts at any time for visitation with children. Most other state visitation laws are more narrowly written, and the Court further limited the impact of its decision by stating that it was not deciding whether visitation statutes should require courts to find that the children will suffer "harm" if grandparents are denied visitation. Such a decision would have affected virtually each state's visitation law, because of all 50 state laws, only Georgia's requires a finding of harm.

LIVING ALONE

Most elderly people who live alone have outlived their spouses, and in some cases, their children and siblings. As a result, the percentage of persons living alone increases with age. According to the 2000 CPS, 30.6 percent of women between age 65 and 74 and 49.4 percent of women aged 75 and over lived alone in 2000. In contrast, only 13.8 percent of 65- to 74-year-old men and 21.4 percent of men over 75 lived alone. These figures reflect the fact that women generally live longer than men, are more likely to be widowed, and less likely to remarry. Nearly half (45.3 percent) of women aged 65 years and older were widowed.

LIVING HOMELESS

Very little research has been conducted on the homeless elderly. Although approximately 12 percent of the homeless population in the United States is over age 65,

only 3 to 5 percent of homeless people who have sought care have been elderly. The relatively low proportion of elderly homeless suggested by this figure may be explained by their access to benefits (such as Social Security, Medicare, and housing), by high death rates once they enter street life, or by their avoidance of high visibility shelters and programs that they fear may be dangerous.

SENIOR HOUSING: NURSING HOMES, ASSISTED LIVING, AND OTHER ALTERNATIVES

Nursing Homes

One of the main reasons for entering a nursing home or similar long-term care facility is to receive medical care. Some experts, however, suggest that between 10 and 60 percent of persons in nursing homes could live in the community if appropriate supportive services (primarily nonmedical) were available. Groups representing the elderly also believe that 30 to 50 percent of those in nursing homes could and would live elsewhere, if such facilities were available. According to the National Nursing Home Survey, only about 4 percent of the older population lives in nursing homes at any given time.

Assisted Living

Assisted living is emerging as the next century's longterm care model.
— Paul Klaassen, CEO of Sunrise Assisted Living

Assisted living housing gets its name from the help provided to residents in the form of housekeeping, meal services, minor medical care, and personal care, such as help getting out of bed, bathing, and/or dressing. Assisted living sprang up to fill a gap in long-term care—elderly people who need some assistance with tasks of daily living (such as cooking and cleaning), but who do not need around-the-clock medical care.

Assisted living facilities can be large or small, institutional or homelike, expensive or affordable. In response to consumer demand, the private sector is increasingly developing facilities that are more like bed-and-breakfasts in appearance than nursing homes. Assisted living facilities try to meet the preference for a residential atmosphere with appropriate, individually tailored services.

Assisted living is the fastest-growing type of senior housing in the United States, with an estimated 15 to 20 percent annual growth rate over the past few years. The American Association of Homes and Services for the Aging estimated that in 1999 assisted living accounted for 75 percent of new senior housing.

According to the National Center for Assisted Living, an industry organization, more than 1 million residents were living in 28,000 assisted living facilities. Fifty-three percent of residents moved to assisted living from private residences, and the average stay in 1997 was 26 months.

The most common reason (44 percent) for discharge was the need for a nursing home stay. Other reasons for discharge included death (26 percent), financial reasons (5 percent), and a move to another assisted living residence (4 percent).

Because of its immense growth, some people have expressed concern about assisted living as an industry. Among the concerns are the potential for serious waste, fraud, and abuse, problems that at times have plagued the nursing home industry and made it among the most regulated of health care components.

Life-Care Communities

Life-care communities provide their residents with housing, personal care, a variety of social and recreational activities, and, ultimately, nursing care. Typically, residents enter into a lifetime contractual arrangement with the facility, for which they pay an entrance fee and a set monthly fee in return for services and benefits. Most facilities are operated by private, nonprofit, and/or religious organizations.

Entrance fees in these communities can vary substantially, from $20,000 to $200,000, and monthly fees range from $500 to $2,000 depending on the size of the facility and the quality and number of services. Services usually do not include acute health care needs such as doctor visits and hospitalization and, with few exceptions, are not covered by government or private insurance.

Shared Housing

Some elderly persons share living quarters to reduce expenses and responsibilities and also for companionship. Many elderly live in the same homes in which they raised their families. These houses may be too large for the needs of one or two persons. Shared housing can be very cost-effective for those who wish to remain in their own homes and for those who cannot afford a home of their own or the cost of a retirement community. About three-fourths of older home-sharing participants are women.

In its most common form, a single homeowner seeks a roommate to share living space and expenses. Shared housing can also include households with three or more roommates and family-like cooperatives in which large groups of people live together.

Unfortunately, the elderly poor who desire to share housing may lose some of their already meager incomes. Under government regulations, supplemental Social Security eligibility and benefits are computed on the basis of the income of the entire household rather than the individual residents, so savings in living expenses may be more than offset by a reduction in benefits and money for food and medicine.

Intergenerational home sharing may fit the needs of younger and older people. While offering the usual benefits of cost-cutting and companionship, home sharers may exchange services—for example, help with household maintenance in exchange for babysitting.

ECHO Units or "Granny Flats"

Elder cottage housing opportunity (ECHO) units or "granny flats" are small, freestanding, removable housing units that are located on the same lot as a single-family house. Another term used in local zoning is "accessory apartments or units." Accessory apartments are self-contained second living units built into or attached to an existing single-family dwelling. They are private, generally smaller than the primary unit, and usually contain one or two bedrooms, a bathroom, sitting room, and kitchen.

Generally, ECHO units or granny flats, and accessory apartments are constructed by a family for an elderly parent or grandparent so that that person can be nearby while each party maintains a degree of independence. Zoning laws and concerns about property values and traffic patterns are major obstacles to granny flats, although as the elderly survive longer and nursing home costs increase, this concept may gain support.

Retirement Communities

A number of developers have experimented with constructing entire cities just for the elderly. Examples include the Sun City communities in Florida, Arizona, and Texas. The Florida and Arizona locations opened in the 1960s, the Texas site in 1996. Homes in these properties are available only to those families in which at least one member is 55 or older, and no one under age 19 is allowed to stay permanently. Sun City offers clubs, golf courses, social organizations, fitness clubs, and recreational complexes. At the Texas location, 45 percent of the land remains open space and natural areas. Medical facilities are located nearby.

Sun City is not for the poor, and many of its residents are wealthy. About 60 percent have had at least some college education, compared with 20 percent of all adults aged 65 years and older.

While cities devoted to the needs and interests of the elderly may seem ideal, they face a unique challenge: everyone is getting older. The demand for social and health services for the thousands of people with a median age of 80 may prove overwhelming.

Cohousing and Intentional Communities

Cohousing, which originated in Denmark, is gaining interest in the United States. What distinguishes the arrangements in this category is planning—a group of individuals design and plan a community. Being in better health and living longer, many seniors wish to maintain their own private residences while also benefiting from certain features helpful to their age group. They may find apartments or townhouses less strenuous to maintain than single-family homes with lawns. They may also enjoy the camaraderie of others their age and some common areas, such as dining facilities.

For such seniors, many communities—or the seniors themselves—are building apartments, townhouses, and condominiums restricted to those over a specified age. Although acute medical needs are not provided for, many such residences are physically equipped for older residents. Furthermore, because of their specific clientele, these communities can accommodate some needs common among the elderly, such as transportation to senior centers, social activities tailored for various stages of aging, and checking on residents when asked. Most of these developments are private enterprises. In fact, in most instances, the seniors plan the community and own not only their own property, but also an interest in the common facilities. There are currently more than 50 cohousing developments in the United States.

Board and Care Facilities

The Subcommittee on Health and Long-Term Care of the Select Committee on Aging of the U.S. House of Representatives defined a board and care facility as one that "provides shelter, food and protection to frail and disabled individuals." Typically, residents have their own bedroom and bathroom, or share them with one other person, but all other rooms are shared space. While the concept is praiseworthy, all too often the board and care business is riddled with fraud and abuses. Totally unregulated in many states, these facilities have frequently become dumping grounds for the old, the ill, the mentally retarded, and the disabled.

Medical experts believe that Supplemental Security Income (SSI) is the only form of income for three-fourths of these residents. It is not uncommon for residents to turn over their entire SSI check to the facility's manager and receive less than minimal care in return.

In an attempt to stem abuses, the federal government passed the Keys Amendment in 1978. Under this law, residents living in board and care facilities that do not provide adequate care are subject to reduced SSI income. The facility's owners would then suffer economically as a result of their tenants' reduced income. In most cases, however, the only ones who have suffered (even more than before) are the residents. While board and care facilities can provide an alternative living arrangement for the elderly, it is one that very few choose.

OWNING AND RENTING A HOME

Owning a Home—The American Dream

According to the American Housing Survey, one in four households contains at least one elderly person. In 2000 most elderly Americans (80.3 percent) owned their own homes, while only 19.7 percent rented. Homeownership peaked between the ages of 70 to 74 (75.7 percent). These rates have risen steadily since the 1990s. (See Table 3.2.) (Note: The U.S. Census Bureau defines a home as "separate living quarters," which may include such dwellings as houses, apartments, and mobile homes, but not quarters in institutions and similar temporary residences.) Homeownership is highest for married-couple families. In 2000, among those aged 65 years and older, 91.9 percent of married couples owned their homes, compared to 65.8 percent of male one-person households, and 69.7 percent of female one-person households.

Elderly householders are less likely than those under age 65 to have mortgage indebtedness. In 2000, 76 percent of elderly homeowners owned their homes free and clear. Even where there is no mortgage remaining on the home, however, the homeowner must still pay taxes, insurance, utility bills, and often high repair costs.

Almost three-quarters, 72.7 percent, of age 65-plus homeowners live in metropolitan areas, with 27.4 percent in central cities and 45.3 percent in the suburbs. The remaining 27.3 percent live in rural areas.

Elderly homeowners tend to live in older housing. In 2000 the median year of purchase for homes owned by the elderly was 1974, compared to 1990 for all homeowners. About half of elderly homeowners paid less than $20,000 for their homes.

Characteristics of Housing and Neighborhoods

The American Housing Survey measures factors such as access to telephones and transportation and perceptions of neighborhood crime in order to get a picture of the quality of housing and neighborhoods. The following findings are for 2000:

- Most housing units in which the head of the household was elderly had telephones (96.8 percent).

- About one-fifth of the households, 20.6 percent, did not have a car, truck, or van available for transportation.

- 51.2 percent of elderly homeowners had access to public transportation, and 8.1 used it at least weekly.

- 5.8 percent of the housing units had moderate to severe physical deficiencies such as plumbing and heating problems.

- 36.7 percent of survey respondents had a very high opinion of the neighborhood they lived in.

- 5.1 percent of survey respondents were bothered by crime in their neighborhoods.

- 90 percent of elderly homeowners felt that they had adequate police protection.

TABLE 3.2

Home ownership rates by age of householder, 1982–99

	1982	1983	1984	1985	1986	1987	1988	1989	1990	1991	1992	1993	1993/r	1994	1995	1996	1997	1998	1999
United States, total	64.8	64.6	64.5	63.9	63.8	64.0	63.8	63.9	63.9	64.1	64.1	64.5	64.0	64.0	64.7	65.4	65.7	66.3	66.8
Less than 25 years	19.3	18.8	17.9	17.2	17.2	16.0	15.8	16.6	15.7	15.3	14.9	15.0	14.8	14.9	15.9	18.0	17.7	18.2	19.9
25 to 29 years	38.6	38.3	38.6	37.7	36.7	36.4	35.9	35.3	35.2	33.8	33.6	34.0	33.6	34.1	34.4	34.7	35.0	36.2	36.5
30 to 34 years	57.1	55.4	54.8	54.0	53.6	53.5	53.2	53.2	51.8	51.2	50.5	51.0	50.8	50.6	53.1	53.0	52.6	53.6	53.8
35 to 39 years	67.6	66.5	66.1	65.4	64.8	64.1	63.6	63.4	63.0	62.2	61.4	62.1	61.8	61.2	62.1	62.1	62.6	63.7	64.4
40 to 44 years	73.0	72.8	72.3	71.4	70.5	70.8	70.7	70.2	69.8	69.5	69.1	69.0	68.6	68.2	68.6	69.0	69.7	70.0	69.9
45 to 49 years	76.0	75.3	74.6	74.3	74.1	74.6	74.4	74.1	73.9	73.7	74.2	73.9	73.7	73.8	73.7	74.4	74.2	73.9	74.5
50 to 54 years	78.8	78.8	78.4	77.5	78.1	77.8	77.1	77.2	76.8	76.1	76.2	77.1	77.2	76.8	77.0	77.2	77.7	77.8	77.8
55 to 59 years	80.0	80.1	80.1	79.2	80.0	80.0	79.3	79.1	78.8	79.5	79.3	78.8	78.9	78.4	78.8	79.4	79.7	79.8	80.7
60 to 64 years	80.1	79.8	79.9	79.9	79.8	80.4	79.8	80.1	79.8	80.5	81.2	80.9	80.9	80.1	80.3	80.7	80.5	82.1	81.3
65 to 69 years	77.9	78.7	79.3	79.5	79.4	79.5	80.0	80.0	80.0	81.4	80.8	80.6	80.7	80.6	81.0	82.4	81.9	81.9	82.9
70 to 74 years	75.2	75.4	75.5	76.8	77.2	77.7	77.7	77.8	78.4	78.8	79.0	79.9	79.9	80.1	80.9	81.4	82.0	82.2	82.8
75 years and over	71.0	71.9	71.5	69.8	70.0	70.8	70.8	71.2	72.3	73.1	73.3	73.3	73.4	73.5	74.6	75.3	75.8	76.2	77.1
Less than 35 years	41.2	40.7	40.5	39.9	39.6	39.5	39.3	39.1	38.5	37.8	37.6	37.9	37.3	37.3	38.6	39.1	38.7	39.3	39.7
35 to 44 years	70.0	69.3	68.9	68.1	67.3	67.2	66.9	66.6	66.3	65.8	65.1	65.4	65.1	64.5	65.2	65.5	66.1	66.9	67.2
45 to 54 years	77.4	77.0	76.5	75.9	76.0	76.1	75.6	75.5	75.2	74.8	75.1	75.4	75.3	75.2	75.2	75.6	75.8	75.7	76.0
55 to 64 years	80.0	79.9	80.0	79.5	79.9	80.2	79.5	79.6	79.3	80.0	80.2	79.8	79.9	79.3	79.5	80.0	80.1	80.9	81.0
65 years and over	74.4	75.0	75.1	74.8	75.0	75.5	75.6	75.8	76.3	77.2	77.1	77.3	77.3	77.4	78.1	78.9	79.1	79.3	80.1

SOURCE: Adapted from "Table 15. Home Ownership Rates for the United States by Age of Householder and by Family Status: 1982 to 1999," in *Housing Vacancies and Homeownership Annual Statistics: 1999*, U.S. Census Bureau, Washington, DC, February, 2001 [Online] http://www.census.gov/hhes/www/housing/hvs/annual99/ann99ind.html [accessed October, 2001]

TABLE 3.3

Least affordable states

State	Housing wage for two bedroom FMR
California	$18.33
District of Columbia	$18.13
New Jersey	$17.87
Massachusetts	$17.65
New York	$17.57
Hawaii	$16.65
Connecticut	$16.45
Alaska	$15.70
Colorado	$15.23
Illinois	$14.92

SOURCE: "Least Affordable States," in *Out of Reach, September 2001,* National Low Income Housing Coalition (NLIHC), Washington, DC [Online] http://www.nlihc.org/oor2001/table1.htm [accessed October 24, 2001]

TABLE 3.4

Least affordable MSAs (Metropolitan Statistical Areas)

MSA	Housing wage for two bedroom FMR
San Francisco, CA	$33.60
San Jose, CA	$30.62
Stamford-Norwalk, CT	$26.62
Oakland, CA	$23.90
Nassau-Suffolk, NY	$23.65
Westchester County, NY	$23.00
Santa Cruz-Watsonville, CA	$22.60
Orange County, CA	$21.10
Boston, MA-NH	$20.21
Bergen-Passaic, NJ	$20.19

SOURCE: "Least Affordable Metropolitan Statistical Areas (MSAs)," in *Out of Reach, September 2001,* National Low Income Housing Coalition (NLIHC), Washington, DC [Online] http://www.nlihc.org/oor2001/table2.htm [accessed October 24, 2001]

- 77.6 of elderly homeowners reported satisfactory neighborhood shopping, and 57.8 percent reported satisfactory shopping within one mile of their home.

- The median value of homes owned by elderly householders was $96,442, compared to $108,300 for all homeowners.

Reverse Mortgages

Like people of all ages, older homeowners need liquid funds to cover expenses. An arrangement known as a reverse mortgage allows older homeowners to "cash in" some of their home equity each month for cash, yet still retain ownership of the home. The money is paid out to a homeowner in monthly installments determined by the amount of home equity borrowed against, the interest rate, and the length of the loan. In most cases, no repayment is due until the homeowner dies, sells the house, or moves permanently.

Sale/Leaseback or Life Tenancy

In a sale/leaseback or life tenancy arrangement, a homeowner sells the home to an investor, who then leases it back to the homeowner. The former homeowner retains the right to live in the house for life as a renter. The investor pays the former owner in monthly installments and also is responsible for property taxes, insurance, maintenance, and repairs.

Renting Is Even More Expensive

The National Low-Income Housing Coalition, in its study *Out of Reach* (2001), collected income and rental housing cost data for the 50 states, the District of Columbia, and Puerto Rico. For each area, the coalition calculated the income that families need in order to be able to afford the fair market rent (FMR) of the housing in that area. The national median housing wage, based on each county's housing wage for a two-bedroom unit at the FMR, was $13.87 an hour in 2001. This was not affordable

for most elderly. Rents were particularly high in some areas, such as California and the District of Columbia (see Table 3.3), and in expensive metropolitan areas such as San Francisco and San Jose, California (see Table 3.4).

Renters generally pay a higher percentage of their incomes for housing than do homeowners. Renters are often faced with several additional drawbacks: mortgage payments on a home generally remain the same over a period of years (often until the entire mortgage is paid off), but rent may increase each year, while the elderly renter remains on a fixed income. Also, homeowners have the equity in their homes to fall back on in times of financial crisis; the renter makes out a monthly check, but none of the money is ever returned as a tangible asset. Finally, mortgage payments are tax deductible, while rent payments are not.

In 2000, 3 in 10 elderly renters received some form of housing assistance, either from the government, such as rent control or public or subsidized housing, or from landlords who voluntarily lower rents to older renters. About 1 in 10 renters over 65 years of age paid no cash rent. For many older renters, meals are part of their rental package.

ADDITIONAL HOUSING PROBLEMS OF THE ELDERLY

Physical Hazards

Features considered desirable by younger householders may be handicaps to the elderly. For example, the staircase in a two-story house may become a formidable obstacle to someone with osteoporosis or a neuromuscular problem. Narrow halls and doorways cannot be navigated in wheelchairs. High cabinets and shelves may be beyond the reach of an arthritis sufferer. While houses can be modified to meet the physical needs of the elderly, not all older houses can be remodeled to accept such modifications, and installing them may be more costly than some elderly can afford. Condominium owners in Florida, whose young-old residents once valued second- and third-floor locations for their breezes and golf-course views, are now being asked to install elevators for residents in their eighties and nineties.

The AARP believes that 85 percent of people over 55 prefer to remain in familiar surroundings rather than move to alternative housing. As a result, those who are able redesign their homes to accommodate the changes that accompany aging—a concept known as "universal design." Its premise is that homes, from their initial blueprints or as modifications, should be equipped for people with disabilities, and should be functional yet aesthetic.

Anticipating the increase in the elderly population in the coming years, some real estate developers are manufacturing experimental houses designed to meet the needs of the elderly and thus prolong independent living. Such houses include nonskid flooring, walls strong enough to support grab bars, light plugs at convenient heights, levers instead of knobs on doors and plumbing fixtures, and wide doors and hallways.

Simple adaptations include replacing doorknobs with levers that can be pushed downward with a fist or elbow, requiring no gripping or twisting; replacing light switches with flat, "touch" switches; placing closet rods at adjustable heights; installing stoves with front or side-mounted controls; and marking steps with bright colors. More complex renovations include replacing a bathroom with a wet room (a tiled space with a showerhead, waterproof chair, and sloping floor for a drain, large enough to accommodate a wheelchair); placing electrical receptacles higher than usual along walls; and widening passageways and doors for wheelchairs or battery-operated carts. Family and friends of disabled and elderly people also benefit from universal design.

Lack of Transportation

When an elderly person's vision and physical reflexes decline, driving a car can be difficult and perilous. Older people whose homes are far from shopping centers or public transportation may have to depend on others for transportation or delivery of the basic necessities, or they may simply have to do without. This is a particularly acute problem for the 27.3 percent of the elderly who live in rural areas. The rural elderly may be isolated not only from food and clothing stores, but also from health and social services.

PUBLIC HOUSING

In 1937 Congress passed the U.S. Housing Act (PL 75-412) to create low-income public housing. Prior to 1956 only 10 percent of available units were occupied by persons aged 65 years or older. Today, the elderly occupy more than 40 percent of available low-income public housing units.

The federal government makes direct loans to private, nonprofit developers to build housing designed specifically for the elderly and the handicapped. At least one-half of the nation's low-income housing units are more than 25 years old. Many were built during the 1930s and 1940s and are in need of major renovation.

Despite federal programs to provide decent, affordable housing, it is still beyond the reach of many millions of elderly. According to the Alliance of Retired Americans (formerly the National Council of Senior Citizens), the average time on a waiting list for elderly housing is 3 to 4 years, and only 1 in 7 elderly poor receives federal housing assistance. For each vacancy in subsidized complexes, there are an estimated 8 elderly people on a waiting list.

CHAPTER 4

WORKING AND RETIREMENT:
NEW OPTIONS FOR THE ELDERLY

Millions of older people are ready, willing, and able to increase their productivity, paid and voluntary. Even now, in taking care of spouses, siblings, and grandchildren, the elderly do the work of three million care givers. For many people, retirement is not the end of a productive life but the beginning of a new one.

— The MacArthur Foundation, 1998

Just because a person reaches the age of 65 does not mean that person's contributions to society are over. The list of older Americans who continue to be high achievers past age 65 is long. A few examples:

- Former Senator John Glenn, the first American to orbit Earth, in 1962, returned to space at age 77 as a payload specialist.

- The current Federal Reserve chairman, Alan Greenspan, is in his seventies and oversees the American economy.

- Benjamin Franklin—writer, scientist, inventor, and statesman—helped draft the Declaration of Independence at the age of 70.

- Thomas Alva Edison worked on such inventions as the light bulb, the microphone, and the phonograph until his death at the age of 84.

- Rear Admiral (Ret.) Grace Hopper, one of the early computer scientists and cocreator of the computer language COBOL, maintained an active speaking and consulting schedule up until her death in her eighties.

- Margaret Mead, the noted anthropologist, returned to New Guinea when she was 72 and exhausted a much younger television filming crew as they tried to keep up with her.

- Albert Einstein, who formulated the theory of relativity, was working on a unifying theory of the universe when he died at age 76.

- Georgia O'Keeffe created masterful paintings when she was past 80 years of age.

More and more, older Americans are not just limited to the traditional idea of "retirement." While many still choose to retire, they may fill their free time with a combination of work, volunteerism, and leisure activities. Many elderly choose not to retire at all, or at least not at age 65. Increasingly, older Americans are following in the footsteps of the great Americans listed above and remaining active well into their golden years.

INCREASING OPTIONS—THE CYCLIC LIFE

Dr. Ken Dychtwald, in *Age Wave: The Challenges and Opportunities of an Aging America* (Bantam, New York City, 1990), likened increasing numbers of elderly to an awakening giant. This wave of age, especially with baby boomers in the wings, affects not only American institutions, but individuals as well. Added longevity often causes people to rethink the pace and plan of their lives, as well as the purposes, goals, and challenges of its various stages.

Throughout human history, the average length of life was short. In a world where most people did not expect to live longer than 40 or 50 years, it was essential that certain key personal and social tasks be accomplished by specific ages. Traditionally, important activities, such as getting an education, job training, parenthood, and retirement, not only were designated to particular periods of life but also were expected to occur only once in a lifetime. The path from childhood to old age was linear—it moved in one direction.

This pattern of life was maintained not only by tradition, but by law. Government regulations and institutional rules and traditions prescribed the ages at which a person should go to school, begin and end work, and receive a pension. This approach to life was based on the assumptions that (1) the activities of life were to be performed on time and in sequence, and (2) most of life's periods of growth occurred in the first half of life, while the second half was, in general, characterized by decline and disinvestment.

Many people believe that as humans live longer, this traditional linear path is evolving into a more flexible pattern, a "cyclic life plan." Having the luxury to arrange one's various life tasks is becoming commonplace. For example:

• Some people are opting to pursue careers throughout their twenties, thirties, and even forties, followed by marriage and child-rearing activities, a reversal of traditional roles (thanks in part to advances in medicine that make it possible to bear children later in life).

• Formal learning was once the province of the young; today, middle-aged and older people are increasingly returning to school.

• People once pursued a single career in their lifetimes; today, workers change jobs and even careers many times. The RAND Corporation, a California-based think tank, predicted that by the year 2020, the average worker would need to be retrained up to 13 times in his or her lifetime. Except for a few specified professions (such as airline piloting), mandatory retirement has become illegal. Many older workers want to continue working (or return to work), and some must do so for financial reasons.

While the linear plan generally included education, work, and recreation/retirement, in that order, a cyclic plan could be a blending, reordering, and repeating of activities, as desired. Although not everyone will choose to do things differently than in the past, people increasingly have the option to do so.

Lydia Bronte, in *The Longevity Factor* (Harper-Collins, New York City, 1993), followed a group of 150 people who chose to work into their seventies, eighties, nineties, and in a few cases, beyond the age of 100. Many had major achievements after age 60. Three-quarters reported that growing old was a positive experience. Bronte suggested that, while scientists in 1900 believed people could not be productive and creative after the age of 40, Americans can expect, a century later, a productive and creative "second middle age" between 50 and 75, and even beyond, that has not existed before.

A CHANGING ECONOMY AND CHANGING ROLES

From Agricultural ...

In early America, there was little correlation between age and work. In that agricultural society, youngsters were put to work as soon as possible to contribute to the family upkeep. At the other end of the age scale, workers who lived beyond age 65 did not retire; they worked as long as they were physically able. Then they were cared for by the younger members of the family. Older people were valued and respected for their accumulated knowledge and experience, and were an integral part of the interconnected family and labor systems.

... to Industrial ...

The Industrial Revolution took people away from the farm and into manufacturing jobs. The work was physically demanding, the hours long, and the tasks strictly structured. Women labored in factories and at home caring for the family. Older people found themselves without a place in the workforce. Their skills and experience were not relevant to new technologies, nor could they physically compete with the large number of young workers eager to take advantage of new economic opportunities.

As industrial workers matured, some of them were promoted to positions as supervisors and managers. Labor unions provided some job security through the seniority system ("first hired, last fired") for older workers who had been with the same company for many years. In an increasingly youth-oriented society, however, older workers were often pushed aside to make way for younger workers. The problem became so severe that Congress passed the Age Discrimination in Employment Act (ADEA; PL 90-202) in 1967 and the Age Discrimination Act Amendment (PL 95-256) in 1978, prohibiting differential treatment of workers based solely on age. In 1987 Congress again amended the act to abolish age-based mandatory retirement for most workers in the private sector as well as those in government employment.

... to Service

The American economy continues its dramatic shift away from manufacturing and toward the service sector. Doctors, data entry workers, travel agents, auto mechanics, and teachers far outnumber coal miners, carpenters, and pipefitters. The number of agricultural employees continues to decline, as does the percentage of manufacturing jobs, while the service industry has doubled its number of employees since 1970. Many service jobs are ideally suited for older workers. These jobs usually do not require heavy labor, and the cumulative experience of years of work is an advantage in almost all service fields.

PARTICIPATION IN THE LABOR FORCE

In 1999 only one in six men aged 65 and over (16.9 percent) worked, compared to two in three men aged 55 to 64 (67.9 percent). (See Table 4.1.) Labor force participation rates for men have shifted over time. In 1950 almost half, or 45.8 percent, of men 65 and over worked, and 86.9 percent of men aged 55 to 64 were in the labor force.

Work patterns of women differ from those of men. In 1999 less than one in ten women aged 65 and over (8.9 percent) were in the labor force, compared to over half (51.5

TABLE 4.1

Labor force participation rates by age and sex, 1950–2008

Year	Men			Women		
	25 to 54 years	55 to 64 years	65 years and older	25 to 54 years	55 to 64 years	65 years and older
1950	96.5	86.9	45.8	36.8	27.0	9.7
1955	97.4	87.9	39.6	39.8	32.5	10.6
1960	97.0	86.8	33.1	42.9	37.2	10.8
1965	96.7	84.6	27.9	45.2	41.1	10.0
1970	95.8	83.0	26.8	50.1	43.0	9.7
1975	94.4	75.6	21.6	55.1	40.9	8.2
1980	94.2	72.1	19.0	64.0	41.3	8.1
1985	93.9	67.9	15.8	69.6	42.0	7.3
1990	93.4	67.8	16.3	74.0	45.2	8.6
1995	91.6	66.0	16.8	75.6	49.2	8.8
1998	91.8	68.1	16.5	76.6	51.2	8.6
1999	91.7	67.9	16.9	76.8	51.5	8.9
2008[1]	91.3	69.4	17.8	79.7	57.7	9.1

[1] Data for 2008 are from the Office of Employment Projections, Bureau of Labor Statistics.

SOURCE: Patrick J. Purcell, "Table 2. Labor Force Participation Rates by Age and Sex, 1950-2008," in "Older Workers: Employment and Retirement Trends," *Monthly Labor Review Online,* vol. 123, no. 10, October, 2000 [Online] http://www.bls.gov/opub/mlr/2000/10/contents.htm [accessed October, 2001]

percent) of women aged 55 to 64. For women 65 and over, workforce participation rates have held relatively steady over the last decades. The rates for women workers aged 55 to 64, however, have increased dramatically. In 1950 one in four women in this age group (27 percent) worked, compared to over half (51.5 percent) in 1999. (See Table 4.1.)

Going in Separate Directions

Women are beginning to realize that by working just a few more years, they can become eligible for good pensions.

— Olivia Mitchell, University of Pennsylvania economist, 1997

Most of today's older women spent some time in the labor force when they were younger. The older the woman, however, the less likely she is to have ever worked outside the home. American women in their late fifties and early sixties, who did leave their houses to work in large numbers, are approaching retirement. If they are single, widowed, or divorced, they often continue to work to support themselves because they do not have enough Social Security credits to retire.

Married older women are also increasingly working after their husbands retire, breaking with the practice of sharing their husbands' retirement. Older husbands and wives are increasingly going in opposite directions. Among the reasons cited are:

• The wives have their own careers.

• They need to secure their retirement and avoid the poverty that has historically come with widowhood.

• Their income helps maintain the family standard of living, particularly if the husband has been pushed out of his job by forced retirement.

• They enjoy the sociability. Building friendships has been found to be more important to women than to men, and women often find retirement more isolating.

According to the National Economic Council Interagency Working Group on Social Security, today 37 percent of older women are entitled to higher pensions than their spousal benefits. The Council predicted that if current trends continued, by 2060 nearly 60 percent of older women would be entitled to higher pensions upon retirement than the spousal benefits they would have received under their husbands' Social Security. Furthermore, 20 percent of the women would qualify for pensions higher than their husbands', up from less than 10 percent today.

CHANGING JOB CHOICES. Women have always been more concentrated than men in fewer occupational fields, primarily service and administrative support, that typically pay lower than average wages and are less likely to provide benefits such as pensions. In recent years, there has been some shift in the occupational distribution of women workers, including those 45 and older. From 1983 to 1995 women of all ages worked less in the administrative support and service sectors and more in executive, managerial, and professional jobs, although the group made up of women aged 65 years and over generally experienced less change than other age groups.

Part-Time Work

The AARP (formerly the American Association of Retired Persons) pointed out in a 2000 article, "Update on Older Workers," that seven out of ten workers aged 55 years and over continued to work full time, and those who worked part time did so by choice. In 2000 just under 2 percent of all nonagricultural older workers were employed part time because they could not find full-time work.

For employers, hiring part-time older workers is often an attractive alternative to hiring younger, full-time workers, partly because of older workers' dependability and experience. In addition, companies often pay part-time workers lower wages and do not provide them with benefits, such as health insurance, pensions, and profit sharing.

Job Tenure

Older people tend to be stable employees who stay in the same job longer than younger employees. Job tenure is measured as the median number of years workers have been with their current employer. According to the U.S. Bureau of Labor Statistics, in January 2000 this figure for workers aged 55 to 64 years was 10 years, and for workers aged 65 years and over it was 9.5 years. In comparison, workers aged 25 to 34 had a job tenure of 2.6 years, those 35 to 44 years of age weighed in at 4.8 years, and those aged 45 to 54 years had a job tenure of 8.2 years. In addition, 53.2 percent of workers aged 54 to 65 and half of workers aged 65 years and over had 10 years or more of job tenure.

MYTHS AND MISPERCEPTIONS ABOUT OLDER WORKERS

All things considered, the older person is in many respects the perfect employee.
— Jeanette Takamira, U.S. Department of Health and Human Services, 1999

Older workers are often stereotyped by the misperception that performance declines with age. Performance studies, however, show that older workers perform intellectually as well as or better than workers 30 or 40 years younger, maintaining their IQ levels, vocabulary, and creative thinking skills.

Dr. Robert Atchley, formerly of Miami University of Ohio's Scripps Gerontology Center, observed in *The Challenge of an Aging Work Force in an Aging Population* (1993) that data documenting the productivity of the older worker have existed for a long time. Numerous studies have found no decline in productivity. Indeed, older employees perform as well as or better than younger ones, except in jobs requiring substantial physical exertion. Dr. Atchley's study concluded that productivity does not peak until the fifties and sixties.

Studies have been conducted to determine whether age can be correlated to job performance in public safety jobs, such as police and fire officers, pilots, and air traffic controllers, or to determine if mandatory retirement at a specific age is necessary to ensure public safety. They have invariably concluded that chronological age is a poor predictor of job performance and limitation, even in situations where public safety is concerned, and the studies have, in general, recommended abolition of mandatory retirement.

A concern about high health insurance costs and the generally higher salaries of older workers, coupled with the notion that an older person will have low productivity, may lead an employer to believe that it is not cost-effective to hire or retain older employees. In most cases, however, this is not true. Very small companies may see higher insurance and benefit costs for older workers, but specialized skills and job experience may more than offset these costs. Other advantages to hiring older workers are their decreased time off for child-care responsibilities and less need for supervision. Also, older workers tend to have lower turnover rates. Employee turnover is very costly for companies because they can put considerable time and money into training each new employee, and there is a learning period before a new employee becomes fully productive.

The Myth of Declining Health, Increased Absenteeism, and Injury

Aging is sometimes associated with higher rates of illnesses and absences from work. In fact, absentee rates are about the same for older full-time wage and salary workers as for younger workers. According to the Bureau of Labor Statistics, during an average work week in 1998, the absence rate for workers aged 55 years and over was 4.2 percent, for those aged 16 to 19 it was 4 percent, and for those aged 20 to 24 it was 3.9 percent. The lowest absence rate was 3.7 percent, among workers 25 to 54 years of age.

Disability rates among the elderly declined during the 1980s and 1990s. As the number of elderly has grown, the number of elderly requiring personal assistance has dropped.

Higher Benefit Costs

While the costs of some benefits, primarily insurance, increase as a person ages, most increased costs of benefits generally associated with age are linked more to seniority and salary. Male workers aged 50 and older usually have more expensive health insurance claims than male workers under 50. On the other hand, female employees over 50 are less expensive to insure than female workers under 50, primarily due to the high costs associated with maternity and child rearing. The rate of insurance claims for workers over age 50 are generally higher than for younger workers. On the other hand, older workers generally do not have as many dependents and are often already covered by other health or pension plans, including Medicare.

The Myth That Older Workers Are Expensive to Train

Dr. Atchley's 1993 study *The Challenge of an Aging Work Force in an Aging Population* found that employers sometimes believed that the elderly are more expensive to train because (1) they are not as bright as young people and (2) they have fewer years to return the employer's investment in training costs.

Atchley found, however, that only 10 percent of Americans over age 65 showed any significant loss of memory, and fewer than half of the 10 percent were seriously impaired. Most losses in mental capacity occur in the oldest-old, not to those in their sixties and seventies, and are not due to age itself but to depression, drug effects, treatable illnesses, or lack of exercise.

Research suggests that older employees value, and therefore focus on, not bits of information but overall relationships. Older employees bring to their jobs a lifetime of learning that is valuable to themselves, their coworkers, and their employers. They have an "organizational" memory—they understand why organizations have evolved in the ways they have. Psychological skills, such as the ability to adapt and find life satisfaction, do not vary by age. Although older workers are somewhat more resistant to change, they can and do adapt; in fact, their greater life experiences have nurtured greater long-term resiliency.

AGE DISCRIMINATION—ILLEGAL YET PERVASIVE

While inaccurate, stereotypes about older workers impel younger workers and the elderly themselves to become fearful of growing old. They can even foster ageism.

— Noreen Hale, *The Older Worker,* 1990

Webster's Ninth New Collegiate Dictionary defines stereotype as a "standardized mental picture that is held in common by members of a group and that represents an oversimplified opinion, affective attitude, or judgment." The nation's preoccupation with youth and stereotypes of age undermine the contribution of experience and knowledge from older workers. America is a youth-oriented culture, and many people shun physical reminders of aging, such as wrinkles and baldness. They also may buy into some of the myths discussed in the previous section, such as lower productivity, higher absenteeism, and higher costs of training for older employees.

The 1967 ADEA and its 1978 amendment were enacted to promote the employment of older workers based on their ability, and to ban discrimination against workers between 40 and 65 years of age. The law made it illegal for employers to discriminate based on age in hiring, discharging, and compensating employees. It also prohibited companies from coercing older workers into accepting incentives to early retirement. In 1987 the act was amended to lift the 65-year-old age limit, making it illegal to discriminate against any worker over 40 years of age, and eliminating mandatory retirement at any age.

The 1990 Older Workers Benefit Protection Act (PL 101-433) strengthens the ADEA. It provides that an employee's waiver of the right to sue for age discrimination, a clause sometimes included in severance packages, is invalid unless "voluntary and knowing."

In 1990 the U.S. Supreme Court (*Public Employees Retirement System of Ohio v. Betts* [492 U.S. 158]) spelled out the terms under which employee benefits may be provided to older workers. In the case before the Court, an employee had been denied disability retirement benefits and was forced instead to accept a less generous early retirement benefit because of her age. The Court ruled that employers may not withhold benefits from older workers, although they may adjust them to offset the higher cost of providing them to older workers.

Although age discrimination in the workplace is against the law, it still exists. More than 15,000 claims of age discrimination are filed with the Equal Employment Opportunity Commission each year. Although most cases involve older workers who believe they were terminated unfairly, a number of the cases involve people who feel they have met age discrimination in hiring practices.

Some workers begin to experience negative attitudes about their age when they are in their fifties, and by the time they reach 60, age discrimination may be obvious. There are many ways an employer (and fellow employees) can exert pressure on an older employee to retire or resign. Age discrimination may be overt, but it can also be covert, subtle, or even unintentional.

Pressure to Retire

Corporations base employment decisions not only on how much an employee contributes to the company, but also on the salary and benefits the company must provide the employee relative to the cost of other employees. Since salary tends to increase with longevity on the job, older workers usually receive higher wages than younger ones. Thus, if two employees are equally productive, but the older one has a higher salary, a company has an economic incentive to encourage the older worker to take early retirement or to lay him or her off.

Employees in this situation find themselves in a difficult position. Early retirement benefits are almost always less than regular retirement benefits, and they may not provide enough financial support to allow a retiree to live comfortably without working. Finding a new job is more difficult for an older person than for a younger one, and older persons are usually unemployed for longer periods than are younger ones. If they refuse to accept early retirement, they may find themselves without jobs at all, perhaps with no pension and no severance pay.

Suing the Company

It is costly to file an age discrimination suit. In addition, employers are reluctant to hire someone who has filed a discrimination suit against a former employer. Workers caught in this position can suffer emotional and financial damage that may adversely affect them for the rest of their lives. Nonetheless, more older workers are choosing to sue their employers. The main classes of issues affecting older workers involve:

- Whether "overqualification" can be grounds (or pretext) for refusing to hire an older person

- Whether a senior worker's higher salary can be used as a basis for discharge

- What preconditions employers can demand from older workers prior to hiring (for example, hiring an older worker with special exemptions from benefits)

A number of sources report that an aging population, coupled with low unemployment, strong demand for experienced workers, and managers who are themselves older are making age less of an issue in the marketplace. Also, older workers have another factor in their favor: the technology gap between younger and older workers is narrowing as personal computers become easier to use.

A CHANGING FUTURE FOR OLDER WORKERS?

As America's population grows older, so will its workforce. During the early years of the twenty-first century, as the baby boomers mature, the median age will increase dramatically. At the same time, the number of workers between the ages of 16 and 24 will decline.

Graying of the Workforce

Within at least the next six or seven years, we'll turn over the entire workforce here.

— Herb Stone, plant manager, General Motors, 1999

Many American companies face a major turnover of their employees. As baby boomers near retirement, companies will be forced to replace them with younger, less experienced workers. In the process, industry will lose important talent. Many experts contend that it is time for corporations to rethink their structure. While employers are glad to see older workers replaced with less expensive younger workers, this may be a bad time economically for them to have to do so.

Some companies are beginning to take notice of the shift. In 1999 the Committee of Economic Development, a New York-based public policy association, issued a call to business and lawmakers to launch a "pro-work agenda" for older workers. It called on employers to make it more attractive for older workers to stay on the job.

RETIREMENT

Retirement requires the invention of a new hedonism, not a return to the hedonism of youth.

— Mason Cooley, *City Aphorisms, Fourteenth Selection*, New York, 1994

Increasing longevity means that people spend more time in all phases of their lives—education, work, and retirement. In 1900 the average male spent only 1.2 years in retirement; by 1980 he was retired an average of 13.6 years. The age of 65 has traditionally been considered "normal retirement age" since the Social Security legislation of 1935 that set that age for receipt of Social Security benefits. Many persons, however, choose to leave the labor force before age 65 for a variety of reasons—health, the retirement of a spouse, the availability of early retirement from Social Security or pension benefits, or the opportunity for leisure activities. Downturns in the economy, mergers, layoffs, downsizing, and bankruptcies can also result in unplanned early retirement. Some companies have reduced staff by offering attractive retirement packages to older workers.

According to the Social Security Administration, the result has been a decline in the retirement age, from around 68 in 1950 to 64 in 1999, although the decline has leveled off since then. Conversely, some elderly, because of improved health, a slight raising of the Social Security retirement age (from 65 to 67), and/or economic need caused by possible cuts in Social Security pension and health insurance benefits may feel they need and want to work longer. In addition, with fewer younger workers available and unemployment rates low, many businesses need older workers.

Some labor economists feel that early retirements deprive the nation of skilled workers needed for robust growth. The government also loses the revenue that those workers would have contributed in income and payroll taxes. For those elderly who must work for economic reasons, forced retirement and unemployment are serious problems. Older workers often experience difficulty in being rehired, and the duration of their unemployment is longer.

Working in Retirement

Work is an essential part of being alive. Your work is your identity. It tells you who you are.

— Kay Stepkin, baker, quoted in *Working,* book 8, by Studs Terkel, 1974

A worker's first retirement may not be his last. Early retirement is often triggered by the onset of pension benefits. These retirees may be back at work at another job within a year, either full or part time, although those jobs often last no more than two or three years. Since people are living longer and experiencing less disability, some retirees find that they miss the work environment, and some use retirement as an opportunity to embark on a second career. Some retirees choose to work but also want more flexibility to pursue outside interests, and hence, take a job that requires fewer hours. Rather than retire altogether, they choose to "phase down" their work lives.

In 1999 the University of Michigan's *Study on Health, Retirement, and Aging* found that of 12,600 workers aged 51 to 61, 73 percent reported they would prefer to continue doing some work, while only 27 percent wanted to stop work entirely. When asked if they thought their employer would allow an older worker to move to a less demanding job, however, 66 percent said "probably not."

LOOKING FOR WORK. Most older Americans who want work may generally be able to find it. The AARP's *Update on the Older Worker: 2000* (Sara E. Rix, June 2001) asserted that "few older Americans who are not currently working say they wish they were. Barely more than 2 percent of the 38.1 million persons 55 and older who were not in the labor force in 2000 reported that they wanted a job, and only slightly more than one-fifth of these had looked for work in the previous year."

According to the Bureau of Labor Statistics, though, when older Americans look for work, it usually takes them longer to find a job than younger people. In 2000 the average duration of unemployment of workers aged 55 and older was 19 weeks, compared to 12 weeks for workers under the age of 55.

Leisure Activities in Retirement

Many recreation and leisure companies already recognize that their industry will need to customize products and services to take advantage of a potentially significant exercise market.

— Kathie Davis, executive director, IDEA (fitness organization), 1998

A longer lifespan gives people the opportunity to spend more time in all the major activities of life, including retirement. For those who do choose to retire, the retirement years can be a period to relax and do many things they have never done (though loss of employment income may limit the pastime activities possible for some older Americans). What do people who are retired do with their time? And how do they express their values when they have more leisure time?

In addition to travel, study, and time with family and friends, television claims a large share of the elderly person's day. According to *Americans 55 and Older: A Changing Market* (Sharon Yntema, ed., 2nd ed., New Strategist Publications, Ithaca, NY, 1999), 64 percent of people aged 65 to 74 watched two to four hours of television a day (based on 1996 data), while 25 percent watched five or more hours. This is the highest percentage for any age group, including children. For people aged 75 and older, 57 percent watched two to four hours a day, while 33 percent watched five or more hours.

Americans 55 and Older also reported that, with the exception of classical music concerts, the elderly are less likely than younger age groups to attend every type of art event, including arts and crafts fairs and opera. On the other hand, older people do attend baseball, football, and related games. The National Survey of Recreation and the

Environment (NSRE) found that in 1994–95 (the most recent statistics available), 28.1 percent of aged 60-plus individuals attended sporting events. NSRE also found that 44.4 percent of people aged 60 and older went sightseeing, 28.8 percent liked bird watching, and 40.7 percent liked to visit beaches and the waterside.

Older people attend religious services in high numbers. In 1996, 45 percent of people aged 65 to 74 and 41 percent of those aged 75 and older attended religious services weekly. Another 14 and 11 percent, respectively, attended one to three times a month.

OUTDOOR RECREATION. Today's elderly are active outdoor enthusiasts. In 1994 and 1995 the NSRE conducted by the U.S. Forest Service interviewed approximately 17,000 Americans over age 15 in random-digit-dialing telephone samplings. The NSRE is the most recent study of outdoor recreation among the American population. Respondents were asked about their participation in 62 specific recreation activities. An analysis of the survey by the Outdoor Products Council of the Sporting Goods Manufacturers Association showed the participation levels of older adults in outdoor activities, such as hiking, biking, fishing, sailing, and swimming. The survey found that 49.7 percent of people over age 60 participated in fitness activities—8.1 percent ran or jogged, 10.6 percent biked, 49.7 percent walked for exercise, and 10.3 percent played golf. These figures were even higher for respondents aged 50 to 59 when the survey was conducted. Sixty-four percent of this group participated in fitness activities: 17.5 percent ran or jogged, 21.9 percent biked, 14.7 percent walked, and 12.1 percent played golf.

Disability does not stop older people from enjoying the outdoors. Another analysis of the 1994 and 1995 NSRE prepared for the National Center on Accessibility found that, in most outdoor recreation activities, people with disabilities in the oldest age groups participated at rates equal to, or greater than, people without disabilities.

Volunteerism in Retirement

One particularly promising and growing group [of volunteers for religious and service organizations] comprises the older, retired members of society. Because Americans are retiring at younger ages, and are in better health and better educated than earlier cohorts of retirees, they are very likely to have the time, skills, and energy to contribute to society through volunteer work.

— A. Regula Herzog and James N. Morgan, *Achieving a Productive Aging Society,* 1993

Every day, millions of older Americans participate in their communities through volunteer work. They make ideal volunteers. They often have free time in a world where time is at a premium; they have wisdom and experience that years of living can bring; and they have

TABLE 4.2

Senior volunteer activity, by age group

	All over 55	Age 55 to 64	Age 65 to 74	Age 75 and over
Senior volunteers (% of senior population)	47.5%	50.3%	46.6%	43.0%
Total number of senior volunteers	27.7 million	11.9 million	8.5 million	7.1 million
Average weekly hours per volunteer	3.3 hours	3.3 hours	3.6 hours	3.1 hours
Total annual hours volunteered	4.8 billion hours	2.0 billion hours	1.6 billion hours	1.1 billion hours
Total dollar value of volunteer time	$71.2 billion	$29.7 billion	$23.7 billion	$16.3 billion

SOURCE: "American Seniors, 1998," in *The New Nonprofit Almanac in Brief*, Independent Sector, Washington, DC, 2001

FIGURE 4.1

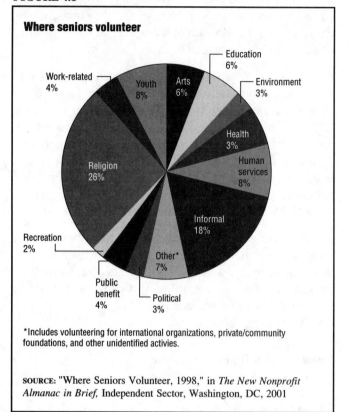

Where seniors volunteer

*Includes volunteering for international organizations, private/community foundations, and other unidentified activies.

SOURCE: "Where Seniors Volunteer, 1998," in *The New Nonprofit Almanac in Brief,* Independent Sector, Washington, DC, 2001

compassion from having encountered many of the same problems with which they are helping others cope.

Volunteerism among older people is a relatively new phenomenon. Historically, the elderly were seen as the segment of society most in need of care and support. As medical technology enables people to live longer, healthier lives and stereotypes about aging crumble, however, the elderly are now recognized as a valuable asset for every type of volunteer activity. Increased education and affluence among the elderly suggest they may be more able and available for volunteer work.

The Independent Sector, a national coalition of philanthropic organizations, reported that in 1998 there were 27.7 million volunteers over age 55. (See Table 4.2.) Slightly over half of all people aged 55 to 64 volunteered, as well as 46.6 percent of people aged 65 to 74, and 43 percent of those 75 and older. All three age groups volunteered three or more hours per week for a total of 4.8 billion hours per year. This is the equivalent of $71.2 billion in contributed labor.

VOLUNTEER PROGRAMS. Volunteer activities take many forms. Many older volunteers work through their churches and community centers or help friends and neighbors informally on a regular basis. Others work with established government and private programs. In 1998 the largest portion of seniors worked for religious causes (26 percent), followed by informal volunteering (such as babysitting for no pay; 18 percent), human services and youth (8 percent each), and arts and education (6 percent each). (See Figure 4.1.)

In 2000, 476 Americans aged 50 and older were serving as Peace Corps volunteers in 77 countries throughout the world, making up 7 percent of the total number of Peace Corps volunteers. The oldest was 79 years of age. Senior volunteers' assignments are similar to those of younger volunteers. Other government programs for senior volunteers include the Senior Corps, Foster Grandparents Program, Retired Senior Volunteer Program, Senior Companion Program, Seniors for Schools, Service Corps of Retired Executives, Environmental Alliance for Senior Involvement, SAVE—Senior Attorney Volunteers for the Elderly, Volunteers of America, Time Dollar Institute, OASIS, and the Experience Corps.

Some metropolitan communities around the country have implemented programs in which senior citizens earn credit for volunteer work. These service credits are earned by performing services for others, ranging from child care to hospital visits. Credits are redeemed when the volunteer needs assistance, which is provided by another volunteer (who in turn receives service credits). Volunteers are thus rewarded for their service, yet there is no expense for either government or private agencies.

NEW TRENDS TOWARD ACTIVISM. "The New Face of Retirement," a national survey of Americans aged 50 to 75 conducted in late 1999 by Peter D. Hart Research Associates, showed that most older Americans have positive attitudes about retirement. The survey, which interviewed 803 Americans aged 50 to 75, including 452 retirees and 351 nonretirees, found that only 28 percent of its respondents viewed retirement in traditional terms, as a time to take it easy and focus on recreation. Instead, 65 percent wanted to stay active, to take on new challenges, and to begin a new chapter in life. According to Civic Ventures, which sponsored the survey, "This new activism crosses virtually all demographic lines; it is expressed by men and women, liberals and conservatives, seniors in every region, people in their fifties and their seventies, those who are healthy and those limited by medical conditions."

Among the findings of "The New Face of Retirement" was that retirees and near-retirees plan to volunteer and perform community service in record numbers. In fact, fully half of older Americans said that volunteering or engaging in community service is very or fairly important to their retirement plans, ranking only behind travel in importance.

An interesting finding from the survey was that 43 percent of respondents, the highest percentage, considered former President Jimmy Carter the best role model for retirement. Carter, an older American himself, has remained active with nonprofit organizations and political service since he left the White House. Other role models of those aged 50 to 75 were Secretary of State Colin Powell (18 percent), and former senator and astronaut John Glenn (11 percent).

WORK VERSUS RETIREMENT

Why Aging Boomers Will Continue to Work

The role of the older worker in America's future is difficult to predict. As fewer young people enter the labor force, industry may have no choice but to retain or hire older workers. In addition, as the age for receiving Social Security benefits is raised and private pensions become more rare, more elderly may need to work longer.

Many sources believe baby boomers are likely to stay in the labor force longer than their parents did. More-educated workers tend to have longer work lives, and boomers are generally well educated. A study of workers in Wisconsin, "Older Workers in the 21st Century: Active and Educated, a Case Study" (*Monthly Labor Review*, June 1996), found a clear association between educational attainment and labor force participation.

Although labor force participation among older adults, especially men, has declined for many years, evidence suggests that the trend has slowed and may be reversing, and some experts have projected a modest rise by 2005 and an even greater rise over the following decades. Among explanations offered for the decline in labor force participation among older adults, especially men, in past decades is that restructuring of the economy has cut the number of blue-collar workers, whose productivity is most likely to decline with advancing age. Job growth is concentrated in white-collar and service occupations, in which age matters less.

Among the factors that will likely cause growth in the proportion of older workers are:

- The proportion of women of all ages in the labor force has been increasing, including among older women.

- Divorce rates among baby boomers are high, so many will not have a spouse's pension income to rely on. In addition, many married couples are finding they need or want the salaries from two jobs.

- Better-educated workers tend to command higher salaries, making a monthly Social Security check a poor substitute for a paycheck. A typical college-educated worker sacrifices more income by retiring than does a worker who failed to finish high school. Higher education thus creates a financial incentive to remain in the labor force.

- Intangible benefits, such as greater job satisfaction, and tangible factors, such as cleaner and safer work conditions, serve to bolster labor force participation among better-educated workers.

A New Model—Will Retirement Be "Out"?

The idea of retiring at 65 is obsolete; it is based on an outdated life expectancy.

— Betty Friedan, Cornell University, 1997

In the past century, people in almost every developed nation came to believe that retirement is a right. Economists worldwide now contend that earlier and earlier retirement is undermining the economic survival of these countries. Peter G. Petersen, chairman of the Institute for International Economics, said, "Unless people can be persuaded to work longer into old age, developed countries will have to accept a loss of productivity, creativity, and even general economic health. Or they will be forced to accept waves of immigration from poorer nations." He contended that in the United States, major hurdles are ageism and the youth culture that pervades many American companies.

With longer life spans, less disability, and more need and desire among many of today's elderly to work, some sources are predicting that the notion of retirement is fast becoming obsolete. In fact, many studies have found that people stay healthier when they work. Workers who continue to work into their eighties may have the opportunity to have two or three careers. Extending the work years would also mesh with proposals to finance Social Security not just by delaying payment, but also by extending productive years and workers' payments into the system.

CHAPTER 5
EDUCATION, VOTING, AND POLITICAL BEHAVIOR

EDUCATION LEVELS OF OLDER AMERICANS

Today the educational levels of the oldest-old reflect the limited opportunities of children born and reared during the early 1900s. After World War I (1914–17), the number of young people who graduated from high school began to increase, a change that is evident in the educational level of today's younger elderly. Tomorrow's elderly will mirror the rapid growth in education that occurred after World War II (1939–45).

According to the U.S. Census Bureau, in March 2000, for 11.7 million Americans aged 65 and older, the highest level of education attained was a high school diploma. (See Table 5.1.) This figure represents 35.8 percent of people aged 65 years and older. Over 3.1 million 65-plus Americans (9.6 percent) were college graduates (with no other higher education degree) and 1.2 million (3.7 percent) had master's degrees. On the other end of the spectrum, the educational level of about 30 percent of those aged 65 and over was less than completion of high school.

Today's 50 to 54 age group will be entering the ranks of the elderly population in the mid-2010s. Eighteen percent of this group (over 3 million individuals) are college graduates and 1.4 million (8.5 percent) have master's degrees. Only 11.7 percent (about 2 million persons) have an educational level less than a high school diploma. (See Table 5.1.)

In most age categories, women and men are equally likely to be high school graduates. According to the Census Bureau's 1999 Current Population Survey, in the 55 to 64 age group, about 81 percent of both women and men had graduated from high school, compared with about 70 percent in the 65 to 84 age category and just over half of those 85 and over. Older men, however, are more likely than older women to have a bachelor's degree or more education. For example, 27 percent of men, but only 19 percent of women, aged 55 to 64 had a bachelor's degree or higher.

Educational attainment is generally correlated with economic and health status in old age. The better educated an elderly person is, the more likely he or she is to be healthier longer and better off financially.

Continuing to Learn

Live as if you were to die tomorrow. Learn as if you were to live forever.
— Gandhi

Campuses are graying. A growing number of older people are going back to school. Retired people are major participants in what was once termed "adult education," that is, courses that do not lead to a formal degree. A number of the 65-plus population have the time and funds to seek learning for personal and social reasons. Some universities allow older people to audit classes without charge. Increasingly, the elderly attend two- and four-year colleges for undergraduate and graduate degrees, as well as to audit courses for no credit. They also attend courses sponsored by community, senior citizen, and recreation facilities. In addition, some seniors are now moving to retirement communities linked to universities.

The reasons for returning to school have changed over time. While the elderly once might have taken courses primarily for pleasure, today's older students may be in school for more practical reasons as well. Many older people are retraining for new careers or to remain competitive in existing occupations. Some older couples have found that they both need to work to afford the activities they enjoy, or they enjoy working and are not ready to retire. Homemakers "displaced" by divorce or widowhood are often seeking careers.

Table 5.2 shows that in 1999, 18.7 percent of people 65 years of age and older participated in adult education at some time in the previous year, up from 10.5 percent in 1991. Most (14.5 percent) participated in adult education

TABLE 5.1

Educational attainment of the population 15 years and over, by age: March, 2000

(Numbers in thousands)

Educational attainment

Age	Total	None	1st–4th grade	5th–6th grade	7th–8th grade	9th grade	10th grade	11th grade	High school graduate	Some college no degree	Associate degree, occupational	Associate degree, academic	Bachelor's degree	Master's degree	Professional degree	Doctorate degree
15 years and over	213,773	911	1,973	3,920	8,644	8,056	9,680	12,741	66,274	39,975	7,722	6,993	31,712	10,527	2,613	2,032
15 to 17 years	12,011	19	4	97	2,395	3,802	3,611	1,909	133	35	–	–	4	–	–	–
18 to 19 years	8,091	14	17	60	100	223	521	2,629	2,294	2,201	19	6	–	4	–	4
20 to 24 years	18,441	28	62	221	253	351	572	1,184	5,761	6,985	482	516	1,867	127	27	4
25 to 29 years	18,268	35	93	298	265	353	401	729	5,435	3,762	821	767	4,313	735	184	75
30 to 34 years	19,518	47	112	308	264	340	420	809	6,111	3,614	871	865	4,250	1,043	294	172
35 to 39 years	22,320	59	161	330	278	352	523	873	7,522	4,097	1,013	1,001	4,245	1,320	319	226
40 to 44 years	22,485	111	173	333	315	329	486	776	7,590	4,134	1,132	1,106	3,999	1,387	320	295
45 to 49 years	19,748	109	125	259	349	259	373	603	6,153	3,694	982	868	3,786	1,595	335	259
50 to 54 years	16,882	46	148	297	360	257	379	492	5,216	3,158	728	705	3,057	1,436	325	279
55 to 59 years	12,868	76	171	250	364	332	367	494	4,548	2,225	444	374	1,756	987	249	230
60 to 64 years	10,519	56	148	318	480	354	397	473	3,810	1,587	375	250	1,302	680	169	122
65 to 69 years	9,352	72	191	255	568	266	426	520	3,576	1,354	235	158	1,001	466	113	151
70 to 74 years	8,444	77	160	259	757	257	428	459	3,073	1,174	239	176	848	320	112	104
75 years and over	14,825	164	409	634	1,895	581	776	790	5,053	1,953	382	201	1,284	426	167	109
15 to 17 years	12,011	19	4	97	2,395	3,802	3,611	1,909	133	35	–	–	4	–	–	–
18 years and over	201,762	892	1,969	3,823	6,249	4,253	6,068	10,832	66,141	39,940	7,722	6,993	31,708	10,527	2,613	2,032
15 to 24 years	38,543	61	83	378	2,748	4,376	4,704	5,722	8,188	9,222	501	522	1,872	131	27	8
25 years and over	175,230	851	1,891	3,542	5,896	3,680	4,975	7,019	58,086	30,753	7,221	6,471	29,840	10,396	2,586	2,023
15 to 64 years	181,152	598	1,213	2,771	5,424	6,952	8,050	10,971	54,572	35,494	6,866	6,458	28,579	9,314	2,221	1,668
65 years and over	32,621	313	760	1,148	3,220	1,104	1,630	1,770	11,701	4,481	856	534	3,133	1,213	393	364

SOURCE: Adapted from "Table 1. Educational Attainment of the Population 15 Years and Over, by Age, Sex, Race, and Hispanic Origin: March, 2000," in *Educational Attainment in the United States: March 2000*, U.S. Census Bureau, Washington, DC, December, 2000 [Online] http://www.census.gov/population/www/socdemo/education/p20-536.html [accessed October, 2001]

TABLE 5.2

Percentage of adults age 18 and above who participated in learning activities in the past 12 months, by educational attainment and age: 1991, 1995, and 1999

Educational attainment and age	1991 Total[1]	1995 Total[1]	1999					
					Type of adult learning activity[2]			
					Credential[3]			
			Total[1]	Basic skills	Full-time	Part-time	Work-related	Personal
Total	37.9	44.3	48.1	1.9	6.5	9.3	22.2	22.2
Educational attainment								
Grade 8 or less	8.0	10.9	14.9	4.7	0	0.7	1.6	6.5
Grades 9–12[4]	16.1	23.5	25.8	7.6	1.4	4.7	6.4	10.3
High school diploma or equivalent	26.7	33.0	38.6	1.3	3.9	6.5	16.6	17.6
Some college, including vocational/ technical	52.6	58.7	58.9	0.8	13.9	13.7	24.3	26.1
Bachelor's degree or higher	56.5	62.1	64.8	(5)	5.6	11.9	37.7	31.9
Age								
18–24	69.1	68.3	69.9	8.9	35.0	13.8	16.7	22.5
25–34	42.2	53.0	60.3	2.2	7.5	15.7	29.7	25.2
35–44	46.6	51.0	51.7	0.9	2.2	10.6	28.7	25.1
45–54	33.3	47.0	49.5	0.7	1.7	7.7	27.0	24.6
55–64	23.0	28.2	35.2	0.4	0.3	4.8	18.9	17.3
65 and above	10.5	15.2	18.7	0.3	0.3	1.2	3.4	14.5

[1] Estimates include participation in basic skills, work-related, credential programs, English as a Second Language, personal interest courses, apprenticeships, or participation in credential program full or part time. Adults who participated in apprenticeships and programs for English as a Second Language are included in the totals but are not shown separately.

[2] Percentages may not add to totals because individuals may have participated in more than one type of adult learning activity.

[3] Includes credential programs provided by either postsecondary institutions or other types of providers.

[4] In 1995 and 1999, includes adults whose highest education level was grades 9–12 who had not received a high school diploma; in 1991, includes only adults whose highest education level was grades 9–11.

[5] Only adults who had not received a high school diploma or equivalent, who received a high school diploma in the past 12 months, or who received a high school diploma in a foreign country and did not have a bachelor's degree were asked about their participation in basic education/General Education Development (GED) activities.

SOURCE: John Wirt, et al., "Table 7-1. Percentage of adults age 18 and above who participated in learning activities in the past 12 months, by educational attainment and age: 1991, 1995, and 1999," in *The Condition of Education: 2001*, U.S. Department of Education, National Center for Education Statistics, Washington, DC, 2001

for personal development, while 3.4 percent took work-related courses.

INCREASING COMPUTER SAVVY. Although computer usage is most frequently associated with the young, many older persons are increasingly using computer technology. The Census Bureau, in *Home Computer Use and Internet Use in the United States: August 2000* (September 2001), reported that 24.3 percent of those 65 and older, the lowest percentage of any age group, had a computer in their homes. (See Table 5.3.) Only 17.7 percent of those 65-plus had access to the Internet at home.

In 1998 SeniorNet, a nonprofit organization that helps the elderly with computers, and Charles Schwab, a discount stockbroker with a large online trading business, conducted a survey, *The 1998 SeniorNet Survey*, to determine computer use among older Americans. The study found that only 18 percent of those 70 and older had ever used a computer, and most said they probably would not do so. Between ages 50 and 70, however, computer ownership rose to 51 percent. Among those 50 and older with a college degree, ownership approached 64 percent. SeniorNet found that older residents were the fastest-growing segment of the computer world.

Fifty-six percent of seniors who were investors had a computer at home. Almost 40 percent of those over 50 had access to the Internet either at home, work, or another site. Nearly 80 percent of those had logged on in the previous month, and spent an average of five hours per week online. One-quarter of seniors who used the Internet said they checked a stock quote the first time they went online. Nevertheless, only one-fifth of senior investors with Internet access used the Internet for financial or investment purposes.

Computer companies are focusing new attention on the over-55 population. Dell Computers has found that older Americans would be more inclined to purchase home computers if they knew someone would be there to help them if they encountered problems. Dell found that 46 percent of seniors would use computers to e-mail friends and family, 33 percent would play computer games, and 26 percent would surf the Internet.

VOTING BEHAVIOR

Retirement often means more leisure time to devote to community affairs such as politics, and Americans are more likely to vote as they get older. In addition, dependence on

TABLE 5.3

Households with computers and Internet access, by age of householder
(Numbers in thousands. Civilian noninstitutional population)

	Total households	Computer in household			Home Internet access		
	Number	Number	Percent	90 percent C.I. (+ −)[1]	Number	Percent	90 percent C.I. (+ −)[1]
TOTAL HOUSEHOLDS	105,247	53,716	51.0	0.4	43,639	41.5	0.4
AGE OF HOUSEHOLDER							
Under 25 years	6,104	2,675	43.8	1.5	2,179	35.7	1.5
25 to 44 years	42,545	25,944	61.0	0.6	21,353	50.2	0.6
45 to 64 years	34,800	19,800	56.9	0.6	16,251	46.7	0.6
65 years and over	21,798	5,297	24.3	0.7	3,856	17.7	0.6

[1]This figure added to or subtracted from the estimate provides the 90-percent confidence interval.

SOURCE: Adapted from Eric C. Newburger, "Table A. Households With Computers and Internet Access by Selected Characteristics: August 2000," in *Home Computers and Internet Use in the United States: August 2000,* U.S. Census Bureau, Washington, DC, September, 2001

Social Security funds by many older people gives them a major personal stake in how the government is run. In 2000, 46 percent of Americans aged 50 and over—32 million people—were members of the AARP (formerly the American Association of Retired Persons), sometimes considered the most powerful lobby on Capitol Hill because of its forceful, nonpartisan political activities. The AARP does not endorse particular candidates but questions candidates on issues such as health care, Social Security and Medicare, long-term care, pension reform, and age discrimination. A candidate's position on each issue is made available to members of AARP, making these older citizens an informed and potentially formidable force in a candidate's bid for election.

Voting participation increases for older age groups until approximately the age of 75, when it declines slightly. The Census Bureau found that in the 1998 election, of those people aged 65 to 74, 77.1 percent were registered to vote and 63.3 percent voted. (See Table 5.4.) Among those 75 years and older, 73.2 percent were registered to vote and 54.8 percent voted.

Because such a large percentage of the elderly vote, they are an important voting bloc. With the growing number of elderly and their increasing education and financial resources, voting participation is expected to increase. Older Americans are projected to become an even more powerful voting group as the aging population swells.

The major reason that people aged 65 and over gave for not voting was illness or disability (40.2 percent). (See Table 5.5.) The second most common reason was being out of town or away from home (10.1 percent). In contrast, the most common reason that people of all ages gave for not voting was "too busy" or "conflicting schedule" (34.9 percent), and the second most frequent answer was "not interested" or "felt vote would not make a difference" (12.7 percent). Only 7.4 percent of the elderly who

were registered to vote but did not cited schedule conflicts as a reason; 12.2 percent said they were not interested or did not feel they could make a difference.

Party Affiliation

The Center for Political Studies, a political think tank, has found differences in political party affiliation based on age. Those persons 64 years and older show a firmer identification with the two major American political parties, Democratic and Republican, than younger Americans. Only half of those younger than 64 years reported attachment to one of those two parties, with a considerable population considering themselves "independent." Among older citizens, fully three-quarters considered themselves either Democrat or Republican.

This may reflect either a greater flexibility among younger voters or less firmly committed opinions and shorter voting histories. It may also indicate a true shift in attitudes toward political parties among American voters. Voters may become more committed to a particular political party as they age, simply due to maturation. On the other hand, today's younger people may have fundamentally different attitudes toward political parties; as they age, they may remain less connected to either of the two major political parties, a trend that could have important political implications.

"GRAY POWER"—A POLITICAL BLOC

People aged 55 to 74 vote more than any other age group and therefore the increasing number of Americans in this age group will have a growing political impact. Organizations such as the AARP already exercise considerable influence in lobbying and in educating political leaders on issues pertinent to older Americans. The AARP, with over 35 million members (about half of all Americans over 50) and an annual budget of over $550

TABLE 5.4

Reported voting and registration, by age, November 1998

(In thousands)

Age	Total	Reported registered Number	Pct	Not registered Number	Pct	Reported voted Number	Pct	Did not vote Number	Pct	U.S. citizen Reported registered Number	Not registered Number	Not a citizen Number
Total 18 years and over	198,228	123,104	62.1	75,125	37.9	83,098	41.9	115,131	58.1	123,104	60,347	14,778
18 to 24 years	25,537	10,014	39.2	15,523	60.8	4,251	16.6	21,286	83.4	10,014	12,979	2,544
25 to 34 years	38,624	20,239	52.4	18,385	47.6	10,816	28.0	27,808	72.0	20,239	13,696	4,689
35 to 44 years	44,369	27,664	62.3	16,705	37.7	18,073	40.7	26,296	59.3	27,664	13,078	3,627
45 to 54 years	34,827	24,137	69.3	10,690	30.7	17,663	50.7	17,164	49.3	24,137	8,678	2,012
55 to 64 years	22,609	16,724	74.0	5,884	26.0	13,095	57.9	9,514	42.1	16,724	4,926	958
65 to 74 years	17,902	13,810	77.1	4,092	22.9	11,333	63.3	6,569	36.7	13,810	3,544	548
75 years and over	14,361	10,516	73.2	3,845	26.8	7,867	54.8	6,494	45.2	10,516	3,445	399

'Not registered' includes 'did not register to vote,' 'do not know,' and 'not reported.' 'Did not vote' includes 'did not vote,' 'do not know,' and 'not reported.'

SOURCE: Adapted from "Table 1. Reported Voting and Registration, by Sex and Single Years of Age: November 1998," in *Voting and Registration in the Election of November 1998, Detailed Tables for Current Population Report, P20-523,* U.S. Census Bureau, Washington, DC, November 2000 [Online] http://www.census.gov/population/socdemo/voting/cps1998/tab01.txt [accessed October, 2001]

million, is the world's second-largest nonprofit organization after the Catholic Church. Its influence will undoubtedly grow as lawmakers, many of whom may themselves be older, respond to the increasing voting power of the elderly. Most economists predict that growing proportions of the American budget will be dedicated to spending for the elderly.

Issues such as age discrimination, quality of care in nursing facilities, Medicare and Medigap coverage, paying for prescription drugs and long-term care, nontraditional living arrangements, and reform in pension plans and Social Security are vital topics for older Americans. Other areas that must be addressed are expansion of senior citizen benefits and discounts, changes in traffic and architectural design, and ethical questions raised by medical technology.

Silver-Haired Legislatures

Twenty-seven states now have Silver-Haired Legislatures. Their members, who must be at least 55, although the average age is 80, include former teachers, judges, doctors, business owners, and even legislators. They take over the House and Senate chambers to consider issues of concern to the elderly. In many cases, they function to educate the real legislators about issues.

One of the largest and most active groups is Florida's Silver-Haired Legislature, founded in 1978. It is a working example of grass-roots politics. For a week every year, the members pick top priority issues and take those to churches, civic clubs, mobile home park organizations, and condominium boards to enlist support. Then they promote these ideas to real state legislators. The members claim that more than 100 of the issues they have promoted have gone on to become state law. Their greatest achievement was the creation in 1988 of a State Department of Elder Affairs. The members have also pushed for bills to eliminate waste, fight consumer fraud, and press for adequate health care. The group has in addition filed a friend-of-the-court brief on physician-assisted suicide.

Town Councils

Across the nation, particularly in small and medium-size towns, more and more older people are being elected to civic positions. There are many reasons for this trend, including growing demands on council members' time (something retired persons often have in abundance), increased numbers of older people, and the growing interest of older people in protecting their resources. One advantage older people offer councils is their greater life experience and long-term perspective.

TABLE 5.5

Reasons for not voting, by age, November 1998

(In thousands)

Reasons for not voting	Total non-voting registered population		Age							
	Number	Percent	18 to 24 years		25 to 44 years		45 to 64 years		65 years and over	
			Number	Percent	Number	Percent	Number	Percent	Number	Percent
ALL REASONS	40,006	100.0	5,763	100.0	19,014	100.0	10,103	100.0	5,126	100.0
Too busy, conflicting schedule	13,948	34.9	2,224	38.6	8,225	43.3	3,118	30.9	381	7.4
Not interested, felt vote would not make a difference	5,076	12.7	562	9.8	2,475	13.0	1,416	14.0	623	12.2
Illness or disability (own or family's)	4,446	11.1	149	2.6	1,093	5.7	1,143	11.3	2,061	40.2
Did not like candidates or campaign issues	2,201	5.5	175	3.0	970	5.1	757	7.5	299	5.8
Out of town or away from home	3,338	8.3	566	9.8	1,232	6.5	1,022	10.1	517	10.1
Forgot to vote (or send in absentee ballot)	2,139	5.3	371	6.4	996	5.2	589	5.8	183	3.6
Transportation problems	737	1.8	71	1.2	238	1.3	153	1.5	274	5.3
Inconvenient polling place or hours or lines too long	433	1.1	68	1.2	219	1.2	110	1.1	36	0.7
Registration problems	1,457	3.6	319	5.5	773	4.1	251	2.5	113	2.2
Bad weather conditions	69	0.2	1	0.0	19	0.1	22	0.2	26	0.5
Other reason, not specified	3,329	8.3	475	8.2	1,560	8.2	876	8.7	418	8.2
Refused or don't know	2,834	7.1	780	13.5	1,214	6.4	645	6.4	195	3.8

SOURCE: Adapted from "Table 12. Reasons for Not Voting, by Sex, Age, Race, and Hispanic Origin, and Educational Attainment: November 1998," in *Voting and Registration in the Election of November 1998, Detailed Tables for Current Population Report, P20-523*, U.S. Census Bureau, Washington, DC, November 2000 [Online] http://www.census.gov/population/socdemo/voting/cps1998/tab01.txt [accessed October, 2001]

CHAPTER 6
ON THE ROAD—ELDERLY DRIVERS

Since the 1990s the number of licensed drivers aged 70 or older has grown by nearly 50 percent. As the nation's population grows older, more older persons are on the streets, both as drivers and as pedestrians. According to the Federal Highway Administration, in 1998 there were 24.8 million licensed drivers over age 65 in the United States, and their ranks were expected to reach 30 million by 2020. In 1998, aged 65-plus drivers accounted for 14 percent of all drivers, up from 10 percent in 1980.

In addition, the number of aged 70-plus drivers continues to increase. In 1978 there were about 8 million drivers over age 70. In 1998 there were almost 18 million.

POTENTIAL SAFETY ISSUES

According to National Highway Traffic Safety Administration official John Eberhard, interviewed in the AARP's (formerly the American Association of Retired Persons) online *Bulletin* (Al Karr, "States Find Ways to Aid Older Drivers," September 2001): "Though involved in fewer accidents than younger people because they drive less often, individuals over 65 are the most likely to die in car wrecks." He added, "Traffic fatalities involving older drivers could triple by 2030."

The Insurance Institute for Highway Safety reported that drivers over age 65 had a higher crash rate per mile driven than all other motorists, except those under 25. Those over 75 had the second-highest fatality rate per mile driven of all drivers after teenagers. Older people who were injured in motor vehicle crashes were more likely to die of their injuries than were people in other age groups. About half of fatal crashes involving drivers 80 and older occurred at intersections and involved more than one vehicle. Drivers over age 65 had a particularly high accident rate when making left turns. Experts attributed that to the fact that older drivers take longer to make the turns, increasing the risk of a crash.

Reduced vision, especially night vision, slower reflexes, reduced hearing, and less flexibility of the head and neck, are common problems of aging that can impair driving performance. Although crash rates are high among older drivers, the actual number of crashes and deaths are relatively low because seniors usually cut down on their driving. In 1998 Eberhard claimed, "If you look at the number of accidents per licensed drivers, those in the 65-and-above group are the safest around."

Vision Problems

A 1999 study at the Johns Hopkins University School of Medicine (*Journal of the American Medical Association*, vol. 282, no. 17), which studied a variety of visual changes in older drivers, found the most dramatic age-related vision changes involve sensitivity to glare and the time it takes the eyes to readjust to normal light after exposure to glare.

Cataracts also play a role in motorist safety. In studies of patients aged 55 and older with cataracts, researchers at the University of Alabama at Birmingham found that those with cataracts were two and one-half times more likely to have been in a crash in the previous five years than those without cataracts. Half the patients with cataracts had surgery to remove them; three years after surgery, their crash rates had leveled off, at a rate of 4.9 crashes per million person-miles of travel. Among those who chose not to have surgery, crash rates increased from 4.8 to 8.3 per million miles of travel in three years.

Safe Driving Habits

Despite some of the statistics given above, older drivers do show a strong interest in automobile safety. Older drivers are more likely than any other age group except infants and preschool children to wear safety belts. Older drivers tend to drive when conditions are safest. They generally limit their driving during bad weather and at night, and they drive fewer miles than younger drivers do. Older drivers are also less likely to drink and drive. The National Center for Health Statistics reported that in 1996 drivers younger than 70 who died in crashes were five times more likely than those 70 and older to be intoxicated (with a blood alcohol concentration of at least .10 per deciliter).

ENSURING THE SAFETY OF OLDER DRIVERS

The trend now is more toward helping those who need it and less toward regulating them out of their cars.

— William Barnhill, *AARP Bulletin*, 1998

Many states, including Arizona, California, Florida, Maryland, Michigan, Oregon, and Pennsylvania, are considering various approaches to reducing risks for older drivers. Some states are implementing roadway enhancements to make driving less hazardous. According to the AARP article "States Find Ways to Aid Older Drivers," cited above, typical improvements include:

- wider highway lanes;

- intersections that give drivers a longer view of oncoming traffic and allow more time for left turns;

- road signs with larger, more visible letters and numbers;

- bigger orange construction-zone cones; and

- more rumble strips to reduce speeding.

Many states are also reviewing licensing requirements for older drivers. The National Conference of State Legislatures counts at least 19 states that call for more frequent license renewals, along with other restrictions, once drivers reach a certain age. Al Karr, in the AARP article cited above, provided other examples of measures states are carrying out:

- In Florida, the Elder Roadway User Program uses reflective pavement markers to illuminate roads when conditions are dark or rainy. Street names are displayed well in advance of intersections. Stop, yield, and warning signs have new, larger lettering.

- The Wisconsin Department of Transportation began making road lanes at least 12 feet wide, testing reflective paints, and designing intersections and road curvatures for easier navigation by older drivers.

- Colorado requires drivers aged 61 and older to renew every 5 years, while younger drivers renew only every 10 years. Hawaii requires 2-year renewals for drivers 72 and older, versus 6 years for others, while in Illinois, drivers 87 and older must renew every year, those 81 to 86 must renew every 2 years, and those under 81 must renew every 4 years.

- Maine drivers aged 40 and over must take a vision test every other time they renew their license until age 62,

and every time after that. Oregon requires a road sign recognition test starting at age 50, while New Hampshire mandates a driving skills test at age 75. In New Mexico, a medical exam is required at age 70 for license renewal.

- All states ask driver's license applicants if they have certain health problems that could impair driving. For a "yes" answer, the applicant may be sent to a physician, or a medical board may decide if driving restrictions are needed.

- Nearly all states heed reports from doctors, family members, courts, police, and motor vehicle departments that identify motorists with health problems that could affect their driving ability. At least five states— California, Delaware, Nevada, North Dakota, and Texas—require physicians to make these types of reports. Other states are considering similar legislation.

Older drivers are encouraged to upgrade their skills with training, such as that offered by the AARP in its 55 ALIVE driver refreshment program, from which millions of Americans have been graduated since 1979. Insurance companies offer reduced premiums to elderly people who enroll in driver's safety classes.

DRIVING SERVICES

I gave up driving this year because my eyes are going. I can't take the bus because I can't see the numbers. I won't take taxis because they smell of smoke and they cost too much. You have to reserve a week in advance for a Regional Transport van, and the seats are tough on my bad back. I'm not frail enough to qualify for some other services. I don't want to impose on my friends or my family. Am I just supposed to sit at home?

— Elderly woman, Portland, Maine

Many aging Americans face the dilemma of being unable to drive and so, despite being otherwise healthy, find themselves prematurely lodged or housed in a nursing facility, simply because they cannot get around their communities to accomplish simple tasks, such as shopping for necessities and keeping doctors' appointments. Two-thirds of the elderly live in suburban and rural areas, and most of their homes are more than two miles from a public transportation stop. There is a large network of individual transportation services, public and private, that will pick up the elderly and disabled at their homes, but these services, known as "paratransit," do not cover the entire country. Most paratransit services rely on vans and paid drivers and run on fixed schedules to specific sites, such as senior centers. They are limited as to whom they can take and where and when they can go.

As the number of elderly people who do not drive has multiplied, federal agencies and organizations devoted to the aging have begun paying attention. AARP's Connections for Independent Living pilot project, using a mix of volunteer and paid drivers, and cars, not vans, is providing on-demand service to the elderly and disabled in Portland, Maine. Clients make a monthly payment or set up an account against which they can draw to pay for service. The network will sell cars the elderly no longer use and start accounts with the money. Entrepreneurs in American communities might also find a market for transporting the elderly.

CHAPTER 7
GENERAL HEALTH AND HEALTH PROBLEMS

One of the fears many people have about growing older is facing the loss of mental and physical abilities. Although the human body does change over time, the rate and amount of this change varies according to the individual. One person may be limited by arthritis at age 65, while another is vigorous and active at 90. Nonetheless, overall health problems and the need for health care are higher in older age groups.

LIFE EXPECTANCY

Americans are living longer than ever before. Life expectancy has increased by 30 years since the beginning of the twentieth century. In 1900 the average life expectancy of a baby born in the United States was 47.3 years, partly because of the high rate of infant mortality. Current estimates from the National Center for Health Statistics (NCHS) are that someone born in 2000 will live almost twice that long, 76.9 years, up from 75.8 in 1995.

During the first half of the twentieth century, increased longevity was a result of reducing or eliminating many diseases that killed infants and children and improved methods of delivering babies, so that more people survived to middle age. Increased life expectancy may also be attributed to decreasing mortality from chronic and acute diseases due to new medical knowledge and technology, healthier diet and exercise habits, and life-sustaining technology.

Improvements in life expectancy have benefited women more than men. The NCHS reported that in 2000 a man could, on average, expect to live 74.1 years and a woman, 79.5 years. Life expectancy for whites (77.4 years) also continued to exceed that of African Americans (71.8 years).

Life Expectancy for the Older Population

According to 2000 estimates by the NCHS, life expectancy at age 65 was an additional 17.9 years. The longevity advantage of women narrowed somewhat for this age group. At 65 years, elderly women had a life expectancy of an additional 19.2 years, compared to 16.3 years for elderly men.

LEADING CAUSES OF DEATH

Six out of every 10 people aged 65 and over die from heart disease, cancer, or stroke. The top 10 leading causes of death for the elderly and the number of deaths from each in 1980 and 1999 are shown in Table 7.1. (Malignant neoplasms refer to cancer, and cerebrovascular diseases include strokes.) Death rates for different age groups for the top 15 causes of death are shown in Table 7.2.

Still Number One: Heart Disease

While there have been great decreases in deaths due to heart disease, it still kills more Americans than any other disease. According to the American Heart Association (AHA), about 85 percent of people who die of heart disease are aged 65 or older.

Table 7.3 includes the death rates attributed to heart disease for selected years between 1950 and 1999. Preliminary 1999 data show that for people aged 65 to 74 there were 709.4 deaths per 100,000 resident population. This is half the 1970 rate for the same age group (1,558.2 deaths per 100,000). The rate for the 75 to 84 age group was also cut roughly in half between 1970 and 1999: there were 1,861.9 deaths per 100,000 resident population for this age group in 1999, down from 3,683.8 in 1970. The improvement was more modest for people aged 85 and older.

Several factors account for the decreasing numbers of deaths from heart disease, primarily including better control of hypertension and cholesterol and changes in exercise and nutrition. Also important is the expanding use of trained mobile emergency personnel (paramedics) in most urban areas. The generalized use of cardiopulmonary resuscitation (CPR) and new emergency medications also increase the likelihood of one's surviving an initial heart attack.

TABLE 7.1

Leading causes of death and numbers of deaths among persons 65 years of age and over, 1980 and 1999

[Data are based on the National Vital Statistics System]

Rank order	1980		Preliminary 1999[1]	
	Cause of death	Deaths	Cause of death	Deaths
...	All causes	1,341,848	All causes	1,797,451
1	Diseases of heart	595,406	Diseases of heart	607,255
2	Malignant neoplasms	258,389	Malignant neoplasms	390,070
3	Cerebrovascular diseases	146,417	Cerebrovascular diseases	148,580
4	Pneumonia and influenza	45,512	Chronic lower respiratory diseases	108,106
5	Chronic obstructive pulmonary diseases	43,587	Influenza and pneumonia	57,270
6	Atherosclerosis	28,081	Diabetes mellitus	51,846
7	Diabetes mellitus	25,216	Alzheimer's disease	43,990
8	Unintentional injuries	24,844	Unintentional injuries	32,147
9	Nephritis, nephrotic syndrome, and nephrosis	12,968	Nephritis, nephrotic syndrome and nephrosis	29,937
10	Chronic liver disease and cirrhosis	9,519	Septicemia	24,621

[1] The rank order of leading causes of death changed somewhat between 1998 and 1999, reflecting in part changes in the coding rules for selecting underlying cause of death between ICD–9 and ICD–10. For example, for persons 65 years and over, Alzheimer's disease rose from 9th to 7th.

NOTES: Cause of death code numbers in 1980 are based on the *International Classification of Diseases, 9th Revision* (ICD–9). Starting in 1999 cause of death code numbers are based on ICD–10.

SOURCE: Adapted from "Table 33. Leading causes of death and numbers of deaths, according to age: United States, 1980 and 1999," in *Health, United States, 2001*, Centers for Disease Control and Prevention, National Center for Health Statistics, Hyattsville, MD, 2001

Increased use of procedures such as heart transplant, cardiac catheterization, coronary bypass surgery, pacemakers, and angioplasty have contributed to extending the lives of those afflicted with heart disease. These procedures also usually improve the quality of life of the individual, who typically suffers less pain and inactivity. According to the AHA, in 2000 the national cost of cardiovascular disease, including coronary heart disease, congestive heart failure, high blood pressure, and "other" heart diseases, was estimated at $326.6 billion. This includes direct costs, such as the cost of physicians and other professionals, hospital and nursing home services, medications, and home health; and indirect costs, such as lost productivity resulting from illness and death.

Most recent studies indicate that postmenopausal women suffer from heart disease as frequently as their male counterparts. Also, according to the AHA, they are more likely to die from heart attacks within a few weeks after the attack. The AHA attributed this to the fact that women tend to have heart attacks at older ages than men do—on average, women do not have heart attacks until 10 years later than men. The reasons for this are not known.

Some observers have suggested that because of the misconception that women do not experience heart disease as frequently, their complaints are not taken as seriously as those of men are. Also, physiological factors, such as hormone effects and small blood vessel size, may increase difficulty during surgical procedures and play a role in women's succumbing to heart disease. Research on heart disease has historically been done on male subjects, but a growing number of studies include women.

Cancer

Cancer is the second-leading cause of death among the elderly. According to the American Cancer Society (ACS), nearly 80 percent of all cancers are diagnosed after age 55. The likelihood of dying of cancer (or malignant neoplasms) increases every decade after the age of 30. (See Table 7.2.) In 1999, among those 65 to 74, there were 836.2 deaths per 100,000 persons; for those 75 to 84, this rate was 1,340 per 100,000 persons; and for those 85 and over, 1,796.7 per 100,000 persons.

Success in curing certain tumors (such as Hodgkin's disease and certain forms of leukemia) has been offset by the rise in rates of other cancers, such as breast and lung cancers. Progress in treating cancer has largely been related to screenings, early diagnoses, and new drug therapies. Table 7.1 shows the increase in the number of cancer deaths among the elderly population between 1980 and 1999. In 1999 there were 390,070 deaths from cancer for those aged 65 and over, compared to 258,389 in 1980.

According to the ACS, one-third of cancer deaths are caused by diet, physical activity, and other lifestyle factors. Some cancers are caused by viral infections such as hepatitis B and human immunodeficiency virus (HIV). In addition, many of the more than 1 million skin cancers that were expected to be diagnosed in 2001 could have been prevented through reduced exposure to the sun.

Strokes

Strokes ("brain attacks," or cerebrovascular disease) are the third-leading cause of death and the primary cause

TABLE 7.2

Death rates by age and age-adjusted death rates for the 15 leading causes of death, 1998 and 1999

[Rates on an annual basis per 100,000 population in specified group; age-adjusted rates per 100,000 U.S. standard population based on year 2000 standard.]

Cause of death (Based on the Tenth Revision, International Classification of Diseases, 1992) and year	All ages[1]	Under 1 year[2]	1-4 years	5-14 years	15-24 years	25-34 years	35-44 years	45-54 years	55-64 years	65-74 years	75-84 years	85 years and over	Age adjusted rate
All causes													
1999	877.0	731.4	34.7	19.2	81.2	108.3	199.2	427.3	1,021.8	2,484.3	5,751.3	15,476.1	881.9
1998 (modified)	864.7	751.3	34.6	19.9	82.3	109.6	199.6	423.5	1,030.7	2,495.1	5,703.2	15,111.7	875.8
1998	864.7	751.3	34.6	19.9	82.3	109.6	199.6	423.5	1,030.7	2,495.1	5,703.2	15,111.7	875.8
Diseases of heart (I00-I09,I11,I13,I20-I51)													
1999	265.9	13.7	1.2	0.7	2.8	8.1	30.3	97.7	274.3	709.5	1,861.8	6,032.5	267.8
1998 (modified)	264.4	15.9	1.4	0.8	2.8	8.2	30.1	100.0	282.8	725.1	1,870.4	5,924.3	268.5
1998	268.2	16.1	1.4	0.8	2.8	8.3	30.5	101.4	286.9	735.5	1,897.3	6,009.6	272.4
Malignant neoplasms (C00-C97)													
1999	201.6	1.8	2.8	2.6	4.6	10.6	37.3	130.4	380.8	836.2	1,340.0	1,796.7	202.7
1998 (modified)	201.7	2.1	2.4	2.6	4.6	11.4	38.5	133.2	386.4	847.0	1,335.3	1,761.3	203.8
1998	200.3	2.1	2.4	2.6	4.6	11.3	38.2	132.3	383.8	841.3	1,326.3	1,749.4	202.4
Cerebrovascular diseases (I60-I69)													
1999	61.4	2.7	0.3	0.2	0.5	1.5	5.7	15.5	41.3	132.2	472.8	1,606.7	61.8
1998 (modified)	61.9	8.3	0.4	0.2	0.5	1.8	6.2	17.5	45.0	137.4	481.0	1,582.6	63.0
1998	58.5	7.8	0.4	0.2	0.5	1.7	5.9	16.5	42.5	129.8	454.3	1,494.7	59.5
Chronic lower respiratory diseases (J40-J47)													
1999	45.5	0.9	0.4	0.4	0.6	0.9	2.0	8.7	48.3	179.2	400.4	642.7	45.8
1998 (modified)	43.6	1.0	0.3	0.4	0.6	0.8	2.1	8.6	46.9	177.1	383.2	596.4	44.0
1998	41.6	1.0	0.3	0.4	0.6	0.8	2.0	8.2	44.8	169.0	365.7	569.2	42.0
Accidents (unintentional injuries) (V01-X59,Y85-Y86)													
1999	35.9	22.1	12.6	7.8	36.2	31.3	34.0	32.5	31.1	45.1	101.1	280.9	35.9
1998 (modified)	36.0	19.7	12.9	8.5	36.8	31.7	34.6	31.7	31.5	45.5	101.3	272.8	36.1
1998	34.9	19.1	12.5	8.2	35.7	30.8	33.6	30.8	30.6	44.2	98.3	264.7	35.0
Diabetes mellitus (E10-E14)													
1999	25.1	*	*	0.1	0.4	1.5	4.3	13.2	38.9	92.8	179.1	315.6	25.2
1998 (modified)	24.2	*	*	0.1	0.4	1.6	4.2	12.8	38.7	90.3	173.2	297.3	24.4
1998	24.0	*	*	0.1	0.4	1.6	4.2	12.7	38.4	89.6	171.8	294.9	24.2
Influenza and pneumonia (J10-J18)													
1999	23.4	8.4	0.9	0.2	0.5	0.9	2.4	4.7	11.2	37.7	158.0	748.0	23.6
1998 (modified)	23.7	8.2	0.7	0.2	0.4	1.0	2.2	4.4	11.9	41.8	168.5	742.8	24.2
1998	34.0	11.7	1.0	0.3	0.6	1.4	3.1	6.3	17.0	59.8	241.4	1,063.9	34.6
Alzheimer's disease (G30)													
1999	16.3	*	*	*	*	*	*	0.2	1.9	17.6	130.4	598.3	16.5
1998 (modified)	13.1	*	*	*	*	*	*	0.2	1.7	16.2	108.8	465.3	13.4
1998	8.4	*	*	*	*	*	*	0.1	1.1	10.4	70.0	299.5	8.6
Nephritis, nephrotic syndrome and nephrosis (N00-N07,N17-N19,N25-N27)													
1999	13.0	4.3	*	0.1	0.2	0.7	1.6	4.1	12.2	37.6	98.2	267.5	13.1
1998 (modified)	12.0	4.6	*	0.1	0.1	0.5	1.2	3.3	9.9	32.0	93.4	267.6	12.1
1998	9.7	3.7	*	0.1	0.1	0.4	1.0	2.7	8.0	26.0	75.8	217.2	9.8
Septicemia (A40-A41)													
1999	11.3	7.4	0.6	0.2	0.3	0.7	1.8	4.7	11.6	31.6	79.9	219.5	11.3
1998 (modified)	10.5	6.8	0.7	0.1	0.4	0.8	1.8	4.3	11.0	29.0	74.3	209.5	10.6
1998	8.8	5.7	0.6	0.1	0.3	0.7	1.5	3.6	9.2	24.3	62.2	175.3	8.9
Intentional self-harm (suicide) (X60-X84,Y87.0)													
1999	10.7	*	*	0.6	10.3	13.5	14.4	14.2	12.4	13.6	18.3	19.2	10.7
1998 (modified)	11.3	*	*	0.8	11.1	13.7	15.3	14.7	13.1	14.0	19.6	20.9	11.3
1998	11.3	*	*	0.8	11.1	13.8	15.4	14.8	13.1	14.1	19.7	21.0	11.3
Chronic liver disease and cirrhosis (K70,K73-K74)													
1999	9.6	*	*	*	0.1	1.1	7.4	17.8	24.1	31.0	32.1	23.1	9.7
1998 (modified)	9.6	*	*	*	0.1	1.3	7.9	17.2	24.2	31.8	32.1	22.7	9.8
1998	9.3	*	*	*	0.1	1.3	7.6	16.6	23.3	30.7	31.0	21.9	9.5
Essential (primary) hypertension and hypertensive renal disease (I10,I12)													
1999	6.2	*	*	*	*	0.2	0.7	2.2	5.6	15.4	43.8	151.3	6.3
1998 (modified)	5.9	*	*	*	*	0.1	0.6	1.9	5.6	15.2	42.9	143.7	6.0
1998	5.3	*	*	*	*	0.1	0.5	1.7	5.0	13.6	38.3	128.4	5.4
Assault (homicide) (X85-Y09,Y87.1)													
1999	6.2	8.7	2.5	1.1	13.2	11.2	7.2	4.7	3.1	2.6	2.5	2.4	6.2
1998 (modified)	6.6	8.5	2.6	1.2	14.6	11.5	7.7	4.9	3.3	2.5	2.7	2.4	6.5
1998	6.6	8.5	2.6	1.2	14.6	11.5	7.7	4.9	3.3	2.5	2.7	2.4	6.5
Aortic aneurysm and dissection (I71)													
1999	5.8	*	*	*	0.1	0.2	0.7	1.8	6.1	22.0	48.9	79.9	5.8
1998 (modified)	6.0	*	*	*	0.1	0.3	0.7	1.7	6.4	23.5	51.6	79.9	6.1
1998	6.0	*	*	*	0.1	0.3	0.7	1.7	6.4	23.5	51.5	79.8	6.1

*Figure does not meet standards of reliability or precision.
. . . Category not applicable.
[1]Figures for age not stated included in "All ages" but not distributed among age groups.
[2]Death rates for "Under 1 year" (based on population estimates) differ from infant mortality rates (based on live births).

SOURCE: D.L. Hoyert et al., "Table 8. Death rates by age and age-adjusted death rates for the 15 leading causes of death in 1999: United States, 1998, modified 1998, and 1999," in "Deaths: Final Data for 1999," *National Vital Statistics Reports,* vol. 49, no. 8, September 21, 2001

TABLE 7.3

Death rates for diseases of the heart, by age, selected years 1950–99

[Data are based on the National Vital Statistics System]

Age	1950[1]	1960[1]	1970	1980	1985	1990	1995	1996	1997	1998	1999[2]
All persons						Deaths per 100,000 resident population					
All ages, age adjusted	586.8	559.0	492.7	412.1	375.0	321.8	296.3	288.3	280.4	272.4	267.7
All ages, crude	355.5	369.0	362.0	336.0	324.1	289.5	280.7	276.4	271.6	268.2	265.8
Under 1 year	3.5	6.6	13.1	22.8	25.0	20.1	17.1	16.6	16.4	16.1	13.7
1–4 years	1.3	1.3	1.7	2.6	2.2	1.9	1.6	1.4	1.4	1.4	1.2
5–14 years	2.1	1.3	0.8	0.9	1.0	0.9	0.8	0.9	0.8	0.8	0.7
15–24 years	6.8	4.0	3.0	2.9	2.8	2.5	2.9	2.7	3.0	2.8	2.8
25–34 years	19.4	15.6	11.4	8.3	8.3	7.6	8.5	8.3	8.3	8.3	8.0
35–44 years	86.4	74.6	66.7	44.6	38.1	31.4	32.0	30.5	30.1	30.5	30.2
45–54 years	308.6	271.8	238.4	180.2	153.8	120.5	111.0	108.2	104.9	101.4	97.5
55–64 years	808.1	737.9	652.3	494.1	443.0	367.3	322.9	315.2	302.4	286.9	274.2
65–74 years	1,839.8	1,740.5	1,558.2	1,218.6	1,089.8	894.3	799.9	776.2	753.7	735.5	709.4
75–84 years	4,310.1	4,089.4	3,683.8	2,993.1	2,693.1	2,295.7	2,064.7	2,010.2	1,943.6	1,897.3	1,861.9
85 years and over	9,150.6	9,317.8	7,891.3	7,777.1	7,384.1	6,739.9	6,484.1	6,314.5	6,198.9	6,009.6	6,032.5

[1] Includes deaths of persons who were not residents of the 50 States and the District of Columbia.

[2] Starting with 1999 data, cause of death is coded according to ICD–10. Discontinuity between 1998 and 1999 due to ICD–10 coding and classification changes is measured by the comparability ratio. To estimate change between 1998 and 1999, compare the 1999 rate with the 1998 rate multiplied by the comparability ratio (0.99).

NOTES: Age-adjusted rates for all years differ from those shown in previous editions of *Health, United States*. Age-adjusted rates are calculated using the year 2000 standard population starting with *Health, United States, 2001*. For data years shown, code numbers for cause of death are based on the then current revision of the *International Classification of Diseases* (ICD). Age groups were selected to minimize the presentation of unstable age-specific death rates based on small numbers of deaths and for consistency among comparison groups. The race groups, white, black, Asian or Pacific Islander, and American Indian or Alaska Native, include persons of Hispanic and non-Hispanic origin. Conversely, persons of Hispanic origin may be of any race. Bias in death rates results from inconsistent race identification between the death certificate (source of data for numerator of death rates) and data from the Census Bureau (denominator); and from undercounts of some population groups in the census. The net effects of misclassification and under coverage result in death rates estimated to be overstated by 1 percent for the white population and 5 percent for the black population; and death rates estimated to be understated by 21 percent for American Indians, 11 percent for Asians, and 2 percent for Hispanics (Rosenberg HM, Maurer JD, Sorlie PD, Johnson NJ, et al. Quality of death rates by race and Hispanic origin: A summary of current research, 1999. National Center for Health Statistics. Vital Health Stat 2(128). 1999). Some rates for the black population in 1950 and for Hispanic and non-Hispanic white for 1985 (and 1986–89, 1991 available electronically) were revised and differ from the previous edition of *Health, United States*.

SOURCE: Adapted from "Table 37. Death rates for diseases of the heart, according to sex, race, Hispanic origin, and age: United States, selected years 1950–99," in *Health, United States, 2001*, Centers for Disease Control and Prevention, National Center for Health Statistics, Hyattsville, MD, 2001

TABLE 7.4

Death rates for cerebrovascular diseases, by age, selected years, 1950–99

[Data are based on the National Vital Statistics System]

Age	1950[1]	1960[1]	1970	1980	1985	1990	1995	1996	1997	1998	Preliminary 1999[2]
					Deaths per 100,000 resident population						
All ages, age adjusted	180.7	177.9	147.7	96.4	76.6	65.5	63.9	63.2	61.8	59.6	61.8
All ages, crude	104.0	108.0	101.9	75.1	64.3	57.9	60.1	60.3	59.7	58.6	61.4
Under 1 year	5.1	4.1	5.0	4.4	3.7	3.8	5.8	6.2	7.0	7.8	2.7
1–4 years	0.9	0.8	1.0	0.5	0.3	0.3	0.4	0.3	0.4	0.4	0.3
5–14 years	0.5	0.7	0.7	0.3	0.2	0.2	0.2	0.2	0.2	0.2	0.2
15–24 years	1.6	1.8	1.6	1.0	0.8	0.6	0.5	0.5	0.5	0.5	0.5
25–34 years	4.2	4.7	4.5	2.6	2.2	2.2	1.8	1.8	1.7	1.7	1.5
35–44 years	18.7	14.7	15.6	8.5	7.2	6.5	6.5	6.3	6.3	6.0	5.7
45–54 years	70.4	49.2	41.6	25.2	21.3	18.7	17.6	17.9	16.9	16.5	15.5
55–64 years	194.2	147.3	115.8	65.2	54.8	48.0	46.1	45.3	44.4	42.6	41.2
65–74 years	554.7	469.2	384.1	219.5	172.8	144.4	137.2	135.5	134.8	130.0	132.2
75–84 years	1,499.6	1,491.3	1,254.2	788.6	601.5	499.3	481.4	477.0	462.0	455.4	472.8
85 years and over	2,990.1	3,680.5	3,014.3	2,288.9	1,865.1	1,633.9	1,636.5	1,612.7	1,584.6	1,500.0	1,606.3

[1] Includes deaths of persons who were not residents of the 50 States and the District of Columbia.

[2] Starting with 1999 data, cause of death is coded according to ICD–10. Discontinuity between 1998 and 1999 due to ICD–10 coding and classification changes is measured by the comparability ratio. Comparability-modified rates should be used to estimate mortality change between 1998 and 1999. For Cerebrovascular diseases, the 1998 age-adjusted comparability-modified death rate for all persons is 63.1.

SOURCE: Adapted from "Table 38. Death rates for cerebrovascular diseases, according to sex, race, Hispanic origin, and age: United States, selected years, 1950–99," in *Health, United States, 2001*, Centers for Disease Control and Prevention, National Center for Health Statistics, Hyattsville, MD, 2001

of disability among the elderly. According to the AHA, about 72 percent of the people who suffer a stroke in a given year are aged 65 and older. About 88 percent of stroke deaths occur in people aged 65 and older. For people over age 55, the incidence of stroke more than doubles in each successive decade.

Table 7.4 shows the death rate for strokes from 1950 to 1999 by age group. Strokes killed 132.2 people per 100,000 resident population in the 65 to 74 age group in 1999 (according to preliminary data). This is one-third the rate of 1970 (384.1 per 100,000). The rate for the 75 to 84 age group was also cut by roughly two-thirds between 1970 and 1999. There were 472.8 deaths per 100,000 resident population for this age group in 1999, down from 1,254.2 in 1970. The improvement was not quite as great for people aged 85 and older. There were 1,606.3 deaths per 100,000 for this age group in 1999, down from 3,014.3 in 1970.

GENERAL HEALTH OF OLDER AMERICANS

The self-perception of poor health among older people has decreased slightly. The NCHS reported that, in 1999, 26.1 percent of noninstitutionalized people aged 65 and over described their health as fair or poor, down from 29 percent in 1991. (See Table 7.5.)

The oldest elderly report higher rates of poor health than younger age groups. In 1999, 22.7 percent of people aged 65 to 74 reported fair or poor health, compared to 30.2 percent of people aged 75 and older.

Although overall rates of disability are decreasing for the elderly, the likelihood of being disabled increases with age. In 1999, 12.8 percent of people aged 65-plus had trouble performing activities of daily living, such as bathing and dressing, compared with only 2.1 percent of people aged 18 to 64. (See Table 7.6.) Among those 65 and over, 19.7 percent had difficulty with instrumental activities of daily living, such as getting around outside the home and preparing meals, while 17.7 percent reported using an assistive device such as a wheelchair, crutches, cane, or walker.

Hospital Usage and Physician Care

The elderly are hospitalized more than younger people, though as for all Americans, the average length of hospitalization for people aged 65 years and older has declined over the years. In 1964 the average length of a hospital stay for older Americans was 12.1 days; in 1999 it was 6 days. Length of stay, however, is still significantly longer for older people than those who are younger. Shorter stays are partly due to the federal government's introduction of diagnosis related groups (categories of illnesses that prescribe/allow for set duration of treatment), which encourage hospitals to release patients as quickly as possible, and partly from increasing use of outpatient procedures instead of hospital admission for those procedures.

The aging of the American population increases demand for physician care, emergency care, and home health visits. In 1999 only 7.9 percent of people aged 65 and over did not make a visit to any of these providers, while 34.3 percent visited 1 to 3 times, 34.1 percent 4 to 9 times, and 23.7 percent 10 or more times. (See Table 7.7.) These figures changed only slightly over the previous two years.

TABLE 7.5

Respondent-assessed health status, by age, selected years 1991–99

[Data are based on household interviews of a sample of the civilian noninstitutionalized population]

Characteristic	Percent with fair or poor health				
	1991	1995	1997	1998	1999[1]
Total[2]	10.4	10.6	9.2	9.1	8.9
Age					
Under 18 years	2.6	2.6	2.1	1.8	1.6
Under 6 years	2.7	2.7	1.9	1.5	1.4
6–17 years	2.6	2.5	2.1	1.9	1.8
18–44 years	6.1	6.6	5.3	5.3	5.1
18–24 years	4.8	4.5	3.4	3.2	3.4
25–44 years	6.4	7.2	5.9	5.9	5.6
45–54 years	13.4	13.4	11.7	11.6	11.5
55–64 years	20.7	21.4	18.2	18.0	18.5
65 years and over	29.0	28.3	26.7	26.7	26.1
65–74 years	26.0	25.6	23.1	23.9	22.7
75 years and over	33.6	32.2	31.5	30.4	30.2

[1] Data starting in 1997 are not strictly comparable with data for earlier years due to the 1997 questionnaire redesign.
[2] Estimates are age adjusted to the year 2000 standard using six age groups: Under 18 years, 18–44 years, 45–54 years, 55–64 years, 65–74 years, and 75 years and over.

SOURCE: Adapted from "Table 58. Respondent-assessed health status according to selected characteristics: United States, selected years 1991–99," in *Health, United States, 2001,* Centers for Disease Control and Prevention, National Center for Health Statistics, Hyattsville, MD, 2001

CHRONIC PHYSICAL PROBLEMS OF THE ELDERLY

Chronic conditions (those that are long lasting or frequently recurring) are a burden of older age. At the start of the twentieth century, acute conditions (severe illnesses of limited duration, such as infections) were predominant and often deadly. With the development of antibiotics and cures for many acute infectious diseases, people are living much longer, and chronic conditions are now the prevalent health problem for the elderly. While many chronic conditions are not life threatening, they pose a substantial burden on the health and financial status of individuals, their families, and the nation as a whole.

Table 7.8 shows the number of major chronic conditions per 1,000 people by age group in 1996. Arthritis is by far the most common chronic condition, with 482.7 occurrences out of every 1,000 people aged 65-plus. Also very common are hearing impairment, high blood pressure, heart disease, and cataracts. Physical ailments can strike anyone at any age, but some conditions, such as the ones mentioned, are more common among the elderly. Chronic conditions account for most deterioration experienced with aging and much use of medical resources.

Arthritis

Arthritis is an umbrella term for a family of more than 100 separate diseases that affect the body's joints and surrounding areas. In common usage, it refers to inflammation of the joints. Arthritis is not a disease solely of the elderly,

TABLE 7.6

Number[1] and prevalence rates[2] of civilian noninstitutionalized persons aged 18 years and older with disability, by age group, 1999

Measure of disability	Persons with disabilities								
	≥18 Years			18–64 Years			≥65 Years		
	No.	Rate	(95% CI[3])	No.	Rate	(95% CI)	No.	Rate	(95% CI)
Difficulty with specified functional activities[4]	**32,191**	**16.0**	**(±0.5)**	**17,110**	**10.2**	**(±0.4)**	**15,081**	**46.3**	**(±1.6)**
Seeing words/letters in newsprint	7,269	3.6	(±0.2)	3,542	2.1	(±0.2)	3,727	11.4	(±1.0)
Hearing normal conversation	6,932	3.5	(±0.2)	3,013	1.8	(±0.2)	3,919	12.0	(±1.0)
Having speech understood	1,982	1.0	(±0.1)	1,326	0.8	(±0.1)	656	2.0	(±0.4)
Lifting/carrying 10 lbs	14,224	7.1	(±0.3)	7,033	4.2	(±0.3)	7,191	22.1	(±1.3)
Climbing a flight of stairs	19,363	9.6	(±0.4)	9,465	5.6	(±0.3)	9,898	30.4	(±1.5)
Walking three city blocks	19,031	9.5	(±0.4)	9,087	5.4	(±0.3)	9,944	30.5	(±1.5)
Difficulty with activities of daily living[4]	**7,690**	**3.8**	**(±0.2)**	**3,514**	**2.1**	**(±0.2)**	**4,176**	**12.8**	**(±1.1)**
Getting around inside home	3,471	1.7	(±0.2)	1,477	0.9	(±0.1)	1,994	6.1	(±0.8)
Getting in/out of bed/chair	5,340	2.7	(±0.2)	2,618	1.6	(±0.2)	2,722	8.4	(±0.9)
Bathing	4,371	2.2	(±0.2)	1,727	1.0	(±0.1)	2,644	8.1	(±0.9)
Dressing	3,130	1.6	(±0.2)	1,387	0.8	(±0.1)	1,743	5.4	(±0.7)
Eating	1,226	0.6	(±0.1)	566	0.3	(±0.1)	661	2.0	(±0.4)
Toileting	2,064	1.0	(±0.1)	922	0.5	(±0.1)	1,143	3.5	(±0.6)
Difficulty with instrumental activities of daily living[4]	**11,795**	**5.9**	**(±0.3)**	**5,370**	**3.2**	**(±0.2)**	**6,425**	**19.7**	**(±1.3)**
Getting around outside of home	8,113	4.0	(±0.3)	3,202	1.9	(±0.2)	4,910	15.1	(±1.1)
Taking care of money and bills	4,492	2.2	(±0.2)	2,205	1.3	(±0.2)	2,286	7.0	(±0.8)
Preparing meals	4,430	2.2	(±0.2)	1,919	1.1	(±0.1)	2,511	7.7	(±0.8)
Doing light housework	6,042	3.0	(±0.2)	2,723	1.6	(±0.2)	3,319	10.2	(±1.0)
Using the telephone	2,597	1.3	(±0.1)	1,001	0.6	(±0.1)	1,597	4.9	(±0.7)
Reporting selected impairments[4]	**11,392**	**5.7**	**(±0.3)**	**8,706**	**5.2**	**(±0.3)**	**2,686**	**8.2**	**(±0.9)**
A learning disability	2,660	1.3	(±0.1)	2,506	1.5	(±0.2)	154	0.5	(±0.2)
Mental retardation	1,544	0.8	(±0.1)	1,417	0.8	(±0.1)	127	0.4	(±0.2)
Other developmental disability	506	0.3	(±0.1)	456	0.3	(±0.1)	—**	—	—
Alzheimer disease/senility/dementia	1,684	0.8	(±0.1)	509	0.3	(±0.1)	1,175	3.6	(±0.6)
Other mental/emotional disability	7,932	4.0	(±0.3)	6,033	3.6	(±0.3)	1,899	5.8	(±0.7)
Use of assistive aid[5]	**9,180**	**4.6**	**(±0.3)**	**3,415**	**2.0**	**(±0.2)**	**5,765**	**17.7**	**(±1.2)**
Wheelchair	2,283	1.1	(±0.1)	1,012	0.6	(±0.1)	1,271	3.9	(±0.6)
Cane, crutches, or walker	6,898	3.4	(±0.2)	2,404	1.4	(±0.2)	4,494	13.8	(±1.1)
Limitation in ability to work around the house	**16,755**	**8.3**	**(±0.4)**	**9,649**	**5.7**	**(±0.3)**	**7,106**	**21.8**	**(±1.3)**
Limitation in ability to work at a job or business	**N/A**	**N/A**	**N/A**	**17,689**	**10.5**	**(±0.4)**	**N/A**	**N/A**	**N/A**
Received federal work disability benefits	**N/A**	**N/A**	**N/A**	**7,611**	**4.5**	**(±0.3)**	**N/A**	**N/A**	**N/A**
Total surveyed	**200,668**	**100.0**		**168,105**	**100.0**		**32,563**	**100.0**	
Total with a disability	**44,088**	**22.0**	**(±0.5)**	**27,781**	**16.5**	**(±0.5)**	**16,307**	**50.1**	**(±1.6)**

[1]In thousands.
[2]Per 100 persons calculated using the civilian, noninstitutionalized U.S. population on July 1, 1999.
[3]Confidence interval.
[4]Number of persons reporting any subcomponent of this category. The category subtotal may be smaller than the components because these categories are not mutually exclusive.
[5]Wheelchair use and use of cane/crutches/walker are mutually exclusive categories.
**Estimates based on <30 unweighted cases and may not be reliable.

SOURCE: "Table 1. Number and prevalence rates of civilian noninstitutionalized persons aged 18 years and older with disability, by age group—Survey of Income Program and Participation, United States, 1999," in "Prevalence of Disabilities and Associated Health Conditions Among Adults—United States, 1999," *Morbidity and Mortality Weekly Report,* vol. 50, no. 7, February 23, 2001

but its prevalence increases with age. Arthritis affects one out of seven people, and nearly half of people aged 65 and over. (See Table 7.8.) According to the Centers for Disease Control and Prevention (CDC), it affects more than 40 million persons in the United States. As the population ages, that number will likely increase to 60 million by 2020.

According to the CDC, approximately 20.7 million adults in the United States have the most common form of arthritis, osteoarthritis, which is also called degenerative joint disease. Most persons over the age of 75 are affected with osteoarthritis in at least one joint, making this condition a leading cause of disability in the United States. Rheumatoid arthritis is an inflammation of the joint lining, and is the most crippling form of arthritis. It affects approximately 2.1 million Americans and two to three times more women than men.

The greatest consequence of arthritis is loss of mobility and deformity in the affected tissues or joints. Patients diagnosed with osteoarthritis generally experience some loss in their ability to perform daily functions, such as household chores, shopping, running errands, and leisure activities. Patients with rheumatoid arthritis often experience more, and more severe, losses in physical ability.

Osteoporosis

Osteoporosis, a bone disorder associated with decrease in bone mass and resulting susceptibility to fracture, and osteopenia, a less serious reduction in bone

TABLE 7.7

Health care visits to doctor's offices, emergency departments, and home visits within the past 12 months, by age, 1997–99

[Data are based on household nterviews of a sample of the civilian noninstitutionalized population]

	Number of health care visits[1]											
	None			1–3 visits			4–9 visits			10 or more visits		
Characteristic	1997	1998	1999	1997	1998	1999	1997	1998	1999	1997	1998	1999
	Percent distribution											
All persons[2,3]	16.5	16.0	17.5	46.2	46.8	45.8	23.6	23.8	23.3	13.7	13.5	13.4
Age												
Under 18 years	11.8	11.7	12.4	54.1	54.5	54.4	25.2	25.6	25.0	8.9	8.2	8.2
Under 6 years	5.0	4.9	5.9	44.9	46.7	45.9	37.0	36.5	36.8	13.0	11.8	11.3
6–17 years	15.3	15.0	15.5	58.7	58.4	58.5	19.3	20.2	19.4	6.8	6.3	6.7
18–44 years	21.7	21.6	24.2	46.7	47.7	45.8	19.0	18.6	17.8	12.6	12.2	12.3
18–24 years	22.0	22.6	24.8	46.8	47.7	46.1	20.0	18.4	17.8	11.2	11.2	11.4
25–44 years	21.6	21.3	24.0	46.7	47.6	45.7	18.7	18.6	17.8	13.0	12.5	12.6
45–64 years	16.9	15.9	16.9	42.9	43.6	42.4	24.7	24.3	25.0	15.5	16.2	15.7
45–54 years	17.9	17.2	18.4	43.9	44.9	43.2	23.4	22.5	22.8	14.8	15.4	15.7
55–64 years	15.3	13.8	14.7	41.3	41.6	41.1	26.7	27.1	28.4	16.7	17.5	15.8
65 years and over	8.9	7.3	7.9	34.7	34.0	34.3	32.5	35.3	34.1	23.8	23.4	23.7
65–74 years	9.8	8.4	8.6	36.9	36.5	36.9	31.6	34.3	33.2	21.6	20.8	21.3
75 years and over	7.7	6.0	7.2	31.8	30.8	31.1	33.8	36.5	35.1	26.6	26.7	26.6

[1] This table presents a summary measure of ambulatory and home health care visits during a 12-month period based on the following questions: "During the past 12 months, how many times have you gone to a hospital emergency room about your own health?"; "During the past 12 months, did you receive care at home from nurse or other health care professional? What was the total number of home visits received?"; "During the past 12 months, how many times have you seen a doctor or other health care professional about your own health at a doctor's office, a clinic, some other place? Do not include times you were hospitalized overnight, visits to hospital emergency rooms, home visits, or telephone calls." For each question respondents were shown a flashcard with response categories of: 0, 1, 2–3, 4–9, 10–12 or 13 or more visits. For this tabulation responses of 2–3 were recoded to 2 and responses of 4–9 were recoded to 6. The summary measure was constructed by adding recoded responses for these questions and categorizing the sum as: none, 1–3, 4–9, or 10 or more health care visits in the past 12 months.

[2] Includes all other races not shown separately, unknown poverty status, and unknown health insurance status.

[3] Estimates are age adjusted to the year 2000 standard using six age groups: Under 18 years, 18–44 years, 45–54 years, 55–64 years, 65–74 years, and 75 years and over.

NOTES: Some numbers for 1998 were revised and differ from the previous edition of *Health, United States*.
In 1997 the National Health Interview Survey questionnaire was redesigned. Data presented in this table are not comparable with data on physician contacts presented in *Health, United States*, 1999 and earlier editions.

SOURCE: Adapted from "Table 72. Health care visits to doctor's offices, emergency departments, and home visits within the past 12 months, according to selected characteristics: United States, 1997–99," in *Health, United States, 2001: Updated Tables*, Centers for Disease Control and Prevention, National Center for Health Statistics, Hyattsville, MD, September, 2001 [Online] http://www.cdc.gov/nchs/products/pubs/pubd/hus/tables/2001/01hus072.pdf [accessed October, 2001]

density, have only recently been recognized as a fairly common condition of old age. They are particularly common among women. (See Figure 7.1.)

According to the National Osteoporosis Foundation (NOF), osteoporosis is defined as about 25 percent bone loss compared to a healthy young adult, or, on a bone density test, 2.5 standard deviations below normal. Although everyone experiences some bone loss with age, many people do not realize that stooped posture (kyphosis) and loss of height (greater than 1–2 inches) are caused by vertebral fractures due to osteoporosis.

According to the NOF, 10 million Americans have osteoporosis and another 18 million have low bone mass, placing them at increased risk of osteoporosis. All totaled, 28 million people may be affected by osteoporosis, and left unchecked, that number was predicted to increase to 41 million by 2015. Eighty percent of those affected by osteoporosis are women. One in two women and one in eight men over age 50 will have an osteoporosis-related fracture in their lifetime.

Osteoporosis is, in fact, the leading cause of bone fractures, resulting in approximately 1.5 million new frac-

tures each year. The estimated national direct expenditures by hospitals and nursing homes for osteoporotic and associated fractures were $13.8 billion in 1995, or $38 million per day.

Diabetes

The elderly are susceptible to type II, or noninsulin dependent, diabetes. According to the American Diabetes Association (ADA), this form of diabetes, also called adult-onset diabetes, accounts for 90 to 95 percent of diabetes. Type II diabetes is nearing epidemic proportions, due to the increased number of older Americans, and a greater prevalence of obesity and sedentary lifestyles. Type I diabetes, also known as insulin-dependent diabetes, generally begins in childhood.

According to the NCHS, diabetes killed 64,751 Americans in 1999. Many more people died from heart disease or strokes resulting from diabetes. The ADA estimated that 16 million Americans have diabetes, and that 5 million of them do not realize they have it.

Frequent complications of diabetes are nerve damage in the legs and feet, sometimes resulting in amputations,

TABLE 7.8

Number of selected reported chronic conditions per 1,000 persons, by age, 1996

[Data are based on household interviews of the civilian noninstitutionalized population.]

Type of chronic condition	All ages	Under 45 years			45–64 years	65 years and over		
		Total	Under 18 years	18–44 years		Total	65–74 years	75 years and over
Selected skin and musculoskeletal conditions		Number of chronic conditions per 1,000 persons						
Arthritis	127.3	30.9	*1.9	50.1	240.1	482.7	453.1	523.6
Gout, including gouty arthritis	9.4	*1.8	*–	*3.0	22.4	30.8	31.7	*29.4
Intervertebral disc disorders	25.4	13.1	*1.0	21.1	62.7	32.2	38.2	*24.0
Bone spur or tendinitis, unspecified	11.1	6.6	*–	10.9	23.2	16.4	*14.6	*18.8
Disorders of bone or cartilage	6.5	*2.1	*0.5	*3.1	10.0	26.2	*15.6	40.6
Trouble with bunions	8.9	4.5	*1.3	6.5	16.2	22.0	*21.2	*23.0
Bursitis, unclassified	18.9	8.2	*0.8	13.1	43.9	38.0	43.0	31.1
Sebaceous skin cyst	4.5	3.6	*0.4	5.7	9.1	*2.0	*3.4	*–
Trouble with acne	18.7	26.3	24.4	27.5	*4.5	*–	*–	*–
Psoriasis	11.1	7.6	*3.2	10.5	20.7	15.0	*16.3	*13.2
Dermatitis	31.2	30.3	30.5	30.1	38.1	25.2	26.6	*23.1
Trouble with dry (itching) skin, unclassified	25.1	19.7	12.7	24.4	28.9	48.9	37.5	64.4
Trouble with ingrown nails	22.0	17.8	*5.2	26.0	26.8	37.7	34.0	42.7
Trouble with corns and calluses	14.3	8.3	*1.1	13.0	25.4	29.7	27.1	33.2
Impairments								
Visual impairment	31.3	17.0	6.3	24.0	48.3	84.2	69.6	104.3
Color blindness	10.6	7.6	*4.0	10.0	16.1	18.8	*20.6	*16.4
Cataracts	26.6	*1.9	*0.5	*2.8	23.3	171.5	151.9	198.6
Glaucoma	9.8	*1.2	*–	*2.0	10.3	57.8	46.7	73.1
Hearing impairment	83.4	30.2	12.6	41.9	131.5	303.4	255.2	369.8
Tinnitus	29.8	10.7	*2.6	16.0	59.6	87.7	96.0	76.2
Speech impairment	10.3	11.1	16.3	7.8	*6.6	*11.7	*10.0	*14.1
Absence of extremities (excludes tips of fingers or toes only)	4.9	*2.0	*1.0	*2.7	5.7	19.4	*21.5	*16.7
Paralysis of extremities, complete or partial	8.1	4.6	*3.8	5.1	13.5	18.9	*12.4	*27.8
Deformity or orthopedic impairment	111.6	83.9	25.6	122.4	177.8	157.6	175.1	133.5
Back	64.0	51.6	7.7	80.6	102.8	68.7	80.0	53.1
Upper extremities	15.8	9.1	*2.6	13.3	29.4	30.9	39.0	*19.8
Lower extremities	48.0	33.5	18.8	43.2	82.5	72.6	77.9	65.3
Selected digestive conditions								
Ulcer	14.0	7.6	*1.3	11.8	26.1	30.1	36.9	*20.7
Hernia of abdominal cavity	16.9	7.2	*1.7	10.8	30.9	48.4	38.3	62.4
Gastritis or duodenitis	14.1	9.4	*3.1	13.5	22.1	27.6	34.0	*18.8
Frequent indigestion	24.3	17.4	*3.3	26.7	42.1	33.5	38.6	*26.4
Enteritis or colitis	6.4	4.8	*1.7	6.9	10.0	*9.2	*8.4	*10.5
Spastic colon	7.9	5.0	*0.7	7.9	13.7	14.3	*16.9	*10.9
Diverticula of intestines	9.6	*1.5	*–	*2.4	17.6	41.9	36.0	50.0
Frequent constipation	11.9	7.2	*5.3	8.5	14.7	33.8	23.9	47.5
Selected conditions of the genitourinary, nervous, endocrine, metabolic, and blood and blood-forming systems								
Goiter or other disorders of the thyroid	17.4	8.2	*1.0	13.0	30.0	48.1	50.3	45.1
Diabetes	28.9	7.6	*1.2	11.8	58.2	100.0	98.4	102.3
Anemias	13.1	12.0	*5.0	16.7	10.7	23.0	*13.7	35.9
Epilepsy	5.1	4.6	*4.9	4.4	*5.8	*6.2	*5.4	*7.4
Migraine headache	43.7	42.2	15.2	60.0	57.9	28.5	28.6	*28.4
Neuralgia or neuritis, unspecified	*1.3	*0.3	*0.2	*0.3	*2.4	*5.6	*2.6	*9.8
Kidney trouble	9.7	8.0	*2.4	11.8	12.8	13.7	*13.7	*13.6
Bladder disorders	11.9	8.1	*3.3	11.3	15.7	26.9	*19.9	36.4
Diseases of prostate	10.6	*1.3	*–	*2.2	14.7	56.1	48.8	66.0
Disease of female genital organs	16.7	15.9	*3.4	24.2	20.7	14.6	*16.5	*12.0
Selected circulatory conditions								
Rheumatic fever with or without heart disease	6.7	4.6	*1.2	6.9	10.4	*11.9	*7.8	*17.5
Heart disease	78.2	33.1	23.6	39.3	116.4	268.7	238.2	310.7
Ischemic heart disease	29.0	2.5	*–	4.2	51.6	140.9	131.0	154.6
Heart rhythm disorders	33.0	24.3	17.0	29.1	40.7	69.1	66.2	73.1
Tachycardia or rapid heart	8.7	3.8	*–	6.4	12.1	30.9	31.0	30.7
Heart murmurs	18.1	18.0	16.6	18.8	17.6	19.6	*21.4	*17.3
Other and unspecified heart rhythm disorders	6.1	2.5	*0.4	3.9	11.0	18.6	*13.9	*25.1
Other selected diseases of heart, excluding hypertension	16.1	6.3	6.6	6.0	24.0	58.7	41.0	83.1
High blood pressure (hypertension)	107.1	30.1	*0.5	49.6	214.1	363.5	356.0	373.8
Cerebrovascular disease	11.3	*1.4	*0.4	*2.0	12.8	65.1	40.2	99.4
Hardening of the arteries	5.9	*–	*–	*–	*6.7	37.8	28.4	50.9
Varicose veins of lower extremities	28.0	13.4	*–	22.2	46.8	79.1	74.0	86.2
Hemorrhoids	32.3	20.8	*0.3	34.4	53.6	61.2	72.8	45.4

TABLE 7.8

Number of selected reported chronic conditions per 1,000 persons, by age, 1996 [CONTINUED]

[Data are based on household interviews of the civilian noninstitutionalized population.]

Type of chronic condition	All ages	Under 45 years			45–64 years	65 years and over		
		Total	Under 18 years	18–44 years		Total	65–74 years	75 years and over
Selected respiratory conditions								
Chronic bronchitis	53.5	50.1	57.3	45.4	59.1	63.5	60.7	67.3
Asthma	55.2	58.9	62.0	56.9	48.6	45.5	43.7	48.0
Hay fever or allergic rhinitis without asthma	89.8	89.2	58.7	109.4	104.8	67.7	61.9	75.7
Chronic sinusitis	125.5	112.6	63.9	144.7	174.1	117.1	127.0	103.5
Deviated nasal septum	7.5	5.5	*1.7	8.0	15.0	*6.2	*3.2	*10.4
Chronic disease of tonsils or adenoids	9.5	13.0	20.2	8.2	*3.0	*0.8	*1.4	*–
Emphysema	6.9	*0.5	*–	*0.8	13.2	32.4	32.3	32.6

*Figure does not meet standard of reliability or precision.
*– Figures does not meet standard of reliability or precision and quantity zero.

SOURCE: P.F. Adams, G.E. Hendershot, and M.A. Marano, "Table 57. Number of selected reported chronic conditions per 1,000 persons, by age: United States, 1996," in *Current Estimates from the National Health Interview Survey, 1996,* Centers for Disease Control and Prevention, National Center for Health Statistics, Hyattsville, MD, 1999

and eye problems that can result in blindness. Both forms of the disease require the daily, sometimes even hourly, monitoring of blood sugar and insulin levels and can often be controlled with diet and a weight reduction program. Currently, there are new methods for administering insulin, such as implants and pumps, and home blood sugar self-test kits are now easily available for diabetic patients. Oral medications have become widely used.

Prostate Problems

Prostate problems in men increase significantly after age 50. The prostate may become enlarged and block the urethra, the canal through which urine leaves the body, making urination difficult. This condition can often be relieved with surgery.

According to the Prostate Cancer Research Institute, prostate cancer strikes over 180,000 men each year, while 40,000 men die from the disease yearly. If found and treated early, cancer of the prostate is generally not life threatening, since it progresses very slowly and remains localized for a long time. Introduction of the PSA (prostatic specific antigen) blood test screening aids in diagnosing cancer of the prostate. Prostate cancer is the third most common cause of death from cancer in men and the most common cause of death from cancer in men 75 and older. The incidence is greatest among African American men over 60.

Urinary Problems

Urinary incontinence, the inability to control bladder function, is not a disease, but rather a symptom of other dysfunctions. According to the National Institute on Aging (NIA), at least 1 out of 10 people aged 65 or older suffers from incontinence. It is a condition that rages from mild leakage to uncontrollable and embarrassing wetting. The problem is more common in women than men.

Urinary problems often have a serious emotional impact. People with urinary problems are more likely to report their health as fair to poor and to report deterioration of their health. About three-fourths of those with urinary problems suffer some limitation of activity.

Incontinence is not a necessary consequence of aging. Specialists report that many people do not reveal their problems with incontinence because they are not aware that help is possible. The aggressive marketing of absorbent undergarments has had the effect of indicating to the elderly that their problem is a normal complication of aging, which discourages many people from seeking help. Treatments are available for treating urinary incontinence, including a new breakthrough medication for stress incontinence. Doctors estimate that 85 to 90 percent of sufferers could be successfully treated.

Malnutrition

Poor nutritional status is a primary concern for the elderly. Nutritionally inadequate diets can contribute to or exacerbate diseases, hasten the development of degenerative diseases associated with aging, and delay recovery from illness. Studies, however, seem to suggest that in general the elderly are more likely than younger persons to try to eat healthfully.

The CDC's *Surveillance for Five Health Risks among Older Adults—United States, 1993–1997* (1999) found that the percentage of those who reported eating fruits and vegetables at least five times per day increased with age. Of those 55 to 64, 26.4 percent ate fruits and vegetables at least five times daily, while 30.4 percent of persons 65 to 74 and 33.6 percent of those 75 or older ate fruits and vegetables at least five times a day. Women were slightly more likely than men to eat at least five portions of fruits

FIGURE 7.1

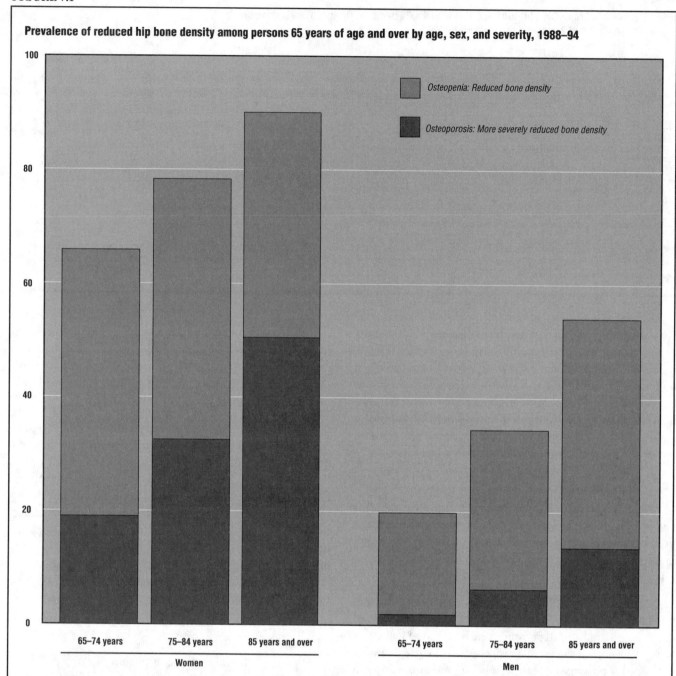

Prevalence of reduced hip bone density among persons 65 years of age and over by age, sex, and severity, 1988–94

Osteopenia: Reduced bone density

Osteoporosis: More severely reduced bone density

65–74 years   75–84 years   85 years and over

Women

65–74 years   75–84 years   85 years and over

Men

SOURCE: "Figure 14. Prevalence of reduced hip bone density among persons 65 years of age and over by age, sex, and severity: United States, 1988–94," in *Health, United States, 1999*, Centers for Disease Control and Prevention, National Center for Health Statistics, Hyattsville, MD, 1999

and vegetables, and whites more likely to do so than African Americans.

Nonetheless, even recent years' emphasis on good nutrition as a major factor contributing to good health, an estimated 30 to 60 percent of all elderly people maintain eating habits that provide them with less than the recommended daily level of nutrients and protein, and a quarter of the elderly suffer from some form of malnutrition. The bodies of those who are inactive become less capable of absorbing and using nutrients in the foods they do eat, and

certain medications increase the body's needs for particular nutrients. Studies show that the protein needs of older people are significantly higher than the daily protein intake recommended by federal agencies. Many hospital stays are for conditions preventable by proper eating. The American Dietetic Association believes that few doctors are trained to recognize malnutrition.

An individual's eating habits can be affected by many factors, including loneliness, depression, poverty, poor appetite, and lack of transportation. Meals provided by

TABLE 7.9

Nutrient intakes of women living alone as compared with women living with others

Nutrient	All ages	Age (years) 19–34	34–54	55–64	65–74	75+
Food energy	L	L	—	—	—	—
Carbohydrate	—	—	—	—	—	—
Protein	L	L	—	L	L	L
Fat	L	L	—	L	—	—
Saturated fat	L	L	L	—	—	—
Vitamin A	H	—	—	H	—	—
Carotenes	—	—	—	—	—	—
Vitamin C	—	—	—	—	—	—
Vitamin E	—	—	—	—	—	—
Thiamin	L	L	—	—	—	—
Riboflavin	—	L	—	—	—	—
Niacin	L	L	—	—	—	—
Vitamin B-6	—	L	—	—	—	—
Vitamin B-12	—	—	—	—	—	—
Folate	—	—	—	—	—	—
Phosphorus	L	L	—	—	—	—
Calcium	L	L	—	—	—	—
Magnesium	—	—	—	—	—	—
Iron	—	L	—	—	—	—
Zinc	L	L	—	L	—	—
Cholesterol	—	—	—	—	—	—
Fiber	—	—	—	—	—	—
Sodium	L	L	—	—	—	L

L = significantly lower; H = significantly higher. From weighted mean 3-day intakes; significant at p < .05. Blank cells indicate no statistically significant relation.

SOURCE: "How Does Living Alone Affect Dietary Quality?" in *Family Ecomonics and Nutrition Review*, vol. 8, no. 4, 1995

TABLE 7.10

Nutrient intakes of men living alone as compared with men living with others

Nutrient	All ages	Age (years) 19–34	34–54	55–64	65–74	75+
Food energy	L	—	—	—	—	—
Carbohydrate	—	—	—	—	—	—
Protein	L	—	—	—	—	L
Fat	L	—	—	—	—	—
Saturated fat	L	L	—	—	—	—
Vitamin A	—	—	—	—	—	—
Carotenes	—	—	—	—	L	—
Vitamin C	—	—	L	—	—	—
Vitamin E	—	—	L	—	L	—
Thiamin	—	L	—	—	—	—
Riboflavin	—	—	—	—	—	—
Niacin	—	—	—	—	—	—
Vitamin B-6	—	—	—	—	—	—
Vitamin B-12	—	L	—	—	—	—
Folate	—	—	—	—	—	—
Phosphorus	L	—	—	—	—	L
Calcium	L	—	L	—	—	L
Magnesium	—	—	—	—	—	—
Iron	—	—	—	—	—	—
Zinc	—	—	H	—	—	L
Cholesterol	—	—	—	—	—	—
Fiber	—	—	—	—	L	—
Sodium	L	—	L	L	—	—

L = significantly lower; H = significantly higher. From weighted mean 3-day intakes; significant at p < .05. Blank cells indicate no statistically significant relation.

SOURCE: "How Does Living Alone Affect Dietary Quality?" in *Family Ecomonics and Nutrition Review*, vol. 8, no. 4, 1995

---

community service organizations, whether they are dinners served at a senior center or home-delivered meals, are one of the most important services offered to the elderly. Experts on nutrition for the elderly, however, increasingly believe that traditional solutions to the problems of hunger and malnutrition, such as Meals on Wheels, may not recognize the whole problem. Chronic illnesses often depress appetites, and in addition, medications can suppress hunger and make older persons lose interest in food. In other words, even if one brings food to the elderly, they will not necessarily eat.

LIVING ALONE AFFECTS DIETARY QUALITY. Many elderly people, especially women, live alone. The U.S. Department of Agriculture reported in 1995 (the most recent statistics available) that the diets of adults living alone were significantly lower in nutrient intakes than the diets of multiperson households. Of those living alone, younger age groups were as likely, or more than likely, as those over 65 not to get adequate nutrients. Women older than 75 and men older than 65 who lived alone had less intake of some nutrients than those who lived with others. (See Table 7.9 and Table 7.10.)

Hearing Loss

There are many causes of hearing loss, the most common being age-related changes in the ear's mecha-

nism. Hearing loss is therefore a very common problem among the elderly. (See Figure 7.2.) In 1995 (the most recent data available) one-third of all people aged 70 and older and not living in institutions were hearing impaired—either deaf or with some trouble hearing in one or both ears. (According to the NCHS, complete deafness in both ears accounts for only about 20 percent of all hearing impairment in the elderly.) Just over one-quarter of people aged 70 to 74 are impaired. This increases to almost half for people aged 85 and over. Elderly men at all ages are more likely than elderly women to be hearing impaired, and white men and women are more likely to have hearing problems than African American men and women.

The NCHS reported that only about one-third of the elderly with hearing loss admitted having used a hearing aid in the last year. In 1995 only 76 percent of persons 70 to 74 with hearing impairments saw a doctor about their problem. In contrast, 98 percent of those with visual impairments saw a doctor about their problem.

People suffering from hearing loss may withdraw from social contact and are sometimes mislabeled as confused or even senile. They are often reluctant to admit to hearing problems, and sometimes hearing loss is so

FIGURE 7.2

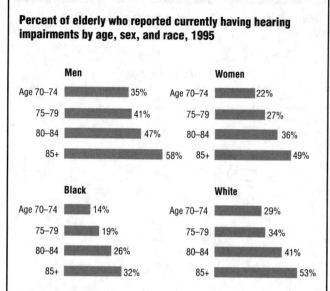

Percent of elderly who reported currently having hearing impairments by age, sex, and race, 1995

Men

Age 70–74	35%
75–79	41%
80–84	47%
85+	58%

Women

Age 70–74	22%
75–79	27%
80–84	36%
85+	49%

Black

Age 70–74	14%
75–79	19%
80–84	26%
85+	32%

White

Age 70–74	29%
75–79	34%
80–84	41%
85+	53%

SOURCE: Mayur Desai et al., "Percent of elderly who reported currently having hearing impairments by age, sex, and race, 1995," in "Trends in Vision and Hearing Among Older Americans," *Aging Trends,* no. 2, March, 2001

FIGURE 7.3

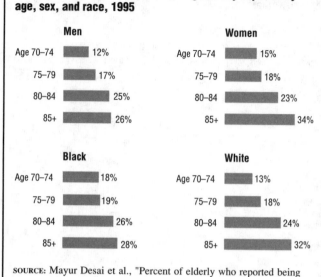

Percent of elderly who reported being visually impaired by age, sex, and race, 1995

Men

Age 70–74	12%
75–79	17%
80–84	25%
85+	26%

Women

Age 70–74	15%
75–79	18%
80–84	23%
85+	34%

Black

Age 70–74	18%
75–79	19%
80–84	26%
85+	28%

White

Age 70–74	13%
75–79	18%
80–84	24%
85+	32%

SOURCE: Mayur Desai et al., "Percent of elderly who reported being visually impaired by age, sex, and race, 1995," in "Trends in Vision and Hearing Among Older Americans," *Aging Trends,* no. 2, March, 2001

gradual that even the afflicted person may not be aware of it for some time.

Treatment is available for increasing numbers of patients, if they seek help, and their options are also increasing. Among the solutions now offered are high-tech hearing aids, amplifiers for doorbells and telephones, infrared amplifiers, and even companion dogs trained to respond to sounds for the owner.

Vision Changes

Almost no one escapes changes in vision as they grow older. By age 40, a person often notices a change in what may have been perfect vision. It becomes increasingly difficult to read small print or thread a needle at the usual distance. For many, night vision declines. This is often caused by a condition called presbyopia (tired eyes) and is a very common occurrence. People who were previously nearsighted may actually find some improvement in eyesight as they become slightly farsighted.

Figure 7.3 shows the percentage of elderly people who reported being visually impaired. Twelve percent of men and 15 percent of women aged 70 to 74 were visually impaired. This number reached 26 percent for men and 34 percent for women at age 85-plus. Rates were similar for whites and African Americans.

Prescription glasses are the norm among the elderly. The NCHS reported that 92 percent of people aged 70 and older wore glasses, and 18 percent also used a magnifying glass for close work and small print. Trouble seeing even

when wearing glasses increases with age from 14 percent among people aged 70 to 74 to 32 percent for those aged 85 and older. Fewer than 2 percent of people aged 70 and over used other equipment, such as telescopic lenses or braille, to help them compensate for loss of vision.

Eye Diseases

Much more serious than simple loss of visual clarity are cataracts, glaucoma, and problems affecting the retina, which frequently occur in elderly people.

CATARACTS. Cataracts occur when the crystalline structure of the eye lens breaks down. The lens becomes clouded, limiting the amount of light reaching the optic nerve and distorting images. Most cataracts develop slowly over time, but they can eventually cause almost total blindness. In recent years there has been a huge increase in lens replacement operations, in which the clouded lens is removed and a plastic lens is substituted. According to the National Eye Institute, over half of all Americans over age 65 have cataracts. They are more common in women than in men. Cataract surgery is one of the most common operations in the United States, with about 1.5 million surgeries performed each year.

GLAUCOMA. Glaucoma is the leading cause of blindness in the United States. Although glaucoma can affect people of any age, it is most common in people older than 60. Among the elderly, approximately 8 percent have glaucoma.

Glaucoma is caused by incomplete drainage of fluids out of the eyeball, causing pressure to build up inside the eyeball. It usually presents no early symptoms, but if undetected in its early stages, it can result in irreversible blindness. There is no cure for glaucoma and no way to restore lost vision. Routine glaucoma tests are especially important for older people. Medication (eye drops or pills) can generally manage the condition. At later stages, laser therapy and surgery are effective in preventing further damage.

PROBLEMS OF THE RETINA. The retina is a thin lining of nerves on the back of the eye. Over time, it can become torn or detached, jeopardizing vision. If treated in time by laser therapy, tears and separations can almost always be repaired. Senile macular degeneration is a condition in which the macula, a specialized part of the retina responsible for sharp central and reading vision, is damaged. Symptoms include blurred vision, a dark spot in the center of the vision field, and vertical line distortion. The NCHS reported that about half of people with macular degeneration are over age 70.

Diabetic retinopathy occurs when the small blood vessels that flourish in the retina do not perform properly. Blood vessels can leak fluid that distorts vision, and sometimes blood is released into the center of the eye, causing blindness. Diabetic retinopathy is a major cause of blindness, but is less common among the elderly than other types of visual impairment. The NCHS reported that about 25 percent of people with diabetic retinopathy are over age 70.

Vision and Hearing Impairments

The CDC reported that 8.6 percent of the elderly population suffer both hearing and vision impairment. Older adults who experience both hearing and sight loss are more likely to report difficulty walking, tending to their daily needs, and managing their medications. They also are more likely to fall and suffer fractures, and are less often able to socialize.

Parkinson's Disease

Once known as "the shaking palsy" but now named after the physician who first described it, Dr. James Parkinson, in 1817, Parkinson's disease (PD) is a disorder of the central nervous system resulting from a degeneration of nerve cells in the brain. Symptoms may occur at any age, although the first symptoms typically begin in the sixties and seventies. The primary symptoms include tremor, rigidity, impaired gait, and balance and speech problems. Such symptoms also increase the likelihood of falling. According to the National Parkinson's Foundation, 1 million Americans have Parkinson's. PD affects 1 in 100 people over age 60.

At present, the cause is unknown, although many researchers believe it may have both a genetic and an environmental component. A history of repeated head trauma has been found more common among PD sufferers than in the general population.

There is no cure for PD, and treatment is aimed at controlling symptoms. The most effective drug for treating the disease is levodopa (L-dopa), and many other medications are being investigated. Surgery is sometimes used in advanced cases, although it is not always successful.

Influenza

Influenza, more commonly known as the flu, is caused by viruses that infect the nose, throat, and lungs. It usually is a mild disease when contracted by healthy children, young adults, and middle-aged people. Flu, however, can be life threatening in older adults and in people of any age who have chronic illnesses such as diabetes or heart, lung, or kidney disease. Most people who get the flu recover completely in one to two weeks, but some people develop serious and possibly life-threatening complications. Older people and people with chronic illnesses run the greatest risk of getting secondary infections, especially pneumonia. According to the NIA, in an average year, flu leads to about 20,000 deaths nationwide (many of which are among the elderly), and many more hospitalizations.

According to NIA, studies have shown that getting a flu shot reduces hospitalization by about 70 percent and death by about 85 percent among older people who are not in nursing homes. Among nursing home residents, the flu shot reduces the risk of hospitalization by about 50 percent, the risk of pneumonia by about 60 percent, and the risk of death by 75 to 80 percent.

Pneumonia

There are two main kinds of pneumonia—viral pneumonia and bacterial pneumonia. Bacterial pneumonia, which includes pneumococcal pneumonia, is more serious. In older people, pneumococcal pneumonia is a common cause of hospitalization and death. According to the NIA, about 20 to 30 percent of people over age 65 who have pneumococcal pneumonia develop bacteremia (bacteria in the blood). At least 20 percent of those with bacteremia die from it, even if they receive antibiotics.

People aged 65 and older are at high risk. The NIA reported that they are two to three times more likely than people in general to get pneumococcal infections. A large study by the National Institutes of Health suggested that vaccination can prevent most cases of pneumococcal pneumonia. The U.S. Public Health Service, the National Coalition for Adult Immunization, and the American Lung Association now recommend that all people aged 65 and older get the pneumonia vaccine, which is covered by Medicare.

DISABILITY AMONG THE ELDERLY

As life expectancy has increased and the number of elderly has grown, some observers have predicted a nation burdened with people living longer who are crippled with disabilities and riddled with pain. Certainly, in some cases, that does occur. The predicted epidemic of pain and disability among the elderly, however, has not materialized to the extent some have feared. Instead, research shows that not only are Americans living longer, but also they are developing fewer chronic diseases and disabilities. America's elderly are defying the stereotype that aging is synonymous with increasing disability and dependence.

Dr. Ken Manton and other researchers at Duke University, in the *1999 National Long-Term Care Survey,* found that disability continued to decline in the 1994 to 1999 period, and that the decline was greater in the 1990s than in the 1980s. The decline in disability rates increased from 1982 to 1989 by .26 percent per year, from 1989 to 1994 by .38 percent per year, and from 1994 to 1999 by .56 percent per year. In addition, disability declined by a greater percentage for African Americans than for respondents in general over the 1989 to 1999 period.

Dr. Manton's study was published in the Proceedings of the National Academy of Sciences. Funded by the National Institute on Aging, it is the most recent round of surveys of a much larger project, the National Long-Term Care Survey, a study of 35,000–40,000 people over the age of 65. This survey, conducted in 1982, 1984, 1989, 1994, and 1999 (and next scheduled for 2004), was designed to track the health status, and changes in the health status, of the U.S. population over 65 both longitudinally (by tracking individuals) and cross-sectionally (by recruiting new samples of people who turned 65 between surveys). The records are linked to both detailed Medicare records and to the Centers for Medicare and Medicaid Services (CMS; formerly the Health Care Financing Administration) vital statistics records to determine exact dates of death.

The analysis also shows a decline in severe dementia of almost 50 percent over the 17-year period, falling from a prevalence of 5.25 percent among the elderly population in 1982 to 2.5 percent of that population in 1999. This represents a decline of almost 1 million cases from previous projections.

These findings have led researchers on aging to ask why it is that older Americans are less frail than before. One answer is that people are either not developing the diseases that cripple or disable them, or they are developing them later in life. Why? Some explanations include:

- The increasing educational levels of the elderly and the greater availability of medical knowledge to the public, in general. Education level has been associated with better health, and also greater wealth, which can enable a person to live a more healthful life and to get adequate health care.

- Better health habits, such as exercising more and eating a more healthful diet, which can improve not only the quality of a person's life but also his or her longevity.

- Improvements in public health (such as nutrition, water quality, and hygiene) that occurred when today's elderly were young.

- Medical advances, such as hip replacements, lens replacements for cataract sufferers, and better pain relievers, which can delay or prevent the burdens of chronic diseases that afflicted previous generations.

- Better management of stroke, heart disease, and vision and hearing deficits, which leads to a decrease in perceptions about the prevalence of dementia.

- A national trend away from nursing homes and toward other alternatives (such as home health care and assisted living facilities), which may be helping older people stay healthy and active longer.

- Treatments for other conditions, such as nonsteroidal anti-inflammatory drugs for arthritis, hormone replacement therapy, and increased use of vitamin E, may also have an effect on dementia.

ORGANIC MENTAL DISEASES OF THE ELDERLY—DEMENTIA

As with other disorders, mental impairments can occur in persons of any age, but certain types of illnesses are much more prevalent in the elderly. The differences between individuals vary dramatically. Some people may never show a decline in mental ability during their older years. Others may experience occasional forgetfulness. A few are robbed of their mental faculties before they reach 60.

Older people with mental impairments were once labeled "senile." Only in recent years have researchers found that physical disorders can cause progressive deterioration of mental and neurological functions. These disorders produce symptoms collectively known as "dementia." Symptoms of dementia include loss of language functions, inability to think abstractly, inability to care for oneself, personality change, emotional instability, and loss of a sense of time or place.

It is important to note that occasional forgetfulness and disorientation are not signs of dementia. True dementia is a disease and is not the inevitable result of growing older. Many disorders may cause or simulate dementia. Senile dementia refers to several impairing diseases and disorders, a small proportion of which are potentially reversible. The CDC reported, in *Surveillance for Morbidity and Mortality among Older Adults—United States, 1995–1996* (December 1999), that the prevalence of dementia increases tenfold from 2.8 percent among adults aged 65 to 74 years to 28 percent among those 85 and older.

Alzheimer's Disease

The most prevalent form of dementia is Alzheimer's disease (AD), named after German neurologist Alois Alzheimer, who in 1906 discovered the "neurofibrillary tangles" now associated with the disease. Alzheimer's is a degenerative disorder of the brain and nervous system; there is no known cause or cure.

Until recently, Alzheimer's was an obscure disease that received little study and still less publicity. Symptoms were generally attributed to aging and the victims diagnosed as senile. Today, Alzheimer's is the subject of intense research and is very much in the public consciousness. Unfortunately, many people have become familiar with the disease because a relative or loved one has been diagnosed with Alzheimer's.

According to the Alzheimer's Association (AA), 4 million Americans have Alzheimer's disease, which is equal to approximately the combined population of Wyoming, Idaho, and Utah. Currently, 1 out of every 10 people over the age of 65 and nearly half of those over 85 have the disease. According to the American Association for Geriatric Psychiatry (AAGP), half of all nursing home patients suffer from AD. If a cure or prevention is not found, more than 14 million of today's baby boomers will develop Alzheimer's disease by the middle of this century.

DEATH RATES. In 1999 the NCHS for the first time included "presenile dementia" in the Alzheimer's classification as a cause of death. The new accounting raised AD from the 12th cause of death to 8th. In 1999 there were 44,507 deaths from Alzheimer's disease.

SYMPTOMS. The diagnosis of Alzheimer's disease can be positively confirmed only after death. An autopsy of the brain of an Alzheimer's victim reveals abnormal tangles of nerve fibers (neurofibrillary tangles), tips of nerve fibers embedded in plaque, and a significant shortage of the enzymes that produce the neurotransmitter acetylcholine. Researchers are now looking for a diagnostic test for Alzheimer's in living subjects.

AD affects the part of the brain called the cerebral cortex, which controls thought, reasoning, memory, and language. It is caused by a loss of nerve cells in areas of the brain central to memory. According to the AAGP, researchers have found that individuals with Alzheimer's have disruptions in their nerve cells—cells stop functioning and lose connections with other nerve cells. Abnormal structures include neuritic plaques (dense deposits of protein) and neurofibrillary tangles. Eventually many areas of the brain are involved.

The symptoms usually begin between the ages of 55 and 80 with mild episodes of forgetfulness and disorientation. As the disease progresses, memory loss increases and mood changes are frequent, accompanied by confusion, irritability, restlessness, and speech impairment. Eventually, the victim may lose all control over his or her mental and bodily functions. Alzheimer's victims survive an average of 8 to 10 years after the first onset of symptoms; some live an additional 25 years.

SUSPECTED CAUSES. Despite intensified research, little is known about the cause (or causes) of Alzheimer's. One thing is certain—it is not a normal consequence of aging. It is, rather, a disease that either strikes older people almost exclusively, or more likely, its symptoms appear and become more pronounced as a person grows older.

There are several theories on the cause(s) of Alzheimer's. Some theories currently being pursued by researchers are:

- A breakdown in the system that produces acetylcholine

- A slow-acting virus that has already left the body before symptoms appear

- A genetic (hereditary) origin

Current research is focusing largely on heredity. Several studies have implicated two specific genes on the chromosomes of Alzheimer's patients. Other studies of twins suggest heredity plays a strong role in the development of the disease.

Research has confirmed a link between Alzheimer's and a high level of certain proteins in cerebrospinal fluid. The protein is not believed to cause the disease but may be a "marker" in diagnosing the disease. Other research suggests that it may be possible to use brain scans to detect mental deterioration years before symptoms become apparent, which would allow the possibility of earlier treatment.

TREATMENT. Major developments in the treatment of AD include the emergence of human gene therapy (to revitalize damaged brain cells) and enzyme-blocking therapy. Some researchers contend that the incidence of AD is lower among people who take anti-inflammatory medications for arthritis and among postmenopausal women who take estrogen as hormone-replacement therapy, although the exact explanation for the lower incidence is still unknown. Many doctors recommend vitamin E because that antioxidant seems to delay symptoms in people already known to have AD.

CARING FOR THE ALZHEIMER'S PATIENT. There are many victims of Alzheimer's besides the person with the disease. While medications such as tranquilizers may reduce some symptoms and occasionally slow the progression of the disease, eventually most Alzheimer's patients need constant care and supervision. Some nursing homes and health care facilities are not equipped to provide this kind of care, and, if they accept Alzheimer's patients at all, they will accept only those in the very earliest stages. A growing number of nursing homes are promoting their institutions as designed to care for Alzheimer's patients, but their cost may be beyond the means of many families, and many children of parents with Alzheimer's desire (or feel a moral obligation) to care for them at home as long as possible.

No matter how willing and devoted the caregiver, the time, patience, and resources required to provide care over a long time are immense, and the task can become overwhelming. Recent studies show that the stress of caring for an Alzheimer's patient can affect the caregiver's immune system, making him or her more vulnerable than normal to infectious diseases. Most observers believe that the public services that could benefit these patients are underused. Once again, the stigma of the illness may prevent people from seeking available help.

ALZHEIMER'S AND DESIGN OF LIVING SPACES. The major challenges to caregivers of Alzheimer's patients are generally the patient's memory loss, disorientation, and wandering. These crises are usually related to confusion states, not to acute medical need. Traditional nursing home care is not designed to deal with such disorientation and wandering; it is rather oriented to immediate physical nursing. Alzheimer's patients, at least in the early stages of the disease, do not require nursing care in the classical sense.

Experiments with Alzheimer's patients are being done with design and architecture. Some authorities suggest that home and institution design can reduce the confusion of these patients and keep them relaxed, safe, and independent as long as possible. The keeping of mementos and familiar objects from the patient's past, involvement in household chores, and rooms designed with toilets in sight are parts of the experiments being carried out. Alzheimer's is becoming an enormous public health and social problem with great social and financial costs. Continued research is vital to understanding the management of this disease.

THE GOVERNMENT'S ROLE. The prevalence of dementia (especially Alzheimer's disease), the profound emotional and financial burden of caring for its victims, and the predicted increase in the older population are putting pressure on the federal government to provide more assistance in caring for current victims and to increase funding for research to find the causes and a cure. Millions of dollars are currently being spent for Alzheimer's research. This figure is dwarfed by the estimated billions of dollars the disease costs in terms of care and the lost productivity of caregivers as well as patients. The CMS estimated that the annual formal and informal cost of caring for those with AD in the United States was $100 billion, with an average per person lifetime cost of $174,000. As the nation's population ages, federally funded health systems will likely be severely strained.

DRUG USE AMONG THE ELDERLY

A broader view of prescribing for seniors recognizes that problems occur from both the overprescribing and underprescribing of drug therapies.

— Paula Rochon, MD, and Jerry Gurwitz, MD, "Prescribing for Seniors: Neither Too Much Nor Too Little," *Journal of the American Medical Association* (July 14, 1999)

According to the Families USA Foundation, 34 percent of all prescriptions are dispensed to the elderly, and they account for 42 percent of all prescription drug expenditures. Many elderly take multiple medications, which greatly increases the risk for drug complications. According to the Kaiser Family Foundation's *Prescription Drug Trends: A Chartbook* (July 2000), the number of prescription medications the average person takes during the course of a year nearly triples between the ages of 45 and 75, from 4.3 to 11.4.

Unique Effect on Elderly

In the last decades of the twentieth century, the pharmaceutical (drug) industry revolutionized the treatment of disease. New medications are released into the market frequently, many for treatment of conditions common to the elderly. Unfortunately, little is known about the unique physiological response of the older body to many chemicals and medications. Most drugs are treated on younger people, not the elderly. As a person ages, the body often responds differently to chemicals than it did at a younger age. Medication taken in incorrect dosages, in combination with other drugs, or on complicated schedules can confuse an elderly person and may result in drug mismanagement. The outcome can be unintentional overdose, a drug reaction, unsuccessful treatment, or even death.

Misuse of Drugs

A major problem for the elderly in drug therapy involves the misuse of drugs. For example, doctors may sedate elderly patients when a nondrug therapy may be appropriate. A number of studies show that sleeping pills are not only overprescribed for many old people but are also abused—they are taken for too long and in alarmingly high doses. Another major medication problem for all age groups, including the elderly, is noncompliance, in which individuals do not take the medications that have been prescribed to treat their conditions or do not take the required dosage.

Prescription Drug Costs

A 2000 national survey by *The NewsHour with Jim Lehrer*, the Kaiser Family Foundation, and the Harvard School of Public Health found that 16 percent of elderly respondents said they had failed to fill a prescription because of the cost; about one in five (21 percent) said they had had to give up things to buy prescription drugs; and 9 percent said they had had to give up such basic necessities as food to pay for their medicines. In total, 23 percent of the elderly said that paying for prescription medicines they needed for themselves or their families was a "serious problem."

The survey also found that the majority of the public (55 percent) correctly recognized that the traditional Medicare program does not pay for prescription drugs for those 65 and over. By comparison, in 1998 far fewer (only 29 percent) were aware that Medicare did not pay for prescription drugs for people aged 65 and older. Over three-fourths (76 percent) of the public favored guaranteeing prescription drug coverage to everyone on Medicare, even if it means more government spending in order to pay for it.

GETTING—AND STAYING—HEALTHY

Because of increased educational efforts and general media coverage of health topics, both older and younger people are becoming more aware of personal habits and lifestyles that may contribute to poor health and accelerate the aging process, particularly over a long period. Many older people are making a conscious effort to change what may be lifelong bad habits, and to acquire new ones that can improve their physical and mental conditions.

Among the health practices useful in helping older people to improve and maintain health are keeping mentally and physically active, proper nutrition, proper use of drugs and alcohol, living in a safe environment, eliminating smoking, and participating in screening programs and tests.

Experts believe that the elderly take better care of themselves than younger people do. They are less likely to smoke, drink, or experience stress than younger people, and the elderly have better eating habits than their younger counterparts. They are, however, less likely to exercise. Increasing evidence suggests that behavior change, even late in life, is beneficial and can improve disease control and enhanced quality of life.

Weight

Obesity is defined as an excessively high amount of body fat or adipose tissue in relation to lean body mass. According to the results of the 2000 National Health Interview (from the NCHS), 22.1 percent of women and 18.8 percent of men aged 60 and over were obese. (See Figure 7.4.) Among the reasons people gain weight as they age are that they tend to exercise less, they may care less about their appearance, and their metabolism slows.

According to the NCHS, overweight and obese individuals are at increased risk for physical ailments such as high blood pressure, hypertension, high blood cholesterol, type II (noninsulin dependent) diabetes, coronary heart disease, congestive heart failure, stroke, and many other serious conditions.

Cholesterol

High blood cholesterol is a major risk factor for heart disease, the leading cause of death in the United States. Lowering cholesterol levels reduces the incidence of heart disease and death among persons with or without coronary heart disease. The NCHS reported in *Health, United States, 2001* (2001) that a smaller percentage of Ameri-

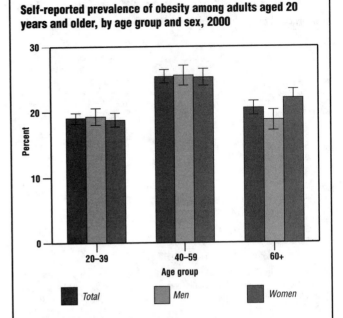

FIGURE 7.4

Self-reported prevalence of obesity among adults aged 20 years and older, by age group and sex, 2000

SOURCE: "Figure 6.2. Self-reported prevalence of obesity among adults aged 20 years and older, by age group and sex: United States, 2000," in *Early Release of Selected Estimates from the National Health Interview Survey: Data from Year 2000 and Early 2001,* Centers for Disease Control and Prevention, National Center for Health Statistics, Hyattsville, MD, October, 2001 [Online] http://www.cdc.gov/nchs/data/nhis/measure06.pdf [accessed October, 2001]

cans now have high levels of blood cholesterol than in previous years, and that average serum cholesterol levels have declined. (See Table 7.11.) In the years 1960–62, 38 percent of men aged 65 to 74 years had high cholesterol levels; in 1988–94, 21.9 percent of men that age had high levels. In 1960–62, 68.5 percent of women aged 65 to 74 years had high cholesterol levels, while in 1988–94, 41.3 percent of women of the same age did. In 1960–62 the mean cholesterol levels for men and women in the 65 to 74 age group were 230 mg/dl and 266 mg/dl, respectively. In 1988–94 the mean cholesterol levels for the same age group were 212 mg/dl for men and 233 mg/dl for women.

Smoking

Per capita tobacco consumption declined in the United States in the last decades of the twentieth century. In 1999 fewer people over 65 (10.5 percent of males and 10.7 percent for females) smoked than all other age groups. These percentages have dropped sharply for men, but increased slightly for women. In 1965, 28.5 percent of males over 65 were smokers, while only 9.6 percent of women 65 and older smoked.

According to the NIA, smoking brings an early death to more than 400,000 people in the United States each year. Lifelong smokers have a one in two chance of dying from a smoking-related disease. Smoking does not simply

TABLE 7.11

Serum cholesterol levels among persons 20 years of age and over, by sex and age, selected years 1960–94

[Data are based on physical examinations of a sample of the civilian noninstitutionalized population]

Sex and age	Percent of population with high serum cholesterol				Mean serum cholesterol level, mg/dL			
	1960–62	1971–74	1976–80	1988–94	1960–62	1971–74	1976–80	1988–94
Male								
20–34 years	15.1	12.4	11.9	8.2	198	194	192	186
35–44 years	33.9	31.8	27.9	19.4	227	221	217	206
45–54 years	39.2	37.5	36.9	26.6	231	229	227	216
55–64 years	41.6	36.2	36.8	28.0	233	229	229	216
65–74 years	38.0	34.7	31.7	21.9	230	226	221	212
75 years and over	- - -	- - -	- - -	20.4	- - -	- - -	- - -	205
Female								
20–34 years	12.4	10.9	9.8	7.3	194	191	189	184
35–44 years	23.1	19.3	20.7	12.3	214	207	207	195
45–54 years	46.9	38.7	40.5	26.7	237	232	232	217
55–64 years	70.1	53.1	52.9	40.9	262	245	249	235
65–74 years	68.5	57.7	51.6	41.3	266	250	246	233
75 years and over	- - -	- - -	- - -	38.2	- - -	- - -	- - -	229

- - - Data not available.

NOTES: High serum cholesterol is defined as greater than or equal to 240 mg/dL (6.20 mmol/L). Risk levels have been defined by the Second report of the National Cholesterol Education Program Expert Panel on Detection, Evaluation and Treatment of High Blood Cholesterol in Adults. National Heart, Lung, and Blood Institute, National Institutes of Health. September 1993.

SOURCE: Adapted from "Table 68. Serum cholesterol levels among persons 20 years of age and over, according to sex, age, race, and Hispanic origin: United States, 1960–62, 1971–74, 1976–80, and 1988–94," in *Health, United States, 2001,* Centers for Disease Control and Prevention, National Center for Health Statistics, Hyattsville, MD, 2001

cut a few months off the end of the smoker's life, but reduces the life of the average smoker by 12 years. Smoking makes millions of Americans sick by causing heart disease, cancer, and respiratory problems. Smokers are also more likely to get the flu (influenza), pneumonia, or other infections (such as colds) that can interfere with breathing, all of which are very dangerous for older people. Smoking can lead to osteoporosis, and can cause the onset of menopause in women smokers sooner than in the average woman.

A 1999 study by the Florida State University Center for Economic Forecasting and Analysis found that smokers entered nursing homes earlier and stayed longer than nonsmokers, while nonsmokers entered nursing homes at later ages and lived longer. Smokers aged 60 to 69 spent, on average, 240 days in nursing homes, compared with 110 days for nonsmokers that age. Among those 70 to 79, smokers spent 225 days in nursing homes, compared with 175 days for nonsmokers. Smokers aged 80 to 89 spent 200 days in a nursing home, compared to 180 days for nonsmokers in that age range. The researchers concluded that smokers became ill sooner.

Exercise

Regular physical activity comes closer to being a fountain of youth than anything modern medicine can offer. Exercise can lower one's risk of heart disease, some cancers, stroke, and diabetes. It can also moderate the effects of osteoporosis, arthritis, and depression, and can

improve sleep quality and memory. Despite the benefits, those over the age of 50 are much less likely than other age groups to exercise.

The CDC, in *Surveillance for Five Health Risks among Older Adults—United States, 1993–1997* (1999), found that physical inactivity increased with age. Thirty-three percent of the elderly aged 55 to 64, 35 percent of those 65 to 74, and 46 percent of those 75 or older reported no physical activity. The prevalence of physical inactivity was greater among African Americans than whites and higher among women than men. Most older people who do exercise engage in low-impact exercises such as walking and swimming.

Use of Preventive Health Services

Use of medical and dental preventive services contributes to the likelihood of healthy aging. The CDC, in *Surveillance for Selected Public Health Indicators Affecting Older Adults—United States* (1999), found that some older Americans underuse preventive procedures and measures.

Most adults—92 percent of those 55 to 64, 95 percent of those 65 to 74, and 96 percent of those 75 and older—reported having a regular source of medical care. Persons with a source of regular care were much more likely to receive basic medical services, such as routine checkups, which present the opportunity to receive preventive services. Men were slightly less likely to report a regular source of care than women. When asked if they had delayed medical care because of cost, few adults—8 percent of those 55 to 64, 4 percent of those 65 to 74, and 2.4 percent of those 75 and older—said that had been the case. The CDC concluded that, overall, cost was not a barrier to care for most older adults.

Nevertheless, considerable numbers of the elderly did not get preventive screenings in 1997 (the most recent statistics available). For breast cancer screenings, the median percentage of women who reported having a mammogram during the preceding two years was 77 percent among those 55 to 64, 75.4 percent among those 65 to 74, and 61.4 percent among those 75 and older. Almost 84 percent of women 55 to 64, 77.4 percent of women 65 to 74, and 58 percent of women 75 and older reported having a Pap test for cervical cancer during the preceding three years.

Screening for hypertension was high among adults 55 and older, at approximately 95 percent. Rates were lower, however, for blood cholesterol checks—from 85 to 90 percent. Among those aged 55 to 64, 25.8 percent had received a fecal occult blood test for colon cancer in the preceding two years, compared to 32 percent of those aged 65 to 74 and 27 percent of those aged 75 and older. Forty percent of Americans between 55 and 64 reported they had ever received a proctoscopy or sigmoidoscopy test for colon cancer. Forty-eight percent of those 65 to 74 and 46 percent of those 75 and older had had the test at some time.

Among those aged 55 to 64, 17 percent received a vaccination against pneumonia, compared to 43 percent of those 65 to 74 and 53.3 percent of those 75 and older. Somewhat larger percentages received influenza vaccinations—38 percent of those 55 to 64, 64 percent of those 65 to 74, and 72 percent of those 75 and older. When asked if they had visited a dentist in the preceding year, 67.5 percent of those aged 55 to 64, 63 percent of those 65 to 74, and 56 percent of those 75 and older said they had done so.

SEXUALITY IN AGING

In 1998 the National Council on the Aging, in *Healthy Sexuality and Vital Aging*, reported on a survey of 1,292 people aged 60 and older. Of the survey respondents, 48 percent said they were sexually active, meaning they had engaged in some type of sexual activity at least once a month in the past year. Among those with partners, 80 percent claimed to be active. Since older men are more likely than older women to have partners, men tended to remain more sexually active throughout their lives. Those women with partners, however, were nearly as active as men when in their sixties and seventies, and even more active in their eighties.

Older men were twice as likely as older women to want more sex—56 percent versus 25 percent. Only 18 percent reported sex was more physically satisfying than when they were in their forties. Of those with partners, 31 percent claimed the physical part of sex was better than it used to be. One in four older Americans said sex was more emotionally satisfying at their current age than when they were in their forties. Men (31 percent) were much more likely than women (17 percent) to report that the emotional benefits of sex were greater than they used to be. At the same time, older men were more likely than women to have partners.

Ninety percent of survey respondents of both sexes claimed an honest, moral character and pleasant personality were desirable in a romantic partner. More than 80 percent claimed to value humor, good physical health, and intelligence. Men, however, placed substantially more importance on sex than did women, at 78 percent and 50 percent, respectively. Men wanted partners who like to have sex. Women, on the other hand, valued financial security in a partner far more than men did (82 percent versus 55 percent).

In 1999 the AARP (formerly the American Association of Retired Persons) studied 1,384 adults aged 45 and older on relationships and sexual attitudes. Most men (67 percent) and women (57 percent) said a satisfying sexual relationship was important to the quality of their lives.

Among those with partners, large majorities (67 percent of men and 57 percent of women) described their partners as "my best friend." Men were slightly more likely than women to describe their partners as "physically attractive" (59 percent versus 53 percent), "exciting" (40 percent versus 33 percent), and "romantic" (39 percent versus 30 percent). The percentage who saw their partners as attractive did not decline with age, but actually increased. Among men, 59 percent of those 45 to 74 and 62 percent of those 75 and over said their partner was "physically attractive," while 52 percent of women 45 to 59 and 57 percent of those 75 and older found their partners to be attractive.

Sexuality seemed to be more important to men than women in the study. Among those aged 45 to 59, 71 percent of men and 44 percent of women agreed that sexual activity was important to their lives. Among those 75 and older, 35 percent of men and 13 percent of women agreed.

Sexual activity declined with age as health declined and people were more likely to have lost their partners. Among those with partners, 62 percent of men and 61 percent of women aged 45 to 59 reported engaging in sex once a week or more, as did 26 percent of men and 24 percent of women 75 and older. Approximately three-fourths of survey respondents reported engaging in sex at least once a month.

Although declining health affects sexual satisfaction and activity, many are not being treated for some ailments that could be affecting their sex lives. Fifty-one percent of those who reported no major illness or depression said they engaged in sex at least once a week, compared to only 30 percent of those with either major disease or depression. Thirty percent of men and 16 percent of women mentioned better health as something that would improve their sex lives, and about 20 percent cited the better health of their partner. Men also mentioned less stress (20 percent) and more free time (19 percent) as factors that would help. For women, less stress (20 percent) and finding a partner (15 percent) also made the list.

Twenty-six percent of men acknowledged being completely or moderately impotent. Only 41 percent of those said they had sought treatment from a medical professional. About 25 percent admitted to using drugs or treatments to enhance sexual performance, including 15 percent who said they had used Viagra.

The researchers found that only a small minority of those with sexual problems were availing themselves of treatments, and large numbers were not even getting treatment for common ailments that can affect sexual performance, such as arthritis. The study concluded, "We can only speculate about what combination of age stereotyping, sexual taboos, lack of access to health care and medications, or other factors, are preventing mid-life and older adults from seeking and/or receiving help."

Changes in Sexual Function

Changes occur in the sexual functioning of elderly men and women. According to an article by O. J. Thienhaus, published in *Geriatrics* (1988), normal changes in aging women include decreases in sex hormones and vaginal lubrication, less pleasure from orgasms, and decrease in arousal after orgasm. Normal changes in aging men include slower and less full erections and a longer break needed before further sexual stimulation is possible following orgasm.

Other factors can greatly affect sexuality in later life. They include but are not limited to excessive alcohol use, use of certain prescription drugs such as antihypertensive agents and psychoactive agents, chronic diseases, lack of a partner, depression, obesity, and surgeries such as mastec-

tomy, ostomy (colon operation), prostatectomy (removal of all or part of the prostate gland), and hysterectomy.

THE SLOW GROWTH OF GERIATRIC MEDICINE

The United States faces an acute shortage of doctors trained to treat older patients, or geriatricians. This shortage will reach serious proportions as the post–World War II baby boom generation reaches retirement age. Currently, the United States has only one-fifth the number of geriatricians needed.

While the demand for geriatrics data grows and specialists and medical students want training in that area, many medical schools have no staff qualified to train them. According to the American Geriatrics Society, there is an urgent need to increase the number of practicing geriatricians in the United States. Currently, there are fewer than 9,000 certified geriatricians, and this number is expected to decline dramatically in the next few years as practicing geriatricians retire at the same time the baby boom generation attains Medicare qualification. The United States will need 36,000 physicians with geriatrics training by 2030 to care for about 76 million older Americans.

Students entering medical school today can expect that at least half the patients they will see will be over 65. Only doctors who have completed fellowships in geriatrics are eligible for certification, which requires a one-year fellowship in geriatrics and passage of an examination by a certifying board. According to a 1996 Alliance for Aging report, only 3 percent of recent medical school graduates had taken elective courses in geriatrics. Only 14 of 128 medical schools require students to take courses in geriatrics, while 86 schools offer geriatrics as an elective course.

Experts believe physicians who are untrained in geriatrics make certain errors in treating the elderly. Common errors include prescribing inappropriately high doses of medications or failing to recognize symptoms of severe and acute conditions, which often present different symptoms in older persons. In addition, some physicians may not know new methods of treating conditions, or may write them off as inevitable diseases of old age when in actuality treatment is available.

CHAPTER 8
MENTAL HEALTH AND ALCOHOL ABUSE

As the nation ages, the physical and mental well-being of older Americans have become topics of increasing interest. Mental illness and alcohol abuse are two major areas of concern that are receiving increased attention from the medical profession.

MENTAL HEALTH

According to the American Association for Geriatric Psychiatry (AAGP), nearly 20 percent of people aged 55 years and older experience mental disorders that are not part of normal aging. The most common disorders, in order of prevalence, are anxiety, severe cognitive impairment, and mood disorders. The AAGP also pointed out that mental disorders in older adults are underreported.

Mental disorders in the elderly may be organic or functional. "Organic" describes a condition that involves detectable or observable changes in the body, while "functional" is used to indicate there is no evidence of an organic disorder. Organic factors may include cerebral arteriosclerosis, chemical imbalances, or tumors. Functional causes include emotional stress, depression, neuroses, or psychoses. Most functional disorders are curable, while an estimated 15 percent of organic disorders are not. Many conditions are manageable with therapy or medication.

The prevalence of major depression declines with age, while depressive symptoms increase. According to the AAGP, 8 to 20 percent of older adults in the community, and up to 37 percent in primary care settings, suffer from depressive symptoms. About 11.4 percent of adults aged 55 years and older meet criteria for an anxiety disorder every year. Phobic anxiety disorders are among the most common in late life, as opposed to panic disorders and obsessive-compulsive disorders. Prevalence of schizophrenia among those 65 years or older is reportedly around .6 percent, compared to 1.3 percent for the population aged 18 to 54 years.

Geriatric medicine, the study of the health problems of older people, is a relatively new field, and research is just beginning in this area. More information is needed on the normal mental ranges and capabilities of older people and the relationship between physiological changes and brain functions, as well as between physical illness and mental confusion. As the number of older people in the United States continues to increase, and especially as the population of baby boomers ages, the demand for geriatric research and resources for physical and mental health care will grow.

PERSPECTIVES OF A LIFETIME MAY CHANGE AS PEOPLE GROW OLDER

Few personal problems disappear with old age, and many become more acute. Marital problems, which may have been kept at bay because one or both of the spouses were away at work, can erupt when a couple spends more time together in retirement. A possible "identity crisis" and reduced income due to retirement can aggravate a tense situation and put a strain on both husband and wife, especially if one of them becomes ill.

Older age can be a period of regrets, of "if onlies" and "could have beens," which can lead to mutual recriminations. With life expectancy rising, married couples can now expect to spend many years together in retirement. Most elderly couples manage the transition, but some have problems.

Along with psychological adjustments to aging, the physical effects must also be confronted. If good health habits and necessary medical treatment have not been maintained in early life, a person's health may decline more rapidly, and disease may worsen the situation. Hearing loss is common, and close correlations have been found between loss of hearing and depression. Vision loss often occurs, which limits the ability to read, watch television, drive, and move. Loss of sight or hearing can cause perceptual disorientation, which in turn may lead to depression, paranoia, fear, and alienation.

A constant awareness of death can also become a problem during retirement years. Although most of the elderly in good health resolve their concerns with death, some acknowledge denial and fear. How well one accepts the inevitability of death can be a major factor in shaping one's aging years.

Satisfaction with Life in General

In 1998 Daniel Mroczek and Christian Kolarz of Fordham University surveyed 2,700 adults from age 25 to 74 about their life satisfaction. They found that the older the respondents, the more frequently they reported feeling positive emotions, such as cheerfulness, good spirits, and happiness. The age correlation existed even when the researchers took into account education, marital status, stress, personality, and economic status. The link was strongest for men, who showed both an increase in positive emotions and a decline in negative emotions (such as sad, nervous, hopeless, or worthless feelings). Older women also reported increased positive emotions with age, but no difference in negative emotions. The happiest subjects were not only older and male, but also married and extroverted.

The researchers theorized that the results could mean several things. It could mean that older Americans represent a generation less willing to reveal unhappiness or dissatisfaction. Or it could mean that people who survived the Great Depression of the 1930s and World War II (1939–45) are happy because they are aware that life could be much worse. It could also be, however, that happiness actually increases with age.

Older Americans Consider Themselves "Survivors"

Because many of today's elderly grew up during the adversity of the Great Depression, most of them do not consider themselves disadvantaged or unable to handle hardship. Instead, many older Americans consider themselves "survivors." This attitude is generally confirmed by studies of older Americans that show that only a small number believe they need counseling or consider loneliness to be a very serious problem. The psychological stress of retirement and physical decline may be of concern to some retirees, but not to most.

In fact, a person's fifties, not his or her sixties and seventies, are more likely to be reported as the years of confrontation with one's mortality and values. Bernice Neugarten, while a psychologist at the University of Chicago, reported that the physical and career shifts that occur when people are in their fifties cause many people to become introspective. By the time they enter their sixties and seventies, many have resolved these conflicts.

Attitudes about Work

The loss of work and the decline in social status that often accompanies the loss of employment are two of the major causes of stress during old age. In a work-oriented society, these losses can create feelings of uselessness and lack of self-worth. Such a sense of worthlessness, if not replaced with something meaningful to the individual, can lead to depression, lowered resistance to disease, and lack of motivation. For those living in poverty, these feelings are compounded by poor housing (often in dangerous surroundings), inadequate diets, and financial worries caused by fixed incomes, making the elderly poor more susceptible to mental problems.

DEPRESSION

Depression is a common disorder. Although many younger people are willing to admit to themselves that they are depressed and to seek treatment, most elderly, who were raised in an era when mental illness was stigmatized, are generally not. As their numbers and influence grow and as mental illness has become less stigmatized, older Americans and their families have become increasingly unwilling to accept mental health problems as inevitable results of aging. The National Institute of Mental Health estimated that 3 percent of Americans over 65 are clinically depressed, while 7 to 12 percent of the elderly suffer from milder forms of depression that impair their quality of life. Experts believe that the percentage of elderly who are depressed is higher than these statistics suggest because depression in the elderly often goes undetected by medical professionals.

A 1997 study (the most recent data available), *Screening for Depression in Elderly Primary Care Patients* (J. M. Lyness, and others), found that 9 percent of elderly patients tested had major depressive disorder and another 8 percent suffered minor depression. Neuropsychiatrist Dr. Martiece Carson, of the University of Oklahoma Health Sciences Center, estimated that in nursing homes the situation was far worse, with 20 to 40 percent of patients being very depressed. The AAGP suggests that more than 50 percent of nursing home residents are affected by depression.

Although many elderly persons are routinely treated by doctors for other conditions, many doctors fail to recognize that their elderly patients are depressed, either because the doctors do not ask or because the elderly do not divulge it.

Some people have a lifelong tendency toward depression that does not become obvious until later in life when the condition may be triggered by circumstances such as retirement, serious illness, or the loss of a loved one—all situations common to aging. Older people face many real-life problems that can compound a biological tendency to depression. While it is natural for a person to feel

FIGURE 8.1

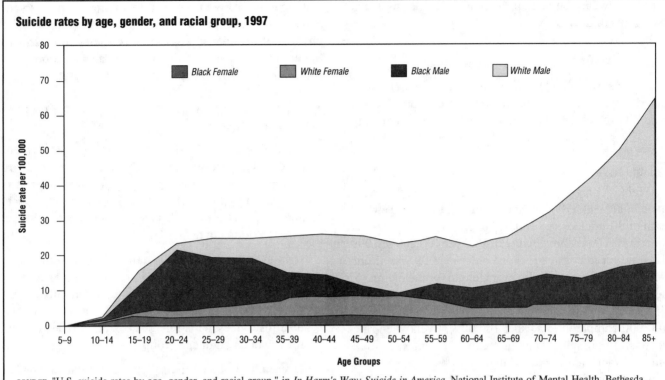

Suicide rates by age, gender, and racial group, 1997

SOURCE: "U.S. suicide rates by age, gender, and racial group," in *In Harm's Way: Suicide in America,* National Institute of Mental Health, Bethesda, MD, January 1, 2001 [Online] http://www.nimh.nih.gov/publicat/harmaway.cfm [accessed October, 2001]

depressed after a traumatic loss, when the depression lingers for months or years, it may be due to a physical or emotional disorder.

Often a physical illness itself can cause depression in the elderly by altering the chemicals in the brain. Among the illnesses that can touch off depression are diabetes, hypothyroidism, kidney or liver dysfunction, heart disease, and infections. In people with these ailments, treating the underlying disease usually eliminates the depression. Sometimes medications, including over-the-counter drugs prescribed for other conditions, precipitate depression.

According to the AAGP, depression affects approximately 25 percent of those with chronic illness and is particularly common in patients with ischemic heart disease, stroke, cancer, chronic lung disease, arthritis, Alzheimer's disease, and Parkinson's disease.

In some elderly people, depression causes them to willfully disregard medical needs, to take medications incorrectly, and to eat poorly. Experts believe these may be "covert" acts of suicide. In addition, depression interferes with the functioning of the immune system.

Treatment of Depression

According to the AAGP, depression is one of the most successfully treated illnesses. When properly diagnosed and treated, more than 80 percent of those suffering from depression recover and return to their normal lives. Only

half of older adults who acknowledge mental health problems, however, receive treatment from any health care provider, and only 3 percent of those receive specialty mental health services.

Treatment for depression begins with the mental health professional who evaluates patients to determine whether depression is a side effect of a preexisting medical condition, a medication, or another cause.

Common treatments for depression include psychotherapy, antidepressant medications, and electroconvulsive therapy (ECT). Psychotherapy can play an important role in the treatment of depression with or without medication. This type of treatment is used in cases of mild to moderate depression and is usually for a defined period (10 to 20 weeks).

Antidepressant medications work by increasing the level of neurotransmitters in the brain. Many feelings such as pain and pleasure are a result of the functioning of the neurotransmitters and when the supply of neurotransmitters is imbalanced, depression may result. ECT is used for life-threatening depression that does not respond to antidepressants. It is safe and effective for severe depression.

According to the AAGP, several studies have found that many older adults who commit suicide have visited a primary care physician very close to the time of the suicide: 20 percent on the same day and 40 percent within one week of the suicide. This fact demonstrates the need for primary care physicians to be alert for the signs and symptoms of depression.

TROUBLE WITH COPING—SUICIDE

The rate of suicide among older adults is higher than that of any other age group, including teenagers. The suicide rate for older white males is particularly alarming. (See Figure 8.1.)

Suicide Rates

Table 8.1 shows that the suicide rate for all age groups, including the elderly, has fluctuated since the 1950s with a high of 30 suicides per 100,000 people aged 65 years and older in 1950, as compared with 15.8 per 100,000 in 1999. The rate for males aged 85 and older in 1999 was almost three times higher than the average rate for the nation (55 per 100,000 compared to 10.6 per 100,000), and is 13 times the rate for females aged 85 and older (55 per 100,000 compared to 4.1 per 100,000). Even when rates dropped in all age groups in previous decades, suicides among older men remained high. By comparison, in the 1990s the rate for women aged 85-plus has been one of the lowest in the country. In 1999 it was the lowest rate of all adults over age 25, 4.1 suicides per 100,000 population.

The Centers for Disease Control and Prevention (CDC) reported in a 1999 study that approximately 20 percent of the 216,631 suicides that occurred in the United States from 1990 through 1996 involved persons 65 and older. Men accounted for 82 percent of suicides in that age group. By race, whites aged 65 and older killed themselves more frequently than African Americans or Hispanics.

Firearms were the most common method of suicide used by both men (77.3 percent) and women (34.4 percent) over age 65. Poisoning was the second most common method among men (12 percent) and women (29 percent). Suicides were highest among divorced/widowed men (76.4 per 100,000), at 2.7 times the rate of suicide by married men.

It is important to note that suicide rates for the elderly are not always reliable since many suicides are "passive." Persons who are sick, lonely, abandoned, or financially troubled have been known to starve themselves, not take medication, or mix medications dangerously. Also, the deaths counted as suicides are only those where suicide is named on the official death certificate, and suicides are often attributed to other causes on death certificates.

Risk Factors

Risk factors for suicide among the elderly differ from those of younger persons. The elderly at risk for suicide often have a higher incidence of alcohol abuse and depression, are socially isolated, and use suicide methods that are more likely to succeed. In addition, older persons make fewer attempts per completed suicide, have more physical illnesses and affective disorders, and, as mentioned above, have often visited a health care provider shortly before their suicide.

A LOOMING CRISIS IN MENTAL HEALTH CARE FOR THE AGING?

Mental health professionals are increasing their focus on the elderly. For example, in 1991 the American Board of Psychiatry and Neurology began certifying geriatric specialists in psychiatry. In 2001, 2,508 psychiatrists were certified as geriatric specialists. Many problems, however, remain. According to the AAGP:

- It is estimated that only half of older adults who acknowledge mental health problems receive treatment from any health care provider, and only a fraction of those (3 percent) receive specialty mental health services. This rate of utilization is lower than for any other adult age group.

- Over half of older persons who receive mental health care receive it from their primary care physicians.

- Older Americans account for only 7 percent of all inpatient mental health services, 6 percent of community-based mental health services, and 9 percent of private psychiatric care, despite comprising 13 percent of the population. Reasons cited for this underutilization include: stigma, denial of problems, access barriers, funding issues, lack of collaboration and coordination between mental health and aging networks, and shortages of appropriate health professionals.

Experts warn that an explosion in psychiatric problems among the elderly is imminent. They believe that by the time the baby boom generation reaches retirement in 2011, 15 million cases of substance abuse, late-onset schizophrenia, anxiety disorders, and depression will present themselves among the elderly. They predicted a 275 percent jump in psychiatrically ill elderly from 1970 to 2030, compared to a 67 percent increase in comparable cases among those 30 to 44 years of age.

Projections of a large increase in mental illness among the elderly follow recent studies showing a relatively high incidence of mental health disorders among those born during the post–World War II boom. Factors indicative of that generation include increasing willingness to seek treatment, less family support, and higher incidence of alcoholism and substance abuse. Historically, use of illicit substances among the elderly has been relatively rare. Nevertheless, the survivors of the drug culture spawned in the 1960s and 1970s are expected to show more use of recreational drugs and the problems associated with them.

TABLE 8.1

Death rates for suicide, by age and sex, selected years, 1950–1999

[Data are based on the National Vital Statistics System]

Sex and age	1950[1]	1960[1]	1970	1980	1985	1990	1995	1996	1997	1998	Preliminary 1999[2]
All persons					Deaths per 100,000 resident population						
All ages, age adjusted	13.2	12.5	13.1	12.2	12.5	12.5	12.0	11.7	11.4	11.3	10.6
All ages, crude	11.4	10.6	11.6	11.9	12.4	12.4	11.9	11.6	11.4	11.3	10.6
Under 1 year	...	...	...	...	...	...	...	...	...	...	...
1–4 years	...	...	...	...	...	...	...	...	...	...	...
5–14 years	0.2	0.3	0.3	0.4	0.8	0.8	0.9	0.8	0.8	0.8	0.6
15–24 years	4.5	5.2	8.8	12.3	12.8	13.2	13.3	12.0	11.4	11.1	10.3
25–44 years	11.6	12.2	15.4	15.6	15.0	15.2	15.3	15.0	14.8	14.6	13.9
25–34 years	9.1	10.0	14.1	16.0	15.3	15.2	15.4	14.5	14.3	13.8	13.4
35–44 years	14.3	14.2	16.9	15.4	14.6	15.3	15.2	15.5	15.3	15.4	14.3
45–64 years	23.5	22.0	20.6	15.9	16.3	15.3	14.1	14.4	14.2	14.1	13.4
45–54 years	20.9	20.7	20.0	15.9	15.7	14.8	14.6	14.9	14.7	14.8	14.1
55–64 years	26.8	23.7	21.4	15.9	16.8	16.0	13.3	13.7	13.5	13.1	12.3
65 years and over	30.0	24.5	20.8	17.6	20.4	20.5	18.1	17.3	16.8	16.9	15.8
65–74 years	29.6	23.0	20.8	16.9	18.7	17.9	15.8	15.0	14.4	14.1	13.5
75–84 years	31.1	27.9	21.2	19.1	23.9	24.9	20.7	20.0	19.3	19.7	18.2
85 years and over	28.8	26.0	19.0	19.2	19.4	22.2	21.6	20.2	20.8	21.0	19.2
Male											
All ages, age adjusted	21.2	20.0	19.8	19.9	21.1	21.5	20.6	20.0	19.4	19.2	18.1
All ages, crude	17.8	16.5	16.8	18.6	20.0	20.4	19.8	19.3	18.7	18.6	17.5
Under 1 year	...	...	...	...	...	...	...	...	...	...	...
1–4 years	...	...	...	...	...	...	...	...	...	...	...
5–14 years	0.3	0.4	0.5	0.6	1.2	1.1	1.3	1.1	1.2	1.2	1.0
15–24 years	6.5	8.2	13.5	20.2	21.0	22.0	22.5	20.0	18.9	18.5	17.1
25–44 years	17.2	17.9	20.9	24.0	23.7	24.4	24.9	24.3	23.8	23.5	22.3
25–34 years	13.4	14.7	19.8	25.0	24.7	24.8	25.6	24.0	23.6	22.9	22.2
35–44 years	21.3	21.0	22.1	22.5	22.3	23.9	24.1	24.6	23.9	24.0	22.4
45–64 years	37.1	34.4	30.0	23.7	25.3	24.3	22.5	23.0	22.5	22.4	21.2
45–54 years	32.0	31.6	27.9	22.9	23.6	23.2	22.8	23.3	22.5	23.1	21.9
55–64 years	43.6	38.1	32.7	24.5	27.1	25.7	22.0	22.7	22.4	21.3	20.1
65 years and over	52.8	44.0	38.4	35.0	40.9	41.6	36.3	35.2	33.9	34.1	32.1
65–74 years	50.5	39.6	36.0	30.4	33.9	32.2	28.7	27.7	26.4	26.2	25.0
75–84 years	58.3	52.5	42.8	42.3	53.1	56.1	44.8	43.4	40.9	42.0	38.3
85 years and over	58.3	57.4	42.4	50.6	56.2	65.9	63.1	59.9	60.3	57.8	55.0
Female											
All ages, age adjusted	5.6	5.6	7.4	5.7	5.2	4.8	4.4	4.3	4.4	4.3	4.0
All ages, crude	5.1	4.9	6.6	5.5	5.2	4.8	4.4	4.4	4.4	4.4	4.1
Under 1 year	...	...	...	...	...	...	...	...	...	...	...
1–4 years	...	...	...	...	...	...	...	...	...	...	...
5–14 years	0.1	0.1	0.2	0.2	0.4	0.4	0.4	0.4	0.4	0.4	0.3
15–24 years	2.6	2.2	4.2	4.3	4.3	3.9	3.7	3.6	3.5	3.3	3.1
25–44 years	6.2	6.6	10.2	7.7	6.5	6.2	5.8	5.8	6.0	6.0	5.6
25–34 years	4.9	5.5	8.6	7.1	5.9	5.6	5.2	5.0	5.0	4.9	4.7
35–44 years	7.5	7.7	11.9	8.5	7.1	6.8	6.5	6.6	6.8	6.9	6.3
45–64 years	9.9	10.2	12.0	8.9	8.0	7.1	6.1	6.4	6.5	6.4	6.0
45–54 years	9.9	10.2	12.6	9.4	8.3	6.9	6.7	7.0	7.3	7.0	6.6
55–64 years	9.9	10.2	11.4	8.4	7.8	7.3	5.3	5.5	5.4	5.5	5.2
65 years and over	9.4	8.4	8.1	6.1	6.6	6.4	5.5	4.8	4.9	4.7	4.3
65–74 years	10.1	8.4	9.0	6.5	6.9	6.7	5.4	4.8	4.7	4.3	4.2
75–84 years	8.1	8.9	7.0	5.5	6.7	6.3	5.5	5.0	5.2	4.9	4.7
85 years and over	8.2	6.0	5.9	5.5	4.7	5.4	5.5	4.4	4.9	5.8	4.1

. . . Category not applicable.

[1] Includes deaths of persons who were not residents of the 50 States and the District of Columbia.

[2] Starting with 1999 data, cause of death is coded according to ICD–10. Discontinuity between 1998 and 1999 due to ICD–10 coding and classification changes is measured by the comparability ratio. The comparability ratio of close to 1.00 denotes no net effect of ICD–10 on this cause.

NOTES: Age-adjusted rates for all years differ from those shown in previous editions of *Health, United States*. Age-adjusted rates are calculated using the year 2000 standard population starting with *Health, United States, 2001*. For data years shown, code numbers for cause of death are based on the then current revision of the *International Classification of Diseases* (ICD). Age groups were selected to minimize the presentation of unstable age-specific death rates based on small numbers of deaths and for consistency among comparison groups.

SOURCE: Adapted from "Table 47. Death Rates for Suicide, According to Sex, Race, Hispanic Origin, and Age: United States, Selected Years, 1950–1999," in *Health, United States, 2001*, Centers for Disease Control and Prevention, National Center for Health Statistics, Hyattsville, MD, 2001

FIGURE 8.2

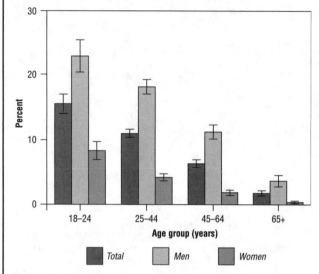

Percentage of adults aged 18 years and older with excessive alcohol consumption, by age group and sex, 2000

NOTE: Excessive alcohol drinkers were defined as those who had ≥12 drinks of any type of alcoholic beverage in their lifetime and consumed ≥ 5 drinks on one occasion at least 12 times during the past 12 months. The analysis excluded 898 adults with unknown alcohol consumption. Brackets indicate 95% confidence intervals.

Age and Sex	Percent	95% Confidence Interval
18-24 years		
Total	15.6	14.1-17.1
Men	23.0	20.5-25.5
Women	8.4	6.9-9.8
25-44 years		
Total	11.0	10.4-11.7
Men	18.3	17.1-19.4
Women	4.2	3.7-4.8
45-64 years		
Total	6.4	5.8-7.0
Men	11.3	10.2-12.4
Women	1.8	1.4-2.3
65 years and older		
Total	1.8	1.4-2.2
Men	3.7	2.8-4.6
Women	0.4	0.2-0.6

SOURCE: "Figure 9.2. Percentage of adults aged 18 years and older with excessive alcohol consumption, by age group and sex: United States, 2000," in *National Health Interview Survey: Data from Year 2000 and Early 2001,* U.S. Department of Health and Human Services, Centers for Disease Control, National Center for Health Statistics, Hyattsville, MD, September 20, 2001 [Online] http://www.cdc.gov/nchs/data/nhis/measure09.pdf [accessed October, 2001]

PROBLEM DRINKING AND ALCOHOLISM

According to the 2000 National Health Interview Survey, the elderly had the lowest rate of excessive alcohol consumption of all age groups. (See Figure 8.2.) Nevertheless, because the measures used for diagnosis for alcohol abuse were developed and validated on young and middle-aged adults, studying the rate of alcoholism among the older population is difficult. The National Institute on Alcohol Abuse and Alcoholism (NIAAA) reported that in contrast to most studies of the general population, surveys conducted in health care settings have found increasing prevalence of alcoholism among the older population. Studies indicated that 6 to 11 percent of elderly patients admitted to hospitals exhibited symptoms of alcoholism, as did 20 percent of elderly patients in psychiatric wards and 14 percent of elderly patients in emergency rooms. In acute-care hospitals, rates of alcohol-related admissions for the elderly were similar to those for heart attacks (myocardial infarction). Yet hospital staff are significantly less likely to recognize alcoholism in an older patient than in a younger patient.

The NIAAA also reported that the prevalence of problem drinking in nursing homes was as high as 49 percent in some studies, depending in part on survey methods. The high prevalence of problem drinking in these facilities may reflect a trend toward using nursing homes for short-term alcoholism rehabilitation stays. Late-onset alcohol problems also occur in some retirement communities, where drinking at social gatherings can be the norm.

Dr. Alison A. Moore, and others, in "Drinking Habits among Older Persons: Findings from the NHANESI Epidemiologic Followup Study (1982–84)" (*Journal of the American Geriatrics Society,* vol. 47, no. 4, April 1999), found that 60 percent of those 65 and older who took part in the National Health and Nutrition Examination Survey I regularly consumed alcohol at some point in their lives. Seventy-nine percent of those were still regular drinkers, one-fourth of whom drank daily. Sixteen percent of the men and 15 percent of the women were heavy drinkers (two or more drinks a day for men and more than one drink per day for women). Ten percent of those 65 and older could be classified as binge drinkers, who consume more than five drinks in one sitting.

Characteristics of Alcoholism among Older People

There are three types of older drinkers, distinguished by the lengths and the patterns of their drinking histories. The first group is made up of those over 60 who have been drinking most of their lives. This group has been termed "survivors" or "early onset problem drinkers." They have beaten the statistical odds by living to an old age despite heavy drinking. These are the persons most likely to show medical problems such as cirrhosis of the liver or brain damage and psychological problems such as depression.

The second group has histories of "bout" drinking between periods of relative sobriety. These are called "intermittents" because they may revert to heavy alcohol use under the stress and loneliness of aging.

The third group has been characterized as "reactors" or "late-onset problem drinkers." The stress of later years, particularly the loss of work or a spouse, may bring about heavy drinking. These people show few of the physical consequences of prolonged drinking and fewer disruptions of their lives. About two-thirds of those 65 and older who suffer from alcoholism have had long-standing alcohol addictions; in the remaining one-third, alcohol abuse develops late in life.

Health-Related Consequences of Alcoholism

Older people generally show a decreased tolerance to alcohol. Consumption of a given amount of alcohol by an elderly person will usually produce a higher blood-alcohol level than it would in a younger individual. Chronic medical problems such as cirrhosis may be present, but the need to detoxify (rid the body of poison) and to treat alcohol-withdrawal problems is less common. One possible explanation may be that those who have heavily abused alcohol do not survive into old age in great numbers.

Alcohol-induced organic brain syndrome (OBS) is characterized by confusion and disorientation. In elderly alcoholics it can be confused with or complicated by a diagnosis of "senility" (infirmity of body and mind associated with old age).

Since elderly people take more medication than other age groups, they are more susceptible to drug/alcohol interactions. Alcohol can reduce the effectiveness and safety of many medications and sometimes result in coma or death. Adverse consequences of alcohol consumption in older people are not restricted to problem drinkers.

Older individuals with medical problems, including diabetes, heart disease, liver disease, and central nervous system degeneration, often do not tolerate alcohol well.

COMPLICATIONS IN DIAGNOSIS AND TREATMENT. Diagnosis of problem drinking among the aging population is complicated by the fact that many psychological, behavioral, and physical symptoms of problem drinking also occur in people who do not have drinking problems. For example, brain damage, heart disease, and gastrointestinal disorders often develop in older adults independent of alcohol use, but may also occur with drinking. In addition, mood disorders, depression, and changes in employment, economic, or marital status often accompany aging but can also be symptoms of alcoholism. A resulting failure to identify the signs of drinking in an older person may aggravate health, relationships, and legal problems associated with alcohol abuse.

Older problem drinkers make up a relatively small proportion of the total number of clients seen by most agencies for treatment of alcohol abuse. Chances for recovery among older drinkers are considered good because older clients tend to complete their therapy more often than younger clients. Problem drinkers with a severe physical disorder or persistent OBS are often placed in nursing homes, although staff members generally have limited experience and training in treating alcoholics.

CHAPTER 9
CARING FOR THE ELDERLY—CAREGIVERS

Societies generally recognize a moral obligation to care for their elderly and needy. The family has historically often included several generations living in close contact with each other and with other members of the community who could share these responsibilities and burdens. Family members were the mainstay of the nation's elder care system.

In America today, family units are much smaller, and family members may live great distances from each other. Communities are often made up of commuters and families with two working parents who may lack the time or desire to care for the elderly. Nonetheless, elder care still usually falls to the family, and more specifically, to the wife, daughter, or daughter-in-law.

For the first time in history, a married couple may spend more years caring for a parent than for a child. Many of those providing elder care will also be rearing children. With the 65-and-older population projected to increase 15 percent by 2010, their offspring, the baby boom generation, can expect to become the most "sandwiched" in history.

The supply of caregivers is not keeping pace with the growth in the older population. The number of elderly persons for every 100 adults of working age (from 18 to 64) is called the old-age dependency ratio. According to the U.S. Census Bureau in 1990, there were 20 elderly persons for every 100 working-aged adults. When the youngest baby boomers approach retirement age in 2025, there will be 32 elderly persons for every 100 people of working age.

DISABILITY AND DEPENDENCY RATES

Rates of disability among the aged are declining, but the likelihood of being disabled is still higher for older age groups. (See Table 7.6 in Chapter 7.) In 1999 almost half (46.3 percent) of the elderly had functional disabilities that affected activities such as lifting 10 pounds or climbing a flight of stairs; 12.8 percent had trouble performing such activities of daily living as bathing and dressing; 19.7 percent had difficulty with instrumental activities of daily living such as getting around outside the home and paying bills; and 17.7 percent reported using an assistive device such as a wheelchair, crutches, a cane, or a walker.

DIFFERING PERCEPTIONS ABOUT CARE

In 1998 ICR Research, Inc., a research organization, and the AARP (formerly the American Association of Retired Persons) surveyed people aged 65 and older who had adult children aged 35 or older. The survey, still the most recent available, assessed how older parents defined independent living, the extent to which different generations have communicated about living independently, and the types of assistance received or needed. The data produced companion studies, *Independent Living: Do Older Parents and Adult Children See It the Same Way?* and *Independent Living: Adult Children's Perceptions of Their Parents' Needs,* from the two different perspectives.

The survey found, in general, a picture of healthy older parents who were able to take care of themselves. It found that adult children do not begin to be concerned about their parents' ability to live independently until their parents begin to experience problems that affect this capacity. Other findings include:

- Adult children and older parents agreed about the meaning of independent living. About half the time, the definitions focused on being able to take care of oneself.

- Adult children and older parents disagreed about the assistance adult children had provided older parents with a problem in the past five years. Older parents were more than twice as likely (36 percent) as the younger generation (16 percent) to say their adult child(ren) did not provide them with any help when they had a problem. Adult children were more likely

TABLE 9.1

Caregiver characteristics, 1997

Age	
18–34 years	22%
35–49 years	39%
50–64 years	26%
>65 years	12%
Gender	
Female	73%
Male	27%
Marital Status	
Married or living with partner	66%
Single, never married	13%
Separated or divorced	13%
Widowed	8%
Employment	
Full-time	52%
Part-time	12%
Retired	16%
Not employed	20%

SOURCE: Sheel M. Pandya and Barbara Coleman, "Figure 1. Caregiver characteristics, 1997" in *Caregiving and Long-Term Care,* American Association of Retired Persons, Washington, DC, December, 2000 [Online] http://research.aarp.org/health/fs82_caregiving.html [accessed October, 2001] © 2002, AARP. Reprinted with permission.

FIGURE 9.1

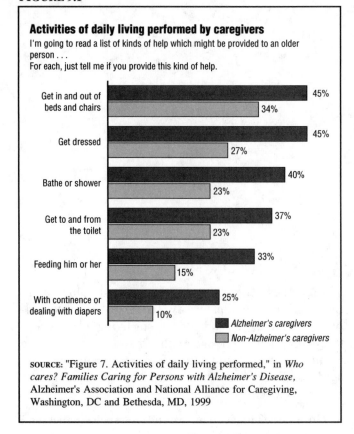

Activities of daily living performed by caregivers

I'm going to read a list of kinds of help which might be provided to an older person . . .
For each, just tell me if you provide this kind of help.

SOURCE: "Figure 7. Activities of daily living performed," in *Who cares? Families Caring for Persons with Alzheimer's Disease,* Alzheimer's Association and National Alliance for Caregiving, Washington, DC and Bethesda, MD, 1999

than older parents to identify specific types of help they provided, such as being there, housekeeping, or money.

- Older parents were generally less concerned than adult children about their own ability to live independently. Older parents (60 percent) were more likely than adult children (41 percent) to say they (the older parents) did not currently receive help from any source to live independently. Older parents (67 percent) were also more likely than adult children (51 percent) to say they (the older parents) did not currently need help to live independently.

- Adult children (52 percent) were more likely to consider giving older parents information regarding assistance to live independently than older parents (34 percent) were to consider asking adult children for such information.

- Most younger respondents (68 percent) said they had not talked with their parents about what it would take for them to live independently, and 71 percent of respondents said their parents had not experienced a problem in the past five years that affected their ability to live independently.

A 1997 study done by Princeton Survey Research Associates, a group funded by Pew Charitable Trusts, surveyed adults with at least one living parent and then surveyed those older parents. The survey, the most recent available on the topic, found that many adults also depend on their older parents. Among adult children aged 65 and older, 4 percent of them said they were more dependent on their parents, 57 percent reported their parents were

more dependent on them, and 29 percent claimed they were equally as dependent on their older parents as their parents were on them. Among those aged 55 to 64, 13 percent said they depended on their older parents, while 50 percent said their parents depended on them more. Thirty-five percent said they were as dependent on their parents as their parents were on them.

PROFILE OF AMERICA'S CAREGIVERS

Families are the backbone of the long-term care system.

— The National Alliance for Caregiving and the Alzheimer's Association, *Who Cares? Families Caring for Persons with Alzheimer's Disease,* 1999

In 1999 the National Alliance for Caregiving and the Alzheimer's Association (NAC/AA) released *Who Cares? Families Caring for Persons with Alzheimer's Disease,* their study on caregiving in the United States in general, and the special requirements for caregivers of persons with Alzheimer's disease. The report found that families generally take personal responsibility for the needs of family members with disabilities, and they do it willingly, but often at great personal cost. Caregivers of Alzheimer's patients contend with special hardships.

Most Caregivers Are Women

The NAC/AA survey found that in 1997 (the most recent statistics available), 22.4 million U.S. households—

FIGURE 9.2

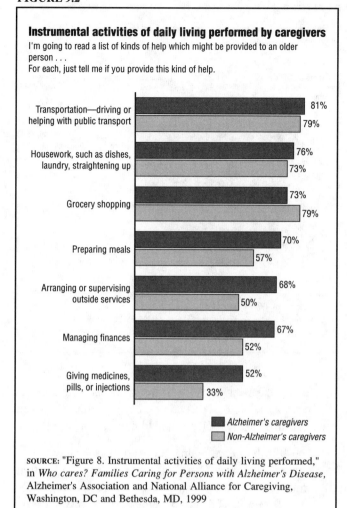

Instrumental activities of daily living performed by caregivers

I'm going to read a list of kinds of help which might be provided to an older person . . .
For each, just tell me if you provide this kind of help.

Transportation—driving or helping with public transport: 81% / 79%

Housework, such as dishes, laundry, straightening up: 76% / 73%

Grocery shopping: 73% / 79%

Preparing meals: 70% / 57%

Arranging or supervising outside services: 68% / 50%

Managing finances: 67% / 52%

Giving medicines, pills, or injections: 52% / 33%

■ Alzheimer's caregivers
□ Non-Alzheimer's caregivers

SOURCE: "Figure 8. Instrumental activities of daily living performed," in *Who cares? Families Caring for Persons with Alzheimer's Disease,* Alzheimer's Association and National Alliance for Caregiving, Washington, DC and Bethesda, MD, 1999

FIGURE 9.3

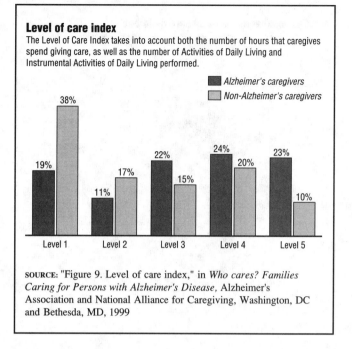

Level of care index

The Level of Care Index takes into account both the number of hours that caregives spend giving care, as well as the number of Activities of Daily Living and Instrumental Activities of Daily Living performed.

■ Alzheimer's caregivers
□ Non-Alzheimer's caregivers

Level 1: 19% / 38%
Level 2: 11% / 17%
Level 3: 22% / 15%
Level 4: 24% / 20%
Level 5: 23% / 10%

SOURCE: "Figure 9. Level of care index," in *Who cares? Families Caring for Persons with Alzheimer's Disease,* Alzheimer's Association and National Alliance for Caregiving, Washington, DC and Bethesda, MD, 1999

nearly one in four—had been involved in family caregiving for individuals 50 years old or older, at some point during the previous 12 months.

The typical caregiver is a married woman in her mid-forties (an average of age 46) who works full-time, is a high school graduate, and has an annual household income of $35,000. Seventy-three percent of caregivers, and 79 percent of the constant (or 40 hours per week) caregivers, are female. (Table 9.1 shows the characteristics of caregivers.) Among Asian Americans, however, almost equal percentages of men and women are caregivers. Asian American caregivers were more highly educated than other racial/ethnic groups.

Women who gave care spent more time than men in caregiving activities—18.8 hours per week for women versus 15.5 hours for men. Asian Americans spent significantly less time weekly than other minority groups in providing care—15.1 hours per week for Asian Americans, 20.6 hours for African Americans, 19.8 hours for Hispanics, and 17.5 hours for whites. Thirty-eight percent of caregivers had been caregivers for 5 years or more; 35

percent, 1 to 4 years; 24 percent, up to 1 year; and the remainder had provided care episodically. Forty percent of caregivers were caring for children under age 18 at the same time they were caring for elderly relatives or friends.

Kinds of Care

The NAC/AA study found that family caregivers provided anything from less than one hour of care per week to "constant care." The average caregiver provided care for 18 hours per week. Alzheimer's patients generally need more hours of care.

Alzheimer's patients required more help with activities of daily living (see Figure 9.1) and instrumental activities of daily living (see Figure 9.2) than other care recipients. Consequently, Alzheimer's patients received more hours of assistance from their caregivers with such activities in the course of each day. These caregivers performed more of the most demanding level of care than caregivers of non-Alzheimer's patients, while caregivers of non-Alzheimer's patients performed more of the least demanding level of care. (See Figure 9.3.) (Level refers to demand and intensity of care. It ranges from level 1 to level 5, with 5 being the highest and most demanding. Level 5 caregivers provided more than 40 hours per week, or "constant care.")

Many caregivers help their patients by giving medicines. Caregivers of Alzheimer's patients reported that 51 percent of their patients had trouble taking medications as directed, compared to only 15 percent of non-Alzheimer's patients. (See Figure 9.4.) Virtually all the caregivers claimed they knew how to give the medications as prescribed and what each medicine was for. Slightly fewer

FIGURE 9.4

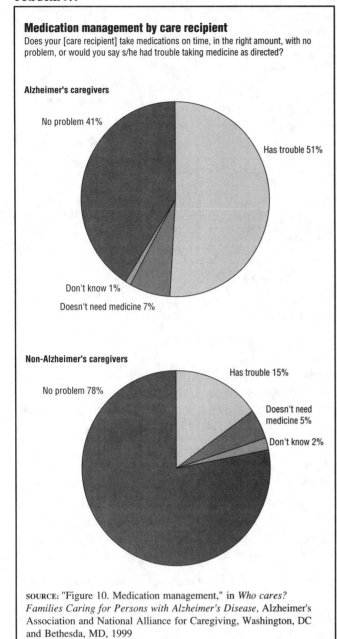

Medication management by care recipient

Does your [care recipient] take medications on time, in the right amount, with no problem, or would you say s/he had trouble taking medicine as directed?

Alzheimer's caregivers

No problem 41%

Has trouble 51%

Don't know 1%

Doesn't need medicine 7%

Non-Alzheimer's caregivers

Has trouble 15%

No problem 78%

Doesn't need medicine 5%

Don't know 2%

SOURCE: "Figure 10. Medication management," in *Who cares? Families Caring for Persons with Alzheimer's Disease,* Alzheimer's Association and National Alliance for Caregiving, Washington, DC and Bethesda, MD, 1999

FIGURE 9.5

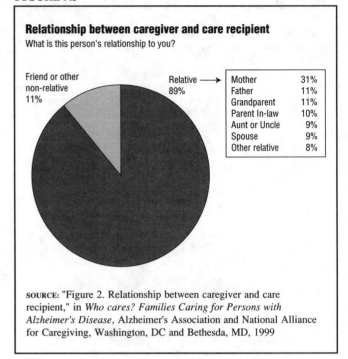

Relationship between caregiver and care recipient

What is this person's relationship to you?

Friend or other non-relative 11%

Relative 89%

Mother	31%
Father	11%
Grandparent	11%
Parent In-law	10%
Aunt or Uncle	9%
Spouse	9%
Other relative	8%

SOURCE: "Figure 2. Relationship between caregiver and care recipient," in *Who cares? Families Caring for Persons with Alzheimer's Disease,* Alzheimer's Association and National Alliance for Caregiving, Washington, DC and Bethesda, MD, 1999

heart disease, cancer, stroke, arthritis, diabetes, lung disease, blindness or vision loss, mental or emotional illness, broken bones, neurological problems, and high blood pressure.

One-fourth of care recipients lived in the same household as their caregiver. Over half (54 percent) lived within 20 minutes of the caregiver's home; 11 percent lived within 20 to 60 minutes' drive; 5 percent, one to two hours away; and 5 percent, more than two hours away. Asian American care recipients were more likely than whites to live with their caregivers.

Competing Demands

Taking care of an elderly person changes the lives of many caregivers. The NAC/AA study found that 60 percent of Alzheimer's caregivers and 65 percent of non-Alzheimer's caregivers worked full or part time. Half of them reported making adjustments to their work schedule (rearranging their work schedules, taking time off without pay, working part time, or quitting their jobs) for caregiving responsibilities. Fifty-seven percent of Alzheimer's caregivers and 47 percent of non-Alzheimer's caregivers went to work late or took time off. Ten percent of Alzheimer's caregivers and 6 percent of non-Alzheimer's caregivers said they gave up work entirely, and 7 percent of Alzheimer's caregivers and 3 percent of non-Alzheimer's caregivers took early retirement. Thirteen percent of Alzheimer's caregivers and 6 percent of non-Alzheimer's caregivers took a less demanding job. (See Figure 9.6.) Although working men also reported these conflicts, fewer men than women rearranged their work lives to accommodate caregiving.

knew the potential side effects of those medications and how they might interact with other medications.

Recipients of Care

Who Cares? also found that 89 percent of caregivers took care of a relative, and 11 percent cared for a friend or neighbor. Thirty-one percent of caregivers took care of their own mothers; 11 percent, their fathers; 11 percent, grandparents; 10 percent, parents-in-law; 9 percent, aunts or uncles; 9 percent, spouses; and 8 percent, other relatives. (See Figure 9.5.) The average age of care recipients was 77 years.

Among those recipients of care who did not have Alzheimer's disease, the main illnesses included dementia,

FIGURE 9.6

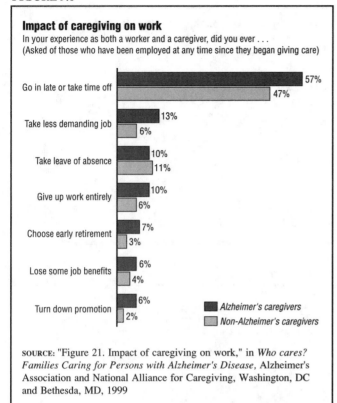

Impact of caregiving on work
In your experience as both a worker and a caregiver, did you ever . . .
(Asked of those who have been employed at any time since they began giving care)

SOURCE: "Figure 21. Impact of caregiving on work," in *Who cares? Families Caring for Persons with Alzheimer's Disease,* Alzheimer's Association and National Alliance for Caregiving, Washington, DC and Bethesda, MD, 1999

FIGURE 9.7

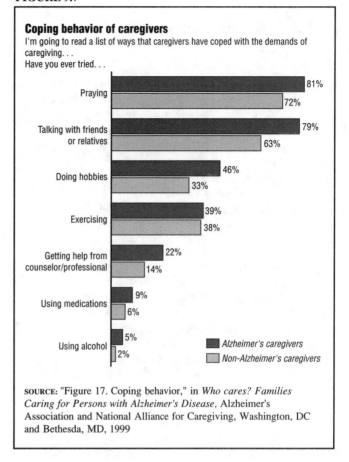

Coping behavior of caregivers
I'm going to read a list of ways that caregivers have coped with the demands of caregiving. . .
Have you ever tried. . .

SOURCE: "Figure 17. Coping behavior," in *Who cares? Families Caring for Persons with Alzheimer's Disease,* Alzheimer's Association and National Alliance for Caregiving, Washington, DC and Bethesda, MD, 1999

Caregivers Need Care Too

For many people, caring for an ill or disabled elderly person can, over time, become an enormous burden. Elder caretakers may neglect their own health and other needs because no one else is available to care for their elderly spouse or parent.

The NAC/AA survey reported that in 1997, 56 percent of Alzheimer's caregivers and 40 percent of non-Alzheimer's caregivers said their caregiving duties caused them to give up time with other family members; 53 percent of Alzheimer's caregivers and 40 percent of non-Alzheimer's caregivers gave up vacations, hobbies, or other activities. Twenty-three percent of Alzheimer's caregivers and 12 percent of non-Alzheimer's caregivers reported experiencing physical or mental health problems due to caregiving. Forty-three percent of Alzheimer's caregivers and 20 percent of non-Alzheimer's caregivers reported "much stress."

The number-one mechanism to cope with stress, mentioned by four out of five survey respondents, was prayer. Talking with friends and relatives, pursuing hobbies, and exercising were also indicated. Some mentioned receiving help from professionals or other counselors or using medications or alcohol. (See Figure 9.7.)

THE CAREGIVER HEALTH EFFECTS STUDY. In 1999 the American Medical Association, in "Caregiving as a Risk Factor for Mortality" (*Journal of the American Medical Association,* vol. 282, no. 23, December 15, 1999), published the results of a study performed by Dr. Richard Schulz and Dr. Scott R. Beach. The study, still the most recent data on the topic, found that after four years of following caregivers aged 66 to 96 (51 percent were women, and 49 percent were men), 103 caregivers had died. After adjusting for socioeconomic factors, existing medical conditions, and subclinical cardiovascular disease, participants who were caregivers and who were experiencing stress (56 percent) had mortality risks 63 percent higher than the noncaregiving control group. Participants who were caregivers but not experiencing strain, as well as those who had disabled spouses but were not providing care for them, did not have elevated mortality rates relative to the noncaregiving control group.

Researchers found that strained caregivers experienced more depression and anxiety and a reduced level of health. They also were less likely to get adequate rest, to have time to rest when they were sick, or to have time to exercise.

The leading difficulty reported by caregivers was seeing the deterioration of their loved one. One in five caregivers mentioned the demands on their time and being unable to do what they wanted; 12 percent said a major problem was the recipient's attitude (uncooperative, demanding).

FIGURE 9.8

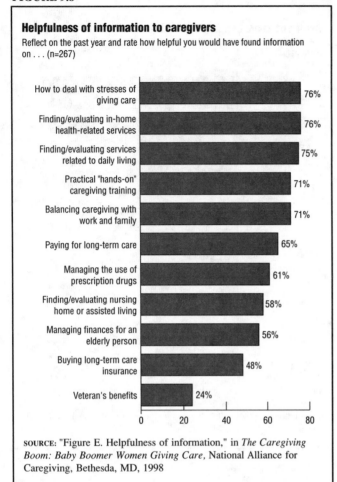

Helpfulness of information to caregivers
Reflect on the past year and rate how helpful you would have found information on . . . (n=267)

SOURCE: "Figure E. Helpfulness of information," in *The Caregiving Boom: Baby Boomer Women Giving Care,* National Alliance for Caregiving, Bethesda, MD, 1998

TABLE 9.2

Influence of caregiving on thinking about the future
How has your thinking about your future been influenced by your caregiving experience? (n=267)

Most Frequent Topics of Thought:

Savings needed	21%
Adequacy of insurance	12
The need to plan	11
Desire not to be a burden to others	7
Taking care of physical health-nutrition and exercise	6
Who might take care of me	5
The future	5

SOURCE: "Table 3. Influence of caregiving on thinking about future," in *The Caregiving Boom: Baby Boomer Women Giving Care,* National Alliance for Caregiving, Bethesda, MD, 1998

FIGURE 9.9

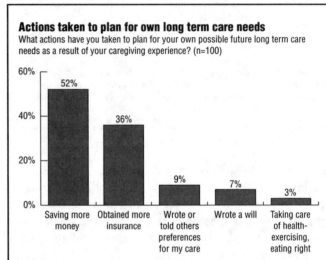

Actions taken to plan for own long term care needs
What actions have you taken to plan for your own possible future long term care needs as a result of your caregiving experience? (n=100)

SOURCE: "Figure J. Actions taken to plan for own long term care needs," in *The Caregiving Boom: Baby Boomer Women Giving Care,* National Alliance for Caregiving, Bethesda, MD, 1998

When asked what were the greatest rewards of caregiving, caregivers cited knowing their recipient was well cared for, the satisfaction of doing a good deed, and the recipient's appreciation. Also mentioned were watching the recipient's health improve, family loyalty, "giving back," fulfilling family obligations, and spending time together.

When asked to describe their caregiving experience in one word, 57 percent chose positive words, such as "rewarding," "thankful," "loving," and "OK." Just over one-third used negative words—"stressful," "burdened," "exhausting"—to describe their caregiving. (Eight percent said they did not know how they felt about caregiving.)

Experts agree that even a small break from the responsibilities of elder care can be of enormous benefit to a caregiver, and many believe that it can prevent older people from being placed in nursing homes prematurely. Recent attention to the special needs of caretakers has resulted in a variety of formal and informal programs designed to provide some relief. While these programs generally provide services to the dependent elderly, their purpose is primarily to assist the caregiver. With hospitals discharging patients sooner and more unwell than in previous years, the role of caregiver has taken on added importance.

THE NEED FOR TRAINING. In 1998, the most recent survey on the topic, the National Alliance for Caregiving, with funding from the Equitable Foundation, in *The Caregiving Boom: Baby Boomer Women Giving Care,* found that women caregivers felt the need for information on a variety of topics. Approximately three-fourths of caregivers reported they would have found it helpful to know how to deal with the stresses of giving care and with finding in-home services to assist with daily living. Seventy-one percent felt they needed "hands-on" training and training in balancing home and work chores with caregiving. Also helpful would have been information on paying for long-term care, the use of prescription drugs, finding assisted living or nursing homes, managing finances, buying insurance, and veteran's benefits. (See Figure 9.8.)

THINKING ABOUT THE FUTURE. *The Caregiving Boom* found that caregiving experiences caused women to

FIGURE 9.10

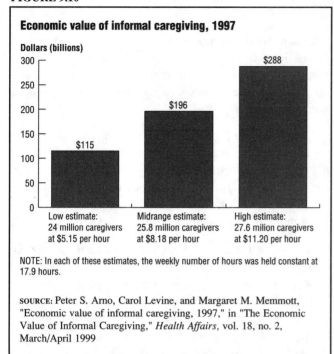

Economic value of informal caregiving, 1997

NOTE: In each of these estimates, the weekly number of hours was held constant at 17.9 hours.

SOURCE: Peter S. Arno, Carol Levine, and Margaret M. Memmott, "Economic value of informal caregiving, 1997," in "The Economic Value of Informal Caregiving," *Health Affairs,* vol. 18, no. 2, March/April 1999

FIGURE 9.11

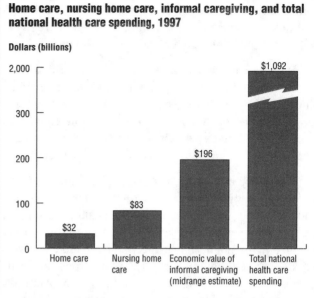

Home care, nursing home care, informal caregiving, and total national health care spending, 1997

SOURCE: Peter S. Arno, Carol Levine, and Margaret M. Memmott, "Home care, nursing home care, informal caregiving, and total national health care spending, 1997," in "The Economic Value of Informal Caregiving," *Health Affairs,* vol. 18, no. 2, March/April 1999

think differently about their own lives. As a result of caring for others, 21 percent said they thought more about the savings needed for their own elder care. Some said they worried about the adequacy of insurance (12 percent), the need to plan (11 percent), and the possibility of being a burden to others (7 percent). Others became more conscious of their own physical health (6 percent), who would take care of them (5 percent), and the future (5 percent). (See Table 9.2.) As a result, many took action to improve their own future, such as saving more money, obtaining more insurance, making sure others knew their preferences for their own care, writing a will, and taking better care of their physical health. (See Figure 9.9.)

THE FINANCIAL COST TO CAREGIVERS. One of America's great assets is the number of family members who provide care for ill or disabled relatives. The millions of informal caregivers save the formal health care system billions of dollars annually. There is a vast discrepancy between government funding allocated to family caregivers and that going to institutions. Of the billions of dollars spent in the field, only a fraction is targeted toward family support services. Most goes to large public and private institutions and group homes.

In a 1997 study that provides the most recent estimates available, *Family Caregiving in the United States: Findings from a National Survey,* conducted by the National Alliance for Caregivers and the National Center for Women and Aging for Metropolitan Life Insurance Company, caregivers reported that taking care of an elderly relative or friend had cut into their earnings. The financial effect was estimated at an average of $659,139 in lost

wages, Social Security, and pension benefits over their lifetimes.

The Caregiving Boom found that 49 percent of women reported that they had suffered a great deal of financial hardship as a result of their caregiver responsibilities.

In 1999 Peter Arno, Carol Levine, and Margaret Memmott, in the "Economic Value of Informal Caregiving" (*Health Affairs,* vol. 18, no. 2, March/April 1999), studied the market value of the care provided by unpaid family and friends to ill and disabled adults. They estimated that the national economic value of caregiving was $196 billion in 1997. Figure 9.10 shows this figure, and the mid-range estimates used to calculate it—25.8 million caregivers in 1997, an average of 17.9 hours of care per caregiver per week, and a "wage" of $8.18 per hour. The $196 billion figure equals approximately 18 percent of the total national health care spending of $1,092 billion. (See Figure 9.11; note that the graphic is not to scale.) Also, that amount does not include the direct costs families pay in unreimbursed health care expenses and loss of income and other benefits (such as Social Security) when a caregiver gives up a job or reduces work hours.

RESPITE CARE. Families caring for elderly relatives may know they need a break, but they may not be aware of the concept of respite care or how to arrange for it. The dictionary definition of respite is "an interval of temporary relief or rest, as from pain, work, duty, etc." The Foundation of Long Term Care (FLTC) has formulated a working definition of geriatric respite care as "the temporary supportive care of an elder who normally lives in the community with a caregiver, by a substitute caregiver, in order to strengthen and maintain the regular caregiver's well-being and ability to maintain care at home."

Respite care takes many forms. In some cases, the respite worker comes to the home to take care of the elderly person so that the caregiver can take a few hours for personal needs, relaxation, or rest. Respite care is also available for longer periods so that caregivers can recuperate from their own illnesses or even take a vacation.

Adult day-care programs around the country provide structured daytime programs through which functionally impaired adults can receive the social, health, and supportive services needed to restore or maintain optimal functioning. While not designed specifically to aid caregivers, adult day-care programs serve a similar purpose as formal respite programs by temporarily giving the caregiver physical and psychological relief from the burden of elder care.

FROM INFORMAL TO FORMAL SERVICES

At the same time that the elderly population is increasing, the segment of the general public available to provide unpaid care, generally made up of family members, is decreasing. The once familiar extended family has become less common in the United States. In addition, several other trends continue to decrease the availability of caregivers, including more women employed outside the home, greater geographical separation of families, higher divorce rates, and smaller families. Fewer caregivers will be available for the increasing number of elderly needing support. As a result, the elderly will likely have to pay for a higher proportion of professional services.

Extensive Care

FOSTER CARE. Although many elderly do not need intensive nursing home care, some of those who need limited assistance are increasingly being cared for in foster homes. It is an alternative that gives an older person safe and comfortable care at approximately one-third the cost of nursing home care.

Foster care for adults is like foster care for children: a person or family is paid to take in other people and provide them a home, including meals, laundry, a place to sleep, and someone to talk to and watch over them. In some programs, the residents pay for the care with their own money, although often a government or nonprofit agency brings the family and the participant together. Some elderly pay for their care with their Social Security or pension income, and some with Supplemental Security Income (SSI). In some cases, states have received Medicaid waivers that allow them to spend federal long-term nursing funds for community-based care programs such

as adult foster homes. Licensing regulations vary from state to state.

There are no overall figures on how many older people are living in foster homes since no single agency monitors the dozens of programs nationwide. Experts estimate that tens of thousands are in foster care, and they see those numbers increasing.

The benefits of foster care, in addition to cost savings, are considerable. Residents report enjoying family life and personal relationships with their foster care families, they tend to focus less on their infirmities and be more independent, and their families are happy not to have to admit them to nursing homes.

CLUSTER CARE. Cluster care is another alternative form of personal care for those elderly who do not need full-time, trained nursing care. Begun as an experiment in New York State in the mid-1980s, cluster care consists of a team of workers employed by one home attendant agency; the team is responsible for the care of a group of clients who live in close proximity. With the supervision of a nurse and a case manager, the clients' schedules are set by evaluating which activities of daily living they need help with and how long it takes to perform those tasks. One worker (a "shared aide") can coordinate visits to several clients in a day. Said one family member, "Cluster care approximates the kind of care we are used to giving those we love in extended families."

Experts predict the program will become increasingly popular across the country as states strapped for money face a population growing older and in greater need of care. Some elderly and disabled, however, cannot be served by such a program, either because they are so frail they need constant monitoring during their waking (and often sleeping) hours, or because they live far from other personal-care clients.

THE ON LOK/PACE PROGRAM. One comprehensive-care program for frail elderly people that is winning support across the country is based on a San Francisco model. The On Lok center in San Francisco's Chinatown weaves medical care, home care, social services, and case management into a single web of care. Founded 20 years ago, the On Lok center derives its name from the Chinese words for "peaceful" and "happy."

"It's not for everyone," said Don Sherwood, who tracked the On Lok program for the Office of Research and Demonstration at the Health Care Financing Administration, the federal agency that manages Medicare and Medicaid (now known as the Centers for Medicare and Medicaid Services). "Only 5 percent of those over 65 are frail enough to be eligible, and many don't want to change doctors and go to a day health center. But for those who want comprehensive care, it's very good."

Clients sign over their Medicaid and Medicare policies. In return, they receive housing and total care, as long as they use the program's doctors and nurses. Central to the On Lok model is the day health center, a vastly expanded version of the social day programs that proliferated in the 1970s. In addition to recreational activities, the centers have added health services with on-site geriatricians, rehabilitation therapists, nurse-practitioners, and other health professionals. When needed, clients are hospitalized. They may also receive, if necessary, intravenous antibiotic or hydration therapy at the center.

Most participants like the program because they are guaranteed health care, including hospitalization or nursing home care, until they die or leave the program. Despite the support services, which are more extensive than would be generally supplied under Medicaid, the program is less expensive than nursing home care. Because the participants' health is constantly monitored, their use of hospitals is so sharply reduced that On Lok facilities cost less than regular care under Medicaid or Medicare, despite all the extra services that the On Lok model provides.

The On Lok model is the basis for a burgeoning program called PACE, the Program of All- Inclusive Care for the Elderly. PACE is almost exactly like the On Lok program. When the Balanced Budget Act of 1997 (PL 105-33) was passed, PACE became a key provider under Medicare and a voluntary state option under Medicaid. At the time the Balanced Budget Act was enacted, there were 15 PACE demonstration programs up and running successfully. Forty were opened in the first year after passage, and about 20 have opened every year thereafter.

Partial Assistance

HELP IN FINDING HELP. The increasing complexity of American society and the growing needs of the aged who have no one to assist them have led to the emergence of two new types of service professions, private care managers and claims companies. These services provide, for a fee, what family members may once have provided. Private care (or case) managers are social workers who provide one-on-one assistance in arranging care, housing, or referral to government agencies that serve the elderly. Care managers oversee home-health staffing needs, monitor the quality of in-home services and equipment, and act as liaison with families living far away. Private care managers can be expensive ($50 to $150 per hour), but they may well be worth the cost. Medical claims companies assist the aged in filling out complicated insurance forms, in exchange for a fee or a percentage of the benefits received.

HELP MANAGING FINANCIAL AFFAIRS. An estimated 500,000 U.S. elderly people need help with financial affairs. In response, new daily money management (DMM) programs have emerged, which provide help to the elderly in paying bills, filling out medical insurance forms, balancing checkbooks, making bank deposits, preparing tax returns, and budgeting. Some managers can even sign checks. The AARP offers free DMM services to low-income families through community agencies. There is, unfortunately, ample opportunity for abuse in this system. Because some elderly may be confused or forgetful, it is easy for them to be taken advantage of.

In 1986 the National Association of Professional Geriatric Care Managers was started in Tucson, Arizona, with 30 members. Today, 1,200 of the nation's estimated 4,000 care managers belong to the organization. Many care managers are now advocating certification.

LEGAL HELP—ELDER LAW. The legal profession has seen the emergence of a new specialty, elder law, which covers the issues that often affect the senior population. The field of elder law includes a wide and growing range of topics. In addition to traditional work in probate, wills, and trust and estate planning, elder law specialists are now involved in such diverse areas as:

- Planning for disability or incapacity through living wills and durable power of attorney

- Establishing eligibility for Social Security, Medicare, and Medicaid benefits

- Long-term care, including patient rights, quality of care, and long-term care insurance

- Elder fraud and abuse

- Grandparents' visitation rights

- Age discrimination at work

- Housing problems (mortgages, housing discrimination)

- Conservatorships and guardianships

- Retirement and pension benefits

CORPORATE INVOLVEMENT

Many corporations are exploring elder care issues. Companies with a high average employee age or more female workers are more likely to have a higher number of caregivers and, hence, more work time lost to elder care tasks. Tardiness and increased use of the telephone frequently occur among some caregivers. These work disruptions can affect the morale of other employees, who may feel they must work harder to compensate for coworkers who assume the duties of caregivers. Employees distracted on the job are more likely to make mistakes and have higher accident rates, as well as increased conflict with fellow employees.

Caregiving problems can also remain hidden from the employer because employees may "cover up" their activities when late or absent. Caregivers may work fewer hours, change schedules, and take time off without pay, which leads to increased hiring and training by the employer. Until recently, however, the additional labor losses attributable to caregiving had not been quantified.

The MetLife Study of Employer Costs for Working Caregivers

Employers, as well as employees, bear a financial burden from personal caregiving. In response to the growing evidence that caregiving for older family members is exacting a cost on U.S. business, the National Alliance for Caregiving and Metropolitan Life Insurance Company (MetLife) conducted a 1997 study, *Family Caregiving in the United States: Findings from a National Survey,* to collect data on the cost of caregiving. The study is the most recent analysis available on the topic. It included only full-time employees and those caregivers who provided the top three (of five) levels of care. These caregivers provided assistance with at least two activities of daily living, or ADLs (bathing, toileting, feeding, transferring, or walking), and at least four instrumental activities of daily living, or IADLs (financial management, transportation, help with medications, shopping, preparing meals, etc.). They provided between 9 and 56 hours of care each week.

According to the study, 23.2 percent (or 22.4 million) of all households were involved in caregiving. The majority of caregivers (64.2 percent) were employed, most (52 percent) full time. Based on these findings, 14.4 million employed caregivers were balancing work with their caregiving roles.

REPLACING EMPLOYEES WHO QUIT. The MetLife study found that over 17 percent of caregivers said they had to quit their jobs or take early retirement because of caregiving tasks. These people provided care an average of four years. Table 9.3 shows the replacement costs, a total of almost $5 billion, for employees who quit.

ABSENTEEISM. The MetLife study found that 10.5 percent of employed caregivers had been absent a minimum of three or more days in the previous six months due to caregiving chores. The total cost to employers was almost $400 million. (See Table 9.4.) Most employed caregivers (59 percent) arrived late for work, left early, took extended lunch breaks, or in some other way altered their work schedule. These caregivers lost an estimated one hour per week that could not be made up, for a total cost to employers of $488 million. (See Table 9.5.)

INTERRUPTIONS AT WORK. Many caregivers interrupted their workdays with phone calls to the care recipient or service providers or with other caregiving chores. These breaks in work were estimated at one hour per week, with a total cost to employers of $3.7 billion. (See Table 9.6.) Sixty percent of caregivers reported experienc-

ing an elder care crisis that caused additional phone calls, loss of concentration, and partial absenteeism (an average loss of three days per year), with a total cost of more than $1 billion. (See Table 9.7.)

SUPERVISING CAREGIVERS. In the MetLife study, 81 percent of employed caregivers said their supervisors were sympathetic regarding their caregiving burdens. Nevertheless, the cost to employers from supervisors providing emotional support, arranging coverage to allow caregivers to be absent, counseling about benefits, and dealing with work disruptions was estimated to be one hour per month and $805 million. (See Table 9.8.)

TOTAL COST TO BUSINESS. The MetLife study estimated that the total cost of caregiving in lost productivity to U.S. business was nearly $11.5 billion per year. (See Table 9.9.) This is a conservative figure, based as it is on median wages and not inclusive of those giving Level I and Level II care or those working part-time. If those caregivers were also included in the calculations, the study concluded that the total costs to U.S. business would exceed $29 billion per year.

PHYSICAL AND MENTAL COSTS TO CAREGIVER. Working caregivers are subject to more frequent headaches, weight loss or gain, and anxiety or depression, and are slightly more likely to be under a physician's care. Caregivers are one-third more likely to report their health as "poor." In the MetLife study, 20 percent of caregivers reported being under a doctor's care, compared to 16 percent of employees who were not caregivers. (It should be noted that caregivers to the elderly may be older than many other workers and perhaps under care for reasons not associated with their caregiving status.) Twenty-two percent of caregivers (compared to 8 percent of noncaregivers) reported anxiety and depression.

Unless the workplace offers some kind of support for the caregiver through assistance programs or other benefits, the employee may not seek help until physical symptoms occur. Thus, health care benefits may end up becoming the major source of corporate support available to most caregivers—a very expensive program for such a purpose.

Caregivers often use their "sick days" or vacation days for caregiving responsibilities. The rigors of caregiving often place these employees in need of time for their own recuperation or recreation, but they may have already used it up for caregiving.

"Trailing Parents"

Just when corporations were getting used to the "trailing spouse," the employee's wife or husband whose career puts obstacles in the way of business moves, a new problem has appeared. The graying of America is creating "trailing parents," who pose even greater relocation

TABLE 9.3

Replacement costs for employees who quit

Full-Time Employed Caregivers by Gender (Levels III, IV, and V)	Number who quit in a given year (4.2%)	Median Weekly Wage	Cost to Employers (75% of annual wage)
Men	59,642	$701	$1,630,553,866
Women	180,981	$468	$3,303,262,439
Total	240,623		$4,933,816,305

SOURCE: "Replacement costs for employees who quit," in *The MetLife Study of Employer Costs for Working Caregivers,* Metropolitan Life Insurance Company, Westport, CT, 1997

TABLE 9.5

Costs due to partial absenteeism

Full-Time Employed Caregivers by Gender (Levels III, IV, and V)	Number experiencing partial absenteeism (59%)	Number unable to make up 50 hours/year (22%)	Median Weekly Wage	Cost to Employers
Men	837,082	184,166	$701	$161,375,558
Women	2,540,085	558,843	$468	$326,923,158
Total	3,377,168	743,009		$488,298,715

SOURCE: "Costs due to partial absenteeism," in *The MetLife Study of Employer Costs for Working Caregivers,* Metropolitan Life Insurance Company, Westport, CT, 1997

TABLE 9.7

Costs due to eldercare crises

Full-Time Employed Caregivers by Gender (Levels III, IV, and V)	Number affected by crises (60%)	Days lost due to crises (3 per year)	Median Weekly Wage	Cost to Employers
Men	852,029	2,556,088	$701	$358,363,487
Women	2,585,441	7,756,322	$468	$725,991,745
Total	3,437,470	10,312,410		$1,084,355,232

SOURCE: "Costs Due to Eldercare Crises," in *The MetLife Study of Employer Costs for Working Caregivers,* Metropolitan Life Insurance Company, Westport, CT, 1997

problems for employees and corporations in an economy that has always depended on a high degree of mobility.

Nobody knows the exact extent of the problem, but already an estimated 20 percent of the workforce is responsible for an aging relative, and that figure will rise. Companies are beginning to deal with the implications of trailing parents. A few, like Apple Computer, have sometimes agreed to foot the bill to relocate elderly relatives rather than settle for a second choice in important personnel appointments.

TABLE 9.4

Costs due to absenteeism

Full-Time Employed Caregivers by Gender (Levels III, IV, and V)	Number absent average 6 days per year (10.5%)	Median Weekly Wage	Cost to Employers
Men	156,205	$701	$131,399,945
Women	473,997	$468	$266,196,973
Total	630,203		$397,596,918

SOURCE: "Costs due to Absenteeism," in *The MetLife Study of Employer Costs for Working Caregivers,* Metropolitan Life Insurance Company, Westport, CT, 1997

TABLE 9.6

Costs due to workday interruptions

Full-Time Employed Caregivers by Gender (Levels III, IV, and V)	Number experiencing workday interruptions	Hours lost due to interruptions (avg. 50 hr/yr)	Median Weekly Wage	Cost to Employers
Men	1,420,049	71,002,434	$701	$1,244,317,663
Women	4,309,068	215,453,391	$468	$2,520,804,670
Total	5,729,117	286,455,825		$3,765,122,333

SOURCE: "Costs Due to workday Interruptions," in *The MetLife Study of Employer Costs for Working Caregivers,* Metropolitan Life Insurance Company, Westport, CT, 1997

TABLE 9.8

Costs associated with supervising caregivers

Full-Time Employed Caregivers by Gender (Levels III, IV, and V)	Number with supportive supervisors (81%)	Supervisor's time (12 hours per year)	Median Weekly Wage	Cost to Employers
Men	1,150,239	13,802,873	$771	$266,084,889
Women	3,490,345	41,884,139	$515	$539,048,871
Total	4,640,584	55,687,012		$805,133,760

SOURCE: "Costs Associated with Supervising Caregivers," in *The MetLife Study of Employer Costs for Working Caregivers,* Metropolitan Life Insurance Company, Westport, CT, 1997

TABLE 9.9

All costs to employers

	Cost per Employee	Total US Employer Costs
Replacing Employees		$4,933,816,305
Absenteeism	$69	$397,596,918
Partial Absenteeism	$85	$488,298,715
Workday Interruptions	$657	$3,765,122,333
Eldercare Crises	$189	$1,084,355,232
Supervisor's Time	$141	$805,133,760
Total	$1,142	$11,474,323,263

SOURCE: "All Costs to Employers," in *The MetLife Study of Employer Costs for Working Caregivers,* Metropolitan Life Insurance Company, Westport, CT, 1997

Meanwhile, corporations are eager for a mobile workforce. Companies move more people each year, not including the outside talent that companies seek to fill crucial slots. With larger numbers of people looking after elderly relatives, corporations are likely to see some of their choices turn down an offer, even at top levels.

Recruiters report that applicants who are caregivers often drop out of the job-changing market (at least temporarily), restrict how far they will move, or both. Relocation specialists claim that people often do not volunteer the information that they are caregivers, lest they be left out of the running for promotions. On a 1995 Atlas Van Lines questionnaire, "family ties," cited by 64 percent of respondents, edged out "spousal employment" for two consecutive years as the primary reason employees turned down relocations.

Many companies have not decided how to respond to the elder care problem. IBM, for example, has no formal policy on moving elderly parents unless they live with an employee (in which case they move with the household). On the Atlas questionnaire, only 3 percent of companies said they would pay to move an elderly relative of a newly hired employee.

Companies sometimes disregard the rules, however, and make decisions on an individual basis. When a manager wants to employ a particular employee, a company often makes an exception and pays for the relocation of family members. The companies may also arrange for referrals to nursing homes and research doctors, hospitals, and home health aides. This is especially true at the upper management level of companies. That fact may explain growing corporate interest in elder care—it affects an increasing number of older, upper-level employees.

Looking for Answers

Employers are beginning to understand they are incurring elder care-related costs in terms of lost work time, impaired productivity, more use of health benefits, higher turnover rates, and size of applicant pools (where some job seekers do not even apply for some jobs because they know in advance that their caregiving responsibilities will interfere). Just as employers now recognize the value of addressing child care issues in the workplace, many of them are also looking for ways to deal with the care of elders, as greater numbers of employees become caregivers over the next few years.

The American Business Collaboration for Quality Dependent Care (ABC) was formed in 1995. It is a business strategy intended to increase the supply and quality of dependent care services in the United States. ABC was formed in response to key labor force changes brought about by the increasing number of women and dual-earner families in the labor force and the increasing caregiving responsibilities of employees. Twenty-one major U.S. national and international corporations, called the "Champions," form the core of the collaboration. The 21 Champion companies are: Aetna Life and Casualty, Allstate Insurance Company, American Express, Amoco, AT&T, Bank of America, ChevronTexaco, Citigroup, Deloitte & Touche, Eastman Kodak, ExxonMobil, GE Capital Services, Hewlett-Packard, IBM, Johnson & Johnson, NYNEX, PricewaterhouseCoopers, Texas Instruments, and Xerox. The collaboration also includes more than 100 regional and local businesses that partner with the Champions in specific initiatives.

CHAPTER 10

PROVIDING HEALTH CARE FOR THE ELDERLY

While providing health care for the elderly is an important issue today, it will become a concern of gigantic proportion as the elderly population of the United States increases. The elderly are the biggest group of users of health services, accounting for more than one-third of the nation's total personal health expenditures. Rising costs, demand for additional services, the further development of life-sustaining technologies, and the role of government are, and will continue to be, subjects of intense debate.

Getting proper health care can be difficult for elderly people. Even if they can afford to pay for the best care, and many cannot, they may not be able to find facilities or skilled health care professionals to provide the services they need. As with living arrangements, there is no single answer as to the best way to deliver health care to the elderly; there are advantages and disadvantages to all the available programs.

HOME AND HOSPICE CARE

In Their Own Homes

Most Americans prefer to live independently as long as possible. Many elderly people with moderate and even severe health problems manage to remain in their own homes for many years by adjusting their lifestyles, modifying their environments, taking the proper medication, and using outside resources, such as relatives, friends, or paid nurses or caregivers, to assist them.

At some point, most elderly people with health problems will need outside assistance. If family members do not have the time or knowledge or are not available to provide the needed care, they must find someone who can. Finding a dependable, skilled caregiver is often very difficult. Paid providers may work directly for clients or for private agencies that contract with the state to serve clients.

HOME CARE ORGANIZATIONS. Home health agencies, home care aide organizations, and hospices are known col-

lectively as "home care organizations." The National Home and Hospice Care Survey (NHHCS) is a continuing series of surveys of home and hospice care agencies in the United States. According to the NHHCS, there were 1,961,000 patients receiving home care services and 8,117,700 patients discharged in 1998. According to the National Association for Home Care, annual expenditures for home health care were estimated to be $36 billion in 1999.

The 1998 NHHCS found 13,300 agencies providing home care service, down from 13,500 in 1996. Of these, 53 percent were proprietary (for profit), 36 percent were nonprofit, and the remainder were government-run or described as "other." Almost two-thirds, 65 percent, were inside metropolitan areas. Over two-thirds, 69 percent, were exclusively home health care agencies, 11 percent were hospices, and the remainder provided mixed or unknown services. The majority, 84 percent, were certified by Medicare and 85 percent were certified by Medicaid. According to the survey, 69 percent of the patients of home health care agencies were elderly.

SERVICES RECEIVED. The 1996 NHHCS provided insight into the types of services that home care patients receive. The most frequent services rendered were bathing or showering (53 percent), dressing (46 percent), transferring to or from a bed or chair (30 percent), and using the toilet (23 percent). The most common instrumental services provided were shopping for groceries or clothes (84 percent), light housework (39 percent), administering medications (23 percent), and preparing meals (23 percent). A few also helped with placing telephone calls and managing money.

Of those discharged from home health care, most no longer needed the services. Some were stabilized or recovered, some were admitted to hospitals, and others had met their goals (recovered or stabilized to the point that they or another person could resume the activities).

Some went on to be transferred to nursing homes, and some died.

PAYING FOR HOME CARE. Medicare pays only for medically related home care. Medicaid or state-financed programs, which are means-tested (available only to those with low incomes), finance some nonmedical home care, such as bathing, meal preparation, dressing, and toileting—the services that people with chronic conditions such as Alzheimer's disease require.

Dramatically rising expenditures caused home health care to consume about $1 of every $12 of Medicare expense in 1997, up dramatically from $1 of every $40 in 1989. Concerns about rising cost and fraud led Congress to pass the Balanced Budget Act of 1997 (PL 105-33). Title IV of that act controls home health care expense by limiting costs and the number of visits allowed. Subsequently, 14 percent of home health care agencies closed. The U.S. General Accounting Office, in *Medicare Home Health Agencies: Closures Continue, with Little Evidence Beneficiary Access Is Impaired* (1999), reported, however, that it found no reason to believe that reductions in the numbers of home health care agencies had compromised care.

Paid home health care will become more important in the years ahead. Three factors account for the growth in home health care:

- Advancements in medical technology that allow for care at home at a lower cost than in an institution

- The availability of the Medicare home health care benefit

- The increase in the number of elderly

HOME CARE WORKERS. In 1999 the Park Ridge Center, a private research organization, reported that among the more than 500,000 home care workers, most are women, poor, and predominantly African American or immigrants. They typically earn the minimum wage and receive no benefits, though unionization and a shortage of workers are changing the situation in many areas.

The elderly often do not want to burden their families and may ask for less help than they need, even to their own peril. Some home care recipients experience discomfort with the presence of "strangers" in their houses. With paid caregivers, they may feel uneasy with the forced intimacy of sharing their private lives. Others become close to their caregivers.

In the Homes of Others

When chronic health problems prevent elderly people from living alone or with spouses, they may move in with their children or other relatives. Families often take ill relatives into their homes because they want to care for them as long as possible or because they cannot find suitable or affordable long-term care facilities. Having an elderly, ill parent or relative in the home can place an emotional and/or financial strain on any family, depending on the type and degree of the health problem. In Alzheimer's cases, for example, the burden can be especially severe and prolonged.

Younger caregivers, most often daughters and daughters-in-law, may struggle with divided loyalties, with unequal contributions among siblings, or the history of a poor relationship with the very parent they must care for. On the other hand, caregivers may view these responsibilities as a last gift to the parent who raised them. Many caregivers experience both conflicting sentiments.

The Olmstead Decision

In July 1999 the Supreme Court of the United States issued the Olmstead decision, which basically makes the statement that the Americans with Disabilities Act prohibits states from discriminating against persons with disabilities, including those disabilities acquired through the aging process. The decision said that states cannot discriminate against the disabled by providing services in long-term care institutions when noninstitutional care is recommended by a treating professional or is requested by the recipient of the services and would be a reasonable accommodation. This ruling was very good news for older people with disabilities. Under this ruling, states can no longer house people in institutionalized care when it is not needed.

HOSPITALS

While most elderly people receive medical treatment in doctors' offices or health clinics, the incidence of hospitalization rises with age. In 1999 people aged 65 to 74 were hospitalized at a rate of 229.8 per 1,000 people; those 75 and older were hospitalized at the rate of 318.5 per 1,000, compared to 125.6 per 1,000 for those 45 to 64. (See Table 10.1.) With some fluctuations, these rates reflect a continuing year-to-year decrease in hospitalizations. For example, in 1997 the rate for people aged 65 years and over was 274.4 per 1,000 compared to 269.7 per 1,000 in 1999.

The average length of a hospital stay in 1999 was 6 days for both those 65 to 74 years old and those older than 75 years. (See Table 10.1.) As with the general population, the average hospital stay of those over 65 has been shortening since the 1980s—from 10.7 days in 1980 to 6 days in 1999.

Part of the cost of hospitalization for most elderly patients is covered under Medicare. After the enactment of the diagnosis related groups system (categories of illnesses that prescribe/allow for set duration of treatment, which encourages hospitals to release patients as quickly as possible), Medicare payments to hospitals fell below

TABLE 10.1

Discharges, days of care, and average length of stay in short-stay hospitals, 1997–99

[Data are based on household interviews of a sample of the civilian noninstitutionalized population]

Characteristic	Discharges			Days of care			Average length of stay		
	1997	1998	1999	1997	1998	1999	1997	1998	1999
	Number per 1,000 population						Number of days		
Total[1,2]	124.3	123.8	119.7	601.2	611.0	555.1	4.8	4.9	4.6
Age									
Under 18 years	90.8	81.9	76.3	319.0	315.6	302.6	3.5	3.9	4.0
Under 6 years	203.5	192.1	183.2	632.6	645.1	664.8	3.1	3.4	3.6
6–17 years	34.0	27.3	24.3	163.1	152.6	*126.5	4.8	5.6	*5.2
18–44 years	96.8	93.1	95.8	358.8	380.5	352.8	3.7	4.1	3.7
45–64 years	124.9	134.0	125.6	631.1	678.6	592.5	5.1	5.1	4.7
45–54 years	99.2	105.5	110.1	527.5	530.8	473.9	5.3	5.0	4.3
55–64 years	164.8	177.9	149.6	792.4	906.1	775.5	4.8	5.1	5.2
65 years and over	274.4	283.4	269.7	1,852.5	1,789.7	1,620.5	6.8	6.3	6.0
65–74 years	249.1	244.3	229.8	1,595.2	1,496.6	1,386.4	6.4	6.1	6.0
75 years and over	307.3	333.0	318.5	2,188.4	2,160.8	1,907.6	7.1	6.5	6.0

*Estimates are considered unreliable. Data preceded by an asterisk have a relative standard error of 20–30 percent.

[1] Includes all other races not shown separately, unknown poverty status, and unknown health insurance status.

[2] Estimates for all persons are age adjusted to the year 2000 standard using six age groups: Under 18 years, 18–44 years, 45–54 years, 55–64 years, 65–74 years, and 75 years of age and over.

SOURCE: Adapted from "Table 90. Discharges, Days of Care, and Average Length of Stay in Short-Stay Hospitals, According to Selected Characteristics: United States: 1997-1999," in *Health United States: 2001 (Updated)*, Department of Health and Human Services, Centers for Disease Control and Prevention, National Center for Health Statistics, Hyattsville, Maryland [Online] http://www.cdc.gov/nchs/products/pubs/pubd/hus/tables/2001/01hus090.pdf [accessed October, 2001]

many of the hospitals' own expenses. This led hospitals to try to make the patient's stay as short as possible in order to make treatment more profitable. It also forced some community hospitals to close. Most of the closures have been in rural communities.

NURSING HOMES—A REVOLUTION IN PROGRESS

Nursing homes provide long-term care for those with health problems so severe that they require specialized, intensive, or prolonged medical treatment.

The Declining Nursing Home Population

According to the National Nursing Home Survey, almost 1.5 million elderly adults were in nursing homes in 1997 (the most recent statistics available), and 9 in 10 nursing home residents were elderly. Approximately 4 percent of the population aged 65 years and older reside in nursing homes at any one time, but more may have lived in nursing homes at some period during their lifetimes.

In the 1980s many investors assumed that growing numbers of the elderly would lead to rapid increases in nursing home populations. As a result, 147,000 new nursing home beds were created between 1985 and 1995 to accommodate an expected 2.1 million elderly. The occupancy rate, however, fell from 92 percent to 87 percent over that time because many of the elderly suffered less disability and were able to live elsewhere, and many nursing homes turned out to be poor investments.

Nursing home use has also declined for another reason—there are now more, and perhaps better, options. With disability rates declining, the elderly are able to be treated in assisted living centers or, with home health care, in their own homes. This also affects length of stay in nursing homes. In 1995 (the most recent data available) nursing home residents were discharged after an average stay of 838 days, compared to 1,026 days in 1985. While most nursing home residents are there because they suffer from serious health problems, some have problems that would not normally require institutionalization, but they may be poor and/or have no one in the community who is able or willing to care for them. Many of these people can now be cared for by home health care providers.

The Cost of Nursing Home Care

Nursing home care is expensive. (See Table 10.2.) In 1999 the average monthly nursing home charge was $3,891, which equals $46,692 a year. Most nursing home residents rely on Medicaid to pay these fees. The second most common source of payment at admission is private insurance, a person's own income, or family support, followed by Medicare. The primary source of payment changes as a stay lengthens. After their funds are "spent down," many of those on Medicare shift to Medicaid, until more than half are Medicaid-funded.

Conditions Have Improved ... Somewhat

For some people, the prospect of living in a nursing home is terrifying. The unsavory reputation of some

TABLE 10.2

Nursing home average monthly charges per resident according to primary source of payments and selected facility characteristics, 1985, 1995, 1999

[Data are based on reporting by a sample of nursing homes]

Facility characteristic	All sources 1999	Own income or family support[1]			Medicare			Medicaid		
	1999	1985	1995	1999	1985	1995	1999	1985	1995	1999
					Average monthly charge[2]					
All facilities	$3,891	$1,450	$3,081	$3,947	$2,141	$5,546	$5,764	$1,504	$2,769	$3,505
Ownership										
Proprietary	3,698	1,444	3,190	3,984	2,058	5,668	5,275	1,363	2,560	3,312
Nonprofit and government	4,225	1,462	2,967	3,903	*	5,304	6,548	1,851	3,201	3,918
Certification[3]										
Both Medicare and Medicaid	4,060	- - -	3,365	4,211	- - -	5,472	5,887	- - -	2,910	3,626
Medicare only	4,437	- - -	3,344	3,873	- - -	*	*	. . .	. . .	. . .
Medicaid only	2,508	- - -	2,352	2,533	. . .	. . .	. . .	- - -	2,069	2,501
Neither	2,360	- - -	2,390	2,685	. . .	. . .	. . .	. . .	. . .	. . .
Bed size										
Less than 50 beds	3,808	886	3,377	3,358	*	*	*	1,335	2,990	3,533
50–99 beds	3,627	1,388	2,849	3,698	1,760	4,929	*	1,323	2,335	3,121
100–199 beds	3,867	1,567	3,138	4,160	2,192	4,918	5,318	1,413	2,659	3,487
200 beds or more	4,281	1,701	3,316	4,029	2,767	4,523	5,912	1,919	3,520	4,011
Geographic region										
Northeast	4,852	1,645	4,117	5,300	2,109	4,883	6,368	2,035	3,671	4,397
Midwest	3,474	1,398	2,650	3,413	2,745	5,439	4,726	1,382	2,478	3,239
South	3,263	1,359	2,945	3,467	2,033	4,889	4,859	1,200	2,333	2,943
West	4,725	1,498	3,666	4,868	1,838	8,825	*	1,501	2,848	3,865

* Data not shown have a relative standard error greater than 30 percent. After 1995 data preceded by an asterisk have a relative standard error of 20–30 percent.
- - - Data not available.
. . . Category not applicable.
[1]Includes private health insurance.
[2]Includes life-care residents and no-charge residents.
[3]Starting in 1995 the certification categories were based on Medicare and Medicaid certification.

SOURCE: Adapted from "Table 124. Nursing Home Average Monthly Charges Per Resident and Percent of Residents, According to Primary Source of Payments and Selected Facility Payments: United States, 1985, 1995, 1997 and 1999," in *Health United States: 2001*, Department of Health and Human Services, Centers for Disease Control and Prevention, National Center for Health Statistics, Hyattsville, Maryland [Online] http://www.cdc.gov/nchs/products/pubs/pubd/hus/tables/2001/01hus124.pdf [accessed October, 2001]

nursing homes is not entirely undeserved. Living conditions in these facilities, however, have improved. Both physical conditions and workers' attitudes toward residents have improved as a result of media attention, government regulation, demands by families, and the concern of the nursing home industry itself.

The industry recognizes the potential market of an aging population and is eager to convey a positive image. A major problem is retaining good employees. Next to child-care facilities, nursing homes have the highest employee turnover rate of any occupation, especially among unskilled and semiskilled workers. Nursing home aides, the people who provide most of the direct patient care, are very poorly paid. In most areas of the country, a person can earn a higher hourly wage at a fast-food restaurant than in a nursing home.

Competition in the Industry

In order to stay competitive with the growing home care industry and the increasing array of services available for the elderly, nursing homes have tried to reinvent themselves, offering additional programs and services along with traditional institutional care. Among those services are adult day care, visiting nurses, respite care (short-term stays when primary caregivers are not available, as on a vacation), transportation, and minimal care apartment units. Craig Duncan, executive director of the Eddy Nursing Home in Troy, New York, explained:

> We are moving away from an institutional base except for the frailest population, and that's because we have better-educated older consumers telling us what they want, and that is to stay out of a nursing home. If we want to maintain and gain a share of that market—and let's face it, all of us are revenue-driven—we had better respond.

Subacute Care

In order to make nursing homes more profitable, nursing home operators have begun to compete with hospitals for subacute care patients. Patients recovering from cancer, heart bypass operations, joint replacement surgery, or serious accidents are increasingly receiving postoperative therapy in nursing homes rather than in hospitals because nursing home care is less expensive.

According to the American Health Care Association, the provision of subacute care grew dramatically during the 1990s. Analysts put the number of subacute beds between 35,000 and 45,000 among 50 national long-term care chains. The majority of subacute units have been opened since 1990.

THE HIGH COST OF HEALTH CARE FOR THE ELDERLY

The elderly make up 12 percent of the U.S. population, but account for one-third of total personal health care expenditures (money spent for the direct consumption of health care goods and services). According to the Centers for Medicare and Medicaid Services, or CMS (formerly the Health Care Financing Administration), total spending for health care topped $1.2 trillion in 1999, up 5.6 percent from 1998, but continuing a six-year trend of growth below 6 percent. (See Table 10.3.) Between 1993 and 1999, health spending averaged increases of .5 percentage points less than the gross domestic product (GDP) as the shift to managed care and impacts from the Balanced Budget Act of 1997 resulted in one-time savings. Coupled with faster real growth in the economy, this resulted in a slight decline in health spending's share of the GDP, from 13.4 percent in 1993 to 13 percent in both 1998 and 1999.

An Especially Severe Burden

The cost of health care in the United States is a serious problem for the elderly. Noted economist Victor R. Fuchs pointed out that if current trends continue, by 2020 the elderly's health care consumption will be approximately $25,000 per person (in 1995 dollars), compared with $9,200 in 1995 ("Health Care for the Elderly, How Much? Who Will Pay For It?," *Health Affairs,* January/February 1999). Fuchs also pointed out that technology is the driving force behind the long-term rise in health care spending.

Health care is the only budget expense for the elderly that constitutes both a higher percentage of income and a greater dollar amount than for the nonelderly. According to 1997 Consumer Expenditure Survey data, health care expenses accounted for 10 to 14 percent of the average senior's household spending. This is more than twice the percentage that younger households spent on health care.

Many elderly Americans are forced into poverty to pay for health care for themselves or for loved ones. Before a family can qualify for some forms of assistance, such as Medicaid, it must often "spend down," that is, spend its assets to the poverty level. This can leave surviving spouses and families in financial ruin. In 1995 Robert M. Ball, chairman of the National Academy of Social Insurance, a non-profit research organization in Washington, D.C., stated,

Sometime in the not-too-distant future, we will get a major national program protecting families against the cost of long term care.... I expect it to come, not primarily because of the potential power of the elderly...but because of pressure from those middle-aged, the sons and daughters of the elderly. They are the ones most at risk.

Where Does the Money Go?

According to 1997 Consumer Expenditure Survey data, more than half of seniors' health care spending was for health insurance. Prescription drugs accounted for an additional 15 to 20 percent. Medical services, such as physician's services, lab tests, and nursing home care, made up another 20 percent.

Where Does the Money Come From?

Almost all Americans 65 years and older receive some help with medical expenses from government programs, such as Medicare and Medicaid, and/or are covered by private medical insurance. Many elderly people mistakenly believe that Medicare will pay for all their health care costs.

No single government or private program covers all health costs. It is possible, however, to obtain total, or almost total, financial coverage for medical costs with a combination of government programs, private health insurance, and out-of-pocket payments by the patient. The cost of such a package, though, can be prohibitive for many elderly people, and qualifications for enrollment in some programs may be difficult or impossible to meet.

Table 10.4 shows the sources of health care coverage for the elderly in 1999. In 1999, 26.3 percent of those 65 and older had Medicare only, and around 64 percent had private insurance. Finally, 7.4 percent had Medicaid. Those over age 65 who qualify for Medicaid can also receive Medicare, and most over 65 who have private insurance also have Medicare (91 percent in 1998). In addition, the family of an elderly person often pays for nursing home care out of their pockets.

EMPLOYER HEALTH INSURANCE. Persons over 65 who are actively employed may be covered under a company health care policy. As shown in Table 10.4, 34.1 percent of age 65-plus Americans had such coverage in 1999. Coverage may not be denied or reduced just because of age or because a person is eligible for benefits under a federal program. Even after retirement, a person may be able to receive continued coverage under a company policy. In 1999, 11.1 million people aged 65 and older carried insurance through a present or previous employer.

MEDIGAP. An increasing number of private insurance companies are offering policies, known as Medigap insurance, that pay for services not included in Medicare. These policies can be expensive and, in some cases, do not provide complete coverage. Abuses in the Medigap insurance field have included overlapping coverage, selling clients more coverage than they need, and deceptive

TABLE 10.3

National Health Expenditure amounts, selected years 1980–2010[1]

Type of Expenditure	1980	1990	1993	1996	1997	1998	1999	2000	2001	2002	2003 (Projected)	2004 (Projected)	2005 (Projected)	2006 (Projected)	2007 (Projected)	2008 (Projected)	2009 (Projected)	2010 (Projected)
							Amount in Billions											
National Health Expenditures	$245.8	$695.6	$887.6	$1,038.0	$1,093.9	$1,146.1	$1,210.7	$1,311.1	$1,424.2	$1,541.9	$1,666.3	$1,789.8	$1,919.4	$2,051.0	$2,186.3	$2,327.4	$2,477.5	$2,637.4
Health Services and Supplies	233.5	669.2	855.8	1,003.8	1,056.5	1,107.9	1,170.8	1,268.2	1,378.1	1,492.8	1,613.7	1,733.6	1,859.6	1,987.6	2,119.3	2,256.6	2,402.8	2,558.4
Personal Health Care	214.6	609.4	775.8	911.9	958.8	1,002.3	1,057.7	1,143.9	1,240.4	1,345.3	1,453.9	1,562.4	1,675.2	1,788.9	1,905.5	2,027.5	2,156.3	2,293.7
Hospital Care	101.5	253.9	320.0	355.9	367.7	377.1	390.9	415.8	442.8	472.5	504.8	534.9	566.8	597.4	626.7	656.8	687.7	720.5
Professional Services	67.3	216.9	280.8	332.9	352.4	373.4	396.5	427.9	463.2	502.5	542.6	583.4	625.2	666.4	709.2	754.3	802.6	854.3
Physician and Clinical Services	47.1	157.5	201.2	229.3	240.9	254.2	269.4	289.2	311.7	337.3	363.3	388.8	414.4	438.8	463.5	489.4	516.9	545.9
Other Professional Services	3.6	18.2	24.5	30.9	33.4	35.9	37.9	41.2	45.1	49.6	54.3	59.2	64.0	68.7	73.5	78.5	83.8	89.4
Dental Services	13.3	31.5	38.9	46.8	50.2	53.1	56.0	60.3	65.4	70.0	74.3	79.0	83.7	88.3	93.2	98.1	103.4	108.9
Other Personal Health Care	3.3	9.7	16.2	25.9	27.9	30.2	33.2	37.1	41.0	45.6	50.8	56.5	63.1	70.6	79.0	88.3	98.5	110.1
Nursing Home and Home Health	20.1	65.3	87.6	113.5	119.6	121.6	123.1	132.8	144.7	158.1	170.5	183.8	197.0	210.5	224.7	239.2	254.3	270.4
Home Health Care	2.4	12.6	21.9	33.6	34.5	33.5	33.1	36.6	41.3	46.6	51.4	56.4	61.1	66.0	71.2	76.2	81.5	87.0
Nursing Home Care	17.7	52.7	65.7	79.9	85.1	88.0	90.0	96.2	103.4	111.5	119.1	127.5	135.9	144.6	153.6	163.0	172.8	183.4
Retail Outlet Sales of Medical Products	25.7	73.3	87.5	109.5	119.2	130.2	147.1	167.6	189.8	212.2	236.0	260.3	286.2	314.6	344.9	377.2	411.6	448.5
Prescription Drugs	12.0	40.3	51.3	67.2	75.1	85.2	99.6	116.9	135.7	155.0	175.8	197.1	219.9	245.3	272.4	301.5	332.6	366.0
Other Medical Products	13.7	33.1	36.2	42.4	44.0	45.0	47.6	50.6	54.1	57.3	60.2	63.2	66.3	69.3	72.5	75.6	79.0	82.5
Durable Medical Equipment	4.0	11.2	13.7	16.4	17.3	17.5	18.1	19.3	20.5	21.7	22.9	24.2	25.5	26.9	28.4	30.0	31.6	33.4
Other Non-Durable Medical Products	9.7	21.9	22.6	26.0	26.7	27.5	29.5	31.3	33.6	35.6	37.3	39.1	40.8	42.4	44.1	45.7	47.4	49.1
Government Administration and Net Cost of Private Health Insurance	12.2	39.6	52.8	59.0	61.6	67.0	72.0	80.0	89.1	94.3	101.5	107.7	115.5	124.1	133.4	142.5	153.2	164.2
Government Public Health Activities	6.7	20.2	27.2	32.9	36.0	38.6	41.1	44.2	48.5	53.3	58.3	63.5	68.9	74.6	80.5	86.7	93.3	100.4
Investment	12.3	26.4	31.8	34.2	37.4	38.2	39.8	43.0	46.1	49.1	52.6	56.1	59.8	63.4	66.9	70.7	74.8	79.0
Research[2]	5.5	12.7	15.6	17.8	18.7	20.5	22.2	24.3	26.1	27.8	29.6	31.5	33.5	35.7	38.0	40.5	43.1	45.9
Construction	6.8	13.7	16.2	16.4	18.7	17.7	17.6	18.7	20.0	21.3	23.0	24.7	26.3	27.7	29.0	30.3	31.6	33.1

[1] The health spending projections were based on the 1999 version of the National Health Expenditures (NHE) released in March 2001.
[2] Research and development expenditures of drug companies and other manufacturers and providers of medical equipment and supplies are excluded from research expenditures. These research expenditures are implicitly included in the expenditure class in which the product falls, in that they are covered by the payment received for that product.
NOTE: Numbers may not add to totals because of rounding.

SOURCE: Adapted from "Table 20. National Health Expenditure Amounts, and Average Annual Percent Change by Type of Expenditure: Selected Calendar Years 1980–2010," in *National Health Care Expenditure Projections: 2000–2010*, Health Care Financing Administration [Online] http://www.cms.gov [accessed October 2001]

TABLE 10.4

Health care coverage for persons 65 years of age and over, according to type of coverage and selected characteristics, selected years 1989–99

[Data are based on household interviews of a sample of the civilian noninstitutionalized population]

Characteristic	Private insurance[1]					Private insurance obtained through workplace[1,2]					Medicaid [1,9]					Medicare only[10]				
	1989	1995[3]	1997[3]	1998	1999	1989	1995[3]	1997[3]	1998	1999	1989	1995[3]	1997[3]	1998	1999	1989	1995[3]	1997[3]	1998	1999
								Number in millions												
Total[4]	22.4	23.5	22.3	21.5	20.8	11.2	12.4	12.0	11.8	11.1	2.0	3.0	2.5	2.6	2.4	4.5	4.6	6.7	7.5	8.5
								Percent of population												
Total, age adjusted[4,5]	76.1	74.5	69.5	66.7	64.0	37.3	38.9	37.0	36.5	34.1	7.2	9.6	7.9	8.1	7.4	15.7	14.8	20.8	23.3	26.3
Total, crude[4]	76.5	74.6	69.5	66.7	64.1	38.4	39.5	37.5	36.7	34.3	7.0	9.4	7.9	8.1	7.3	15.4	14.7	20.8	23.2	26.3
Age																				
65–74 years	78.2	75.1	69.9	66.6	64.5	43.7	43.3	42.0	39.7	37.9	6.3	8.4	7.5	7.8	6.6	13.8	14.4	20.3	22.7	25.9
75 years and over	73.9	73.9	69.1	66.8	63.5	30.2	34.1	31.6	33.0	29.9	8.2	10.9	8.4	8.4	8.1	17.8	15.2	21.5	24.0	26.8
75–84 years	75.9	75.7	70.2	68.1	64.6	32.0	36.0	33.2	35.1	31.9	7.9	9.9	7.9	7.8	7.2	16.2	14.1	20.5	22.9	26.3
85 years and over	65.5	67.3	64.7	61.8	59.6	22.8	27.3	25.6	25.3	23.0	9.7	14.3	10.2	10.5	11.4	24.9	19.2	25.2	27.9	28.5
Sex[5]																				
Male	77.4	76.6	72.1	68.5	64.5	42.1	43.3	42.0	40.7	37.8	5.2	5.8	5.1	6.2	5.3	14.9	14.3	19.6	21.9	26.2
Female	75.4	73.2	67.7	65.5	63.8	34.0	35.8	33.5	33.6	31.4	8.6	12.2	9.9	9.5	8.8	16.2	15.0	21.7	24.3	26.3
Race[5,6]																				
White	79.8	78.3	72.7	70.3	67.5	38.7	40.4	37.9	37.9	35.1	5.6	7.4	6.5	6.4	5.7	13.9	13.5	19.3	21.8	25.1
Black	42.3	40.3	42.5	40.3	40.2	23.7	24.6	30.8	27.3	27.3	21.2	28.4	19.7	18.0	18.2	34.9	29.0	34.8	38.1	37.0
Hispanic origin and race[5]																				
All Hispanic[6]	42.3	39.8	30.6	29.1	26.9	22.2	18.4	17.7	17.8	17.3	26.4	32.7	29.0	27.2	24.0	22.7	23.6	35.1	38.4	42.5
Mexican	33.5	31.8	31.8	26.5	27.4	20.2	15.9	17.7	17.2	16.8										
White, non-Hispanic	81.0	80.3	74.9	72.3	69.6	39.3	41.7	39.0	38.8	36.2	4.9	6.1	5.4	5.4	4.7	13.6	12.9	18.4	20.9	24.0
Black, non-Hispanic	42.4	40.1	42.6	40.5	40.4	23.7	24.4	30.7	27.6	27.4	21.1	28.5	19.5	18.0	18.1	34.9	29.1	34.8	37.9	37.1
Percent of poverty level[5,7]																				
Below 100 percent	46.1	40.0	31.9	32.8	28.3	11.6	13.8	7.2	10.0	8.5	28.2	36.4	40.0	36.7	35.7	26.4	23.4	27.0	28.4	32.7
100–149 percent	67.7	67.6	54.5	48.7	44.6	22.2	26.7	17.4	19.1	14.7	9.0	12.8	13.9	14.1	15.3	20.7	18.6	28.3	33.2	35.9
150–199 percent	81.1	76.0	69.8	65.6	62.0	39.0	38.7	33.3	30.9	27.0	4.7	5.9	5.1	6.1	4.2	13.6	16.8	22.7	26.1	31.5
200 percent or more	85.5	85.3	81.8	78.6	75.5	49.4	49.3	48.5	49.1	44.6	2.4	2.4	2.7	3.5	2.9	11.0	10.8	14.6	16.7	19.7
Geographic region[5]																				
Northeast	76.1	76.2	72.7	72.0	66.0	42.2	44.6	42.3	43.0	39.2	5.4	8.9	6.5	7.5	7.3	17.4	15.3	19.8	19.3	25.5
Midwest	81.9	82.3	78.5	78.3	77.0	40.0	44.7	40.7	40.7	37.9	3.7	5.8	5.0	4.9	5.7	13.8	11.0	15.4	16.3	15.7
South	73.0	70.7	66.0	62.0	60.2	32.0	33.7	32.9	33.1	30.5	9.7	11.8	10.0	9.6	8.2	16.6	15.9	21.6	26.0	29.0
West	74.7	68.8	59.9	54.9	51.5	37.1	33.6	33.6	30.3	29.9	9.4	11.5	9.9	10.2	8.2	14.4	17.2	28.3	31.4	36.4
Location of residence[5]																				
Within MSA[8]	76.6	74.7	68.4	65.5	62.8	39.9	40.9	38.6	38.2	35.5	6.5	8.9	7.5	8.0	6.9	15.9	14.9	22.3	24.4	28.0
Outside MSA[8]	74.8	73.9	73.2	70.6	68.2	30.2	32.2	31.8	31.1	29.4	8.8	11.7	9.4	8.4	8.8	15.5	14.2	15.9	19.7	20.6

[1] Almost all persons 65 years of age and over are covered by Medicare also. In 1998, 91 percent of older persons with private insurance also had Medicare.
[2] Private insurance originally obtained through a present or former employer or union. Starting in 1997 also includes private insurance obtained through workplace, self-employed, or professional association.
[3] The questionnaire changed compared with previous years.
[4] Includes all other races not shown separately and unknown poverty level.
[5] Estimates are age adjusted to the year 2000 standard using two age groups: 65–74 years and 75 years and over.
[6] The race groups white and black include persons of Hispanic and non-Hispanic origin; persons of Hispanic origin may be of any race. Other race groups are not shown because sample sizes are too small to obtain reliable estimates.
[7] Prior to 1997 percent of poverty level is based on family income and family size using Bureau of the Census poverty thresholds. Beginning in 1997 percent of poverty level is based on family income, family size, number of children in the family, and, for families with two or fewer adults, the age of adults in the family. Missing family income data were imputed for 25 percent of the sample 65 years of age and over in 1994, 22 percent in 1995, and 24 percent in 1996. Percent of poverty level was unknown for 29 percent of sample persons 65 or older in 1997, 34 percent in 1998, and 38 percent in 1999.
[8] MSA is metropolitan statistical area.
[9] Includes public assistance through 1996. Starting in 1997 includes state-sponsored health plans. In 1999 the age-adjusted percent of the population 65 years of age and over covered by Medicaid was 7.4 percent, and 0.4 percent were covered by state-sponsored health plans.
[10] Persons covered by Medicare but not covered by private health insurance, Medicaid, public assistance (through 1996), state-sponsored or other government-sponsored health plans (starting in 1997), or military plans.
NOTES: Percents do not add to 100 because persons with both private health insurance and Medicaid appear in more than one column, and because the percent of persons without health insurance (1.1 percent in 1999) is not shown.

SOURCE: Adapted from "Table 131. Health Care Coverage for Persons 65 Years of Age and Over, According to Type of Coverage and Selected Characteristics: United States: Selected Years 1989-1999," in *Health United States: 2001 (Updated)*, Department of Health and Human Services, Centers for Disease Control and Prevention, National Center for Health Statistics, Hyattsville, Maryland [Online] http://www.cdc.gov/nchs/products/pubs/pubd/hus/tables/2001/01hus131.pdf [accessed October, 2001]

advertising. Because federal and state laws set a minimum level of benefits for a supplemental policy, one such policy is enough in virtually every case, although some policyholders have more than one policy.

The Omnibus Budget Reconciliation Act of 1990 (PL 101-508) allows people reaching the age of 65 to buy Medigap policies regardless of the condition of their health, provided they do so within six months after

FIGURE 10.1

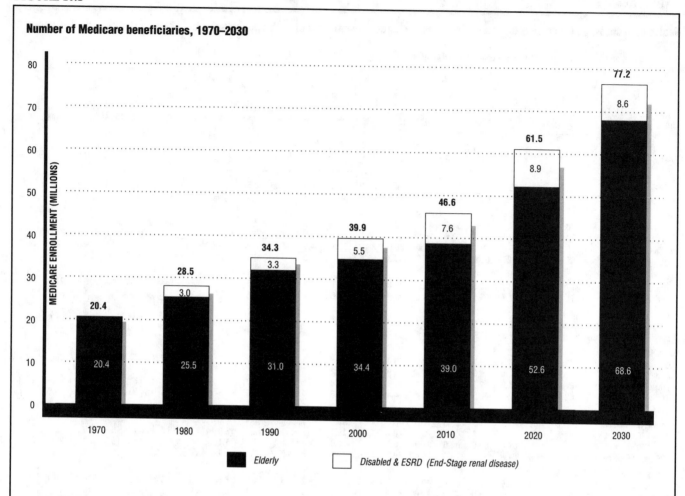

Number of Medicare beneficiaries, 1970–2030

SOURCE: "Figure 1. Number of Medicare Beneficiaries, CY 1970–2030," in *Medicare: A Profile*, Health Care Financing Administration, July, 2000 [Online] http://www.cms.gov [accessed October, 2001]

enrolling in Medicare. These protections apply to new beneficiaries, approximately 2 million people a year. About 64 percent of the elderly have some form of private insurance in addition to Medicare. African Americans are only half as likely to have supplemental coverage as their white counterparts.

NO HEALTH INSURANCE. The U.S. Census Bureau reported in 1998 that only 1.1 percent of all Americans over age 65 had no health insurance. Of poor people over 65, 3.2 percent had no health insurance.

GOVERNMENT HEALTH CARE PROGRAMS

The United States is one of the few industrialized nations that does not have a national health care program. In most other developed countries, government programs cover almost all health-related costs, from maternity care to long-term care.

In the United States, the two major government health care programs are Medicare and Medicaid. They provide financial assistance for the elderly, the poor, and the disabled. Before the existence of these programs, a large number of older Americans could not afford adequate medical care.

Medicare

The spirit in which this law is written draws deeply upon the ancient dreams of all mankind. In Leviticus, it is written, "Thou shall rise up before the hoary head, and honor the face of an old man."

— Russell B. Long, Democratic senator from Louisiana, at the original vote for Medicare in 1965

The Medicare program, enacted under Title XVIII ("Health Insurance for the Aged") of the Social Security Act, was signed into law by President Lyndon B. Johnson and went into effect on July 1, 1966. That year, 19 million elderly entered the program. CMS forecast that by 2030 the number of Americans insured by Medicare would be over 68 million. (See Figure 10.1.)

The Medicare program is composed of three parts.

- Part A provides hospital insurance. Coverage includes doctors' fees, nursing services, meals, a semiprivate room, special care units, operating room costs, laboratory tests, and some drugs and supplies. Part A also covers rehabilitation services, limited posthospital skilled nursing facility care, home health care, and hospice care for the terminally ill.

- Part B (Supplemental Medical Insurance or SMI) is elective medical insurance; enrollees must pay premiums to get coverage. It covers private physicians' services, diagnostic tests, outpatient hospital services, outpatient physical therapy, speech pathology services, home health services, and medical equipment and supplies.

- A new, third part of Medicare, sometimes known as Part C, is the Medicare + Choice program, which was established by the Balanced Budget Act of 1997. It expands beneficiaries' options for participation in private-sector health care plans.

In 2001 about 40 million people were enrolled in one or both of Parts A and B of the Medicare program, and 5.7 million of them chose to participate in a Medicare + Choice plan. According to CMS, in 1999 the average enrollee received $5,410 in benefits, although, in a typical year approximately 17 percent of the elderly covered by Medicare do not file a single claim. The fastest-growing segment of Medicare enrollees is the 85-plus age group. The impact of an aging Medicare population on health care expenditures is significant since, on the average, the aged tend to be sicker and incur much greater expense per capita.

PROVIDING ONLY LIMITED PROTECTION. Medicare has been an extremely successful program. In 1965, when President Johnson signed the bill into law, only half of America's elderly had any health insurance. Today, Medicare pays hospital and doctor bills for about 40 million Americans over 65, or approximately 97 percent of the elderly, making this age group the only one in America with virtually universal coverage. Medicare, along with increased Social Security benefits, has helped transform an age group that has suffered from high rates of poverty into a more economically secure group. It is also a key source of health care financing for older Americans with limited incomes. In 1997 nearly three-quarters of Medicare expenses went to individuals with average incomes of $25,000 or less. (See Figure 10.2.)

Medicare, however, does not provide complete health care coverage. The plan does not pay for basic medical expenses such as routine physical examinations, prescription drugs, eyeglasses, prostheses (artificial body parts), and, perhaps most importantly, long-term care. Figure 10.3 shows health expenditures and the percentage paid by Medicare. According to the CMS, paying for long-term care (44 percent) outpaced all other out-of-pocket expens-

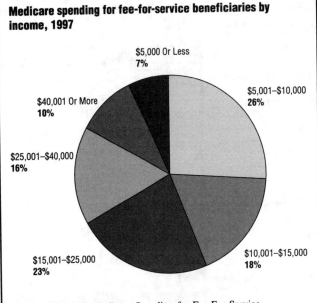

FIGURE 10.2

Medicare spending for fee-for-service beneficiaries by income, 1997

SOURCE: "Figure 5. Medicare Spending for Fee-For-Service Beneficiaries by Income, 1997," in *Medicare: A Profile*, Health Care Financing Administration, July, 2000 [Online] http://www.cms.gov [accessed October, 2001]

es for Medicare beneficiaries in 1997. Prescription drugs followed with 18.7 percent, physician care with 18.5 percent, dental care with 9.1 percent, hospital outpatient with 4.4 percent, hospital inpatient with 4.1 percent, and home health with 1.2 percent. (Note: these tabulations do not include the cost of Medigap insurance and the Medicare Part B premium.) Due to these shortcomings, older Americans are, in fact, spending a higher proportion of their incomes on health care now than they were in 1965 before Medicare and Medicaid were enacted.

The costs of prescription drugs are frequently a burden for elderly health consumers, as Medicare does not cover them. Figure 10.4 shows lower drug utilization levels among those without drug coverage. Beneficiaries without drug coverage average nearly eight fewer prescriptions per year than those with coverage. The Henry J. Kaiser Family Foundation points out that lower use of drugs by Medicare beneficiaries without drug coverage may negatively affect health and result in increased use of other health services. For example, beneficiaries with hypertension who lack drug coverage are 40 percent less likely to purchase antihypertensive medications.

Figure 10.5 shows the sources of payments used by Medicare beneficiaries for health care. On average, Medicare pays only slightly over half of the health care costs of its beneficiaries ($5,114). Beneficiaries pay 18 percent out of their own pockets, an average of $1,681 in 1997. In addition, Medicaid covers 11.9 percent ($1,107), private insurance covers 10 percent ($922), and other sources cover the remaining 5 percent ($516).

FIGURE 10.3

National personal health expenditures by type of service and percent Medicare paid, 1998

Category of spending

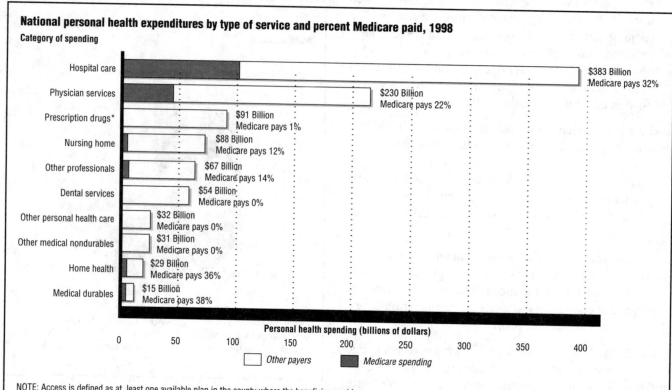

NOTE: Access is defined as at least one available plan in the county where the beneficiary resides.

*NOTE: Medicare payments are from managed care plans only, since fee-for-service Medicare does not generally cover outpatient prescription drugs.

SOURCE: "Figure 20. National Personal Health Expenditures by Type of Service and Percent Medicare Paid, 1998," in *Medicare: A Profile*, Health Care Financing Administration, July, 2000 [Online] http://www.cms.gov [accessed October, 2001]

FIGURE 10.4

Average prescriptions filled by Medicare beneficiaries, with and without drug coverage, 1998

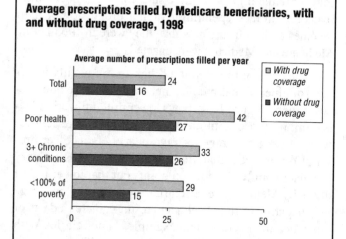

SOURCE: "Figure 3. Average Prescriptions Filled by Medicare Beneficiaries, with and without Drug Coverage, by Selected Characteristics, 1998, in *Medicare and Prescription Drugs*, The Henry J. Kaiser Family Foundation, Washington, DC, May 2001 [Online] http://www.kff.org/content/2001/1583-03/1583_03rx.pdf [accessed October, 2001]. This information was reprinted with permission of the Henry J. Kaiser Family Foundation of Menlo Park, California. The Kaiser Family Foundation is an independent national health care philanthropy dedicated to providing information and analysis on health issues to policymakers, the media, and the general public. The Foundation is not associated with Kaiser Permanente or Kaiser Industries.

FIGURE 10.5

Sources of payment for Medicare beneficiaries' use of medical services, 1997

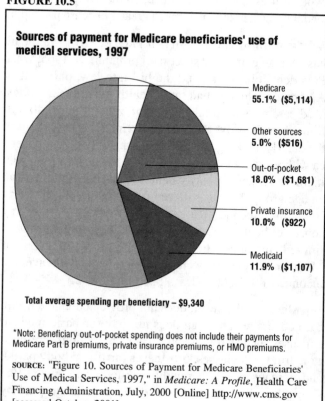

*Note: Beneficiary out-of-pocket spending does not include their payments for Medicare Part B premiums, private insurance premiums, or HMO premiums.

SOURCE: "Figure 10. Sources of Payment for Medicare Beneficiaries' Use of Medical Services, 1997," in *Medicare: A Profile*, Health Care Financing Administration, July, 2000 [Online] http://www.cms.gov [accessed October, 2001]

FIGURE 10.6

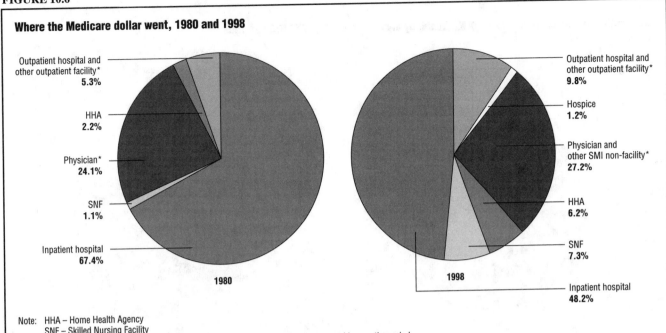

Where the Medicare dollar went, 1980 and 1998

Outpatient hospital and other outpatient facility*
5.3%

HHA
2.2%

Physician*
24.1%

SNF
1.1%

Inpatient hospital
67.4%

1980

Outpatient hospital and other outpatient facility*
9.8%

Hospice
1.2%

Physician and other SMI non-facility*
27.2%

HHA
6.2%

SNF
7.3%

Inpatient hospital
48.2%

1998

Note: HHA – Home Health Agency
SNF – Skilled Nursing Facility
*The definition of these categories has changed over time, so they are not directly comparable over the period.

SOURCE: "Figure 9. Where the Medicare Dollar Went, 1980 and 1998," in *Medicare: A Profile*, Health Care Financing Administration, July, 2000 [Online] http://www.cms.gov [accessed October, 2001]

Figure 10.6 shows the recent shift in Medicare spending away from inpatient hospital services and toward outpatient and other services. In 1980, 67.4 percent of Medicare spending was for inpatient hospital service, compared to 48.2 percent in 1998. In 1980, 2.2 percent of spending went to home health agencies (HHAs). In 1998, 6.2 percent of spending went to HHAs and 1.2 percent went to hospice care. (Medicare did not pay for hospice care in 1980.) And, in 1980, 1.1 percent of Medicare spending went to nursing home care (SNF, or skilled nursing facility), compared to 7.3 percent in 1998.

A PROGRAM IN CRISIS. Policy makers generally agree that Medicare cannot be sustained in its current form. Its costs are rising and must be controlled before the baby boomers begin receiving benefits around 2010. The costs for medical procedures often used by the elderly, such as angioplasty and coronary bypass surgery, have increased. In addition, people are living longer. In 1995, for the first time since 1972, Medicare's trust fund lost money, a sign that the financial condition of Medicare was worse than assumed. The CMS, which runs Medicare, had not expected a deficit until 1997. Income to the trust fund, primarily from payroll taxes, was less than expected, and spending was higher.

The deficit is significant because losses are expected to grow from year to year. No tax increases are scheduled under current law, and federal officials do not expect a reduction in the rate of spending unless a budget deal is reached between President George W. Bush and the Con-

gress. No such solution seems likely. There are enough assets to cover the shortfall over the next few years, but once the assets of the trust fund are depleted, there is no way to pay all the benefits that are due.

Politicians and policy makers are bitterly divided over how Medicare should be changed, and how quickly. The Medicare payroll tax has not been increased since 1986. Some Democrats have argued that only a true social insurance program, financed by payroll taxes and covering everyone, would spread the risk sufficiently and ensure that all the elderly, rich and poor, could receive complete medical coverage. Republicans, by and large, have argued for a voluntary system. Both Democrats and Republicans, in general, believe that recipients should have more choices and more financial responsibility for what they choose.

While almost no one advocates an abrupt withdrawal of benefits from today's retirees, the benefits cannot last forever in their current form. Recipients will likely have to contribute more, benefits will have to decline, or Medicare payments to doctors and hospitals, already very low, will have to be cut even more. None of these options are politically appealing to a congressperson running for reelection.

In 1997 Congress passed the Balanced Budget Act, which expanded health plan options and lowered program spending. The act encouraged wider availability of health maintenance organizations and permitted other types of plans, such as preferred provider organizations, provider sponsored organizations, private fee-for-service plans,

FIGURE 10.7

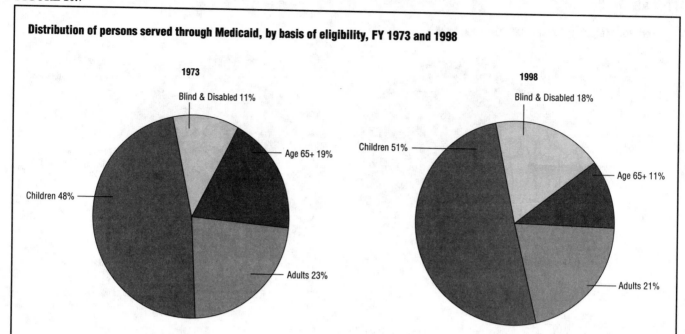

Distribution of persons served through Medicaid, by basis of eligibility, FY 1973 and 1998

1973

Blind & Disabled 11%
Age 65+ 19%
Children 48%
Adults 23%

1998

Blind & Disabled 18%
Children 51%
Age 65+ 11%
Adults 21%

Note: (1) The percentage distribution for 1973 does not include 1.5 million persons served by Medicaid whose basis of eligibility is reported as "other," and the percentage distribution for 1998 does not include 3.1 million persons served whose basis of eligibility is unknown; (2) percentages may not sum to 100 due to rounding; (3) the term "adults," refers to non-elderly, non-disabled adults; (4) disabled children are included in the blind & disabled category shown above.

SOURCE: "Figure 1.9. Distribution of Persons Served Through Medicaid, by Basis of Eligibility, Fiscal Years 1973 and 1998," in *A Profile of Medicaid*, Health Care Financing Administration, September 2000 [Online] http://www.cms.gov [accessed October, 2001]

and medical savings accounts, to participate in Medicare. (As of fall 2001, however, availability of these plans was close to nonexistent.) It also modified the way plan payments are figured and created the Medicare + Choice program. Under the Medicare + Choice plan, a member receives not only the required package of benefits available under Medicare, but also coverage for prescription drugs, routine physical exams, and dental care.

Congress, however, underestimated the savings that would be produced when they passed the Balanced Budget Act. The budget cuts to payments for many services have hurt many health care providers. Some providers, faced with drastic declines in revenues, have lobbied Congress to restore money cut from their payments.

Taking all these factors into account, Medicare faces significant financing hurdles in the future. The projected doubling of the Medicare population to 77 million by 2030 will require increased funding to maintain present benefits. In addition, there is a great need and demand for an additional prescription drug benefit, and there are other badly needed improvements, such as financing of long-term care.

MEDICARE HEALTH MAINTENANCE ORGANIZATIONS. Medicare's fee-for-service system was the method of payment for medicine in 1965, but is no longer. Since 1985 Medicare beneficiaries have had the option of receiving

health care through health maintenance organizations (HMOs). HMOs provide health care services for a fixed prepayment. For monthly prepaid premiums, HMO enrollees receive benefits not available under Medicare alone, such as free prescription drugs, dental care, eyeglasses, hearing aids, and hospitalization. The HMOs, in turn, receive fixed payments from the CMS. This managed care system was intended to control costs while maintaining quality medical care.

Effective in 1998, following the Balanced Budget Act, many HMOs cut back popular benefits, such as free prescription drugs, eyeglasses, and dental care, and/or raised fees for their services. Many private insurers, such as employers, have eliminated drug benefits for retired persons as well. Some health care providers claim their patients are sometimes unable to afford needed medications, and their health consequently suffers. Furthermore, many HMOs that are no longer able to make a profit insuring older Americans have withdrawn their programs.

According to the Kaiser Family Foundation, in 1999 approximately 16 percent of Medicare recipients had enrolled in an HMO, 71 percent lived in an area where a Medicare HMO was available, and 61 percent had a choice of at least two HMOs.

PUBLIC OPINION. In 2000 the Commonwealth Fund surveyed 2,000 adults aged 50 to 70 in order to understand

FIGURE 10.8

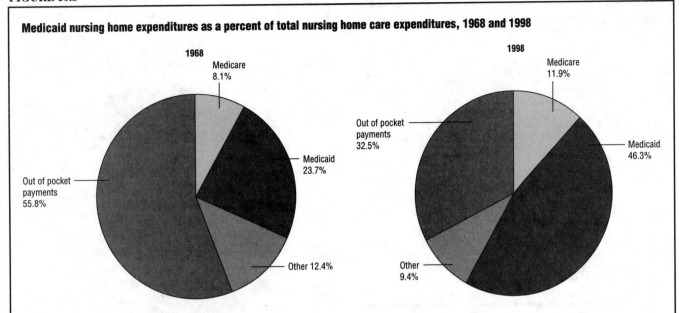

Medicaid nursing home expenditures as a percent of total nursing home care expenditures, 1968 and 1998

Note: Medicaid spending includes the state and federal shares. Total U.S. spending on nursing home care was $87.8 billion in 1998 compared to $2.9 billion in 1968. The 1998 "other" expenditures primarily consists of private health insurance and Veteran's Administration spending. The 1968 "other" consisted largely of non-Medicaid general funds from state/local and federal governments. Percentages may not sum to 100 due to rounding.

SOURCE: "Figure 4.4. Medicaid Nursing Home Expenditures as a Percent of Total U.S. Nursing Home Care Expenditures, Calendar Years 1968 and 1998," in *A Profile of Medicaid*, Health Care Financing Administration, September 2000 [Online] http://www.cms.gov [accessed October, 2001]

how Medicare is perceived (Cathy Shoen, Elisabeth Simantov, Lisa Duchon, and Karen Davis, "Counting on Medicare: Perspectives and Concerns of Americans Ages 50 to 70," July 2000). The survey found that Americans in this age group have a high opinion of the Medicare program. Sixty-eight percent of current Medicare beneficiaries considered becoming eligible for Medicare an important event in their lives. The survey also found that 63 percent of individuals in the 50 to 70 age group who were not eligible for Medicare would be interested in enrolling before age 65 if the option were offered.

Medicaid

Medicaid, Title XIX of the Social Security Act, is a program established in 1966 to provide medical assistance to certain categories of low-income Americans: the aged, blind, disabled, or members of families with dependent children. The costs of the Medicaid program are financed jointly by the federal government and the states. Medicaid covers hospitalization, doctors' fees, laboratory fees, X rays, and long-term nursing home care. It is the largest source of funds for medical and health-related services to America's poorest people and the second-largest public payer of health care costs, after Medicare.

According to the CMS, in 1998, 41.4 million people were enrolled in Medicaid. The elderly accounted for 11 percent (3.9 million people) of those receiving Medicaid,

down from 19 percent in 1973. (See Figure 10.7.) Of all Medicaid beneficiaries, 8.5 percent were aged 65 to 84 and 2.8 percent were aged 85-plus.

Medicaid spent $175 billion on health care costs in 1998. Medicaid's growth rate in spending was 5.9 percent in the 1980s. During the 1990s the average annual real growth rate increased to 9.8 percent. Most of this growth occurred in the early 1990s and growth is now slower. According to the CMS, a variety of factors contribute to this growth in spending, including changes in federal and state policy, congressionally mandated expansions in eligibility, and increases in program spending. Some of the reasons for the more recent decreased growth in spending include slower enrollment growth, lower medical price inflation, and the expansion of managed care.

In 1998 Medicaid was the principal source (46.3 percent) of financing for nursing home care. (See Figure 10.8.) By comparison, Medicaid covered less than a quarter of nursing home expenses in 1968, three years after the program was funded.

With the average cost of a year's nursing home residency exceeding $46,000, it generally does not take long for most Americans to deplete their savings and qualify for Medicaid coverage; half of them do so within six months. "The fact is," said Jeff Eagan, executive director of the Long-Term Care Campaign, a coalition representing the

TABLE 10.5

National veteran population, by age, selected years 1990–2020

Year[1]	Total	Under Age 45	Age 45-64	Age 65-84	Age 85 +	Median Age
1990	27,958,000	8,913,000	11,617,000	7,271,000	156,000	54.4
1995	27,133,000	7,137,000	11,441,000	8,502,000	223,000	55.7
2000	25,498,000	5,701,000	10,266,000	9,020,000	511,000	57.4
2005	23,150,000	4,684,000	9,705,000	7,824,000	937,000	59.1
2010	20,821,000	3,920,000	8,663,000	7,005,000	1,233,000	61.2
2015	18,696,000	3,487,000	6,941,000	7,104,000	1,164,000	61.8
2020	16,880,000	3,392,000	5,919,000	6,570,000	999,000	62.1
% Change[2]	-39.6%	-61.9%	-49.1%	-9.6%	539.0%	14.2%

[1]All data are as of 9/30 of each year. VetPop2000 data from 4/1/90 through 6/30/99 have been interpolated to yield values for 9/30/90 through 9/30/98.
[2]"% Change" refers to change over the period 1990-2020.

SOURCE: Adapted from "Supplemental Table 3. National Veteran Population by Age (1990–2020)", in *Veteran Data and Information,* Department of Veterans Affairs, Washington, DC, July 31, 2001 [Online] http://www.va.gov/vetdata/Demographics/VPwelcome.htm [accessed October, 2001

disabled, "Right now, Medicaid is the long-term care safety net." In addition, it is the primary source of prescription drug coverage for a large number of the poor elderly. Although home health services currently account for only a small share of Medicaid expenditures for the aged, it is the fastest-growing sector.

Veterans' Benefits

Those who have served in the U.S. military are entitled to medical treatment at any of the many veterans' facilities around the nation. According to the Department of Veterans Affairs (VA), in 1999 there were about 9.2 million veterans aged 65 to 84 and 451,000 aged 85-plus. The number of veterans in the 65 to 84 age group was expected to decrease between 2000 and 2020, but the number of 85-plus veterans was expected to more than double in the same period. (See Table 10.5.)

In recent years the VA has shifted health care emphasis from inpatient to outpatient care. From fiscal year 1989 to fiscal year 1999 the total number of patients treated in VA hospitals decreased from 1,059,979 to 597,259. In 1999 there were 172 VA hospitals.

The number of veterans in nursing homes has decreased in recent years after historical highs, in part due to the VA's de-emphasis on its traditional nursing home care. There were 12,724 patients in VA nursing homes in 1999, down from a peak of 13,642 in 1996. The VA was given broader authority by Congress in 1999 to provide a range of extended care options, including adult day health care and respite care, to qualified veterans.

LONG-TERM HEALTH CARE

The majority of Americans see an important role for the government in long-term care, both in regulating the

FIGURE 10.9

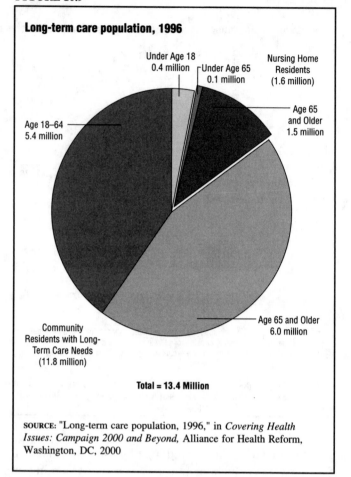

Long-term care population, 1996

Under Age 18 0.4 million
Under Age 65 0.1 million
Nursing Home Residents (1.6 million)
Age 18–64 5.4 million
Age 65 and Older 1.5 million
Community Residents with Long-Term Care Needs (11.8 million)
Age 65 and Older 6.0 million

Total = 13.4 Million

SOURCE: "Long-term care population, 1996," in *Covering Health Issues: Campaign 2000 and Beyond,* Alliance for Health Reform, Washington, DC, 2000

quality of long-term care facilities and in helping finance the costs for nursing home care.

— *The NewsHour with Jim Lehrer,* the Kaiser Family Foundation, and the Harvard School of Public Health, *National Survey on Nursing Homes,* October 2001

Perhaps the most pressing and most difficult health care problem facing America today is long-term care. Long-term care includes a wide range of services for persons who need assistance from day to day with basic living activities such as dressing, eating, and toileting. In 1996 (the most recent data available) about 13 million seniors and persons with disabilities required long-term care. (See Figure 10.9.) Of those 13 million, a significant majority—about 60 percent—were over age 65. Only 1.6 million people in need of long-term care lived in a nursing home or similar facility in 1996, but 90 percent of nursing home residents were elderly.

In 1996 the John Hancock Mutual Life Insurance Company, in conjunction with the National Council on Aging, surveyed Americans about their plans for future long-term medical needs. The study found that less than half of all adults had planned for the possibility of debilitating illness. Among the reasons given for lack of planning were "the issue is difficult to face," more immediate

FIGURE 10.10

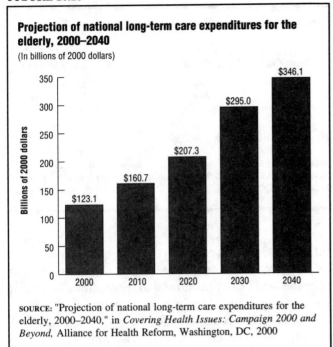

Projection of national long-term care expenditures for the elderly, 2000–2040

(In billions of 2000 dollars)

SOURCE: "Projection of national long-term care expenditures for the elderly, 2000–2040," in *Covering Health Issues: Campaign 2000 and Beyond,* Alliance for Health Reform, Washington, DC, 2000

FIGURE 10.11

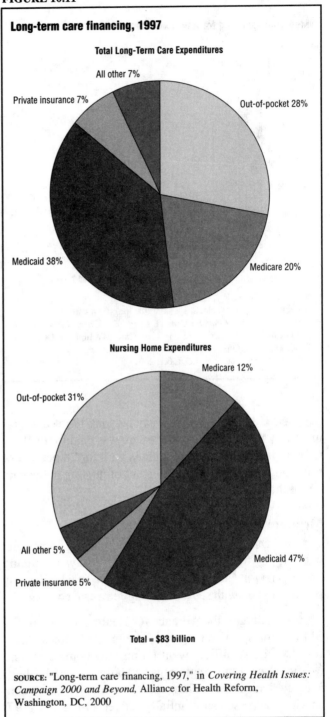

Long-term care financing, 1997

Total Long-Term Care Expenditures

All other 7%
Private insurance 7%
Out-of-pocket 28%
Medicare 20%
Medicaid 38%

Nursing Home Expenditures

Medicare 12%
Out-of-pocket 31%
All other 5%
Private insurance 5%
Medicaid 47%

Total = $83 billion

SOURCE: "Long-term care financing, 1997," in *Covering Health Issues: Campaign 2000 and Beyond,* Alliance for Health Reform, Washington, DC, 2000

needs, procrastination, lack of affordability, and unwillingness to take financial risks.

Predominating reasons varied by age group. Baby boomers most often (75 percent) cited being too busy, although the youngest boomers claimed to have more pressing needs associated with child rearing. Those aged 51 to 75 said the issue was better dealt with when it arises, and two-thirds of that group said the issue was too hard to face. The oldest Americans, born before 1925, believed it was too late to save meaningfully toward the possibility of need. Three-fourths of respondents of working age claimed they would take advantage of long-term care insurance if their employers offered it.

Options Are Limited and Expensive

The options for good, affordable long-term care in the United States are few. One year's stay in a nursing home costs more than $46,000 a year. Even hiring an unskilled caregiver who makes home visits can cost more than $25,000 a year; skilled care costs much more. Most elderly people and young families cannot afford this expense. Lifetime savings can be consumed before the need for care ends.

The Future of Spending for Long-Term Care

The Congressional Budget Office (CBO) reported that the population over age 85, those most likely to require long-term care, would more than triple by 2040. Even though elderly disability rates have fallen in recent years, reducing somewhat the need for long-term care, the CBO projected that spending for long-term care would grow by more than two and one-half times by 2040, reaching $346 billion (in inflation-adjusted dollars) that year for the elderly alone. (See Figure 10.10.)

Who Pays for Long-Term Care?

Long-term care, especially nursing home care, is costly, as noted. One reason long-term care is such an explosive issue is the patchwork arrangements in place to pay those big bills. Medicare and Medigap insurance, whether supplied through an employer or privately

FIGURE 10.12

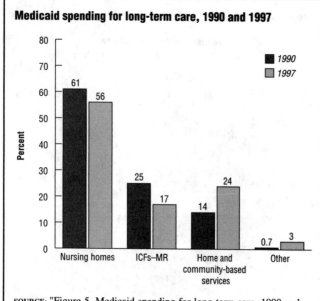

Medicaid spending for long-term care, 1990 and 1997

■ 1990
■ 1997

SOURCE: "Figure 5. Medicaid spending for long-term care, 1990 and 1997," in *Defining Common Ground: Long Term Care Financing Reform in 2001*, Citizens for Long Term Care, Washington, DC, February, 2001 [Online] http://www.citizensforltc.org/whitepapers.html [accessed October, 2001]

TABLE 10.6

Long-term care insurance average annual premium

Average Age	Base Policy	With 5% Inflation Protection
40	$247	$589
50	$364	$802
65	$980	$1,829
79	$3,907	$5,592

4-year policy, $100/day, 20-day "deductible"

SOURCE: "Long-term care insurance average annual premium," in *Covering Health Issues: Campaign 2000 and Beyond*, Alliance for Health Reform, Washington, DC, 2000

purchased, do not completely pay for long-term care. Figure 10.11 shows how long-term care was paid for in 1997. Of note is the fact that individuals paid for 28 percent of total long-term care and 31 percent of nursing home care out of their own pockets.

Medicare and Medicaid

Medicare does not cover custodial nursing home care, but will pay for short-term rehabilitative stays in nursing homes, and for some home health care. Medicaid is the only public program with substantial long-term care coverage.

According to the Alliance for Health Reform, of the $115 billion spent on long-term care in 1997, almost three-fourths, or $83 billion, went for nursing home care, and Medicaid paid the single biggest share, just under half. Medicaid spending on home and community-based care services increased substantially between 1990 and 1997. (See Figure 10.12.) In 1990 only 14 percent of spending went for home and community-based services. In 1997 almost a quarter, 24 percent, was spent on such services.

Medicaid, however, does not work like insurance, which offers protection from catastrophic expense. Middle-income persons needing nursing home care, for example, become eligible for Medicaid only after they "spend down" their own personal income and assets (to $2,000 or less for an unmarried individual). Medicaid begins paying, in that case, only after the person is impoverished.

Even then, Medicaid will not necessarily pay the entire nursing home bill. People must meet income eligi-

bility standards as well. In some states, people with incomes too high for regular Medicaid eligibility, but with high medical bills, are allowed to spend down into being income-eligible for Medicaid. They must incur medical bills until their income for a given period, minus the medical expenses, falls below the Medicaid limit.

While every state's Medicaid program covers long-term care, each has made different choices about the shape of its program. Eligibility rules vary. Protection for the finances of a spouse of a nursing home resident vary widely. Even the mix and quantity of services differ. Thus the levels of Medicaid long-term care spending per beneficiary vary substantially. New York, California, Massachusetts, and Texas accounted for 60 percent of Medicaid home care spending in 1995, almost twice their combined 33 percent share of elderly Medicaid beneficiaries.

Private Long-Term Care Insurance

In 2000 the Alliance for Health Reform predicted that about 4 percent of long-term care bills would be paid from private long-term care insurance that year, and that some 6 to 7 percent of those over age 65 had such policies. The high costs of policies are often prohibitive for older people. In 1996 a policy with four years' benefits at $100 per day and limited inflation protection cost $67 a month for someone age 50, but more than $466 a month for someone age 79. Table 10.6 shows how average annual premiums increase with the age of the policyholder.

Long-term care policy sales have grown (600,000 policies were sold in 1996), especially since favorable tax treatment was clarified in 1996 legislation. Average premiums have been stable, even declining, and benefits in average policies have improved. But insurers have found it tough to convince middle-aged Americans, for whom premiums are more affordable, that they need long-term care insurance at that stage in their lives. Few employers have offered to help pay for long-term care insurance, unlike health insurance, for their workers.

The Crisis in Long-Term Care

Most industry analysts believe progress has been made in meeting the health care demands of an aging population. Nonetheless, governmental budget cuts to Medicare, Medicaid, and Social Security, along with attempts in Congress to lessen regulation, may threaten the quality of long-term care. The AARP (formerly the American Association of Retired Persons), the nation's largest organization of older people, predicted that more than 2 million people could lose coverage for long-term care—including nursing home coverage and assistance at home—if budget cuts occurred. The supporters of less regulation countered that strict regulation is no longer necessary and that free-market conditions will both improve the quality of care and decrease the cost of nursing home care.

FALLING THROUGH THE CRACKS

A 1997 Public Health Service study found that 6 percent, or 3.3 million, of the elderly reported that they did not have a regular source of medical care. Older persons with Medicare and private or public health insurance coverage were more likely to have a regular source of care than those who had Medicare only or who were uninsured. Among the reasons cited for lack of care were "does not need a doctor" (47 percent), inconvenience (23 percent), "does not trust doctor" (7 percent), cannot afford (7 percent), and other (10 percent).

Unmet needs were most likely to include dental care (1.4 million elderly), glasses (1 million), medical care (500,000), and prescription medications (600,000). Although the majority of elderly people had a regular source of care, many did not get routine preventive services such as immunizations, Pap smears, or mammograms. Almost 41 percent did not get influenza immunizations, 62.7 percent did not get pneumonia immunizations, 32.1 percent of women did not get mammograms, and 49.6 percent did not receive digital rectal examinations for colon or prostate cancer. For whatever reasons, many elderly are not getting preventive care services.

PROVIDING HEALTH CARE—A POLITICAL AND ETHICAL CONCERN

Health care costs continue to rise mainly because of increased prices for services, more sophisticated technologies, rising demand for services, and inflation. How much and what kind of health care protection should be available are ongoing questions with no easy answers. The problems have not gone unnoticed by Congress. A wide array of bills have been introduced with proposals ranging from almost total protection under federal programs to almost complete dependence on the private sector. There is little consensus on a solution. Faced with an aging population and ever-rising medical costs, the nation's health care predicament is a major challenge for policy makers.

CHAPTER 11
CRIME AND THE ELDERLY

CRIMES AGAINST THE ELDERLY

The U.S. Department of Justice, in *Crimes against Persons Age 65 or Older, 1992–97* (Washington, DC, January 2000), reported that Americans 65 years and older were considerably less likely to be crime victims than younger people. The elderly make up 12 percent of the population, but accounted for only 7 percent of crime victims between 1992 and 1997. During this time, the elderly were victims of almost 2.7 million property and violent crimes. (See Table 11.1.)

In average numbers for the period 1992–97, people over age 65 experienced violent crime at the rate of 5.3 violent crimes per 1,000 persons, compared to a rate of more than 100 violent crimes per 1,000 people for those under 25, a rate of 48 per 1,000 in those aged 25 to 49, and 15 per 1,000 among those aged 50 to 64. (See Figure 11.1.) For property crimes over the same period (1992–97), households headed by the elderly were victimized at an average rate of 117.3 per 1,000 households, compared to almost 500 per 1,000 for those households headed by someone aged 12 to 24, 350 per 1,000 among those households headed by a person aged 25 to 49, and almost 250 per 1,000 for households headed by someone aged 50 to 64. (See Figure 11.2.)

TABLE 11.1

Crimes against persons or heads of household age 65 or older, by type of crime

	Average number per year, 1992-97	Percent
Total crimes	2,694,290	100.0%
Personal crimes	212,420	7.9%
Crimes of violence	166,330	6.2
Murder	1,000	0.04
Nonfatal violence	165,330	6.1
Rape/Sexual assault	3,280	0.12
Robbery	40,950	1.5
Total assault	121,100	4.5
Aggravated assault	34,050	1.3
Simple assault	87,050	3.2
Personal theft	46,090	1.7
Number of persons age 65 or older	31,296,350	
Property crimes	2,481,870	92.1%
Household burglary	623,790	23.2
Motor vehicle theft	124,930	4.6
Theft	1,733,160	64.3
Households heads age 65 or older	21,161,850	

SOURCE: Patsy Klaus, "Victimizations of persons age 65 or older or of households with a head of household age 65 or older," in *Crimes Against Persons Age 65 or Older, 1992–97*, U.S. Department of Justice, Bureau of Justice Statistics, Washington, DC, 2000

FIGURE 11.1

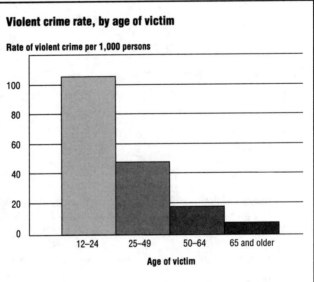

Violent crime rate, by age of victim

Rate of violent crime per 1,000 persons

Age of victim

Note: Violence includes murder, rape and sexual assault, robbery, and simple and aggravated assault.

SOURCE: Patsy Klaus, "Violent crimes per 1,000 persons age 65 or older," in *Crimes Against Persons Age 65 or Older, 1992–97*, U.S. Department of Justice, Bureau of Justice Statistics, Washington, DC, 2000

FIGURE 11.2

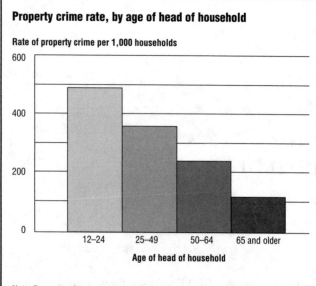

Property crime rate, by age of head of household

Rate of property crime per 1,000 households

Age of head of household

Note: Property crime includes household burglary, motor vehicle theft, and theft.

SOURCE: Patsy Klaus, "Property crimes per 1,000 households with a household head age 65 or older," in *Crimes Against Persons Age 65 or Older, 1992–97*, U.S. Department of Justice, Bureau of Justice Statistics, Washington, DC, 2000

FIGURE 11.3

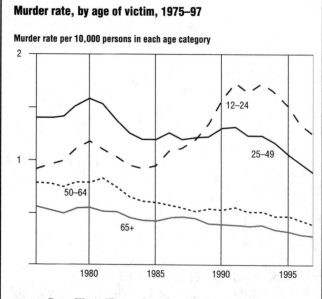

Murder rate, by age of victim, 1975–97

Murder rate per 10,000 persons in each age category

SOURCE: Patsy Klaus, "Rates of murder against persons age 65 or older declined after 1976 while those against persons ages 12–24 fluctuated," in *Crimes Against Persons Age 65 or Older, 1992–97*, U.S. Department of Justice, Bureau of Justice Statistics, Washington, DC, 2000

FIGURE 11.4

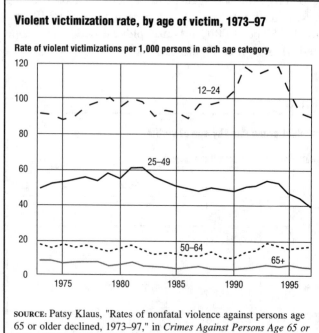

Violent victimization rate, by age of victim, 1973–97

Rate of violent victimizations per 1,000 persons in each age category

SOURCE: Patsy Klaus, "Rates of nonfatal violence against persons age 65 or older declined, 1973–97," in *Crimes Against Persons Age 65 or Older, 1992–97*, U.S. Department of Justice, Bureau of Justice Statistics, Washington, DC, 2000

FIGURE 11.5

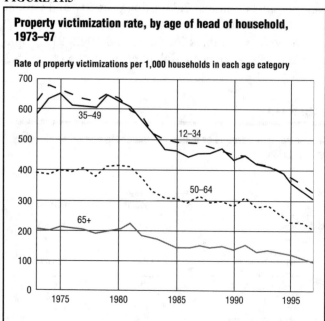

Property victimization rate, by age of head of household, 1973–97

Rate of property victimizations per 1,000 households in each age category

SOURCE: Patsy Klaus, "For a household with a person age 65 or older as head, property crimes in 1997 occurred at half the 1973 rate," in *Crimes Against Persons Age 65 or Older, 1992–97*, U.S. Department of Justice, Bureau of Justice Statistics, Washington, DC, 2000

Crime victimization rates among the elderly have generally declined by half since 1973. Murders of those over 65 dropped by half from 1976 to 1997 (see Figure 11.3), nonfatal violence fell from 9 incidents per 1,000 persons in 1973 to 4.5 incidents per 1,000 persons in 1997 (see Figure 11.4), and property crimes decreased from 205 per 1,000 in 1973 to 96 per 1,000 persons in 1997 (see Figure 11.5).

Experts believe that some economic crimes, such as fraud and confidence schemes, disproportionately affect persons aged 65 and older, although statistics on these

TABLE 11.2

Victim-offender relationship

Type of violence and victim-offender relationship	Age of victim	
	65 or older	12-64
Murder	100.0%	100.0%
Nonstranger total	50.1	45.8
Relative, intimate	26.4	13.5
Other known	23.7	32.3
Stranger	14.6	14.3
Unknown relationship	35.3	39.9
Total nonlethal violence	100.0%	100.0%
Relatives or intimates	9.1	15.0
Well known	12.9	15.3
Casual acquaintances	14.5	18.0
Strangers	56.2	48.4
Unknown relationship	7.4	3.3

Note: "Other known" murder victims includes a wide variety of relationships. These data cannot be classified into "well known" and "casual acquaintances." For nonlethal violence, the victim identified the nature of the relationship as "well known" or "casual acquaintance."

SOURCE: Patsy Klaus, "Relatives of intimates committed more than 1 in 4 of the murders and 1 in 10 of the incidents of nonlethal violence against persons age 65 or older," in *Crimes Against Persons Age 65 or Older, 1992–97*, U.S. Department of Justice, Bureau of Justice Statistics, Washington, DC, 2000

FIGURE 11.6

Place of victimization

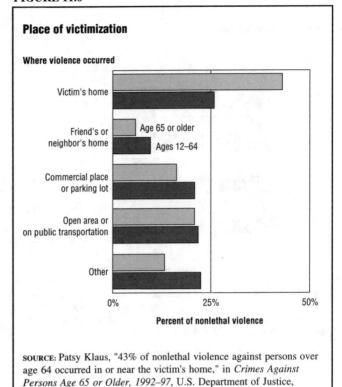

SOURCE: Patsy Klaus, "43% of nonlethal violence against persons over age 64 occurred in or near the victim's home," in *Crimes Against Persons Age 65 or Older, 1992–97*, U.S. Department of Justice, Bureau of Justice Statistics, Washington, DC, 2000

---

crimes are not collected by the major crime reporting agencies. The elderly often live on fixed incomes and limited savings. "Get rich" schemes can appear very attractive to the elderly because they offer the promise of economic security.

The Emotional Impact of Crime

Incidents of virtually every major type of crime in the United States decreased significantly between 1993 and 2000. According to the Federal Bureau of Investigation's Uniform Crime Reports, the crime rate fell for the ninth straight year in 2000, declining 3.3 percent from 1999, 18.9 percent from 1996, and 30.1 percent from 1991. Victimization is, however, a severe problem for the elderly. Speaking before the House Select Committee on Aging in 1995, Irwin I. Kimmelman, attorney general for the New Jersey Department of Law and Safety, noted that it is not the number of crimes, but the "terrible and tragic impact that crime has on [the elderly] that is significant. Crime causes much more fear among the elderly and has a far more deleterious impact on the quality of their lives."

Crimes against the elderly are particularly devastating because older people are often less resilient than younger people. Even so-called nonviolent crimes, such as purse snatching, vandalism, and burglary, can be devastating. Stolen or damaged articles and property are often irreplaceable, either because of sentimental or monetary value. Even nonviolent crimes leave victims with a sense of violation and vulnerability.

Once victimized, an elderly person can be reluctant to leave his or her home, due to fear of strangers. This may be justified in some cases and not justified in others: Only 14.6 percent of murders of the elderly between 1992 and 1997 were committed by a person who was a total stranger to them, but 56.2 percent of nonlethal violence incidents were perpetrated by strangers. (See Table 11.2.)

CHARACTERISTICS OF ELDERLY CRIME VICTIMS

Among the elderly, certain groups are more likely to experience a crime than others. More than 60 percent of the elderly live in metropolitan areas, and many live in inner cities, where crime rates are the highest. From 1992 to 1997, 43 percent of violent, nonlethal crimes against older people occurred in or near their homes (compared to 26 percent for younger victims). (See Figure 11.6.) For the elderly, the homes and neighborhoods where they generally spend most of their time do not necessarily offer escape from victimization, but, in fact, may make them especially vulnerable.

As a group, the elderly are more dependent on walking and public transportation, which increases their exposure to possible criminal attack. People aged 65 and older were about six times more likely than younger persons to "never" go out at night. Crimes against the elderly were far more likely to occur during the day (70 percent) than

FIGURE 11.7

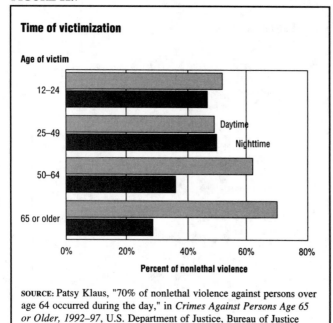

Time of victimization

SOURCE: Patsy Klaus, "70% of nonlethal violence against persons over age 64 occurred during the day," in *Crimes Against Persons Age 65 or Older, 1992–97*, U.S. Department of Justice, Bureau of Justice Statistics, Washington, DC, 2000

FIGURE 11.8

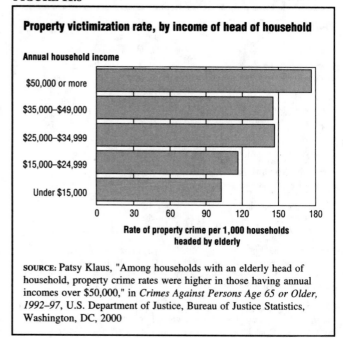

Property victimization rate, by income of head of household

SOURCE: Patsy Klaus, "Among households with an elderly head of household, property crime rates were higher in those having annual incomes over $50,000," in *Crimes Against Persons Age 65 or Older, 1992–97*, U.S. Department of Justice, Bureau of Justice Statistics, Washington, DC, 2000

at night (30 percent). (See Figure 11.7.) Most personal theft from elderly persons took place in stores or other businesses and occurred during the day.

Crimes of violence were highest among those who lived in a city, rented their homes, were divorced or separated, were African American or Hispanic, and had incomes below $7,500. Crimes of theft were greatest for those elderly with incomes over $25,000, those who lived in cities, and those who were divorced or separated. Property crime rates were highest for those with incomes above $50,000. (See Figure 11.8.) Elderly whites had both the lowest violent crime (see Figure 11.9) and property crime rates (see Figure 11.10).

Elderly persons were about as likely as younger persons to sustain serious injuries from violent crimes. Among people aged 65 and older who were victims of violence, about 22 percent were injured, approximately half of those required treatment at the scene or in a doctor's office or hospital, and about 1 percent were hospitalized overnight. (See Figure 11.11.)

Weapons were somewhat more likely to be used against elderly victims of violence (32 percent) than against younger victims (28 percent). Firearms comprised 42 percent of the weapons used against the elderly. Knives accounted for 17 percent; the remainder were other weapons or unknown.

The Elderly Are More Likely to Report Crime

People aged 65 and older were more likely to report violence (52 percent), personal theft (45 percent), and

property crimes (36 percent) to the police than were younger victims (who reported 43 percent of violent crimes, 29 percent of personal thefts, and 32 percent of property crimes). (See Figure 11.12.)

Older People Are Considered Easy Prey

Because of their physical limitations, older people are often considered easy prey. The elderly usually do not resist a criminal attack. They are aware that they may lack the strength to repel a younger aggressor and that they are particularly susceptible to broken bones and fractured hips, which could permanently cripple them. The U.S. Bureau of Justice reported that victims aged 65 and older took protective measures in about half of their victimizations, compared to 73 percent of younger victims. Those over 65 who try to protect themselves most often use nonphysical action, such as arguing, reasoning, screaming, or running away. Younger victims are more likely to use physical action, such as attacking, resisting, or chasing the offender. Most criminals are likely less concerned about nonphysical defenses than they are about physical resistance.

Treatment by the Courts

Elderly victims are sometimes treated poorly by the criminal justice system. Because of physical impairments such as poor hearing and vision and slowness of movement and speech, older persons can encounter impatience and insensitivity when they attempt to report a crime. This kind of treatment adds to their frustration and sense of helplessness.

Victim compensation for crimes against the elderly is currently provided on the state level, and amounts vary

FIGURE 11.9

Violent victimization rate, by age, sex, and race of victim

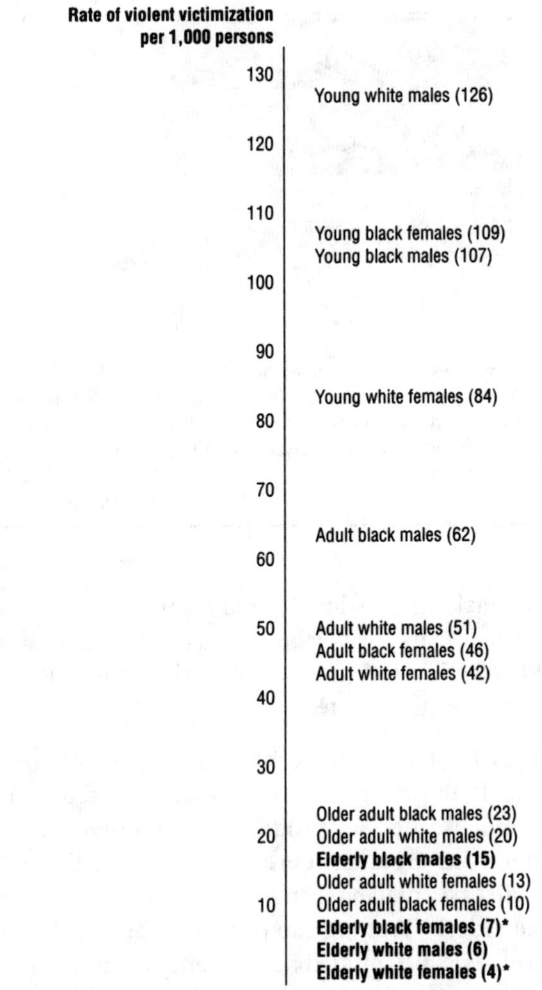

Rate of violent victimization
per 1,000 persons

130	Young white males (126)
120	
110	Young black females (109)
100	Young black males (107)
90	
80	Young white females (84)
70	
60	Adult black males (62)
50	Adult white males (51)
	Adult black females (46)
40	Adult white females (42)
30	
20	Older adult black males (23)
	Older adult white males (20)
	Elderly black males (15)
10	Older adult white females (13)
	Older adult black females (10)
	Elderly black females (7)*
	Elderly white males (6)
	Elderly white females (4)*

Note: This report applies the following age categories: Young (ages 12–24); Adult (ages 24–49); Older adult (ages 50–64); Elderly (age 65 or older)

*The apparent difference between elderly females is not statistically significant.

SOURCE: Patsy Klaus, "White women age 65 or older had the lowest rate of nonlethal violent victimization, 1992–97," in *Crimes Against Persons Age 65 or Older, 1992–97*, U.S. Department of Justice, Bureau of Justice Statistics, Washington, DC, 2000

FIGURE 11.10

Property crime rate, by age, sex, and race of head of household

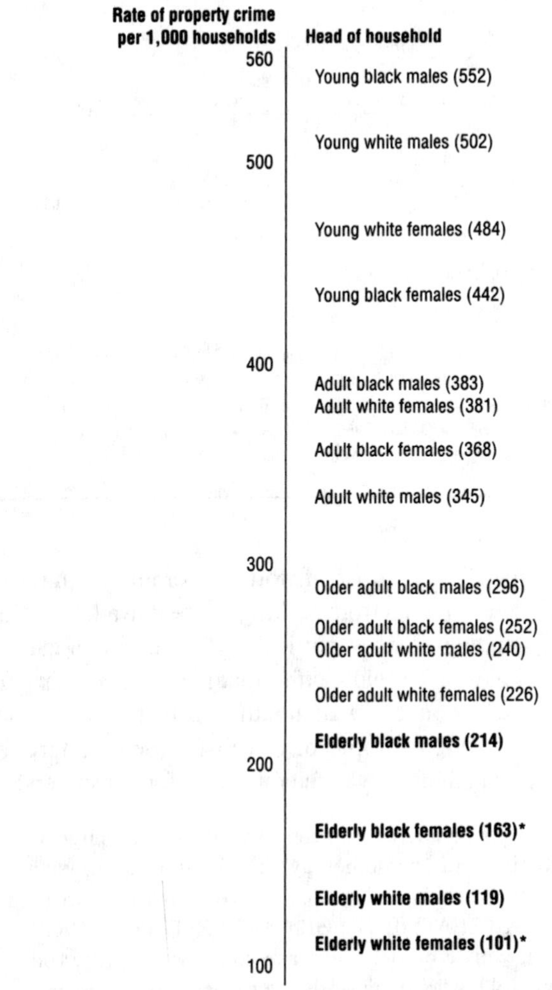

Rate of property crime
per 1,000 households | Head of household

560	Young black males (552)
500	Young white males (502)
	Young white females (484)
	Young black females (442)
400	Adult black males (383)
	Adult white females (381)
	Adult black females (368)
	Adult white males (345)
300	Older adult black males (296)
	Older adult black females (252)
	Older adult white males (240)
	Older adult white females (226)
	Elderly black males (214)
200	
	Elderly black females (163)*
	Elderly white males (119)
	Elderly white females (101)*
100	

Note: This report applies the following age categories: Young (ages 12–24); Adult (ages 24–49); Older adult (ages 50–64); Elderly (age 65 or older)

*The apparent difference between elderly females is not statistically significant.

SOURCE: Patsy Klaus, "Households with a white female head of household age 65 or older had the lowest property crime rates, 1992–97," in *Crimes Against Persons Age 65 or Older, 1992–97*, U.S. Department of Justice, Bureau of Justice Statistics, Washington, DC, 2000

from state to state. Most states compensate for medical, counseling, and physical therapy expenses associated with the crime and reimburse for lost wages, loss of support to dependents, and for funeral expenses.

FRAUD

Health Fraud

On September 10, 2001, Howard Beales, director of the U.S. Bureau of Consumer Protection of the Federal Trade Commission (FTC), testified before the U.S. Senate Special Committee on Aging for its hearing "Health Fraud and the Elderly: A Continuing Health Epidemic." The FTC enforces a variety of federal antitrust and con-

sumer protection laws. Beales's remarks focused on the FTC's work to combat fraudulent claims for products marketed as treatments or cures for serious diseases. Many of these diseases, including cancer, heart disease, and arthritis, are particularly prevalent among the elderly.

Beales pointed out that at the consumer level, the costs of these products and services range from a few dollars to tens of thousands of dollars for cancer treatments offered in foreign "clinics." In most cases, these products and services are not covered by insurance. In addition to economic injury, some products and services can pose a serious

FIGURE 11.11

Injury and treatment rate of elderly victims of violence

Not injured	Injured
77.9%	22.1%

Not treated	Treated
10.9%	11.2%

	Doctor's		
At scene	office*	Hospital	Elsewhere*
2.9%	2.1%	5.6%	0.6%

Released from	
emergency room	Hospitalized*
4.7%	0.9%

*Based on 10 or fewer cases.

SOURCE: Patsy Klaus, "On average each year 1992–97, of persons age 65 or older who reported being a victim of violence, 22% were injured and 1% were hospitalized overnight," in *Crimes Against Persons Age 65 or Older, 1992–97*, U.S. Department of Justice, Bureau of Justice Statistics, Washington, DC, 2000

FIGURE 11.12

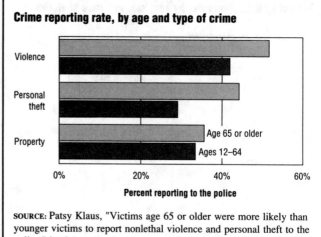

Crime reporting rate, by age and type of crime

SOURCE: Patsy Klaus, "Victims age 65 or older were more likely than younger victims to report nonlethal violence and personal theft to the police," in *Crimes Against Persons Age 65 or Older, 1992–97*, U.S. Department of Justice, Bureau of Justice Statistics, Washington, DC, 2000

health threat. The promise of worthless or unproven remedies can deter victims from seeking the best available treatments. In some instances, particularly in the area of cancer, marketers have even told victims that it is not necessary for them to seek conventional treatment. In his testimony, Beales gave this example of a website for an unproven treatment, which displayed the following for consumers:

> Does this mean you can cancel your date for surgery, radiation and chemotherapy? YES! After curing your cancer with this recipe it cannot come back. THIS IS NOT A TREATMENT FOR CANCER: IT IS A CURE! But if you do not wish to make your doctor angry, you could follow her or his wishes, too. Be careful not to lose ANY VITAL ANATOMICAL PARTS in surgery though, because you may need them later when you are healthy!

In some patients, delaying treatment may worsen the condition. Deferred treatment is not the only risk, however; some products and services are themselves dangerous. The FTC has brought recent cases against marketers of products containing comfrey, an herbal product that can lead to serious liver damage when taken internally.

The FTC, U.S. Food and Drug Administration (FDA), U.S. Postal Service, and state law enforcement and regulatory agencies all play a role in protecting consumers, especially seniors, from health fraud. To combat health fraud on the Internet, the FTC started Operation Cure.All, an initiative targeting deceptive and misleading Internet promotion of products and services as cures or treatments for serious diseases. In addition to the FTC, participants in Operation Cure.All include the FDA, several state attorneys general, and Health Canada.

Operation Cure.All conducted two rounds of Internet surfing in 1997 and 1998. They found over 1600 sites worldwide making questionable claims for products marketed as treatments for various diseases. Of these sites, over 800 were located in North America, with the vast majority in the United States.

In 2001 the FTC filed eight cases as part of Operation Cure.All, targeting companies that marketed a variety of devices, herbal products, and other dietary supplements to treat or cure cancer, arthritis, Alzheimer's disease, diabetes, and many other diseases that affect the elderly. Among the products for which marketers made unsubstantiated health benefit claims were a DHEA (dehydroepiandrosterone) hormonal supplement, St. John's wort, various multiherbal supplements, colloidal silver, comfrey, and a variety of electrical therapy devices. Prior to 2001, the FTC had filed eight Operation Cure.All cases. The challenged products include Cat's Claw, shark cartilage, cetylmyristoleate (CMO), Essiac Tea, and magnetic therapies. In all these cases, the companies made strong claims about treatments or cures for serious diseases with little or no evidence to support the claims.

Financial Fraud

Financial crimes against the elderly are on the rise. Such crimes include telemarketing, mail fraud, Internet scams, health care and insurance fraud, pension and trust fund fraud, mail theft, reverse mortgage fraud, and many others. The National Fraud Information Center estimated that there were 14,000 illegal telemarketing operations in the United States alone annually, bilking the elderly out of $40 billion each year. Surveys by the AARP (formerly the American Association of Retired Persons) revealed that over half of telemarketing fraud victims were aged 50 or older.

Dennis M. Lormel, chief of the Financial Crimes Section of the Federal Bureau of Investigation (FBI) also testified before the U.S. Senate Special Committee on Aging for its hearing on frauds against the elderly. Lormel reported that "it has been the experience of the FBI that the elderly are preyed upon by...unscrupulous individuals for several reasons":

- The elderly are generally more likely than others to have substantial financial savings, home equity, or credit, all of which are tempting to fraud perpetrators.

- Those who grew up in the first half of the twentieth century are often reluctant to be rude to others, so they may be more likely to hear out a con's story. They can also be overly trusting.

- The elderly are less likely to report frauds, due to embarrassment, not knowing who to report to, or fear of appearing mentally incapable to handle their own affairs.

- Older Americans who do report fraud may not make very good witnesses. Their memories may fade over the often-extended span of time between the actual crime and the trial, and on the witness stand, they may not be able to provide detailed enough information to lead to a conviction.

- Finally, the elderly are likely to be very interested in products that claim to enhance mental or physical functioning, or that offer cures for health problems. Lormel pointed out that in a society where technology advances every day, "it is not so unbelievable that the products offered by these con men can do what they say they can do."

In its annual report *Developments in Aging* (106th Congress), the U.S. Senate Special Committee on Aging described one common financial scheme frequently used by fraudulent marketers. It is called the "sweepstakes" or "free giveaways" scheme. A consumer receives a postcard, which announces that he or she is entitled to claim one or more prizes. The award notice is professionally designed to appear legitimate. The postcard bears a toll-free telephone number and the consumer is instructed that he or she must simply call to claim the prizes. Once the toll-free number is accessed, a recording instructs the consumer to touch numbers on the telephone that correspond with a "claim number" that appears on the postcard.

Ultimately, the consumer receives no prize. What is received is a "telephone bill" that reflects a substantial charge for the call, just as if a 900 number had been called. The entry of the sequence of numbers that matched the claim number engages an automated information service for which the consumer is charged.

The AARP described another financial scheme, called the "dishonest teller" scheme. The scheme begins when the caller, who claims to be a bank official or "bank examiner," informs the elderly person that his or her checking or savings account has had some unusual withdrawals. The con waits for a reaction to see if the person on the other end of the line believes that the caller is really a bank examiner who is trying to help him or her. If so, the caller asks the call recipient for private account information—the caller claims to "assist" the bank, but in actuality, this information allows the illegal withdrawal of cash from the older person's account.

Some bank examiner cons have been known to approach people leaving a shopping center and ask, under the pretense of a survey, how they paid for their purchases. If cash was used, other cons, posing as law enforcement officers, follow the potential victims home and accuse them of using counterfeit money. They then follow up with a story that the victims' account has been manipulated by a dishonest teller.

Medicare Fraud

Medicare loses millions of dollars every year due to fraud and abuse. The most common forms of Medicare fraud are:

- Billing for services not furnished

- Misrepresenting a diagnosis to justify a higher payment

- Soliciting, offering, or receiving a kickback

- Charging Medicare higher fees than normal for certain procedures

- Falsifying certificates of medical necessity, plans of treatment, and medical records to justify payment

- Billing for a service not furnished as billed

In 1996 Congress enacted the Health Insurance Portability and Accountability Act (HIPAA), which created funding to protect Medicare's program integrity. In one of the largest efforts in the history of Medicare, the program has undertaken a major campaign to help eliminate Medicare fraud, waste, and abuse. According to the Office of Inspector General, as a result of the campaign, the federal government recovered $1.2 billion in fines, settlements, and judgments for the Medicare program during fiscal year 2000.

In order to combat Medicare fraud on the level of the beneficiary, the U.S. Administration on Aging (AoA) provides grants to 48 local organizations to help older Americans be better health care consumers and to help identify and prevent fraudulent health care practices. These Senior Medicare Patrol projects train volunteer retired professionals, such as doctors, nurses, accountants, investigators, law enforcement personnel, attorneys, and teachers, to help Medicare and Medicaid beneficiaries become better health care consumers. Since 1997 these projects and other AoA grants have trained more than 25,000 volunteers, conducted more than 60,000 community education events, and counseled more than 1 million beneficiaries.

The "Who Pays? You Pay" campaign is an example of a successful outreach effort to combat Medicare fraud. It is a unique partnership between the AARP, the U.S. Department of Health and Human Services, and the U.S. Department of Justice. It establishes a line of defense against a problem that costs the Medicare program billions of dollars each year.

The campaign asks beneficiaries to regularly review their Medicare statements and ask such questions as "Did I receive the services or products for which Medicare is being billed? Did my doctor order the service or product for me? And, to the best of my judgment, is the service or product necessary given my health condition?" If the answer to any of these questions is no, the partners emphasize working first with the health care provider or Medicare insurance company. If there is still doubt, beneficiaries are to call a hotline (1-800-HHS-TIPS). Medicare beneficiaries receive rewards up to $1,000 for successfully identifying fraud and abuse.

DOMESTIC ABUSE AND MISTREATMENT OF THE ELDERLY

Domestic violence against the elderly is a phenomenon that has only recently gained public attention. It is impossible to determine exactly how many elderly people are the victims of domestic violence. As with child abuse, the number of actual cases is larger than the number of reported cases. Experts agree, however, that elder abuse is far less likely to be reported than child or spousal abuse. Definitions of abuse and reporting methods vary greatly both between states and among different government agencies.

Nationwide, reports of domestic elder abuse have increased. The National Center on Elder Abuse (NCEA) reported 117,000 incidents in 1986. By 1996 (the most recent statistics available), 293,000 cases were reported, an increase of 150 percent over the 10 years.

The NCEA estimated, however, that despite the lower reported numbers, in 1996 approximately 1.01 million elders were victims of domestic abuse. Another 1.15 million elders are believed to have been victims of self-neglect, bringing the total number of abuse victims to 2.16 million individuals that year. Many of these cases have gone unreported. With enhanced public awareness and improved reporting systems, experts anticipate reports of elder domestic abuse will continue to increase.

Types of Mistreatment

Research on domestic elder abuse is still in its infancy, but studies conducted over the past 15 years have revealed several recurring forms of abuse. Federal definitions of elder abuse, neglect, and exploitation appeared for the first time in 1987 amendments to the Older Americans Act. Broadly defined, there are three basic categories of abuse: (1) domestic elder abuse, (2) institutional elder abuse, and (3) self-neglect or self-abuse.

Domestic elder abuse generally refers to any form of maltreatment of an older person by someone who has a special relationship with the elder (a spouse, sibling, child, friend, or caregiver). Most sources have identified the following categories of domestic elder mistreatment:

- Physical abuse—inflicting physical pain or injury

- Sexual abuse—nonconsensual sexual contact of any kind with an older person

- Emotional or psychological abuse—inflicting mental anguish by, for example, name calling, humiliation, threats, or isolation

- Neglect—willful or unintentional failure to provide basic necessities, such as food and medical care, due to caregiver indifference, inability, or ignorance

- Material or financial abuse—exploiting or misusing an older person's money or assets

- Abandonment—the desertion of an elderly person by an individual who has physical custody of the elder or who has assumed responsibility for providing care to the elder

- Self-neglect—behaviors of an elderly person that threaten his or her own health or safety

The NCEA reported that most of the confirmed cases, or about 55 percent of all reports of elder abuse in 1996 (the most recent existing data), turned out to be self-neglect or self-abuse. The remaining types of domestic elder maltreatment in 1996 were physical abuse (15 percent), sexual abuse (0.4 percent), emotional abuse (8 percent), financial exploitation (12.4 percent), all other types (6 percent), and unknown (4 percent).

Theft by Family and Friends

Criminal justice professionals are finding that money and property are being stolen from today's elderly at alarming rates and that a large portion of the crimes are being committed not by professional criminals but by relatives, friends, health aides, household workers, and neighbors. In-home care for elderly persons often allows other persons access to the financial and property assets of those cared for. Like child abuse and sexual abuse crimes, many crimes against the elderly are not reported because the victims are physically or mentally unable to summon help or because they are reluctant or afraid to publicly accuse relatives or those they are dependent upon.

Medical advances are lengthening lives and resulting in greater numbers of older and, in many cases, infirm persons. Increasing numbers of these elderly people have substantial bank and investment accounts. Those too sick to manage even their Social Security or pension checks are particularly vulnerable. Financial exploitation is likely to grow as the number of older Americans who are most vulnerable to it, the lonely and those in poor health, rises.

Women are frequent victims of such crimes, primarily because there are so many more elderly women. Loneliness causes many victims not to report the crimes, even when they are aware of them, simply because they are afraid to lose the companionship of the perpetrator. When a case of financial abuse is reported, the source of the information is likely to be someone other than the victim—a police officer, ambulance attendant, bank teller, neighbor, or other family member.

Most states require doctors and other social service professionals to report evidence of abuse. The most common outcome of intervention is that the victim is moved to an institution. Many elderly, however, refuse to be removed from an abusive situation in order to be put in an alternative setting, and without the victim's cooperation, little can be done.

Who Are the Abusers of the Elderly?

The NCEA reported that adult children were the most frequent perpetrators, making up 40 percent of all elder abusers in 1996. (See Figure 11.13.) Fifteen percent of abusers were spouses. Other family members, including siblings, parents, and grandchildren, comprised 29 percent. In addition, professional caretakers in the home sometimes abuse the elderly in their care. There may be a significant number of elderly who are abused by two or more people.

SEX OF PERPETRATORS. The NCEA reported that in 1990 the majority—54.7 percent—of perpetrators of abuse toward the elderly were male. By 1996 there was no significant difference between the sexes in likelihood of elder abuse—47.4 percent of perpetrators were male, and 48.9 percent were female.

Who Are the Abuse Victims?

About two-thirds of elder abuse victims in domestic settings are female, according to the NCEA. Data from 36 states showed that 67.4 percent of the elderly who were abused in 1996 were females. In addition, older elders are more likely to be victims. Elderly persons over the age of 80 made up more than one-third of victims in 1996. The median age of elder victims was 77.9 years. The NCEA reported that 62.4 percent of self-abusers were women. The median age of these self-neglecting elders was 77.4 years.

FIGURE 11.13

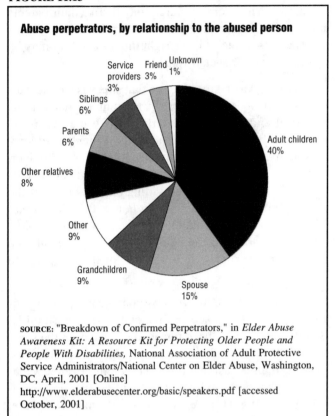

Abuse perpetrators, by relationship to the abused person

SOURCE: "Breakdown of Confirmed Perpetrators," in *Elder Abuse Awareness Kit: A Resource Kit for Protecting Older People and People With Disabilities,* National Association of Adult Protective Service Administrators/National Center on Elder Abuse, Washington, DC, April, 2001 [Online] http://www.elderabusecenter.org/basic/speakers.pdf [accessed October, 2001]

By race, in 1996, 66.4 percent of the victims of domestic elder abuse were white, while 18.7 percent were African American. Hispanic elders accounted for 10.4 percent of the victims; Native American and Asian American/Pacific Islanders each constituted less than 1 percent.

Reporting of Elder Abuse

In most states, certain professionals—adult protective service/human service workers, social service workers, law enforcement agencies, and medical workers—are required to report domestic elder abuse, neglect, and exploitation. The NCEA reported that in 1996, 22.5 percent of all reports of elder abuse came from physicians and other health-care professionals. Another 15.1 percent came from service providers, and family members and relatives of victims reported 16.3 percent of suspected elder abuse cases. Friends, neighbors, law enforcement personnel, clergy, banks/financial institutions, and abuse victims made the remainder of reports. The NCEA reported that most elder abuse reports were substantiated after being investigated. In 1996, 64.2 percent of all reports were proven.

Causes of Elder Abuse

According to the NCEA, no single theory can explain why older people are abused. The causes of elder abuse are diverse and complicated. Some relate to the personality of the abuser, some reflect the relationship between the abuser and the abused, and some are reactions to stressful situations. While some children truly dislike their parents and the role of caregiver, many others want to care for their parents or feel it is the right thing to do, but may be emotionally or financially unable.

STRESS. Most experts agree that stress is a contributing factor in abuse of the elderly. Meeting the daily needs of a frail and dependent elderly relative may be overwhelming for some family members. When the elderly person lives in the same household as the caregiver, crowding, differences of opinion, and constant demands often add to the strain of providing physical care. If the elderly person lives in a different house, the added pressure of having to commute between two households, doing extra housekeeping chores, and being on call at a moment's notice may be too much for the caregiver to cope with.

THE FINANCIAL BURDEN. In many cases, caring for an elderly person places a financial strain on a family. Elderly parents may need financial assistance at the same time that their children are raising their own families. Instead of an occasional night out, a long-awaited vacation, or a badly needed new car, families may find themselves paying for ever-increasing medical care, prescription drugs, physical aids, special dietary supplements, extra food and clothing, or therapy. Saving for their children's college education, for a daughter's wedding, or for retirement becomes difficult. Resentment can build quickly, and it can lead to emotional if not outright physical abuse of the elderly by caregivers.

THE CYCLE OF ABUSE. Some experts believe that persons who abuse an elderly parent or relative were themselves abused as children. Dr. Suzanne K. Steinmetz, director for Resources for Older Americans at the University of Delaware and a recognized expert on domestic violence, found such a pattern in her studies of elderly abusers. She found that only 1 out of 400 children treated nonviolently when they were raised attacked their elderly parents; on the other hand, 1 out of 2 children who were violently mistreated as they grew up abused their elderly parents.

Chicago psychiatrist Mitchell Messer, who treats adults who care for elderly parents, noted, "We find parent beatings when the parents set the example of solving problems through brutality when the children were growing up.... The response is simply following the example...set." As adults, formerly abused children often have financial, marital, or drug problems that they blame on their parents and which make them even more abusive.

INVASION OF PRIVACY. Most Americans believe that home is a place a person should be able to call his or her own. When that home must be shared, there is an inevitable loss of a certain amount of control and privacy. Movement may be restricted, habits may need to be changed, rivalry frequently develops between generations over decision making, and young children may play the adults against each other to get what they want. Frustration and anxiety result as both parent and supporting child try to suppress angry feelings, sometimes unsuccessfully.

LOSS OF FREEDOM. An adult child may be obligated to care for an adult parent just at the time when his or her own children are leaving home. The resentment of being once again tied to the home, this time to care for a frail, perhaps bedridden, parent pushes many caregivers to the breaking point. To make matters worse, they may feel guilty and ashamed of their negative feelings. The dependent parent, in turn, often senses this resentment and may respond by withdrawing or becoming even more demanding. The average length of home care for a severely dependent person who is over 70 is between five and six years. In many cases, it is much longer.

Additionally, an adult child (usually a daughter) with children still in the home may find herself in the position of caring also for an elderly parent. The term "sandwich generation" (those persons who have both a younger generation and an older generation to care for) has been coined to describe these caregivers who may have anticipated enjoyment of their own interests at exactly the same time they are required to assume care for an aged parent. At the same time, it should be emphasized that the overwhelming majority of caregivers who suffer these many types of stress do not abuse the elderly people they are caring for.

REVERSE DEPENDENCY. Some sources believe that people who abuse an elderly person may actually be quite dependent on that person. Some experts have found that abused elderly people were no more likely to have had a recent decline in health or be seriously ill or hospitalized previously than the nonabused elderly. In fact, as a group, the abused elderly were more self-sufficient in preparing meals, doing ordinary housework, and climbing stairs than were the nonabused elderly.

On the other hand, abusing caregivers often seem more dependent on their victims for housing, financial assistance, and transportation than were nonabusing caregivers. They often seem to have fewer resources and are frequently unable to meet their own basic needs. Rather than having power in the relationship, they are relatively powerless. From these observations, some authorities have concluded that abusing caregivers may not always be driven to violence by the physical and emotional burden of caring for a seriously disabled elderly person, but may have emotional problems of their own that can lead to violent behavior.

The Abusive Spouse

The high rate of spousal abuse among the elderly is possibly the result of the fact that many elderly people live with spouses, so the opportunity for spousal violence is great. Violence against an elderly spouse may be the continuation of an abusive relationship that began years earlier—abuse does not end simply because a couple gets older. Sometimes, however, the abuse may not begin until later years, in which case it is often associated with alcohol abuse, unemployment, postretirement depression, and/or loss of self-esteem.

Intervention and Prevention

All 50 states and the District of Columbia have laws dealing specifically with adult abuse, but as with laws concerning child abuse and spousal abuse among younger couples, they are often ineffective. The effectiveness of laws and the enforcing agencies vary from state to state and even from county to county within a given state. No standard definition of abuse exists among enforcement agencies. In many cases, authorities cannot legally intervene and terminate an abusive condition unless a report is filed, the abuse is verified, and the victim files a formal complaint. An elderly person could understandably be reluctant, physically unable, or too fearful to accuse or prosecute an abuser. At the present time, 42 states and the District of Columbia operate "mandatory reporting systems," making it mandatory for certain professionals to report suspected abuse. In eight states, reporting is voluntary.

The best way to stop elder abuse is to prevent its occurrence. As noted above, researchers have identified specific situations where abuse is likely to occur and the type of person who is likely to be an abuser. Older people who know that they will eventually need outside help should carefully analyze the potential difficulties of living with a child and, if necessary and possible, make alternate arrangements. In any event, they should take care to protect their money and assets to ensure that their valuables cannot be easily taken over by someone else.

Young families or persons who must care for an older person, voluntarily or otherwise, must realize that their frustration and despair do not have to result in abuse. Social agencies can often work with families to help relieve anger and stress. Sometimes there are ways to offset the financial burden of elder care, for example, through tax deductions or subsidies for respite care.

Elder Shelters

In 1999, Rosalie S. Wolf, of the Institute on Aging, in *Elder Shelters: United States, Canada, and Japan,* reported that little study had been done on the subject of sheltering elderly abuse victims. Virtually no listing of shelters for the elderly existed. She was able to identify 17 programs—8 in operation, 6 in the planning stage, and 3 closed. The oldest program dated from 1986; the newest had opened in May 1998. Since the original count, 3 additional shelters have been identified, 2 in Tokyo, Japan, and 1 in Montreal (it opened in 1992 but closed in 1995). The Japanese shelters had opened earlier than any of the others, in 1981.

Dr. Wolf's study found that few older women have been served in battered women's shelters, although age was not a criterion for eligibility. Shelters typically cannot accept people who cannot take care of themselves. They rarely provide 24-hour supervision, and they often close during the daytime.

INSTITUTIONAL ABUSE—
A FORGOTTEN POPULATION?

The greatest threat that many older Americans face is not a criminal armed with a gun but a telemarketer armed with a deceptive rap. And our most defenseless seniors, those who are sick or disabled and living in nursing homes, cannot lock the door against abuse and neglect by people paid to care for them.

— President Bill Clinton, 1999

Abuse of the elderly can also occur outside the private home, in nursing homes charged with the care of the aged and ill patient. "Institutional abuse" generally refers to the same forms of abuse as domestic abuse crimes but perpetrated by persons who have a legal or contractual obligation to provide elders with care and protection. Despite the fact that, by law, nursing homes must take steps to attain or maintain the "highest practicable physical, mental, and psychosocial well-being of each resident," too many residents are the victims of neglect or abuse by these facilities or their employees.

Types of Abuse and Neglect

Nursing home neglect and/or abuse can take many forms including:

- Failure to provide proper diet and hydration

- Failure to assist with personal hygiene

- Overmedication or undermedication

- Failure to answer call lights promptly

- Failure to turn residents in their beds to promote circulation

- Slapping or other physical abuse

- Leaving the residents in soiled garments or beds or failure to take them to the toilet

- Use of unwarranted restraints

- Emotional or verbal abuse

- Retaliation for making a complaint

- Failure to provide appropriate medical care

- Sexual assault or rape of the resident

- Theft of the resident's property or money

A Snapshot of Nursing Home Abuse

In the most recent study on the subject, Brian Payne and Richard Cikovic studied 488 cases of nursing home abuse reported to Medicaid Fraud Control Units ("An Empirical Examination of the Characteristics, Consequences, and Causes of Elder Abuse in Nursing Homes," *Journal of Elder Abuse & Neglect,* vol. 7, no. 4, 1995). Forty-two states have Medicaid Fraud Control Units responsible for detecting, investigating, and prosecuting Medicaid fraud and abuse. The study found that 84.2 percent of the abuse was physical, including slapping; hitting with an object such as a hairbrush, wet towel, or spatula; kicking; and spitting. The remaining acts were sexual (8.8 percent), monetary (1.4 percent), or duty-related, in which an employee misperformed specific duties, such as removing bandages in a rough manner. The most recent statistics from the U.S. Department of Aging reported there were 548 complaints of sexual abuse between October 1, 1995, and September 30, 1996.

Although nurses' aides comprised the largest group of abusers (62 percent), they were also the single most numerous employee group in nursing homes. Of the 488 incidents, 63 percent involved a male employee. Males were also slightly more likely to be victims (57 percent). Male employees tended to abuse male residents; female employees tended to abuse female victims.

Some experts suggest that in an attempt to squeeze more profit from the operation, too many nursing homes do not hire adequate numbers of qualified staff. Poorly qualified, untrained, or overworked staffs are often unable to cope with the demands of nursing home residents. Exposing abuse in those situations is often more difficult than in other health care environments because the victims are sometimes unable to communicate their abuse or neglect because of their physical or mental disabilities.

Efforts to Control Abuse

In an effort to improve the quality of care and eliminate abuse in nursing homes, government regulations and laws are requiring greater supervision of nursing homes. In 1987 President Ronald Reagan signed into effect a landmark law, the Omnibus Budget Reconciliation Act (PL 100-203), which included sections that protected patient rights and treatment. The law went into effect October 1990. Compliance with the law varies from state to state and from one nursing facility to another. Families are increasingly filing (and winning) court suits against irresponsible nursing facilities. New York State enacted "Kathy's Law," which created the new felony-level crime of "abuse of a vulnerable elderly person." In 1999 President Bill Clinton announced a crackdown on nursing homes and states that do a poor job of regulating them.

EVEN CRIMINALS GET OLDER

The Nation's prison population is aging.

— Allen J. Beck and Christopher J. Mumola, *Prisoners in 1998*

The growing number of the aging in the nation's penal system raises some questions for the future. Some experts believe stricter sentencing laws mean prisons will be housing more elderly convicts and paying more money to do so. With the increasing introduction of "three strikes and you're out" programs that sentence habitual felons to life sentences, the 1987 abolition of parole for federal crimes, and the growing use of mandatory life sentences, the problems of the elderly will become a major problem for the nation's prisons.

Eighty-six-year-old Viva LeRoy Nash is believed to be the nation's oldest death-row inmate, incarcerated at Arizona State Prison. He has suffered numerous heart attacks since the 1980s, and like many others his age, he takes a number of medications each day and requires a low-fat diet. He is part of a growing number of older inmates.

According to a Bureau of Justice Statistics report (Allen J. Beck and Christopher J. Mumola, *Prisoners in 1998,* August 1999), the nation's older prison population is small but significant. About 3 percent of the 1.3 million federal and state inmates in the country in 1997 were aged 55 years or older. This means there were 155 prisoners aged 55-plus per 100,000 people in that age group. A small but growing number of these inmates (10 percent) will serve 20 or more years in prison before release and 5 percent will never be released.

As the inmate population grows older, prisoners require additional medical, dietary, and psychological services that will further stretch the already huge cost of inmate care. Older inmates often suffer from more health problems than the general aged population. They are more likely to be infected with HIV and tuberculosis and to have histories of drug abuse. They are often less mobile, and prisons are not designed for easy access. Aged inmates are also more affected by violence within the prison. Experts estimate that caring for aging convicts can be two to three times as expensive as caring for younger prisoners. In addition, when elderly inmates are released, where do they go? Who will care for them?

Others have questioned the value of incarcerating older inmates at all. Many criminologists claim that most prisoners become less violent with age. They contend that the money spent to imprison a 60-year-old who is likely no longer a threat to society could be better spent to incarcerate an 18-year-old with a budding career in crime. Taxpayers may ask themselves if they are willing to pay to maintain older offenders in prison for their lifetimes as corrections take a growing proportion of public money.

Other critics observe that retaining prisoners in prison for years creates people who are conditioned to being told what to do and who have no independent support systems. They often have no skills with which to support themselves, and for some of them, their only friends are fellow inmates. They may be out of touch with the outside world and unable to adjust to life as free persons.

CHAPTER 12
DEATH, DYING, FUNERALS, AND BURIALS

DEATH AND DYING

In contemporary American society death is something that primarily happens in old age.
— George E. Dickinson, *Social Gerontology*, 1998

Funerals, burials, and cremations are all too frequent events in the lives of older people. According to a 1999 survey conducted for the AARP (formerly the American Association of Retired Persons), one in five Americans aged 50 and older was involved in arranging or preplanning a funeral from January 1998 to June 1999. On the other hand, death is a less threatening presence for older people as compared to younger age groups. A survey conducted by International Communications Research for AARP and *Modern Maturity* magazine (September–October 2000) among 1,815 Americans aged 45 and older found that the older the respondents, the less afraid they were of dying and being in pain at the end of life. The survey also found that women were more fearful than men of dying, being in pain at the end of life, and having the dying process prolonged by artificial means.

Advances in Medical Technology and Pain Reduction

By far, the most frequent beneficiaries of advances in medical technology are the elderly. Unfortunately, while technology can enhance life in certain circumstances, it may prolong life (as well as the dying process) at the expense of quality of life and without regard for individual wishes. The legal, ethical, religious, and economic questions raised by such technology have yet to be resolved and will certainly touch the lives of an ever-growing number of older Americans. Among those technologies at issue are cardiopulmonary resuscitation (CPR), respiratory ventilation, organ transplants, dialysis, nutritional support and hydration, antibiotics, and recently, euthanasia and suicide-enabling paraphernalia and procedures.

According to the AARP/*Modern Maturity* survey cited above, three-fourths of people aged 45 and older

agreed that doctors should be able to use controlled substances to manage pain at the end of life. Almost this number believe there is a point at which costly health treatments should be stopped, and nature should be allowed to take its course, even if that means a patient will die. Only half of the 45-plus age group is supportive of voluntary euthanasia (patients actively taking their own lives) and less than half are supportive of physician-assisted suicide (where a doctor helps someone to commit suicide by prescribing a fatal dose of drugs or administering a lethal injection).

The AARP survey also found that the percentage of people who believed that voluntary euthanasia and physician-assisted suicide should be made legal decreases significantly among older people, especially for physician-assisted suicide. More than half of adults aged 45 to 54 believed that voluntary euthanasia or physician-assisted suicide should be legal, compared with 35 to 42 percent of those aged 75 and older. The study also found that 67 percent of respondents believed that doctors could accurately predict how long a patient has to live.

The Patient Self-Determination Act and the Death with Dignity Act

In October 1990 Congress passed the Patient Self-Determination Act, which was the first federal legislation to ensure that patients are informed of their right to accept or refuse medical care. To receive reimbursement through Medicare and Medicaid programs, hospitals and other organizations must comply with the federal law.

In addition, in November 1994 Oregon voters passed the Death with Dignity Act. This act allows competent, terminally-ill adult patients in the state to obtain a physician's prescription for drugs to end their lives. According to the *Fourth Annual Report on Oregon's Death with Dignity Act* (February 6, 2002), from the Oregon Department of Human Services, 21 Oregonians chose physician-assisted suicide under the Death with Dignity Act in 2001, 27 in 2000, 27 in 1999, and 16 in 1998. Though those who chose this option ranged in age from 25 to 94, the median age of all participants was 69.

The course of the Death with Dignity Act has not been smooth, however. Then-Attorney General Janet Reno declared in 1998 that Oregon doctors acting under the Death with Dignity Act were not in violation of Drug Enforcement Agency rules. The current Attorney General, John Ashcroft, however, reinterpreted the Controlled Substances Act on November 6, 2001, and made doctors who prescribed drugs under the Death with Dignity Act subject to prosecution. On November 20, 2001, an Oregon state judge extended a temporary restraining order on Ashcroft's directive, pending a new hearing within five months. As of February 2002 the Act stands, but its future may be uncertain.

A study conducted in Oregon looked at the impact of laws such as the Death with Dignity Act (Maria J. Silveira, et al., "Patients' Knowledge of Options at the End of Life, Ignorance in the Face of Death," *JAMA*, vol. 284, no. 19, November 15, 2000). The study examined 1,000 outpatients' understanding of legal options like advance directives and the Death with Dignity Act. Results of the study show that a significant proportion of outpatients surveyed appear to misunderstand their options at the end of life.

Most understood that they could refuse life-sustaining medical care. Many, however, did not understand that life support could be withdrawn once started, or that pain could be managed aggressively by increasing medication doses, even with the possibility of a double effect (giving pain medications with the goal of relieving pain and suffering, even if death may occur as a result). According to the study's scoring system, less than half (46 percent) of patients aged 66 to 69 were knowledgeable about such issues, compared with 50 percent of those aged 51 to 65, 48 percent of those aged 31 to 50, and 36 percent of those aged 18 to 30.

FUNERALS AND BURIALS

Funeral Expenses

The National Funeral Directors Association estimated that the average cost of a funeral was between $5,000 and $5,700, not including burial or cremation costs. An AARP Andrus Foundation study (Mercedes Bern-Klug, *The Funeral Information Project*, May 4, 1998) on funeral home and cemetery decision making found that in the Kansas City, Missouri area, combined funeral home and burial costs ranged from $195 to $14,000, with an average of $2,300 for cremation and $6,500 for burials.

Caskets are the most expensive funeral item. According to a 1996 Federal Trade Commission (FTC) report ("Consumer Access to Price Information about Funerals to Get Major Boost under New FTC/Industry Program"),

although an average casket costs slightly more than $2,000, some mahogany, bronze, or copper caskets sell for as much as $10,000. Until recently, caskets were sold only by funeral homes, but now cemeteries and others also sell them.

Advance Funeral Planning

In 1995 and 1998 the AARP conducted two studies to assess various aspects of preneed funeral and burial arrangements for the population aged 50 and older ("Older Americans and Preneed Funeral and Burial Arrangements: Findings from a 1998 National Telephone Survey and Comparison with a 1995 Survey," May 1999). The surveys found that 43 percent of Americans aged 50 and older, or 28.4 million people, were solicited by telephone, mail, or in person about purchasing advance funeral arrangements in 1998. The study also found that 39 percent of Americans aged 50 and older, or 25.7 million people, had been solicited about purchasing a burial or other final disposition in advance, an increase of 11 percentage points in three years.

The AARP studies found that in 1998, 32 percent of Americans aged 50 and over, or roughly 21 million people, had prepaid some or all of their funeral and/or burial expenses. This remained essentially unchanged from 1995 (when the figure was 28 percent). Those who prepay for funeral or burial goods and services tend to be older (aged 65-plus), and tend to have low to moderate annual household incomes of between $15,000 and $40,000.

Funeral Practices

Funeral homes are required by the FTC's Funeral Rule to give consumers a list of prices for the merchandise and services they offer. In 1997 the FTC's Funeral Rule Offender Program test-shopped over 300 funeral homes nationwide and found that over 85 percent of the homes were substantially complying with the Funeral Rule.

A 1999 AARP study, however, found some serious compliance problems in the funeral industry. In part to assess whether funeral homes are complying with the FTC rule, the AARP conducted a survey of individuals who had arranged or prearranged a funeral or burial in the 18 months preceding their interviews. Results of the survey showed that a significant proportion of funeral homes were not in compliance with the rule. Other survey results also demonstrated that older consumers should be wary when arranging funerals:

• Of those funeral arrangers who viewed caskets on display for purchase or rental, one-third were not given written casket price lists before they began looking at the merchandise.

• One-third of funeral arrangers in the study did not receive price information before talking about specific funeral goods and services.

- One-fourth of the funeral arrangers indicated they were not asked for their permission before a loved one's body was embalmed.

- One-third of the persons who had arranged a funeral within the past 18 months reported being told by a funeral director that protective features of a casket would help preserve the body indefinitely, which is a falsehood.

Cemetery Practices

The AARP's study also looked at cemetery practices. Cemeteries are not bound by the FTC's Funeral Rule. The study found that 36 percent of those purchasing a burial plot from cemeteries did not receive a price list, nor did one in five of those purchasing other cemetery goods and services. In addition, more than one-fourth of respondents (29 percent) said that they were incorrectly told that the protective features of a grave liner or burial vault would help preserve the body indefinitely.

Cremations

Cremations continue to grow in popularity. A survey conducted by the National Funeral Directors Association in 2000 found that 26 percent of 1,002 consumers surveyed said they would prefer cremation to earth burial—an 8 percentage point increase from the previous 10 years. Nearly 75 percent said they would choose cremation for reasons other than cost.

According to the Cremation Association of North America, 25 percent of deaths resulted in cremations in 1999. In 1996 and 1997 the median age of the deceased who were cremated was 74 years.

IMPORTANT NAMES AND ADDRESSES

AARP (formerly American Association of Retired Persons)
601 E St., NW
Washington, DC 20049
(202) 434-2277
(800) 424-3410
FAX: (202) 728-4573
E-mail: member@aarp.org
URL: http://www.aarp.org

Administration on Aging
330 Independence Ave., SW
Washington, DC 20201
(202) 619-7501
FAX: (202) 260-1012
E-mail: AoAInfo@aoa.gov
URL: http://www.aoa.dhhs.gov

Alliance for Aging Research
2021 K St., NW, Suite 305
Washington, DC 20006
(202) 293-2856
(800) 639-2421
FAX: (202) 785-8574
E-mail: info@agingresearch.org
URL: http://www.agingresearch.org

Alzheimer's Association
919 N. Michigan Ave., Suite 1100
Chicago, IL 60611-1676
(312) 335-8700
(800) 272-3900
FAX: (312) 335-1110
E-mail: info@alz.org
URL: http://www.alz.org

American Association for Geriatric Psychiatry
7910 Woodmont Ave., Suite 1050
Bethesda, MD 20814-3004
(301) 654-7850
FAX: (301) 654-4137
E-mail: main@aagponline.org
URL: http://www.aagponline.org

American Association of Homes and Services for the Aging
2519 Connecticut Ave., NW
Washington, DC 20008-1520
(202) 783-2242
FAX: (202) 783-2255
E-mail: memberservices@aahsa.org
URL: http://www.aahsa.org

American Geriatrics Society
350 5th Ave., Suite 801
New York, NY 10118
(212) 308-1414
FAX: (212) 832-8646
E-mail: info@americangeriatrics.org
URL: http://www.americangeriatrics.org

American Society on Aging
833 Market St., Suite 511
San Francisco, CA 94103-1824
(415) 974-9600
FAX: (415) 974-0300
E-mail: info@asaging.org
URL: http://www.asaging.org

Asociacion Nacional pro Personas Mayores/National Association for Hispanic Elderly
234 E. Colorado Blvd., Suite 300
Pasadena, CA 91104
(213) 487-1922
(800) 953-8553 (in-state only)
FAX: (213) 385-8553

Assisted Living Federation of America
11200 Waples Mill Rd., Suite 150
Fairfax, VA 22030
(703) 691-8100
FAX: (703) 691-8106
E-mail: info@alfa.org
URL: http://www.alfa.org

Centers for Medicare & Medicaid Services
7500 Security Blvd.
Baltimore, MD 21244-1850
(410) 786-3000
URL: http://www.cms.gov

Children of Aging Parents
1609 Woodbourne Rd., Suite 302A
Levittown, PA 19057
(800) 227-7294
URL: http://www.caps4caregivers.org

Eldercare Locator Directory
(800) 677-1116
FAX: (202) 296-8134
URL: http://www.eldercare.gov

Family Caregiver Alliance
690 Market St., Suite 600
San Francisco, CA 94104
(415) 434-3388
FAX: (415) 434-3508
E-mail: info@caregiver.org
URL: http://www.caregiver.org

Gerontological Society of America
1030 15th St., NW, Suite 250
Washington, DC 20005
(202) 842-1275
FAX: (202) 842-1150
E-mail: geron@geron.org
URL: http://www.geron.org

Gray Panthers
733 15th St., NW, Suite 437
Washington, DC 20005
(202) 737-6637
(800) 280-5362
FAX: (202) 737-1160
E-mail: info@graypanthers.org
URL: http://www.graypanthers.org

Jewish Council for the Aging
11820 Parklawn Dr., Suite 200
Rockville, MD 20852
(301) 255-4200
FAX: (301) 231-9360
E-mail: jcagw@jcagw.org
URL: http://www.jcagw.org

Medicare Rights Center
1460 Broadway, 11th Floor
New York, NY 10036
(212) 869-3850

(800) 333-4114
FAX: (212) 869-3532
E-mail: info@medicarerights.org
URL: http://www.medicarerights.org

National Academy of Elder Law Attorneys, Inc.
1604 N. Country Club Rd.
Tucson, AZ 85716
(520) 881-4005
FAX: (520) 325-7925
URL: http://www.naela.org

National Alliance for Caregiving
4720 Montgomery Ln., Suite 642
Bethesda, MD 20814
(301) 718-8444
FAX: (301) 652-7711
E-mail: gailhunt.nac@erols.com
URL: http://www.caregiving.org

National Alliance of Senior Citizens
2525 Wilson Blvd.
Arlington, VA 22201
FAX: (703) 528-4380

National Association for Home Care
228 7th St., SE
Washington, DC 20003
(202) 547-7424
FAX: (202) 547-3540
URL: http://www.nahc.org

National Caregiving Foundation
801 N. Pitt St., Suite 116
Alexandria, VA 22314-1765
(703) 299-9300
(800) 930-1357

National Caucus and Center on Black Aged
1220 L St., NW, Suite 800
Washington, DC 20005
(202) 637-8400
FAX: (202) 347-0895
URL: http://www.ncba-aged.org

National Center on Elder Abuse
1201 15th St., NW, Suite 350
Washington, DC 20005-2800
(202) 898-2586
FAX: (202) 898-2583
E-mail: NCEA@nasua.org
URL: http://www.elderabusecenter.org

National Center for Health Statistics Division of Data Services
6525 Belcrest Rd.
Hyattsville, MD 20782-2003
(301) 458-4636
URL: http://www.cdc.gov/nchs

National Citizens' Coalition for Nursing Home Reform
1424 16th St., NW, Suite 202
Washington, DC 20036
(202) 332-2275
FAX: (202) 332-2949
URL: http://www.nccnhr.org

National Council on the Aging
409 3rd St., SW, Suite 200
Washington, DC 20024
(202) 479-1200
FAX: (202) 479-0735
E-mail: info@ncoa.org
URL: http://www.ncoa.org

National Family Caregivers Association
10400 Connecticut Ave., Suite 500
Kensington, MD 20895-3944
(800) 896-3650
FAX: (301) 942-2302
E-mail: info@nfcacares.org
URL: http://www.nfcacares.org

National Hispanic Council on Aging
2713 Ontario Rd., NW
Washington, DC 20009
(202) 265-1288
FAX: (202) 745-2522
E-mail: nhcoa@worldnet.att.net
URL: http://www.nhcoa.org

National Hospice and Palliative Care Organization
1700 Diagonal Rd., Suite 625
Alexandria, VA 22314
(703) 837-1500
FAX: (703) 837-1233
E-mail: info@nhpco.org
URL: http://www.nhpco.org

National Indian Council on Aging
10501 Montgomery Blvd., NE, Suite 210
Albuquerque, NM 87111-3846
(505) 292-2001
FAX: (505) 292-1922
URL: http://www.nicoa.org/

National Institute on Aging
Building 31, Room 5C27
31 Center Dr., MSC 2292
Bethesda, MD 20892
(301) 496-1752
(800) 222-2225
FAX: 301-589-3014
URL: http://www.nih.gov/nia

National PACE Association
801 N. Fairfax St., Suite 309
Alexandria, VA 22314
(703) 535-1565
FAX: (703) 535-1566
E-mail: info@npaonline.org
URL: http://www.natlpaceassn.org

National Respite Locator Service ARCH National Respite Network and Resource Center Chapel Hill Training-Outreach Project
800 Eastowne Dr., Suite 105
Chapel Hill, NC 27514
(800) 773-5433
URL: http://www.chtop.com/locator.htm

National Senior Citizens Law Center
1101 14th St., NW, Suite 400
Washington, DC 20005
(202) 289-6976
FAX: (202) 289-7224
URL: http://www.nsclc.org

National Society for American Indian Elderly
2214 N. Central, Suite 250
Phoenix, AZ 85004
(602) 307-1865
E-mail: info@nsaie.org
URL: http://www.nsaie.org

National Urban League, Inc.
120 Wall St.
New York, NY 10005
(212) 558-5300
FAX: (212) 344-5332
E-mail: info@nul.org
URL: http://www.nul.org

OWL
666 11th St., NW, Suite 700
Washington, DC 20001
(202) 783-6686
(800) 825-3695
FAX: (202) 638-2356
E-mail: owlinfo@owl-national.org
URL: http://www.owl-national.org

Pension Benefit Guaranty Corporation
1200 K St., NW
Washington, DC 20005-4026
(202) 326-4000
URL: http://www.pbgc.gov

Pension Rights Center
1140 19th St., NW, Suite 602
Washington, DC 20036-6608
(202) 296-3776
FAX: (202) 833-2472
E-mail: PnsnRights@aol.com
URL: http://www.pensionrights.org

SeniorNet
121 2nd St., 7th Floor
San Francisco, CA 94105
(415) 495-4990
FAX: (415) 495-3999
URL: http://www.seniornet.org

Service Corps of Retired Executives
409 3rd St., SW, 6th Floor
Washington, DC 20024
(800) 634-0245
FAX: (202) 205-7636
URL: http://www.score.org

U.S. Census Bureau
Washington, DC 20233
E-mail: webmaster@census.gov
URL: http://www.census.gov

U.S. Department of Veterans Affairs
810 Vermont Ave., NW
Washington, DC 20420
(202) 273-5700
(800) 827-1000
URL: http://www.va.gov

RESOURCES

The stated mission of the U.S. Census Bureau, part of the U.S. Department of Commerce, is "to be the preeminent collector and provider of timely, relevant, and quality data about the people and economy of the United States." Many Census Bureau publications include useful data about the elderly in America, including: *The 65 Years and Over Population: 2000; Age 2000; Aging in the Americas into the XXI Century; Aging in the United States—Past, Present, and Future; America's Families and Living Arrangements: 2000; American Housing Survey for the United States: 1999; Americans with Disabilities: 1994-95; Asset Ownership of Households: 1993; Centenarians in the United States, 1990; Computer Use in the United States, 1997; Consumer Expenditure Survey, 1999; Educational Attainment in the United States: March 2000; Global Aging into the 21st Century; Health Insurance Coverage: 1998; Household Net Worth and Asset Ownership: 1993-1995; Households with Computers and Internet Access by Selected Characteristics; Housing Vacancies and Homeownership: 2000; Money Income in the United States: 2000; Population Projections for States, by Age, Sex, Race, and Hispanic Origin: 1995 to 2025; Poverty in the United States: 2000; Resident Population Estimates of the United States by Age and Sex: 1990-1999; Selected Characteristics of People 15 Years and Over by Total Money Income in 2000 by Race, Hispanic Origin, and Sex;* and *Voting and Registration in the Election of November 1996.*

The Centers for Medicare and Medicaid Services (CMS), formerly known as the Health Care Financing Administration, is the part of the U.S. Department of Health and Human Services that coordinates Medicare and Medicaid. Significant CMS publications include: *Health Care Financing Review; The Medicare and Medicaid Supplement; Medicare 2000: 35 Years of Improving Americans' Health and Security; Medicare: A Profile; National Health Care Expenditure and Projections; National Health Expenditures: 2000;* and *A Profile of Medicaid.*

Another agency within the Department of Health and Human Services is the National Center for Health Statistics (NCHS), part of the Centers for Disease Control and Prevention (CDC). The job of the NCHS is to provide vital and health statistics. Publications of interest in the study of older Americans are: *Advance Data and Mortality Trends for Alzheimer's Disease; Health 2001; Health and Aging Chartbook, 1999; Morbidity and Mortality Weekly Reports; National Vital Statistics Reports; National Health Interview Survey; National Home and Hospice Care Survey; Trends in Causes of Death among the Elderly; Trends in Vision and Hearing among the Elderly;* and *Vital and Health Statistics—Access to Health Care, Part 3: Older Adults.*

Other useful resources from government agencies include: *Private Pension Plan Bulletin Abstract of 1997 Form 5500 Annual Reports* (Pension and Welfare Benefits Administration); *Fast Facts and Figures about Social Security* and *Income of the Aged Population: 1998* (Social Security Administration); *A Profile of Older Americans* (U.S. Administration on Aging); *Age Patterns of Victims of Serious Violent Crime, Change in Criminal Victimization: 1994-95, Crime against Persons Age 65 or Older, 1992-1997,* and *Prisoners in 1998,* by Allen J. Beck and Christopher J. Mumola (U.S. Bureau of Justice Statistics); *Monthly Labor Review* (U.S. Bureau of Labor Statistics); *Adult Education Survey, The Condition of Education 1998,* and *Digest of Education Statistics 1997* (U.S. Department of Education); *Data on the Socioeconomic Status of Veterans and on VA Program Usage,* by Robert E. Klein, et al., and "National Veteran Population by Age: 1990-2020" (U.S. Department of Veterans Affairs); *The National Survey of Recreation and the Environment* (U.S. Forest Service); *Alzheimer's Disease—Estimates of Prevalence in the United States: 1998* (U.S. General Accounting Office); *Surveillance for Selected Public Health Indicators Affecting Older Adults—United States,* by Judy Stevens, et al.,

Morbidity and Mortality Weekly Report, vol. 48, no. SS-8, December 17, 1999 (CDC); *Alcohol Alert* (National Institute on Alcohol Abuse and Alcoholism); *Age Pages* (National Institutes of Health/National Institute on Aging); and *If You're Over 65 and Feeling Depressed: Treatment Brings New Hope* (National Institutes of Health/National Institute on Mental Health).

The AARP (formerly the American Association of Retired Persons) funds many studies and surveys on topics about and of interest to older Americans. Some notable examples are: *AARP/Modern Maturity Sexuality Survey; Caregiving and Long-Term Care; Comparisons of Grandparent Visitation Statutes Nationwide; Older Americans and Preneed Funeral and Burial Arrangements: Findings from a 1998 National Telephone Survey and Comparison with a 1995 Survey; Out of Pocket Spending on Health Care by Medicare Beneficiaries Age 65 and Older: 1999 Projections;* and *States Find Ways to Aid Older Drivers* by Al Karr. Also of interest is *The Funeral Information Project,* by Mercedes Bern-Klug, published by the AARP Andrus Foundation.

For information on caregiving, good resources include the National Alliance for Caregiving (*The Caregiving Boom: Baby Boomer Women Giving Care; Family Caregiving in the United States;* and *Who Cares? Families Caring for Persons with Alzheimer's Disease*). The National Alliance for Caregiving and Metropolitan Life Insurance Company worked together to produce *The MetLife Study of Employer Costs for Working Caregivers.* Also useful is *Defining Common Ground* by Citizens for Long Term Care.

Many organizations and publications provide information on specific health and wellness issues for the elderly, including mental health and physical capability. Some notable publications are: *2000 Heart and Stroke Statistical Update* and *Biostatistical Fact Sheet—Older Americans and Cardiovascular Diseases* (American Heart Association); *Boomers Age* (Alzheimer's Association); *Cancer Facts and Figures: 2001* (American Cancer Society); *Fast Facts on Osteoporosis* (National Osteoporosis Foundation); *Parkinson's Disease: What You and Your Family Should Know,* by Paul Nausieda, M.D., and Gloria Bock, M.S.N., R.N. (National Parkinson Founda-

tion); *I Will Manage* (Simon Foundation for Continence); *Changes in the Prevalence of Chronic Disability in the United States Black and Nonblack Population above Age 65 from 1982 to 1999,* by Kenneth G. Manton and XiLiang Gu (National Academy of Sciences); *Fact Sheets* (American Association for Geriatric Psychiatry); *The Prevention Index: 1996 Summary Report* (*Prevention Magazine*); "Patients' Knowledge of Options at the End of Life, Ignorance in the Face of Death," by Maria J. Silveira, et al. (*Journal of the American Medical Association,* vol. 284, no. 19, November 15, 2000); and "Practical Overview of Sexual Function and Advancing Age," by O.J. Thienhaus (*Geriatrics,* 1988).

Information on elder abuse can be found in the following sources: *Elder Abuse Awareness Kit* (National Association of Adult Protective Service Administrators); *Elder Abuse Information Series* and *Elder Abuse: Questions and Answers* (National Center on Elder Abuse); and "An Empirical Examination of the Characteristics, Consequences, and Causes of Elder Abuse in Nursing Homes" (*Journal of Elder Abuse & Neglect,* vol. 7, no. 4, 1995).

Other useful publications and resources for the study of aging Americans are: *The 1998 SeniorNet Survey* (SeniorNet and Charles Schwab); *Americans 55 and Older: A Changing Market,* second edition (New Strategist Publications, Ithaca, NY, 1999); *America's Senior Volunteers* and *The New Nonprofit Almanac in Brief* (Independent Sector); *Long-Term Care: Is Demography Destiny?* (Alliance for Health Care Reform); *Medicare and Prescription Drugs* and *Prescription Drug Trends: A Chartbook* (Henry J. Kaiser Family Foundation); *Myths and Realities of Aging 2000* (National Council on the Aging); *National Survey on Prescription Drugs* (*News Hour with Jim Lehrer*/Kaiser Family Foundation/Harvard School of Public Health); *The New Face of Retirement* (Peter D. Hart Research Associates); *Saving—And Not Saving—For Retirement* (Employee Benefit Research Institute); and *World Population Prospects, the 2000 Revision* (United Nations).

Information Plus sincerely thanks all of the organizations listed above for the invaluable information they provide.

INDEX